Strategic Studies Institute Book

RUSSIAN NUCLEAR WEAPONS:
PAST, PRESENT, AND FUTURE

Stephen J. Blank
Editor

November 2011

*****

*****

Comments pertaining to this report are invited and should be forwarded to: Director, Strategic Studies Institute, U.S. Army War College, 632 Wright Ave, Carlisle, PA 17013-5046.

*****

Published by Books Express Publishing
Books Express Publishing, 2011
ISBN 978-1-78039-992-8

Books Express publications are available from all good retail and online booksellers. For publishing proposals and direct ordering please contact us at: info@books-express.com

CONTENTS

Foreword v

Introduction vii
    Stephen J. Blank

Part I

1. Russian Nuclear and Conventional Weapons:
   The Broken Relationship 1
       Dale R. Herspring

2. Russia's Conventional Armed Forces:
   Reform and Nuclear Posture to 2020 33
       Roger N. McDermott

Part II

3. Nuclear Weapons in Russian Strategy and
   Doctrine 99
       Andrei Shoumikhin

4. Russia's Security Relations with the
   United States: Futures Planned and
   Unplanned...161
       Pavel K. Baev

5. Nuclear Weapons in Russian National
   Security Strategy 187
       Nikolai Sokov

Part III

6. Caught between Scylla and Charybdis: The
   Relationship between Conventional and
   Nuclear Capabilities in Russian Military
   Thought 261
   Daniel Goure

7. Russia and Nuclear Weapons..............................293
   Stephen J. Blank

8. Russian Tactical Nuclear Weapons: Current
   Policies and Future Trends..................................365
   Richard Weitz

9. New START and Nonproliferation: Suitors or
   Separate Tables?...417
   Stephen J. Cimbala

10. Russia's Nuclear Posture and the Threat
    that Dare Not Speak its Name............................459
    Jacob W. Kipp

About the Contributors 505

FOREWORD

While the Cold War is long past, the importance of arms control in Russo-American relations and the related issue of nuclear weapons for Russia remain vital concerns. Indeed, without an appreciation of the multiple dimensions of the latter, progress in the former domain is inconceivable. With this in mind, the Strategic Studies Institute (SSI) is very pleased to present the following essays, which were presented at a conference at the National Defense University on June 28, 2010. These essays explore many, if not all, of the issues connected with Russia's relatively greater reliance on nuclear weapons for its security. As such, they constitute an important contribution to the analysis of the Obama administration's reset policy, Russo-American relations, Russian foreign and defense policy, and international security in both Europe and Asia. Additionally, questions concerning the approach taken by other nuclear power nations in reference to the arms control agenda provide a crucial backdrop for the progress toward curbing the proliferation of nuclear weapons, a long-standing central goal of U.S. security policy.

We offer these essays to our readers in the belief that the information and analyses contained herein will strengthen our understanding of Russia's extensive nuclear agenda and provide a deeper understanding of the many issues in international security connected with Russia and its nuclear posture.

DOUGLAS C. LOVELACE, JR.
Director
Strategic Studies Institute

INTRODUCTION

As of November 2010, the so-called "New START (Strategic Arms Reduction Treaty)" treaty between the United States and Russia that was signed in Prague, Czech Republic, on April 8, 2010, awaits a ratification vote in the Senate. Regardless of the arguments pro and con that have emerged since it was signed, it is clear that the outcome of the ratification vote will not only materially affect the Obama administration's reset policy towards Russia, but also the strategic nuclear forces of both signatories. Indeed, throughout the Cold War, both sides built up their forces based on what each was thought to have or be building. Although the Bush administration (2001-09) rhetorically announced its intention to sever this mutual hostage relationship, it failed in that regard. As a result, critical aspects of that relationship still survive in Russia's orientation to the United States and in the language of the treaty, especially in its preamble, which explicitly affirms a link between nuclear offense and defense.[1]

Therefore, whatever the fate of the treaty and the reset policy, it is clear that both Moscow and Washington stand before crossroads in regard to the future of their strategic nuclear programs and force structures. Moreover, each side's course of action will tangibly affect the future course of action of the other side regarding the panoply of issues and policies connected with the development of nuclear weapons and the missions for them. With this in mind, the Office of the Secretary of Defense (OSD) organized a conference bringing together several distinguished experts on Russian nuclear weapons. The conference took place at the National Defense University, Fort Lesley J. McNair, Washington, DC, on June 28, 2010, and the papers that follow are the revised versions of the papers presented at this conference.

Each author was asked to answer several different questions pertaining to the present and future posture of Russia's nuclear weapons (including tactical nuclear weapons). Moreover, it quickly became clear that Russia's nuclear future in many ways, large and small, depends greatly on the degree of success that Moscow will have in its current large-scale efforts at comprehensive military reform. These reforms encompass virtually the entire military structure and are the most thoroughgoing reforms since Mikhail Frunze's reforms in 1924-25. Consequently, no analysis of nuclear present and future posture is possible without a systematic analysis of those reforms and their impact. Therefore, the following chapters provide an examination of Russia's military and political motives behind nuclear weapons policy as they pertain not only to the U.S./North Atlantic Treaty Organization (NATO), but also to China, whose rising power has clearly caught the Kremlin's attention.

Dale Herspring and Roger McDermott present a systematic exposition and analysis of the reforms of the conventional forces and the impact this might have on nuclear issues. Andrei Shoumikhin, Pavel Baev, and Nikolai Sokov closely examine the ways in which Russia has previously thought about nuclear weapons, how it does so at present, and as well as how it might think about them in the future. Daniel Goure and Stephen Blank analyze some of the larger strategic issues driving Russian security and defense policy and their connection to nuclear weapons. Stephen Cimbala relates both the U.S. and Russian structures to issues tied to nonproliferation and to what future reductions to a 1,000 warhead level might look like, while Jacob Kipp analyzes the deep-seated strategic challenges that Russia faces in its Asian-Pacific Far East. Richard Weitz provides an in-depth analysis of the vexing issue of tactical nuclear weapons (TNW) that are already a source of friction between the two sides and one that will figure prominently in any future arms control negotiation.

In many cases, it will become clear that in the attempt to answer the questions asked of them, the authors of this book have produced a considerable amount of overlap, i.e., more than one author addressing the same point. However, what is equally as clear is that there is no agreement among them. There was a deliberate attempt to avoid a "pre-cooked" consensus. Rather, each author's individual view is asserted in their chapters, underscoring the inherent opacity of Russian programs and the different analytical approaches of each writer. This outcome is hardly surprising in view of the strategic importance, complexity, many-sidedness, and ambiguity of Russia's approach to nuclear weapons. While the differences among the writers may produce difficulties for readers not necessarily versed in the intricacies of Russian strategic thinking and policy, they reflect the true reality of the material and the issues, which are inherently difficult and contentious in the United States (as the debate over the NEW Start treaty clearly illustrates). The difficulty and complexity is inherent in the subject matter, and we deliberately sought to avoid imposing predetermined outcomes or conclusions in organizing the conference and these papers. We hope that these papers serve to illuminate some of the most important, yet also intractable, defense policy issues facing the United States (and other states as well, not just Russia) and that they contribute to an even richer discussion and debate here in the United States, if not abroad.

ENDNOTE

1. Stephen Blank, "Cold Obstruction: The Legacy of US-Russia Relations Under George W. Bush," in Stephen J. Cimbala, ed., *The George W. Bush Defense Program: Policy, Strategy, & War*, Washington, DC: Potomac Books, 2010, pp. 113-138; TREATY BETWEEN THE UNITED STATES OF AMERICA AND THE RUSSIAN FEDERATION ON MEASURES FOR THE FURTHER REDUCTION AND LIMITATION OF STRATEGIC OFFENSIVE ARMS, available from *www.state.gov/documents/organization/140035.pdf*; PROTOCOL TO THE TREATY BETWEEN THE UNITED STATES OF AMERICA AND THE RUSSIAN FEDERATION ON MEASURES FOR THE FURTHER REDUCTION AND LIMITATION OF STRATEGIC OFFENSIVE ARMS, available from *www.state.gov/documents/organization/140047.pdf*.

CHAPTER 1

RUSSIAN NUCLEAR AND CONVENTIONAL WEAPONS: THE BROKEN RELATIONSHIP

Dale R. Herspring

Since the collapse of the Soviet Union, the Kremlin's leaders and generals have consistently believed that whatever happens to their conventional forces, if worst comes to worst, they can rely on their nuclear weapons as a deterrent. After all, no country was about to attack the Russian Federation with its triad of nuclear weapons. Unfortunately, for the Russians this was more of an illusion than a reality because in spite of some minor improvements (e.g. the addition of the Topol-M, and the SS-24), the fact is that its nuclear forces are deteriorating along with its conventional forces. Indeed, at present, Moscow has neither a competent conventional nor a nuclear force. The former are in the midst of a major reform project—encouraged by Moscow's poor performance in the war with Georgia—while two-thirds of its nuclear triad is for the most part unusable.

BACKGROUND

When the Strategic Rocket Forces (SRF)/(RVSN) were created in 1959, they were primarily an extension of the Soviet Army's long-range artillery. Indeed, most of the officers came from that tradition, and it would be the ground leg of the nuclear triad that would be the most important. Of the other two legs of the triad, the Navy was second in importance, followed by the air force.[1] This meant that the land-based intercontinental ballistic missiles (ICBMs) were the most powerful components of the Soviet and later the Russian military's nuclear forces. As a consequence, over the years they received the majority of resources and attention. Indeed, the domination of the ground based systems led the Soviets to ignore or at least pay minimal attention to coordinating the three legs. For practical purposes, they were three independent arms.

By the beginning of the 1990s, a significant part of the Russian nuclear triad had come to the end of their service life. After all, the majority of the missiles had been deployed in the 1960s and 1970s. Even the sea-based ballistic missile submarines, the Yankee, Delta I, and Delta II had been put into operation in 1968-74.[2] The Soviets were well aware of the need to modernize their nuclear forces, but the collapse of the Union of Soviet Socialist Republics (USSR) interrupted the nuclear modernization process. Moscow had planned to deploy new types of missiles with shorter delivery times and a shorter booster phase, and to equip them with multi-element last stages, or "buses" to saturate and thus disable the information processing systems and destruction capabilities of the future American antiballistic missile (ABM) defense.[3] Unfortunately for the Russians, by the time the regime collapsed in 1991, the ICBM modernization program was not completed. The same was true of the other two legs of the triad.

In 1991, Gorbachev established the Strategic Deterrence Forces (SDF) which unified the three legs. However, the collapse of the USSR meant that the SDF were located all over the country, as well as in many of the newly independent countries. There was an attempt to save the SDF by creating a combined military force under control of the Commonwealth of Independent

2

States (CIS). For a number of reasons, by the beginning of 1992, it was clear that the CIS option was dead on delivery.[4] Indeed, by the middle of 1992, the key question was how to withdraw the nuclear weapons from CIS countries—how to get them back to Russia. New countries like Kazakhstan, Ukraine, and Belarus wanted no part of the nuclear force. However, the process of withdrawing and re-stationing these missiles on Russian soil undermined whatever progress had been made in coordinating the actions of the three legs. To make matters worse, budgetary allocations were insufficient just to maintain these systems, let alone modernize them.

NUKES AND CONVENTIONAL WEAPONS IN THE 1990s

The 1990s were a difficult time for the SDF. For example, Moscow's nuclear arsenal fell to a level 4-4.5 times below its once impressive figure. The reason was simple: the collapse of the Russian economy made it increasingly difficult for Russia to purchase and maintain its nuclear stockpiles. In 2002, one Russian source claimed that since 1991, "Russia has no resources to maintain the previous nuclear force of about 10 thousand on strategic delivery vehicles and about 20 thousand of sub-strategic nukes."[5]

The situation confronting Moscow's conventional forces was dismal at best. Consequently, Russia's generals had to watch American conventional forces roll unopposed through Iraqi troops during Operation DESERT STORM in 1991. They realized that Russia's chances for keeping up with the West were dimming quickly. This was obvious in the area of procurement, which fell by more than 80 percent between 1991 and

1994.[6] Similarly, by October 1994, "some 85 nuclear submarines were docked because the Navy could not afford to turn to conventional forces, consider the following. In 1991 the military ordered and received 585 combat aircraft. In 1995 it received only 2 combat aircraft."[7] This was not only the case in the air force but throughout the armed forces. To quote the same source, "In most developed countries, between 60 and 80 percent of all weapons are new: in Russia the figure is 30 percent. Assuming this situation remains unchanged, by the year 2005, the military will have only 5.7 percent new weapons. Gradually, we will slide toward the category of armies of third-world countries."[8]

THE MILITARY DOCTRINE OF 1993

Something had to be done. Accordingly, Moscow decided to modify its military doctrine. Thus on November 2, 1993, the Russian government issued a document entitled, *Principle Guidance on the Military Doctrine of the Russian Federation* (PGMD).[9] This statement of military doctrine was based on the first ever National Security Concept (*The Basic Provisions of a Foreign Policy Concept*) previously adopted by the Security Council. In it, Moscow essentially stated that it had no alternative but to rely on nuclear weapons in an emergency, and that it was prepared to use them first if the country's survival was at stake. This was Moscow's form of deterrence. Indeed, the only mission assigned to the nuclear forces was to "remove the threat of nuclear war by deterring its initiation against the Russian Federation and its allies."[10]

It would be wrong to think that Russian military experts seriously believed that Russia could get along with nuclear weapons alone. General Makmut Gareev, generally considered one of Russia's leading military thinkers provided the following observation:

> But it is impossible to ensure a reliable defense with nuclear weapons alone. First, many countries have even now the ability (to be increased in the future) of developing a surprise attack not only with nuclear, but also with conventional precision weapons, in order to destroy the nuclear bases of other countries, depriving them of the ability to retaliate or carry out nuclear retribution.[11]

Regardless of how desperate the Kremlin was for new conventional-type weapons, the 1990s would continue to be a disaster for the Russian military for both conventional and nuclear weapons. To quote Rose Gottemoeller: "The debate over the role of nuclear weapons in Russian national security has been at the center of military reform, with the key questions very much in play."[12]

YELTSIN IGNORES THE MILITARY

Gottemoeller was right. The problem, however, was that Boris Yeltsin did not take military reform, whether on the nuclear or conventional level seriously. He did not consider the West to be a threat, and thus, unlike his generals, was more concerned with his domestic power or the economy than he was with upgrading and reforming the military. In fact, he ignored the military and regularly provided it with far less than even a subsistence budget—the military might only get 40-50 percent of what it was authorized because the tax collection system in Russia was broken. It led to situations where soldiers were sent out to pick mushrooms to supplement their diet.[13]

5

In 1996, the budget shortfall was 25,000 billion rubles (R). The situation inside the military was so bad that the average officer was due about R10,000 in back pay.[14] The next year, the shortfall was R34,000 billion.[15] Because of budgets like the foregoing, there was no money for procurement. What money there was, had to be spent on maintenance and provisions for the troops. As Alexei Arbatov put it, the budgets from 1997 to 1999 allocated up to 70 percent for maintenance, while cutting personnel by 30 percent. This left almost nothing for research and development. Funds allocated to them "were barely sufficient for modernization of the minimal strategic forces."[16] With this background, it is not surprising that there were serious differences between advocates of conventional and strategic forces. In fact, the battle was bitter, made worse by the personal dislike between the two main actors: General Anatoly Kvashnin and Igor Marshal Sergeyev.

THE BATTLE BETWEEN KVASHNIN AND SERGEYEV

General Anatoly Kvashnin was an army officer, a man who had worked his way up serving in a variety of posts in the infantry (Ground Forces) to become Chief of the General Staff. It should also be noted that Kvashnin's personality matched his infantry background. He was open and blunt, and a person willing to engage in bureaucratic fisticuffs even if that meant being insubordinate vis-à-vis his boss.

Meanwhile, the defense minister, Igor Sergeyev, was a career missile officer. Indeed, he spent his entire career concerned about nuclear weapons. He was a polished officer who eschewed the kind of bureaucratic politics that Kvashnin reveled in. It was his job to advise Yeltsin, while attempting to keep the defense establishment on an even keel. Not surprisingly, the outcome was constant conflict between these two men with Sergeyev constantly touting the value of nuclear weapons, while Kvashnin argued in favor of expanding conventional forces.

As with so many other areas, Yeltsin was a major part of the problem. First, he changed the law to place both the defense minister and the Chief of the General Staff directly under him. As a result, the Chief of the General Staff was no longer subordinate to the defense minister. That meant that while the defense minister could do his best to convince the Chief to carry out a specific policy, he could not force him to do so. Furthermore, since the General Staff was primarily in charge of operational matters, the Chief could implement his orders as he saw fit. From a military policy standpoint, the result was bureaucratic chaos. No one knew for certain what Yeltsin's policy was, nor what the Ministry of Defense (MoD) policy was on a variety of issues.

In fact, Yeltsin's only policy was to keep the military off balance, to create a situation in which the military would never threaten his position domestically. After all, he was well aware that it was the military that came to his aid in the 1993 coup attempt. Had the generals decided to sit that conflict out, the outcome might have been very different — with Yeltsin sitting in a Russian jail. He was not about to take a chance with these generals and admirals. If that meant a weaker military, that was too bad, but it was not that important during the 1990s.

One of the few positive things Yeltsin did vis-à-vis the military was to order the Security Council to come up with a new National Security Concept. It was completed on May 7, 1997, and enacted by presidential decree on December 17, 1997.[17] While the Concept laid the basis for a revision of military doctrine, it was far too broad and ambiguous when it came to setting priorities, national interests, and responsibilities.

Meanwhile, in an effort to make structural changes, Sergeyev sought and achieved permission to recreate the SDF. The purpose was to establish a force that combined the strategic nuclear capabilities of the Strategic Rocket Forces, the Navy, and the Air Force, as well as other units having responsibility for early warning command and control units. Additionally, the country's reconnaissance satellites would be subordinated to the SDF.

Finally on March 15, 1999, Yelstin approved a document called "Main Provisions of Russia's Nuclear Deterrence Policy." The document made it clear that Russia's nuclear forces were the guarantor of the country's national security.[18] The problem with the Concept was that it did not bring about the stability and predictability (*stabil'nost' i predvidenie*) that is so much a part of military thinking the world over. Generals and admirals cannot plan for the future if they do not know what kind of a conflict they are preparing for, or if they do not know what kind of weapons systems and personnel they will have at their disposal. If there were two words that would describe the 1990s from the generals' and admirals' point of view, they were confusion and chaos. It was clearly time for a new military doctrine.

PUTIN AND THE MILITARY DOCTRINE OF 2000

When Vladimir Putin took over as president of Russia, he faced a military that was in need of just about everything. Ships did not sail, planes did not fly, and tanks were not in working order. Indeed, the country did not carry out a single division level exercise during the 1990s, and there were many officers at the lieutenant colonel and colonel level that had not commanded an active unit larger than a company. This lack of military experience would come back to haunt the Russian military, for example, in the war against Georgia. Meanwhile, Putin took as one of his primary tasks the stabilizing of the Russian military. After all, Russia was fighting a war in Chechnya, and its military problems could not be ignored.

The *2000 Military Doctrine* was approved by Russian Presidential Edict 706 on April 21, 2000.[19] As it would on other occasions, the Russians refused to clarify the issue of a nuclear threshold. The document made clear that Moscow "keep the right to use nuclear weapons in response to the use of nuclear weapons or other WMD [weapons of mass destruction] against Russia or its allies, as well as in response to large-scale conventional aggression in critical situations for Russian national security."[20] Given the desperate condition of its conventional weapons, it is not surprising that the Russians wanted to preserve freedom of maneuver. That included the use of nuclear weapons, even if a conventional war deteriorated badly. In fact, the Russian military included such an option in its exercises — West 99 and Autumn 2002.[21] The document did not resolve the question of which side the Kremlin should or would favor — nuclear or conventional. Indeed, if there was anything new in it, it was the recognition of the threat presented by international terrorism.

While Washington may not have realized it at the time, its decision to withdraw from the 1972 ABM Treaty meant that the Kremlin did not have to get rid of its multiple warhead missiles as demanded by the treaty. From a policy standpoint, the urgency of modernizing existing missiles disappeared. The current ones would suffice. The Kremlin had found a way to maintain its nuclear weapons "on the cheap." Such a policy may work over the short run, but to remain effective the missiles had to be modernized and new ones had to be developed to counter the other side's countermeasures.

Meanwhile, the very expensive naval arm of the Russian triad suffered one problem after another. First was the sinking of the submarine *Kursk*—one of the modern submarines in the Russian fleet—in August 2000, which presumably was the result of an onboard missile explosion Then there was the case of the *Yuri Dogorukiy*, a strategic submarine that was under construction throughout the 1990s. The intention was for it to enter service in 2001. However, when the missile that was designed for it (the SS NB-28) failed, it was redesigned for the Bulava missile. It was not until February 13, 2008, that it was finally launched. As a consequence, there was no way the Navy could argue for a dominant position in the Russian strategic arsenal.

This brings us back to the ongoing battle between Kvashnin and Sergeyev, which had major overtones for the relationship between nuclear and conventional weapons. The battle between the two men reached the point where, to quote Alexei Arbatov: "In reality, under the umbrellas of the official Russian doctrine, there are now two military doctrines, with all the consequences flowing therefrom."[22] The battle was over the heart of the Russian military—which side would be favored: nuclear weapons as favored by Sergeyev or conventional forces as favored by Kvashnin? The former maintained that, given Russia's weak conventional forces, Moscow's only alternative was to develop its nuclear capabilities to the point where no other state or organization would consider attacking Russia. Kvashnin, on the other hand, maintained that Russia was already faced with threats that could only be handled by conventional forces. After all, one could not seriously consider using nuclear weapons in Chechnya or Bosnia. The military had to have modern conventional weapons to meet these challenges.

For his part, Sergeyev made the familiar argument that all of the conventional forces in the world would not protect Russia in the face of an opponent who had nuclear weapons and the will to use them. To quote Arbatov: "Russia's nuclear arsenal should be sufficient to inflict pre-set damage to any aggressor under any circumstances."[23] However, according to Federov, an analysis of Moscow's nuclear capabilities at that time led to "the major conclusion that Russia's nuclear weapons cannot perform the mission of deterrence against the hypothetical aggression at the regional level."[24] The obvious problem, as pointed out by Alexandr Golts, is that "nuclear weapons are less capable against terrorism than any other."[25]

The simple fact is that "Moscow lacks a coherent military strategy. In particular, the *Military Doctrine of the Russian Federation* was approved only in April 2000, while the *Naval Doctrine of the Russian Federation* was approved in July 2001. Programs and plans of military construction were out of proportion to Russia's economic capabilities."[26] To make matters worse,

Russia's generals could not get rid of the idea of a large scale conflict requiring mass armies. They were still mentally tied to fighting the North Atlantic Treaty Organization (NATO). To quote Locksley:

> There are consistent allegations that the doctrine and training sections of the General Staff are governed by 'Germans', veterans of the Group of Soviet Forces in Germany, who are nostalgic about planning and conducting big multi-theatre warfare rather than setting the doctrinal conditions and introducing suitable training regulations. Russian military forces have not fully reformed and adapted to the changed threat environment.[27]

Regardless of what approach Moscow adopted, Putin had to find a way to stop the constant bickering between Sergeyev and Kvashnin.

On July 12, 2000, there was a meeting in the Kremlin, in which Kvashnin argued in favor of disbanding the SRF. He had in mind cutting the number of intercontinental missile divisions from 19 to 2. ICBMs would go from 756 to only 150 by 2003. This would also decrease the SRF's share of the budget from 18 percent to 15 percent. Sergeyev responded in a newspaper article in which he called Kvashnin's plan, "criminal stupidity and an attack on Russia's national interests." The next day Putin ordered both generals to "silence their debate and come up with realistic policy proposals."[28]

Kvashnin repeated his criticism at an August 11 Security Council meeting attended by Putin. The latter was frustrated, but realized that he would have to do something. He stated, "I have been rather tolerant of the debates in the defense ministry and society as a whole. . . . Now is the time to bring the matter to its rightful conclusion."[29] In the meantime, matters appeared to be going Kvashnin's way. For example, the 1997 decision by Sergeyev to get rid of the Ground Forces as a separate service was reversed.

There was a particularly important meeting of the Security Council on November 9, 2000. During the meeting, Putin acknowledged the importance of nuclear weapons, but he also mentioned the need to "see other challenges." It was clear from his comments that his primary concern was improving the Army's conventional capabilities. The plan adopted at the meeting foresaw a two-staged process. Phase one covered 2001 to 2005 and would focus primarily on personnel. The second focused on giving the military the logistical support it needed.

On March 24, 2001, it was announced that Putin had signed Decree No. 337, "On Supporting the Plan for Conversion and Development of the RF Armed Forces and Improving Their Structure." The decree broke the SRF in two commands: The Strategic Missile Troops and the Space Troops. Four days later Putin fired Sergeyev, making him a presidential advisor. He was replaced by Sergei Ivanov, a former KGB general and close confidant of Putin. Ivanov's task was to smooth matters over with Kvashnin, while helping to create stability inside the military.

In spite of Ivanov's best efforts, it soon became obvious that he could not work with Kvashnin. The latter ignored him just as he had Sergeyev. As noted above, the problem was that the Law on Defense stated that Kvashnin worked for the president, and did not have to clear his actions or ideas with Ivanov. Then on June 14, at Putin's urging, the Duma changed Article 13 of the Law on Defense to mention only the Defense Ministry: "Oversight for the Armed Forces of the Russian Federation is carried out by the defense minister via the Defense Ministry."[30] Furthermore, Article 15, which had listed the main functions of the General Staff, was declared null and void. This meant that henceforth the Chief of the General Staff worked for the Defense Minister. Several weeks later Kvashnin was fired as well.

RUSSIA'S NUCLEAR FORCES

According to Institute for International Security Studies (IISS) figures, in 2000, the SRF had a total of 771 ICBM launchers. However, there were problems with the Navy's new follow-on submarine-launched ballistic missiles (SLBMs), and it was cancelled in August 1998 after three test failures.[31] During the same year, Vladimir Yakovlev, head of the SRF, stated that Moscow "would have 20-30 Topol-Ms each year for 3 years and 30-40 in each of the subsequent 3 years."[32] In fact, Russia deployed only 10 during 1998 and 1999, and six during 2000.

By 2004, matters had further deteriorated. As one observer noted:

> The situation in the manufacturing sector is so serious, that in 2004 serial production of the Topol-M had to be stopped twice. This was the last straw. . . . If the government does not make the necessary steps in the next 2-3 months, the strategic nuclear force's development program will be disrupted.[33]

In fact, Ivanov tried to put a good face on matters, noting in 2005 that the Kremlin intended to acquire six ICBMs and one Tu-160 strategic bomber.[34] From a strategic standpoint, this was a joke as one writer noted:

14

The words about the priority of nuclear deterrence are as usual hanging in the air, because the plan to buy six intercontinental ballistic missiles and one strategic Tu-160 missile carrier in 2006 means nothing to anyone. Vladimir Dvorkin, who earlier headed the 4th Defense Ministry's research for strategic arms stated. With such tempos there is absolutely no certainty about what will remain of Russia's strategic nuclear forces in 2012-2015, after the completely outdated weapons are withdrawn, and whether we will be able to maintain the nuclear balance with the United States at 2,200 warheads determined by the Russian-U.S. Strategic Offensive Reduction Treaty.[35]

On May 29, 2007, Moscow tested a new ground based missile. The SS-24 multiple warhead ballistic missile is similar to the Topol-M except that its primary purpose is to overcome air defense systems such as the one the United States previously intended to deploy in Europe. To quote the now former defense minister Ivanov: "These complexes are capable of penetrating all existing and perspective anti-missile systems."[36] It was tested in its MIRVed (multiple independently targetable reentry vehicle) form in November of 2008.

THE SITUATION WITH THE BULAVA

Just as the SRF needed a new, more modern missile, so did the Navy. New submarines were being constructed, and a new missile had to be developed. Each of the new Project 955 submarines would carry 12 of these new missiles. In addition, these new missiles would be back-fitted into the Project 941 submarines. The Bulava, however, was to become a major headache for the Kremlin. In the beginning, Moscow was convinced that this new missile would be a savior for the Russian submarine fleet.

15

Defense Minister Sergei Ivanov announced that in 2007 the armed forces will acquire a new strategic ballistic missile, the S-30 Bulava . . . . Ivanov said that the new supersonic MIRV missile has no equivalent in the world. On 27 September, a Northern Fleet submarine in the White Sea launched a Bulava, which after a 30 minute flight successfully hit a target in the testing ground in Kamchatka. . . . That same day, President Vladimir Putin said during his nationwide teleconference that the Bulava can change its route and altitude in such a way that it makes the missile invulnerable to the strategic-missile-defense systems of 'some of our partner countries'.[37]

Reality, however, would be quite different from Ivanov's and Putin's predictions. For example, a few days later, the MoD reported that "several minutes after the launch, the automatic system of self-destruction was triggered as a result of a deviation of the mission from its trajectory."[38]

Some background is needed before discussing the Bulava's problems. In 1998 when the decision was made to build this missile, cost was a key concern. Yuri Solomonov, the chief designer at the Moscow Institute of Thermal Technology (MITT), promised to create a new system, the Bulava-30, which is both a land and sea missile. As a consequence, the project was transferred from the Makeyev Design Bureau, which had been building the Topol-M, to MITT. The amount of money sunk into this project by 2009 was $7 billion.[39] Believe it or not, according to some estimates, 40 percent of the MoD's budget was being devoted to the Bulava project.[40] Still, as late as 2008, the MoD was reportedly commenting privately that "the strategic nuclear forces are in particularly catastrophic situation."[41]

If the constant failures by the Bulava were not enough, the Navy was becoming increasingly embarrassed. Why? Because the Kremlin was building submarines to be equipped with the Bulava missile. The MoD expected to have them in service in 2008. The submarine *Dmitri Donskoy* had been refitted in time to accommodate the Bulava missiles. In addition, a new submarine, the *Yuri Dolgorukiy*, was launched in 2009 and ready to go to sea by 2010. Moscow had also begun work on two additional submarines, the *Aleksandr Nevsky* and the *Vladimir Monomakh*. This meant that the Kremlin was faced with the very embarrassing situation of having one submarine that was supposed to be equipped with Bulava missiles going to sea with its missile tubes empty — with two more on the way!

For his part, Admiral Vladimir Vysotskiy maintained that one of the major problems confronting the military in Russia was the decrepit state of its military-industrial complex. There is a lot of truth in his comments — the technology in many of the industrial plants is from the 1970s or 1980s. Furthermore, the average age of most of those who are competent to work in most of those factories is over 60. The majority of the younger qualified workers left the military factories to work in better paying jobs elsewhere.

Faced with this dismal situation, Yuri Solomonov, the Chief Designer who in 1998 claimed that he could design the new missile, was fired. After all, the missile had failed 7 times out of 11 launches since 2004. Despite the poor performance , Moscow appears to be stuck with the Bulava missile. There was talk of inserting the Sineva missile, but it is a completely different system. Furthermore, taking the Bulava tubes and related equipment out of submarines like the *Yuri Dolgorukiy* and replacing them with tubes that would fire the Sineva missiles would be cost prohibitive.

In 2008, Moscow tried to test the Bulava missile once again with one successful attempt in September and yet another failure in December. In the latter case, not one of the reentry vehicles hit their targets at the Kamchatka range. It marked the fifth failure out of 10 launches. As one Russian source put it, "the 10th graded launch from on board the submarine missile-carrier *Dmitry Donskoy* ended in full-scale disaster."[42]

The bottom line stated by Admiral Vysotskiy was that "The Navy has nothing to replace it with." According to Vysotskiy, in spite of the unsuccessful tests, the Navy had no choice but to press ahead with the program. The missile is slated to be the mainstay of the sea leg of Russia's nuclear deterrent through 2040-45.[43]

According to Russian sources, the next test of a Bulava was scheduled for the end of June 2010 on board the *Dmitri Donskoy*. But this was modified in May when it was announced that the missile would be tested "no earlier than November this year [2010]."[44] The reason, according to the Navy, is that they have still not been able to determine "the reason for the previous launch failures."[45] The Navy suspects that the problem is in the assembly of the missile; the only way they can explain why some missiles have worked successfully, while others have not. In the future, the Navy stated that it will launch three Bulava missiles at the same time in an effort to pinpoint the problem. In the meantime, the new submarines will undergo sea trials, but not really put to sea doing the job they were intended to perform until the Bulava is perfected, whenever that happens.

LONG-RANGE AVIATION

Using the one or two Tu-160s available to him, General Igor Khovorov, the commander of Long-Range Aviation (LRA), stated that during 2006, he planned to carry out 10 launches of cruise missiles; not exactly what one would expect from the air force of a superpower.[46] The next year, the commander of the Air Force announced that an upgraded Tu-160 would enter service with the Air Force, and that another one was in the pipeline.[47] Imagine if the effective air arm of the Russian nuclear triad consisted of only four or five old, if modernized, strategic aircraft!

The situation did not improve over time. For example, every time a senior Air Force officer spoke of new planes, his comments were clearly focused on fighter aircraft, which appears to be the major concern of the Air Force at present—the Fifth Generation Fighter. Consider the follow comments from a critic of LRA:

> Strategic missile-armed aircraft are designed to destroy enemy targets with …known coordinates. Recently within the scope of the LRA command and staff drill conducted under the direction of DA (LRA) Commander Major-General Anatoliy Zhikharev, crews took up Tu-95MSs with practice cruise missiles aboard from Engles Airbase. They unsuccessfully executed launches to maximum range (around 2,500) against targets on the northern Pemboy Range (Vorkuta). It was "whispered" to me that the missiles' deviation from the center of the target did not exceed 20m. This is something of which to be proud![48]

The bottom line is that LRA has a very long way to go before it can be considered a critical part of the strategic nuclear triad.

19

THE SEARCH FOR A NEW MILITARY DOCTRINE 2010

Even though it had only been in effect for 3 years, by 2003 there were calls for an updating of Russian military doctrine. As General Anatoliy Kulikov put it:

> Bearing in mind the recent war in Iraq, the current military doctrine of Russia does not meet modern requirements for national security. It should be the basis for drafting a national security doctrine of Russia to clearly define modern threats and challenges to Russian armed forces.[49]

From an organizational standpoint, Putin and Ivanov had succeeded in stabilizing the military. However, there were continued problems—funding for the military was increased, but there was still not enough to purchase the weapons needed either to modernize the country's conventional forces, or to build the nuclear forces the country needed. As a result, in 2005 Putin formally charged Russia's military leaders to come up with a new military doctrine.

One of the key factors of any nuclear doctrine is preemption. Putin had made his position on this issue very clear in 2003, when he remarked, "If the practice of preventive strikes should *de facto* become widespread and grow stronger, Russia reserves the right to such practice." He continued, remarking, that "We are against this, but we retain the right to carry out preventive strikes."[50]

So what were the major—problems beyond the reoccurring issue of preemption? First, as Arbatov noted, was the failure of the doctrine to tell the Armed Forces "what kind of enemy they are supposed to prepare themselves against."[51] A second factor was the absence of a discussion of the threat of terrorism. Meanwhile, under Ivanov's direction (as President of the Security Council), the latter was preparing a new concept of national security, which according to the Russian constitution is supposed to proceed and guide the drafting of military doctrine. In fact, the drafting of both documents would turn out to be more lengthy than anticipated.

There was little change in the concept of nuclear deterrence. Theoreticians like General Gareyev maintained that it was critical to continue to build up Russia's nuclear deterrent. Interestingly, he also noted that it would be important for the doctrine to pay attention to "the development of general-purpose forces; the Air Force, the Navy, and ground troops."[52]

In May 2009, Medvedev signed the *National Security Strategy Document*, which laid the basis for the new *Military Doctrine* document that he signed on February 5, 2010. Insofar as nuclear weapons were concerned, the doctrine of preemption was not mentioned, but the idea was retained. As the document states:

> The Russian Federation reserves the right to utilize nuclear weapons in response to the utilization of nuclear and other types of weapons of mass destruction against it and (or) its allies, and also in the event of aggression against the Russian Federation involving the use of conventional weapons when the very existence of the state is under threat.[53]

This led one commentator to call Russia's new military doctrine "An Exercise in Public Relations"—a reference to the avoidance of the term preemption.[54] Otherwise, when it comes to nuclear weapons, the document is not significantly different from previous editions.

THE SHRINKING NUCLEAR FORCES

Throughout the 1990s and into the next century, not only did Moscow experience problems with particular weapons systems, the number of nuclear weapons was decreasing. Note the following criticism:

> At the start of 1992, the Russian Federation had 6,347 nuclear warheads. When Boris Yeltsin resigned at the end of 1999, he left his successor 5,842 warheads. At the start of 2007, Russia had 681 ICBMs (including SLBMs carried by submarines) with 2,460 warheads and 79 strategic aircraft with 884 cruise missiles. That's a total of 3,344 warheads. If current trends persist (new missiles are being built at an extremely slow rate, while the withdrawal of old missiles is accelerating), the Strategic Nuclear Forces might have no more than 300 ICBMs by the middle of the next decade with no more than 600 warheads.[55]

In short, insofar as Moscow's nuclear forces were concerned, the future looked anything but bright.

THE STATUS OF CONVENTIONAL WEAPONS, 2010

If there were problems with nuclear forces, the problems with conventional weapons were even greater. This was brought home to the Kremlin in great clarity by the War with Georgia. The war began in chaos—especially among the high command in Moscow. As one Russian source put it:

> The Main Operations Directorate and the Main Organization Directorate found themselves on August 8, 2008, in the street in the direct sense of the word. On

that day the directorates were engaged in carrying out a very strict directive of Defense Minister Anatioliy Serdyukov. Ten KAMAZs [a type of Russian truck] were lined up at entrances, and property of the General Staff's two main directorates, packed in boxes and bundles, was being loaded into them.[56]

The result was that "many officers learned the news that Georgia had begun military operations against South Ossetia from morning news publications."[57]

When the generals sat down to evaluate Russian performance during the war, they were shocked and quite vocal in discussing problems. This discussion became the impetus for the greatest change in Russian conventional forces since World War II. In an interview in May 2009, a former Russian Airborne Troop (VDV) intelligence chief, Colonel Pavel Popovskikh, underscored the dated condition of combat training within the elite airborne forces, as well as reflecting on the situation within conventional forces.

> Our army is still being trained based upon regulations, which were written in the 1960s! The regulations, manuals, combat training programmes, and the volumes of standards have become obsolete. An old friend recently sent me the volume of standards that is in force, which we wrote in 1984, 25 years ago. This volume is a reflection of the operation and combat training of the troops and their operating tactics. If the Airborne Troops have remained at the prehistoric level, then we can confidently say that the General Staff and the rest of the troops continue to train for a past war.

The Georgian War was a watershed for Russia. It was clear that the Russian military was plagued with aged equipment, hardware, and weaponry, which were dangerously coupled with ineffective command and control systems, poor communications, and interservice coordination. There were also intelligence support failings, failure of the global satellite navigation system (GLONASS), and higher than anticipated casualties partly as a result of problems with inadequate Identification of Friend or Foe (IFF) equipment. In August 2008, the independent Russian military newspaper, *Nezavisimoye voyennoye obozreniye,* noted that 60-75 percent of 58th Army tanks deployed in Georgia were the old T-62, T-72M, and T-72BM, none of which could withstand Georgian antitank warheads.

There was even controversy among the new weapons that were being produced: when discussing the new T-90 tank in July 2008, then commander-in-chief of Ground Forces Army General Alexei Maslov openly admitted that Russian tanks were lagging behind other countries in the use of modern electronics. As he put it, "although work to develop a tank battlefield information management system is already under way, its installation on outdated tank models is too costly and therefore not recommended."[58]

One could go on, but the bottom line is that weapons and equipment in the current Russian Army is antiquated at best. In June 2009, the MoD stated that "the outfitting of troops (forces) with arms and with military and special equipment currently remains at a level of from 60 to 100 percent, but the proportion of modern models is around 10 percent."[59] It will be many years—perhaps not until 2020, a year often suggested by Russian military analysts—before the military that has been reduced to close to one million personnel and is undergoing major structural changes will have a relatively modern armed force once again.

USING STRATEGIC NUCLEAR FORCES TO OFFSET CONVENTIONAL WEAKNESSES

It is clear that the Kremlin's attempt to maintain a strong nuclear deterrent to provide an umbrella while Russia's conventional forces were modernized failed on both grounds. First, while Russia maintained a nuclear deterrent of sorts, if anything it decreased during the Yeltsin, Putin, and Medvedev periods. As long as one has the option of a nuclear first use, Moscow has a nuclear deterrent, but it is far less than it was in 1993 or even 2000. Furthermore, for practical purposes, it is limited to ground based ICBMs for the immediate future. The other two legs of the nuclear triad — the Bulava naval variant is dysfunctional to this point, and the few obsolete Tu-95MS and TU-160 LAR bombers — for all practical purposes are irrelevant.

Turning to the conventional forces, the military is clearly in a period of transition. Defense Minister Serdyukov has undertaken a major restructuring of the Russian military and faces a monumental task in updating and modernizing its weapons systems. If anything, the quality of the current inventory has continued to deteriorate despite some efforts to modernize them. Weapons systems from the 1970s, 1980s, and even 1990s are everywhere, but they are of little use against weapons systems based on technology from the 21st century.

There is a major problem facing both the modernization of nuclear and conventional weapons, and that is the sad state in which the military-industrial complex finds itself. As a Russian general put it in April 2010, "The Defense Ministry cannot buy something that does not guarantee parity in the event of a conflict. . . . The army cannot buy artillery with a range of

20 kilometers when the enemy has 70 kilometers."[60] In another instance, the same officer made it clear that if incompetence and corruption mean that Russia cannot find quality conventional weapons in Russia, it will have to purchase them abroad—a stinging indictment of the country's domestic industrial complex. To quote him again:

> Vladimir Popovkin said . . . that the military paid defense industry a R5 billion advance for the building of unmanned aerial vehicles, but never did acquire the vehicles, which are so much needed by the field. And this is why it was forced to purchase them in Israel. The problem is not a lack of know-how or ability, it is the backwardness of the available technology of enterprises of the OPK (defense industrial complex). The fact is that certain directors of design bureaus and plants, instead of channeling the allocated funds into the purchase of modern production lines, put them into the bank to obtain interest to build up their margins.[61]

How and when Russian industry will be in a position to produce quality weapons, whether it is a Bulava missile or a modern fighter jet or an armored vehicle, is uncertain. Until it is able to do so, however, the chances of Moscow catching up with the West in either area are minimal unless it purchases all of its weapons abroad.

ENDNOTES - CHAPTER 1

1. Rose Gottemoeller, "Nuclear Weapons in Current Russian Policy," in Steven E. Miller and Dmitri Trenin, eds., *The Russian Military: Power and Policy*, Cambridge, MA: MIT Press, 2004, pp. 183-186.

2. Vladimir Dvorkin, "Russia's Strategic Nuclear Forces after the USSR: Reforming and Prospects," in Yuri Fedorov and Bertil Nygren, eds., *Russian Military Reform and Russia's New Security Environment,* Stockholm, Sweden: Swedish National Defense College, 2003, p. 114..

3. *Ibid.*, p. 115.

4. For a discussion of the problems from a Russian perspective, see Dale R. Herspring, *The Kremlin and the High Command: Presidential Impact on the Russian Military from Gorbachev to Putin,* Lawrence, KS: University Press of Kansas, 2006, esp. chap. 3.

5. Yuri Federov, *No First Use of Nuclear Weapons,* London, UK, *Pugwash Meeting No. 27,* November 15-17, 2002, p. 2.

6. "Defense Ministry on Reform Efforts - Budget," *RFE/RL Daily Report,* August 22, 1994.

7. "Conversation without Middlemen," Moscow TV, September 14, 1995, *Foreign Broadcast Information Service Central Eurasia (FBIS SOV),* September 18, 1995.

8. *Ibid.*

9. For a copy of this doctrine in English, see "The Basic Provisions of the Military Doctrine of the Russian Federation," available from *www.fas.org/nuke/guide/russia/doctrine/russia-mil-doc.html.*

10. *Ibid.*, p. 3.

11. General Makmut Gareev, Jacob Kipp, ed., *If War Comes Tomorrow: The Contours of Future Armed Conflict,* London, UK: Cass, 1998, p. 84.

12. Gottemoeller, in Miller and Trenin, p. 186.

13. Herspring, *The Kremlin and the High Command,* pp. 79-119.

14. As cited in Michael J. Orr, *The Deepest Crisis: The Problem of the Russian Army Today,* Surrey, UK: Conflict Studies Research Centre, Royal Military Academy Sandhurst, October 4, 1996, p. 1.

15. "The Sword of Crisis Over the Military Budget," *Krasnaya zvezda*, January 30, 1999, available from *FBIS SOV*, February 1, 1999.

16. Alexei Arbatov, "The Transformation of Russian Military Doctrine: Lessons Learned from Kosovo and Chechnya," *Marshall Center Papers*, No. 2, July 20, 2000, p. 8.

17. For a detailed discussion of the politics involved with this Concept, see David J. Betz, *Civil-Military Relations in Russia and Eastern Europe*, London, UK: RoutledgeCurzon, 2004, p. 61.

18. See "New Military Doctrine Still Includes Nuclear First Strike," *The Russia Journal*, May 12, 1999, available from *www.therussiajournal.com.index.htm?cat'4&type'3"obj'529*.

19. A copy of the 2000 document is as *Document*, available from *www.scrf.gov.ru.April*.

20. Fedorov, *No First Use of Nuclear Weapons*, p. 3.

21. *Ibid.*

22. Alexei Arbatov, "The Dilemma of Military Policy in Russia," *Nezavisimaya gazeta*, November 6, 2000, available from *ng.ru/printed/ideas/2000-11-16/8_dilemma.html*.

23. *Ibid.*, p. 2.

24. Federov, *No First Use of Nuclear Weapons*, p. 6.

25. Alexandr Golts, *Armiya rossi: 11 poteryannykh let*, Moscow, Russia: Zakharov, 2004, p. 139.

26. Victor I. Esin, "The Military Reform in the Russian Federation: Problems, Decisions and Prospects," in Federov and Nygren, p. 102.

27. Christopher Locksley, "Concept, Algorithm, Indecision: Why Military Reform Has Failed in Russia since 1992," *Slavic Military Studies*, Vol. 14, No. 1, March 2001, p. 16.

28. "Hope Glimmers for Reform," *Moscow Times*, March 29, 2001, Johnson's List, March 29, 2001.

29. "Development Strategy of the Armed Forces Defined," *Military News Bulletin*, No. 8, August 2000.

30. "*Federalnyi zakon ob oborone*" April 24, 1996, available from *www.mil.ru/articles/articles3863.shtml*.

31. International Institute For Strategic Studies, *The Military Balance, 1999-2000,* London, UK: Oxford University Press, 1999, p. 111.

32. Arms Control Association, "Russia Deploys Six Topol-M Long-Range Missiles," January/February 2001.

33. "Development of Russia's Nuclear Forces Said Threatened by Lack of Funding," *Agentstvo Voynnykh Novostey*, October 29, 2004, available from *FBIS SOV*, November 2, 2004.

34. "*Stenograficheskiy otchet o soveshchanii rukovodyashchego sostave Vooruzhennykh Sil*," available from *president.kremlin.ru/appears/2005/11/09/2022_trebe6337tyre63381_969885.shtml*.

35. "Russia's Rearming Too Slow to Compete," *Interfax*, November 11, 2005, available from *FBIS SOV,* November 12, 2005.

36. "Russia Tests Missile Able to Penetrate Defense as Putin Warns of European Powder Keg," *Space War*, May 29, 2007.

37. "Defense Minister Presents New Strategic Missile," *RFE/RL Report*, September 29, 2005.

38. "Russian Navy Official Confirms Failure of Bulava Missile System," *Interfax*, October 25, 2006.

39. See "The 'Bulava' Should Be Put in the Kremlin: It Does Not Fly," *Moskovskiy Komsomolets Online*, August 2, 2009, available from *FBIS SOV, August 4, 2009.*

40. *Ibid.*

41. "Ministry of Defense has Written Latest Concept," *Nezavi-*

simoye vooyennoye obozreinye, August 19, 2008, available from *FBIS SOV,* August 20, 2008.

42. "Programmed for Failure," *Pravda-KPRF,* February 2, 2009.

43. "Navy Commander in Chief: There's Nothing with which to Replace the Bulava," *Grani.ru,* December 16, 2009, available from *FBIS SOV,* December 17, 2009.

44. "Three-Way Error Method," *Kommersant Online,* May 25, 2010, available from *FBIS SOV,* May 26, 2010.

45. *Ibid.*

46. "Commander of Long-Range Aviation Outlines Future Plans," *RIA-Novosti,* December 21, 2005, available from *FBIS SOV,* December 22, 2005.

47. "Russian Air Force Getting New Bombers, Fighters and Helicopters," *Agentstvo voyennykh novostey,* June 17, 2006, available from *FBIS SOV,* June 18, 2006.

48. "Strategic Aviation Maintain Formation! Supersonic Tu-160s Over the Ocean Broke Away from NATO Interceptors," *Argumenty Nedeli Online,* May 10, 2010, available from *FBIS SOV,* May 11, 2010.

49. "Russian General Calls for Drafting New National Security Doctrine," Interfax, April 17, 2003, available from *FBIS SOV,* April 18, 2003.

50. "Putin on Preemption" *AFP,* available from Johnson's List, October 9, 2003.

51. "True Military Reforms are Entirely Up to the President," *Novye Izvestiya,* April 6, 2004, available from Johnson's List, April 6, 2004.

52. "General Gareyev Says Russia Changing its Military Doctrine," *RIA-Novosti,* January 8, 2007, available from *FBIS SOV,* January 8, 2007.

53. "The Military Doctrine of the Russian Federation Approved by Russian Federation Presidential Edict on 5 February 2010," available from *www.sras.org/military_doctrine_russian_federation_2010*.

54. Dmitry Gorenburg, "Russia's New Military Doctrine: An Exercise in Public Relations," February 8, 2010, available from *russiamil.wordpress.com/2010/02/08/russias-new-military-doc*.

55. "Eight Years of Falling Behind and Weakening," *Nezavisimaya gazeta*, No. 27, February 13, 2008, available from *FBIS SOV*, February 14, 2008.

56. "Sword of the Empire," *Zavtra*, October 5, 2008, available from *FBIS SOV*, October 6, 2008.

57. *Ibid.*

58. "Russian General Outlines Plan to Supply Army with New Armored Equipment," *Interfax*, November 15, 2008, available from *FBIS SOV*, November 16, 2008.

59. "National Security Priorities: Improving Legislative Support for Military Organizational Development," *Voyenno-Promyshlennyy Kuryer*, June 20, 2009, available from *FBIS SOV*, June 21, 2009.

60. "Russian Military Refuses to Buy Russian Army's Inferior to Foreign Counterparts," *Interfax,* April 19, 2010, available from *FBIS SOV*, April 22, 2010.

61. "Ultimatum to Defense Industry: The Russian Army Has Already Been Forced to Purchase Weapons form Overseas Firms," *Nezavisimaya gazeta*, April 11, 2010, available from *FBIS SOV*, April 12, 2010.

CHAPTER 2

RUSSIA'S CONVENTIONAL ARMED FORCES: REFORM AND NUCLEAR POSTURE TO 2020

Roger N. McDermott

Although Russian defense reform was already in its advanced planning stages prior to August 2008, the Russia-Georgia war served to facilitate launching the new effort to reform and modernize the conventional armed forces. This reform, repackaged as the "new look," was not only ambitious in its scope and aims but would, if implemented, fundamentally transform the Russian military. Formally announced in October 2008, with the administrative or organizational elements rapidly carried out throughout 2009, and progressing towards achieving key targets by 2012, Defense Minister Anatoliy Serdyukov's reforms have revealed contradictions and unforeseen challenges, while the resulting corrective processes exposed a degree of reconceptualization.[1] The delicate balance achieved in avoiding the reform being undermined, either through institutional inertia or until now largely ineffective or at times irrationally-inspired critics, will continue until these issues are resolved; most likely, not before 2012.[2]

SERDYUKOV'S REFORM

On October 14, 2008, after leaks about the reform agenda and a period of reflecting on the operational lessons of the campaign in Georgia, Serdyukov briefed the defense ministry collegium in closed session. Viktor Zavarzin, the Head of the Duma's Defense Committee, and Viktor Ozerov, the Head of the Defense and Security Committee of the Federal Council, were reportedly not permitted to attend.[3] As the agenda emerged, Viktor Ilyukhin, a member of the State Duma, said its success would largely depend upon developing improved social conditions for servicemen, procuring modern weapons, and enhancing the manageability and discipline of the troops. Aleksandr Vladimirov, the Vice-President of the College of Military Experts, advocated developing new programs and styles of teaching officers aimed at producing a generation of officers with a deep understanding of geopolitics and global trends.[4] The trouble is that few understood the agenda precisely, which often resulted in criticism not really matching what was unfolding, or focusing upon one aspect at the expense of the broader picture.

Serdyukov secured the formal approval of the collegium, briefing them on *Perspektivny oblik Vooruzhennykh Sil RF i pervoocherednye mery po ego formirovaniu na 2009-2020 gody* (*The Future Outlook of the Russian Federation Armed Forces and Priorities for its Creation in the period 2009-2020*). At its heart, the reform concept meant the abandonment of the mass mobilization principle that had served the interests of the state since the 19th century reforms conducted by Dmitry Milyutin. This being the case, it would no longer make sense to argue that the North Atlantic Treaty Organization (NATO) posed any military threat to Russia that required mobilization. That controversy was well-concealed beneath plans to downsize, or more accurately "streamline," the officer corps.[5]

In Orenburg on September 26, 2008, Russian President Dmitry Medvedev met with the commanders of military districts, outlined the reasons for reforming the armed forces, and referred to five decisive factors in military development.[6] These were:

1. Improving the organization and structure of the forces by converting all divisions and brigades to permanent readiness brigades, abolishing the mass mobilization principle and abandoning the division-based system.

2. Enhancing the overall efficiency of command and control (C^2) (later interpreted as opting for a three-tiered structure: operational command-military district-brigade).

3. Improving the personnel training system, including military education and military science.

4. Equipping the armed forces with the latest weapon systems and intelligence assets, primarily high-technology, in order to "achieve air superiority, deliver precision strikes on ground and maritime targets, and ensure operational force deployment."

5. Improving the social status of military personnel, including pay and allowances, housing, and everyday living conditions as well as a broad range of support packages.[7]

Careful analysis of the structure of foreign, including NATO, militaries had convinced the reformers to adopt an officer to enlisted personnel ratio of 1:15. The pre-reform 355,000 officer positions would thus be pared back to only 150,000 and new demands would be placed on these officers.[8] As not all positions were filled, the planning envisaged shedding 205,000 officer posts by 2012 in order to optimize the system by addressing its "top heavy" features that resulted in having more colonels and lieutenant-colonels than junior officers.[9] The officer reductions were severe: the number of serving generals was to be reduced from

1,107 as of September 1, 2008, to 886 by 2012. Colonel posts were slashed from 25,665 to 9,114; majors from 99,550 to 25,000; and captains from 90,000 to 40,000. The only increase was to affect lieutenants, increasing from 50,000 to 60,000. In an interview with *Rossiya TV* in March 2010, Serdyukov explained that another 3 years were required, and he reported that 67,000 officers had been dismissed from service in 2009.[10] If that figure was reliable, they were approximately 50,000 away from the set target by the spring of 2010 (allowing for shedding the 2-year officers) and on course to complete the downsizing by 2012. However, some defense officials questioned whether 15 percent was the correct target and even suggested further paring back the officer corps to 9 percent of the overall manning structure.[11]

Upon completion, the "new look" would abandon the traditional division-based system and replace it with a brigade-based structure geared towards maneuverability. Cadre units were to be jettisoned and in their place only "permanent readiness" formations would remain. Although the transformation impacted on the air force and navy, the greatest impact was on the ground forces, with 85 brigades formed in 2009 and divisions disbanded, while their pre-reform total of 1,890 units was earmarked for reduction to only 172 units and formations. In the air force, which converted to a squadron-based system, only 180 of the 340 units would remain; while the navy was scheduled to move from 240 units to 123. The Strategic Rocket Forces (SRF) (*Raketnye Voyska Strategicheskogo Naznacheniya* [RVSN]) were to be streamlined from 12 to 8 divisions. The airborne forces (*Vozdushno Desantnye Voyska* [VDV]) were reduced from 6 to 5 and faced a brigade-based restructuring, an indication of a one-

size-fits-all approach, although this was later successfully resisted by the VDV, despite the fact that it had
always deployed at sub-divisional level with a brigade headquarters in its recent combat history.[12] The
air force had to shed 50,000 positions,[13] or around 30
percent of existing air force officer positions. In January 2009, Colonel-General Alexander Zelin, the Commander in Chief (CINC) of the *Voyenno-Vozdushnyye
Sily* (VVS) confirmed that the restructuring of the air
force was underway: reforming 80 percent of units,
among which 10 percent were to be disbanded, 22
percent redeployed, and 68 percent would experience
staff changes.[14] The overall driving force in the transition to the brigade-based structure was to enhance the
maneuverability of the ground forces.[15]

Serdyukov also targeted the navy. Initially this
centered on relocating its headquarters to St. Petersburg, though the costly move was postponed in response to concern over the recession and opposition
from serving admirals.[16] In April 2009, the transfer
process was "suspended": of the main command's
800 staffers, only 20 favored the move.[17] Rear Services
were downsized, losing 40 percent of all officers, including a number of generals: 12,500 posts including
5,600 officers and warrant officers. Between 23 to 40
percent of all civilian posts were eliminated,[18] leaving
around 300 individuals in the Rear Services central
apparatus.[19] Many of its functions were civilianized,
ranging from catering services, using civilian enterprises to provide fuel, to the provision of bathing and
laundry services for the troops.[20]

Implementation.

Chief of the General Staff (CGS) Army-General Nikolai Makarov, a critical supportive figure in the reform, noted in December 2008 that to oversee and monitor the implementation of the reform, the General Staff sent its representatives into line units. Their sole task was to report on any instances of individuals seeking to sabotage the reform.[21] During 2009, the structural reforms planned as part of Serdyukov's reforms were largely successful, in what by any standard represented a significant *organizational* achievement. In the process the mass mobilization system, cadres, and divisions (apart from the VDV) all passed quietly into history. Officer downsizing proved more complex, with various figures cited at different times as it progressed. However, by late 2009, officially, 85 permanent readiness brigades had been formed as well and the new three-tiered command and control system was in place. Medical staff lost 10,000 officer posts and 22 military hospitals were closed.[22] Additionally, 80 percent of all lawyers were dismissed, and only 20 officer positions in military media organizations remained—preserving those working for the official defense ministry publication, *Krasnaya Zvezda*. Military educational institutions were also earmarked for reduction from 65 to 10; three military educational centers, six academies, and one military university (streamlining the General Staff Academy), which was needed to serve a new role based on filling the brigades with effective commanders and promoting efficiency and higher standards in these institutions. Deputy Defense Minister Army-General Nikolay Pankov said most of the previous 65 institutions were only 60-70 percent full, and consequently they were combined.[23] The prestigious General Staff Academy had its 17 chairs reduced to two (the art of war and national security and defense) and instead of its usual 100-120 annual graduates, admitted only 16 students at the one-star level in 2009-10. These were taught a revised curriculum (for example, students no longer needed to study the division).[24]

It is also worth noting that, just as President Medvedev and Prime Minister Vladimir Putin are commonly referred to as the ruling "tandem," so too in defense terms there is also an effective tandem: Serdyukov and Makarov. The latter had his service extended by presidential decree after reaching retirement age (60) in October 2009. This partnership between the first truly civilian Russian defense minister (Sergei Ivanov was a former Federal Security Service *(Federal'naya Sluzhba Bezopasnosti)* [FSB] officer) and the Chief of the General Staff (CGS) may well be instrumental in promoting and conducting the reform, but it would be misleading to characterize the reform as being the work of a small or maverick elite: it simply could not be enacted without the active participation of many other actors; particularly the *siloviki* (military politicians).

Contradictions and Challenges.

Almost 2 years into the reform, numerous contradictions and challenges have surfaced. How can such high levels of readiness be achieved if the manning of such brigades is mostly based upon 12-month-service conscripts? Is this enough time to train and achieve necessary standards? There is no consensus within the defense ministry and General Staff on the precise nature of the manning system: a widespread recognition that the experiment with contract personnel has failed has not been followed by any obvious solution. There is disagreement over the length of conscript service, or, faced with a dwindling conscript pool, whether to increase the maximum age for service from 27 years of age to 30.

Much has been made of extensive planning to introduce a new professional non-commissioned officer (NCO), with the first of these being trained in a new NCO training center at the elite Ryazan airborne school. The Commander of the VDV, Lieutenant-General Vladimir Shamanov, was specifically tasked with inculcating the "spirit" of the VDV among these new NCOs. All were required to make parachute jumps and were meticulously trained in a course lasting 2 years and 10 months. Yet, despite the shortage of entrants to the center (it opened in December 2009 with under 260 students), there are also contradictory statements concerning the underlying NCO concept: will these NCOs in the future take on the burden of commanding their units, and will their commanding officers come to terms with delegating authority? Addressing the defense ministry collegium on March 5, 2010, President Medvedev said such NCOs in the future may take on command roles, which does not help to clarify their actual role. Medvedev stated that: "NCOs should be capable, *if required,* to substitute for officers of the primary level."[25]

Another critical factor in measuring the success of Serdyukov's reform will be the transformation of the officer corps. Yet, there is also no clear consensus on what model officer Russian defense planners have in mind, nor has there been any planning for how to achieve this. Instead, there are loosely framed aspirations calling for better types of officers. Reportedly, corruption persists within the officer corps. If there is a concerted effort to minimize or eliminate this scourge, how will the defense ministry conduct such a policy? Will an officer known for his competence and command abilities be sacked if he is found guilty of corruption? Indeed, the challenges facing the new look may be more rooted in manning issues such as these than in overcoming the problems associated with equipment and weapons modernization. Of course, these demands are emerging from the drive to modernize the inventory, as well as from efforts to upgrade command and control and adopt network-centric warfare capabilities. Such a technological and information-based military environment will necessitate a significantly higher level of education to equip officers to meet such demanding challenges.

Surprisingly in this context, the defense ministry expended substantial energy and time on paper chasing. Serdyukov commissioned the drafting of a written code of honor. In November 2010, the 3rd All-Army Conference of army and navy officers was scheduled in Moscow to discuss formulating principles of corporate ethics among Russian officers in the longer-term look of the armed forces. That debate was encouraged within units. This is an important step, as Colonel (Retired) Vitaliy Shlykov believes that a code of corporate ethics will result in a fundamentally "new level" of professionalism within the Russian military. Nonetheless, the development of an ethos and a code of ethics among officers will take time to develop. It is a positive initiative to introduce a clear code for officers. However, as American officers say, they need to "walk the walk," not simply be aware of a codified approach to their important role, but also to live and serve as an inspirational example to their men. Higher standards of justice and moral character are demanded from officers compared with society and those whom they lead, and the formulation of a codified document in Russia will no doubt set a benchmark against which officer standards can be outlined and measured, though the longer-term task is to encourage a constant striving for excellence among officers through a variety of mechanisms including incentives.[26] As these issues are examined by Russian officers, all too often they regard society simply as a source of problems for the military, failing to appreciate just how much Russian society has changed over the past 20 years. This institutional myopia will likely persist until an effort is made to adapt any agreed officer model to reflect societal realities.

An analysis of the reform in the period 2009-10 highlights numerous obstacles and ongoing challenges:

- The downsizing of the Russian officer corps, planned well in advance of the current reforms, is being ruthlessly implemented. Its unintended consequence has been to reduce officer morale and place additional burdens on those serving.
- Senior defense and military officials have avoided offering precise detail on how the downsizing is being conducted, and consequently official statements and figures are often misleading and contradictory.
- Senior level officer rotations, dismissals, or retirements since the reform began reveal a systematic campaign to avoid the emergence of any coherent and organized anti-reform movement.
- The officer cuts were driven by the need to enhance C^2, and improve the efficiency of the manning system and were rooted in a Russian analysis of the structure of western militaries.

- The General Staff wants to develop a new type of officer, more akin to their western counterparts, but presently lack any clearly defined model for officer development.
- Corruption and ill-discipline has increased since the reform began.
- The General Staff has identified that the mentality of serving officers is the main stumbling block in the path of officer reform.
- Russian operational-strategic exercises conducted since the reform was launched confirm that an unstated aim of the "new look" is the adoption of network-centric warfare capabilities.
- Elements of testing network-centric command, control, and communications (C^3) systems established the need to adjust officer training and exposed design flaws in the new technology.
- Exercises, however, remained mostly focused on contact warfare, including both offensive and defensive operations.
- Officers are now being rapidly taught the principles and practical skills needed in order to transition towards network-centric warfare.
- Weaknesses in tactical level capabilities were also revealed and resulted in shifting the training focus in 2010 towards improving individual skills.
- The independence and capability of the "new look" brigades are likely to be impaired for many years by the slow rate of modernization and by further efforts to improve the manning system and reform the officer corps.[27]

Many of these challenges are unlikely to be overcome rapidly. In the case of officer reform for example, rather than achieving the leadership's objectives (if clearly defined) by 2020, it is more realistic to expect the process (if pursued consistently) to take a generation. Perhaps one of the central challenges facing the reform relates to its undeclared aim, which is evident in military exercises and several aspects of officer training and procurement: the adoption of network-centric warfare principles.

While Russian military theorists have long written about and advocated network-centric warfare, this has intensified in two stages, with the first following an analysis of the U.S.-led intervention in Iraq in 2003, and, more recently, after the announcement of the "new look." Although there is clearly theoretical understanding, even sophistication within this "debate," it is equally accurate to designate the Russian military as currently being at the beginning of a very long road towards fully adopting such concepts and applying them within their structures. This is not, as some commentators or government officials appear inclined to believe, merely a question of technology, procuring the necessary high-technology assets including having enough *GLObal'naya NAvigatsionnaya Sputnikovaya Sistema* (GLONASS) satellites in orbit, but it also places demands on the culture of the armed forces extending into thought processes and attitudes.[28]

Russia is still in the early stages of adopting network-centric warfare, which will transition from the current contact-based capabilities towards being able to conduct noncontact operations. However, it is necessary to stress that there are reasons to suggest this will not happen as rapidly as the Russian leadership might like. This is not only linked to the slow rate of procurement (estimates within the Russian defense industry suggest that there is capacity to transfer five brigades per annum to automated C^3 systems) but also raises important defense planning issues.[29] If network-centric warfare capabilities are the central aim of the reform, has this been adequately factored into current procurement plans? In other words is the state prioritizing the correct equipment and weapons systems? Officers receiving additional training during 2010 on how to issue orders using such automated technology reported that the software is overly complicated and the icons and other aspects of the systems need to be simplified. If officers are experiencing such user issues it raises fundamental questions about the end-user being a 12-month conscript. This seems to be more than mere teething issues.[30]

An additional, deeper, and more complex problem, or rather set of problems, relates to the division, disagreement, and misunderstanding that currently exists on how simple or complex these challenges really are and what it means for force structure and training. Reading Russian writers on network-centric warfare, it is quite striking how advanced and sophisticated their knowledge can be, revealing deep understanding of these developments in the U.S. and Chinese armed forces in particular. However, there are gaps and a lack of fully agreed approaches to overcoming such issues, which may well serve to complicate planning decisions. Here the risk is, to paraphrase the former Russian Prime Minister, Viktor Chernomyrdin, "we wanted the best, and ended up with what usually happens." In a recent article in *Nezavisimoye Voyennoye Obozreniye* assessing the contours of this debate, Major-General Vasiliy Burenok, the Director of the Defense Ministry's 46th Research and Development

Institute, examined some of these inconsistencies. Noting that the model of network-centric warfare is formed of three grids (sensor, information, and combat) he then demonstrated the way that many theorists over-simplify the issues.[31]

He noted that some Russian military scientists attempt to prove that adopting network-centric warfare requires no changes to the plans to develop the armed forces and their weapons systems or combat manuals and instructions. Others argue precisely the opposite, and recommend procuring next generation armaments as well as mass-produced network-centric robotic technologies that are not even available in western armies. Burenok succinctly encapsulated the sheer complexity in forming armed forces oriented towards network-centric operations, since it entails seeking a synergy between human and technologically advanced factors. Yet, some theorists persist, in his view, in claiming that progress can be achieved by making a massive and sudden jump to introduce such new concepts and technology. He concludes that if there is no real understanding of how this type of war should be fought, then it is impossible to verbalize and formulate algorithms for conducting network-centric wars. The scientific understanding must *precede* software development and procurement decisions.[32]

After the transition to the new model of the armed forces, we have found ourselves at the beginning of the journey, because both the structure and the composition of the military formations have changed considerably (*and continue to change*).[33] And what about information compatibility? It begins with the unified information space (standard classifications, vocabularies and databases of models, their tactical and technical performance characteristics and so on), whose creation in Russia progresses at a pace which requires considerable acceleration. And the situation with information transferability is far from the ideal altogether, given our mind-boggling diversity of auto-mated systems and means of data transfer which were designed using different fundamental, design, and software principles.[34]

Resolving such issues and making appropriate refinements where needed also, as Burenok stressed, has implications for force structure and development. Thus, while the "new look" is marked by its switch from the system it displaced, it is not yet in its final form: it will continue to change in response to the de-mands of network-centric warfare models and how this is achieved practically and in a way that suits Rus-sian requirements.

Reconceptualization.

Considering the overall conceptual basis of Serdyukov's reform revolving around restructuring and focusing on permanent readiness brigades with enhanced combat capability and combat readiness, it is worth tracing the formative intellectual influences that led to adopting and planning the new look. Of course, brigades were not "new" as such in the Rus-sian military experience. They were, after all, actively utilized in mechanized formations during the Great Patriotic War, and, more recently, Soviet and Russian defense ministers had certainly toyed with the idea of either enhancing the number of brigades or even transitioning more fully to a brigade-based system. In October 1990, Defense Minister Dmitry Yazov signed a draft reform program envisaging such a transition, Pavel Grachev later planned to increase the number of brigades in the table of organization and equipment (TOE) and he, as well as Igor Sergeyev and Sergei Ivanov, considered forming operational-strategic commands. Nonetheless, the most striking feature of Serdyukov's reforms is the extent to which they draw upon an analysis of foreign military experience.

In April 2004, the Foreign and Defense Policy Council (SVOP) in Moscow published an important 70-page study. Colonel (Retired) Vitaliy Shlykov headed the team of writers, including Alexei Arbatov, Alexander Belkin, Major-General (Retired) Vladimir Dvorkin, Sergei Karaganov, Mikhail Khodorenok, and Andrei Kokoshin.[35] The report, *Voyennoye stroitel-stvo i moderinzatsiya Vooruzhennykh sil russiy* (The Development and Modernization of the Russian Armed Forces), identified 15 traits present in the world's leading militaries, though absent from the Russian armed forces, and recommended dramatically reducing the officer corps, abolishing warrant officers, training professional NCOs, introducing military police, and a number of other measures (later featuring in Serdyukov's reform).[36]

This was referred to in a letter from Serdyukov to Sergei Karaganov, the Chairman of SVOP, on September 30, 2009:

> The issues which are raised in the report are important during the period of profound reforms in the Russian Federation armed forces. In the process of the transition to the new model of the Russian Federation armed forces, the Russian defense ministry is *currently implementing the most important measures which are proposed in the report, including the transition to the new TOE and establishment of the military formations, optimization of the command and control bodies, comprehensive technological rearmament of the troops (forces), improvement of*

*the system of staffing, optimization of the system of military
education, improvement of the system of mobilization planning and other measures.*[37]

Serdyukov's letter also promised that the defense
ministry planned to involve SVOP experts in future
development and modernization of the Russian military in the broader, "consultative interaction within
the framework of the activities of the Public Council of the Russian Federation defense ministry."[38] In
April 2010, while attempting to explain why the defense ministry had suspended its plans to introduce a
military police structure, Serdyukov interestingly said
that additional time was required to "study foreign
experience."[39]

It is important to emphasize, however, that there
was and is no Russian effort to copy western experience. Although this analysis is playing a formative
role in the current reform, it is highly unlikely that the
Russian armed forces will ever simply become a copy
of any western model. Although the report cannot be
seen as representing sole justification for aspects of the
reform concept, it is nevertheless possible to discern
many of its features and identify both the strength and
weakness of the new look. For many western observers, the conceptual approach involved in Serdyukov's
reform makes sense precisely because it does draw
upon western experience. As the reform concept was
applied, the defense ministry and General Staff discovered weaknesses or unforeseen problems requiring correction or revision to the original concept.
Absent from the original declaratory concept, for instance, was the intention recently outlined by the General Staff, to replace the existing six military districts
with four enlarged operational-strategic commands
(by December 1, 2010).

The performance of the brigades, for instance, during operational-strategic exercises in 2009 (Kavkaz, Ladoga, and Zapad 2009) revealed that they were heavy and cumbersome, consequently taking longer than anticipated to move over large distances. Such brigades, retaining the firepower of a division and in many cases as much heavy artillery, seemed more like small divisions. This "one size fits all" approach was unsustainable. Senior commanders publicly admitted that recalculation was required. Notably, the CINC of the Russian ground forces, Colonel-General Aleksandr Postnikov, appointed in January 2010, stated that further refinements were needed in order to make the forces more flexible and mobile. He particularly recommended that instead of maintaining such heavy brigades, three types were required: heavy, multirole, and light.[40] Postnikov was effectively saying that a key feature of the reform, rapidly conducted throughout 2009, now required refinement, or additional reform. For critics of this reform, this appeared to admit inadequate planning. Yet, the opposite is probably more accurate: it showed that the planners were implementing, assessing, re-evaluating, discussing, and where necessary making corrections, even if that involved altering key concepts. In other words, paradoxically, it confirms that a real and systemic reform is in progress with mistakes being made, adjustments demanded, and new challenges encountered. Postnikov, in fact, described the brigades as less than perfect, and said that the defense ministry was actively working to correct mistakes. He said the brigades were badly equipped (after all, at the start of the reform, there was only 10 percent modern weapons and equipment in the TOE) and characterized readiness levels as "low."[41] Postnikov was not isolated in holding such views, as an interview by the Deputy Defense Minister for Armament, Vladimir Popovkin, confirmed. On February 20, 2010, Popovkin told *Ekho Moskvy* that the new brigade structure had turned out to be "cumbersome, they are all heavy." He added that "light brigades with light equipment" were needed in order to correct this imbalance. In turn, this would demand a diverse approach toward training, adopting new combat training models, and might also add to the procurement needs of the brigades.[42]

Such calls to further fine tune the brigade structure were also present in work by highly respected military theorists such as Major-General (Retired) Ivan Vorobyev, co-writing in *Voyennaya Mysl,* (along with Colonel Valeriy Kiselev) in the spring of 2010, advocating three brigade types based on enhancing their maneuverability. The co-authored article began with a brief overview of brigade development in the U.S. armed forces and then turned to the history of Soviet brigades during the Great Patriotic War. It highlighted the fact that deficiencies within the TOE can result in military defeat and noted in passing the five TOE reorganizations during the first 6 months of the Great Patriotic War. The article then recommended adopting three types of brigade (heavy, medium, and light) depending on the operational axis.[43] They also stressed that the restructuring of the TOE was no panacea, and the effectiveness of these brigades would depend on several factors:

> Much will depend on technical outfitting, the quality and combat effectiveness of arms and military *equipment,* brigade *manning,* the personnel's proficiency and moral-psychological and combat qualities, materiel support, and above all the *officers' professional training,* which cannot be improved overnight. Brigade

51

employment will be effective when they are trained to preempt the enemy, deliver surprise attacks, and execute swift maneuvers, and when they have high protection and survivability.[44]

It is also worth highlighting in passing the way in which the authors utilized the legacy of World War II as a basis to advocate changing the TOE rather than retaining the pre-existing structures. The experience gained during the war, in their view, had exposed the inadequacies of the TOE and compelled its displacement in order to meet new requirements. Thus, Vorobyev and Kiselev centered their argument on the often unifying legacy of the Great Patriotic War and simultaneously advocated restructuring the TOE.[45]

CGS Makarov has already lamented the low quality of brigade commanders, saying that many of those appointed in 2009 have been sacked because they were simply not up to the task. If Vorobyev and Kiselev's model were adopted, which would certainly contribute to mobility and maneuverability, it would actually result in the basic building block of the new look becoming the *battalion* rather than the brigade. Consequently, the training burden would expose deeper problems; since finding suitable brigade commanders is clearly proving difficult.

As the reform concept is reconceptualized, moving from a uniform brigade size towards perhaps three basic types and determining their mission type and operational utility, it is equally possible that the claim regarding permanent readiness brigades may also require adjustment. The likelihood is that in future there will be a stratified approach to readiness levels on differing strategic axes. Equally, these structures need to be optimized to suit the development and adoption of network-centric warfare capabilities, and as this is introduced and experience is gained, it may well elicit further adjustments. In short, having successfully abandoned the mass mobilization principle, jettisoning cadre units, and forming the new brigade-based structure, the leadership is now reviewing the reform concept itself in order to correct weaknesses discovered after assessing these new structures. The timescale to complete this process is likely to be between 2012 to 2016, while more significant challenges lie ahead in relation to developing the officer corps, educating and training brigade commanders, forming professional NCOs and modernizing the TOE. Despite the officially declared target of reaching a 70:30 ratio of modern equipment and weapons by 2020, progress to date has proved much slower than expected. Rather than the 9-11 percent modernization per annum, the rate appears to be closer to 2 percent. How will this mismatch be corrected? Will the defense ministry opt for more upgrades? Will there be a greater appetite for foreign procurement? Can the problems facing the Russian defense industry be overcome?

Analyzing and assessing foreign military experience and calibrating these features into reform planning, however, will only take Russian defense reform so far. They may understand, often quite thoroughly, the principles involved, but without practical experience they will not appreciate why it works or exactly how. The reform processes could be cut short or facilitated by asking for foreign defense reform assistance, even though such a step is potentially controversial, especially if that assistance were to be provided by NATO or Alliance members, it is nonetheless possible at least in theory, and could form part of intensified trust building measures.

RUSSIAN MILITARY DOCTRINE 2010: "STRATEGIC DISCONNECT"

The long awaited new Russian military doctrine, first mooted by the then President Vladimir Putin in the spring of 2005 and intended to replace its previous version in 2000, was finally signed by President Medvedev on February 5, 2010.[46] Although western and Russian analysts focused their speculation on the nuclear elements of the doctrine, there was no explicit move toward lowering the nuclear threshold, though as many noted there can be no certainty on the issue since further detail on the nuclear posture was contained a classified addendum (*The Foundations of State Policy in the Area of Nuclear Deterrence to 2020*). The military doctrine, tactically released during the ongoing START negotiations and sandwiched between the publication of the U.S. *Quadrennial Defense Review* and the 46th Munich Security Conference, appeared balanced, encapsulating a compromise between hawks and doves and really offering something in its text for everyone, avoiding being either too provocative or controversial. Little in its content fitted with the image of a "resurgent Russia."[47]

Nonetheless, as many Russian analysts and commentators noted, the doctrine is remarkable for a number of less positive reasons. First, and perhaps most striking, it bears no resemblance to the new look armed forces. In fact, it is quite the opposite since it is almost entirely divergent from the actual ongoing military reform.[48] The gap between official theory and practice is therefore staggering by any rational measurement. Moreover, the doctrine occasionally contradicts the May 2009 *National Security Strategy* (NSS) and even contains self-contradictory statements, offering little clarity on the nature of warfare or threats that the armed forces should be prepared to meet. Parts of its content simply make no sense whatsoever. One example of this confused approach, which exposes the dichotomy between the doctrine and Serdyukov's military reform, can be demonstrated by the latter having abolished the mass mobilization principle as a result of the organizational transformation in the armed forces in 2009, while the former document mentions "mobilize" or "mobilization" more than 50 times. The 2000 doctrine specified the role of the General Staff in terms of command and control, also referring to the function of the defense ministry and the military districts. All this has been jettisoned in the new doctrine and in its place there is a vacuum. The new doctrine notes the potential hazard posed by information warfare and the need for the state to possess the means to conduct such operations, yet information warfare is largely ignored in the doctrine, while its only counterpart (*The Information Security Doctrine*, 2000) now appears somewhat dated. The "balance," if this was what was intended on the part of those drafting the doctrine, is in reality a sea of confusion, in which the military are tossed to and fro and any sense of strategy is left helplessly sinking. Long-term trends, clear guidance, or nuanced interpretation in this context must be treated cautiously and often with multiple caveats.

The sense of strategic disconnect contained in the new military doctrine is perhaps better understood by examining certain features of its content coupled with how the document was formulated, noting which actors were involved, and finally linking the doctrine to the actual condition of the conventional armed forces.

The Search for the "New:" Defining "Dangers" and "Threats."

The military doctrine takes account of its previous 2000 version as well as other strategic planning documents (*Concept for the Long-Term Socioeconomic Development of the Russian Federation for the Period through 2020, National Security Strategy through 2020,* and relevant provisions of the 2008 *Russian Foreign Policy Concept* and the *Russian Federation Maritime Doctrine for the Period through 2020*). In general terms, the doctrine appeared too loosely constructed, lacking specificity. This prompted Colonel-General (Retired) Leonid Ivashov to observe: "This doctrine can be used in military academies for seminars on the subject of how to compile such documents, but this doctrine has little to do with Russian reality."[49] However, the doctrine contained little that was fundamentally "new," though there were shifts, text left unchanged since the 2000 version, and aspects that failed to connect with changes in the strategic environment since 2000.[50] Unlike the 2000 doctrine, the new military doctrine makes a crucial distinction between *opasnosti* (dangers) and *ugrozy* (threats) facing Russia. This allows Moscow to continue to designate NATO enlargement, as opposed to the existence of the Alliance *per se,* as a danger, rather than an imminent threat. In so doing, however, and by placing this as the primary "danger," Moscow has signaled that the previously anti-western paradigm evolving within its doctrinal thinking persists, albeit in a slightly more muted manner.[51] Allowing for the innovation of distinguishing the difference between dangers and threats, as well as the general less specific framing of language regarding the latter, it is worth noting the perception of the Russian security elite that the dangers facing the state have grown.

To begin with, the doctrine defines how these terms are used: a military danger is "a state of interstate or intrastate relations characterized by an aggregate of factors that can, under certain conditions, lead to the emergence of a military threat." Whereas a military threat is:

> a state of interstate or intrastate relations, character-ized by the real possibility of the emergence of a mili-tary conflict between opposing sides, a high degree of readiness of some state (group of states) or separatist (terrorist) organizations for the use of military forces (violence with the use of weaponry).[52]

In other words, in certain situations the former may evolve into the latter more serious scenario.

Dangers and Threats.

These dangers are delineated into 11 points. Pole position, as already noted, is given to NATO (in the 2000 doctrine not specified, only referred to as a "bloc"), especially the aim of assigning global func-tions to the Alliance, both violating international law and moving relentlessly towards Russia's borders by its expansion; attempts to destabilize individual states or regions, or undermine strategic stability; deploy-ment or build-up of foreign troops on the territories or waters of states contiguous with Russia and its al-lies; creating and planning to deploy strategic missile defense systems to undermine global stability and nuclear parity, militarizing outer-space and the de-ployment of strategic non-nuclear precision weapon systems; territorial claims on Russia or its allies and interference in their internal affairs; proliferation of weapons of masss destruction (WMD), missiles, and related technology, and the increase in nuclear weapon states; individual states violating international accords and noncompliance with existing treaties; the use of military force close to Russia in violation of the United Nations (UN) Charter or other norms of international law; the emergence of armed conflict and possible escalation of such conflicts on the territories of states close to Russia and its allies; the spread of international terrorism; and the emergence interfaith tension, international armed radical groups in areas adjacent to Russian borders and those of its allies, and the growth of separatism and religious extremism in various parts of the world. Internal dangers stem from efforts to compel change to the constitution; undermine the sovereignty, unity, and territorial integrity of the state; and disrupt the functioning of the organs of state power, state and military facilities, and the information infrastructure of Russia (Section II.8.a-k; 9.a-c).[53] The proliferation of WMD and the increase in the number of states with nuclear weapons as well as international terrorism, according to the military doctrine, pale in comparison with NATO.

As noted, the reference to NATO is not new. What is new is the way it is presented more exactly as a "danger," which probably also reflects dissatisfaction with the lack of western interest to date in Medvedev's European security architecture initiative. The second seems to be an insertion that fails to make clear to what it might refer, while the next appears a more nebulous variant on a similar statement in the previous doctrine. An additional new danger appears to relate not only to Ballistic Missile Defense (BMD) but also obliquely to U.S. "global strike" planning. Reference to territorial claims against Russia has been condensed in the new doctrine, since the old formula had an additional element concerning a multipolar world. The next two dangers were absent in the old doctrine:

WMD proliferation and related technology and the violation of international treaties and agreements. The first of these could be explained by reference to North Korea and possibly Iran, while the latter seems linked to the abrogation of the 1972 ABM (antiballistic missile) Treaty and the collapse of the Conventional Forces in Europe (CFE) Treaty. The danger posed by the use of military force near Russia in violation of the UN Charter follows a similar formula used in the old doctrine. Finally, the references to interfaith tension and international armed radical groups must surely have Afghanistan in mind. Internal dangers relate to separatism and terrorism mainly in the North Caucasus, as well as possible attempts to penetrate information security.

The main military threats stem from a drastic deterioration in the (interstate) military-political situation resulting in escalation to the use of military force; impeding the functioning of command and control systems in the country; disrupting the functioning of the Strategic Rocket Forces, missile early warning systems, space-based monitoring systems, nuclear weapons storage facilities, and other potentially hazardous facilities; forming and training illegal armed formations on Russian territory or on the territory of its allies or contiguous state; demonstrations of military force during military exercises on the territories of states contiguous with Russia; and, finally, increased activity on the part of armed forces of individual states or group of states involving partial or complete mobilization and the transitioning of the states' organs of state and command and control to wartime conditions (Section II.10.a-e).[54]

The first of these threats does not appear in the 2000 doctrine, while the second follows the earlier formula almost verbatim. The third threat, though present in the old doctrine, seems to signal concern that an enemy may try to establish and train illegal armed formations on Russian territory. However, the fourth and fifth threats are new and, in terms of the latter, while the doctrine does not explicitly mention China, which is taboo in Russian security documents, it might reflect growing concern in Moscow over military exercises conducted by the People's Liberation Army (PLA), that appear to have rehearsed future Chinese military intervention in Russia and Central Asia.[55] Thus, as the military doctrine outlines the dangers and threats facing the Russian state, these are often contradictory, give rise to questions concerning their order of importance, countermand other strategic planning documents such as the *Foreign Policy Concept 2008* or the *NSS 2009*, and are so loosely framed as to appear nebulous. NATO is represented as a danger and its global functions decried, while the same doctrine advocates a much firmer version of Article 5 in relation to the Moscow-led Collective Security Treaty Organization (CSTO) and, in its list of multilateral organizations with which to pursue cooperation, mentions NATO (albeit in last place after the CSTO, Commonwealth of Independent States [CIS], Organization for Security and Cooperation in Europe [OSCE], Shanghai Cooperation Organization [SCO] and the European Union [EU]) (Section III.19.e).[56]

Lengthy Gestation Period: Infighting, Military Reform and Other Factors.

The terrorist attacks on New York and Washington on September 11, 2001 (9/11), followed by the global war on terrorism, and intervention in Afghanistan and Iraq, combined with the progress of the second

Chechen war and instances of domestic terrorism in Russia such as the Nord Ost theater attack in Moscow in October 2002 or the Beslan school siege in September 2004 appeared to necessitate revision of the military doctrine passed in 2000. Adjustment to the post-9/11 security environment, enhanced for a time by Moscow's willingness to pursue international counterterrorist cooperation, finally resulted in the then President Vladimir Putin ordering a new military doctrine in June 2005. That the gestation period for this new doctrine was so long, almost 5 years, requires some explanation. In seeking that bureaucratic insight, it is necessary to scrutinize, as far as possible, features of the drafting process to understand how the "balance" represented in the new doctrine was achieved and where the sensitivities were located.

On January 20, 2007, a consultative conference was held in Moscow to examine the issue of formulating a new military doctrine. Those attending the conference were representative of the bodies with vested interests in the military doctrine: the presidential staff, government, Duma, Federation Council, Security Council, Ministry of Defense, Interior Ministry, Emergencies Ministry, the Federal Security Service, Federal Protection Service, Academy of Sciences, and Academy of Military Sciences. In January 2008, the Academy of Military Sciences held an additional conference that also paid close attention to such issues. In December 2008, more formal plans for a new military doctrine were announced. During a meeting of the Russian Security Council a working group was formed consisting of delegates from state bodies and civilian and military academic experts and led by the Deputy Secretary of the Security Council, Army-General Yuri Baluyevsky (former Chief of the General Staff). Colonel-General Anatoliy Nogovitsyn headed the defense ministry working group. Army-General Makhmut Gareev, President of the Academy of Military Sciences and one of the country's foremost military theorists, also played a key role in drafting the doctrine. Thus, the most significant players leading the process shared a military background and probably brought military interests to the fore. What is remarkable is that the reporting on the drafting in 2007-08 bears a striking resemblance to the final content of the 2010 military doctrine.[57]

A key paper in the January 2007 conference entitled "Doctrinal Views of NATO on the Nature of Wars and on Security" presented by an unnamed Main Intelligence Directorate (GRU) officer, reportedly stressed the issue of NATO expansion. Another paper, "The Role and Place of Strategic Nuclear Arms in Russia's Military Doctrine," asserted that the security of the Russian state is *90 percent* dependent upon nuclear deterrence. Colonel-General Aleksandr Rukshin, the then Chief of the General Staff's Main Operations Directorate, covered the organizational development and use of Russia's armed forces. Papers were given in order of importance, with air and space defense placed above naval aspects of doctrine. Papers on international terrorism were therefore given less priority, in part since the armed forces saw this as a function of the interior ministry and intelligence services, while a paper on military education failed to reach the top 10. Yet, Baluyevsky emphasized that the main threat was hidden in the fact that the conduct of hostile information activity against Russia has incommensurately grown, the initiator of such activity appeared clear to all military chiefs assembled in the hall. Critically, following the conference, Major-General (Retired) Vladimir Belous, Professor in the Academy of Military Sciences, said that he saw few differences between the military doctrine in 2000 and that being worked out:

> There was no military doctrine in Soviet times, but there was a powerful army. The organizational work of the top was aimed at increasing the professional capabilities of the armed forces. Now in the post-Soviet period the Chief of the General Staff is motivated by the assessments of the Americans on the highest state of the Russian armed forces. Apparently he does not realize that this is said to a great extent in order to increase the Pentagon's budget. And meanwhile the organizational work of the highest military circle degenerates into primitive paperwork, as if the paper itself will solve the problems of the armed forces.[58]

The die was largely cast then during 2007-08 and there were intermittent rumors that the new doctrine would be signed in the latter part of each year. The question arises, why was it delayed? Some analysts suggested that evaluating BMD, or the presidential transition from Putin to Medvedev, or indeed waiting to assess the outcome of the U.S. presidential election may have played some part in shelving the doctrine. However, the necessity for the new doctrine emerged more sharply after the Russia-Georgia war in August 2008 and the launching of Serdyukov's new look reforms in October 2008. For instance, the inclusion in the doctrine of the affirmation of the right to deploy troops abroad "to defend the interests of the Russian Federation and its citizens, and to protect international peace and security," directly follows Medvedev's December 2008 (Section III.26) change to the law on defense permitting this type of intervention.[59]

Nuclear Posture and Redrafting.

Despite the reset in U.S.-Russian relations that largely took place in the fall of 2009 around the on-going START talks, senior Russian security officials not only implied that consideration was being given to lowering the nuclear threshold, but also to the extension of nuclear deterrence to involve local conflicts. Although he was not intending to promote an image of continued conventional military weakness, Secretary of the Security Council and former Director of the FSB, Nikolai Patrushev, revealed details of changes to the draft military doctrine in relation to the country's nuclear posture. In an interview with journalists in Novosibirsk on October 8, 2009, Patrushev signaled that the doctrine was being "fine-tuned," and may include the right to use a "preventative nuclear strike."[60] He also stated that Moscow's greatest priority was to "keep its nuclear state status" and that "conditions of the deployment of nuclear weapons" were corrected to allow their use "not only in global but also regional and even local conflicts." He also said: "The conditions for the use of nuclear weapons to repel aggression with the use of conventional weaponry in large-scale, but also in regional and even in a local war have been corrected. Moreover, in situations critical for national security, the inflicting of a preventive nuclear strike upon an aggressor is not excluded." However, his meaning was clear, since during his interview he left little scope for doubt, using the word *preventivnyy* (preventive) several times and only once using the term *uprezhdayuschiy* (preemptive).[61] It is also important to note that General Baluyevsky provided tacit support for these comments, confirming on October

15, 2009, that such revisions were being made to the draft doctrine.[62] Such comments aroused trepidation even on the part of Russia's closest allies.[63]

Russian commentators were also uneasy about Patrushev's comments, though largely in agreement that despite Serdyukov's reform agenda, it implied continued conventional weakness. Konstantin Sivkov, the Vice-President of the Academy of Geopolitical Problems, said that due to the serious problems in the armed forces, "Russia can ensure its national security and ward off military threats on the scale of local wars and above [regional and large-scale] only by recourse to the threat or direct use of nuclear weapons."[64] Aleksandr Pikayev, a government critic and a high-ranking member of the Russian Academy of Science, said that the planned shift in the new doctrine reflected conventional weakness and an admission that the armed forces simply were unable to carry out their "assigned missions." Igor Korotchenko, a member of the Defense Ministry's Public Council and the then editor of *Voyenno-Promyshlennyy Kuryer*, said that the new doctrine had to "compensate for the degradation of the Russian armed forces," adding that to preserve its great power status Russia "is ready to use nuclear weapons."[65] Some even suggested that the lack of progress in military reform had increased reliance upon nuclear weapons as the only possible way to deter aggression against Russia.[66]

Other officials and experts were more guarded in their assessments, linking any possible inclusion of Patrushev's leaks in the new doctrine, once finalized, to progress in the START talks. An unnamed source in the presidential administration, for instance, told *Vedomosti* that the new doctrine was "still being worked out," and the final decision would be left to

65

Medvedev.[67] Although much of the doctrine had already been drafted, it appears on closer examination that some redrafting occurred following the meeting between Obama and Medvedev in Moscow on July 7, 2009, and that these revisions were further affected by the ongoing START negotiations. In February 2009, Serdyukov claimed the new doctrine would be ready for signing in September 2009, while later in the same month CGS Makarov explained that doctrine had been "worked out" and "will remain in its current form."[68] By May 2009, Colonel-General (Retired) Vladimir Karabushin, the Vice-President of the Academy of Military Sciences, said the new doctrine would receive Medvedev's signature in early August.[69] Nonetheless, in early August Patrushev, far from implying imminent signature, said that in fact "substantial revisions" were made and claimed that the latest draft bore little resemblance to the earlier one. It is likely that the point of neuralgia and disagreement related to the nuclear issue.[70]

The abandonment of the mass mobilization system and transition from the division-based structure in the ground forces to the brigade-based replacement, implemented rapidly throughout 2009 meant the doctrine could only realistically be signed at the end of that year.[71] As that organizational transition occurred and the new brigades were tested in operational-strategic exercises in 2009 (Kavkaz, Ladoga, and Zapad 2009), the General Staff had to contend with convincing skeptics that the new look may result in lowering readiness levels. That in turn led to the hawks pushing the nuclear threshold and preemptive strike issues onto the agenda, while the General Staff leadership attempted to portray the new brigades as more combat capable and combat ready.[72] Despite the public claims that the conventional transformation had resulted in achieving the capability to deploy brigades within "1 hour," it seems that a tenuous consensus was reached amounting to recognition that the reforms had not damaged readiness levels (which were very low prior to launching Serdyukov's reform).[73] An additional area of widespread disagreement related to abandoning Russia's traditional self-reliance on its defense industry for its procurement needs. The admission in September 2009 that talks were underway between Moscow and Paris on the possible procurement of the *Mistral* class amphibious assault ship brought the controversy over seeking foreign armaments and equipment to the fore and this internal tussle most likely carried over into the issue of finalizing the military doctrine.[74] The reformers also knew the draft paid scant regard to the new look and had to brace themselves to press ahead with the reform despite the impending publication of a doctrine that seems at odds with the agenda.

While nuclear preemption and lowering the threshold was clearly on the agenda, an event in early December 2009 in Moscow may well have proven to be an opportunity to move a voice of reason center stage. On December 8, 2009, an assembly of the Academy of Military Sciences held in Moscow examined urgent problems in the development of military science and improving the country's defense. In the presence of many of the military top brass, the keynote speech was given by the President of the Academy, Army-General (Retired) Makhmut Gareev. His wide-ranging speech covered the situation in Afghanistan, the expansion of NATO, the South Caucasus, Central Asia, transnational threats, and changes in the strategic environment. Gareev said that insufficient attention was given to identifying the intentions and forecasting the practical actions of numerous international and transnational forces, particularly the western think tanks producing closed work for government. "This is why many important processes end up outside our field of view," he asserted. However, he noted forms of opposition, economic, information-based, and psychological, having a substantial impact on the nature of warfare and the development and training of armed forces. Stressing that nuclear weapons remain the most important and reliable means to ensure the security of the Russian state, he said that with the nature of new threats nuclear weapons could not be regarded in absolute terms. Gareev noted:

> Having a mindset that Russia's security is guaranteed as long as there are nuclear weapons do not conform fully to the new realities. We know the Soviet Union had nuclear weapons, but nuclear weapons remain and there is no union state.[75]

Moreover, he emphasized that such weapons cannot be general-purpose, stressing their use is futile in local situations such as Chechnya or to neutralize economic and information threats or all types of subversive activity. Drawing on the experience of the Great Patriotic War, Gareev said it was time to assess the merits of the decisive importance not only of the initial period of war, but above all the first strategic strike. Reminding his audience of the difficulties the Red Army faced in the first few months following the German invasion in 1941, then referring to more recent conflicts in the Persian Gulf and Yugoslavia (1991 and 1999 respectively), he said in modern conditions it is impossible to withstand a massive first strike. "Therefore, as in the fight against terrorism, more aggressive actions are needed and preemptive actions as well, if necessary," he concluded.[76] His appeal seemed less nuclear than it did conventional. An aspect later taken up in April 2010 by Andrei Kokoshin, a member of the Russian Academy of Sciences and former member of the Security Council: "The new Russian-U.S. treaty on strategic offensive armaments lays the basis for strategic stability for the foreseeable future. However, this is not an automatically achievable objective. It can only be achieved if Russia continues to carry out a whole range of improvements to its strategic forces." He explained that Russia should keep its strategic forces secure against attacks and increase their capacity to penetrate any potential missile defense, adding: "Strategic stability will largely depend on precision weapons with conventional warheads, to which a great deal of attention should also be paid, providing Russia with a potential for non-nuclear or *pre-nuclear deterrence*."[77] "The latter by the way, is prescribed by the new Russian military doctrine," he said.[78] His reference to *pre-nuclear deterrence* drew upon Gareev's thinking, but it is still a long way off, as the conventional modernization of the Russian armed forces faces technological and defense industry-related challenges. In any case, Gareev's was a voice of reason: nuclear weapons cannot be considered as general-purpose options.

Patrushev's leaks were ultimately absent from the new military doctrine which, if anything, assumes a more cautious stance on the nuclear issue than did its previous version in 2000. There is no commitment to preventive or preemptive strikes, or reference to local conflict. Its comment on the issue, briefer than in 2000, describes nuclear use "when the very existence of the state is under threat," instead of the earlier: "in situations critical to the national security of the Russian Federation."(Section III.22).[79]

The Russian Federation reserves the right to utilize nuclear weapons in response to the utilization of nuclear and other types of weapons of mass destruction against it and (or) its allies, and also in the event of aggression against the Russian Federation involving the use of conventional weapons when the very existence of the state is under threat. (Section III.22).[80]

As if to stress still further the level of extreme caution involved, the doctrine also adds: "The decision to utilize nuclear weapons is made by the Russian Federation president." Its inclusion seems calibrated to remind the military that the decision rests with the supreme political leadership. Despite the controversy in the fall of 2009, the doctrine did not adopt a more aggressive nuclear posture, suggesting that a struggle occurred in the hiatus resulting in the victory of more moderate forces in the Russian security elite.[81] While there was a fudge on the issue of the new look, on the nuclear issue and foreign procurement the hawks were plucked and their hopes for rapid feather growth lay in questioning whether the new look will prove successful in the future and in clinging dogmatically to nuclear deterrence. Paradoxically, the new doctrine subsequently allowed slightly more scope to those advocating reform to openly discuss the "teething" problems of the new look armed forces.

PANDORA'S BOX AND GROWING INTERNATIONAL STRATEGIC CONFUSION

This uneasy consensus reflected in the new military doctrine, which appears weighed in favor of old approaches, manifests itself in a curious way in the country's nuclear posture. Military justification for such reluctance to reduce or eliminate Russian tactical nuclear weapons (TNW) is less rooted in strategic deterrence capabilities than either Russian politicians or experts admit. The Defense Ministry's 12th Main Directorate (*Glavnoye Upravleniye Ministerstvo Oborony*—GUMO) tasked with responsibility for nuclear weapons, maintains that such weapons are needed in the Kola Peninsula at naval facilities. Equally, it is fair to say that within the Russian armed forces, the navy is the main advocate of maintaining these capabilities, since they are considered as a necessary part of confronting the U.S. Navy in any conflict. In August 2009, the naval main staff indicated that the role of TNW was set to expand on attack nuclear submarines for that very reason.[82] GUMO and the uniformed armed forces, however, would place much greater currency upon long-range systems, rather than on tactical weapons when attempting to relate nuclear strategy to actual military planning. As the Russian state seeks to update and modernize its strategic nuclear forces by 2020, many are expressing skepticism that this will be fully implemented, not only owing to budgetary setbacks, but also due to the ongoing design problems experienced in connection with the Bulava submarine-launched ballistic missile (SLBM). Nevertheless, the political inertia and sensitivity surrounding the issue of nonstrategic weapons has long resonance after previous futile efforts to make progress on the issue.

While many have questioned the military value of TNW, a belief in such military value most certainly persists in the Russian strategic context, but primarily in relation to China. This is due to several factors all linked to Russian conventional weakness vis-à-vis the PLA. In the first instance, in any military conflict the Russian VVS cannot guarantee air superiority against the Chinese. Moreover, they do not possess sensor-fused cluster munitions, though in theory their surface to surface missiles (SSM's) could deliver cluster munitions depending on whether the missile troops remained intact long enough. Faced with an advancing PLA division or divisions, early use of TNW would present a viable option.

In February 2010, Aleksey Arbatov, the Head of the Moscow-based World Economics and International Relations Institute of the Center for International Security, explained that such weapons are for Moscow, "the chief guarantee for maintaining a balance of forces with the United States," adding: "Considering the colossal U.S. superiority in conventional weapons and the growing lag above all in delivery vehicles of the strategic forces, the role of TNW only grows as an instrument of foreign policy." Yet, the military significance of the tactical weapons is far eclipsed by the issue of how to verify and monitor any binding joint reductions, since, as he admits, this is in order of magnitude much more complex than any reduction in strategic nuclear forces. "Technically it is practically impossible to verify a reduction," he suggested. "While intercontinental missiles simply can be destroyed, you cannot do it so simply with dual-purpose delivery systems," Arbatov believes, pointing out that frontal aviation artillery and the navy can be equipped with such capabilities, but monitoring their storage facilities would be "unprecedented."[83]

Colonel-General (Retired) Viktor Yesin, a former Chief of the Main Staff of the RVSN, linking recent assurances over U.S. BMD plans with the possible future participation of Russia, expressed the need for caution on the part of Moscow:

When the issue is national security, attention must be given to the capabilities of the arms system being developed and not to assurances, which can change in 1 hour. Moscow should not fall into the same trap that it fell into in the past when the West promised that, after the unification of Germany, NATO would not advance to the East.[84]

Such skepticism, distrust, and outright opposition to cooperation with the United States or NATO in the areas traditionally featuring in Russian anti-western foreign policy rhetoric is more pronounced in the discussion on TNW. Any sense that such discussions may serve to benefit Russian security is at best a minority view. While its U.S. and European advocates appear to suggest that the reduction of U.S. TNW based in Europe would result in strong pressure on Moscow to reciprocate, Russian experts adopt a more nuanced stance, partly based on attacking western thinking or in pointing out the contradictions in the strategic thinking at play. Major-General (Retired) Vladimir Dvorkin, a senior researcher at the Institute of World Economy and International Relations of the Russian Academy of Sciences,[85] recently encapsulated that approach by noting that Russia need not respond to any future withdrawal of such weapons from Europe, since, as he suggested, this would take the form of a unilateral action, and Russia has no such weapons deployed beyond its territory. Only after a unilateral withdrawal of U.S. TNW from Europe could bilateral talks commence between Moscow and Washington aimed at a balanced reduction of these weapons. As Dvorkin stated in what could only have been a passing reference to the China factor, "This does not mean that we must achieve the same ceilings (that is, the same levels of TNW), since, in comparison with the

United States, Russia is in a different regional situation." Yesin also supports such a position, arguing that Moscow must set as a pre-condition to any talks, that all strategic and TNW must be located exclusively on the national territories of those states possessing them.[86] Dvorkin implied that any policy designed to "place the onus on Russia" would be doomed from the outset.

On April 21, 2010, prior to traveling to Washington for talks on a range of security issues, CGS General Makarov indicated that this represents official policy, stating that any future negotiation must be preceded by withdrawing U.S. weapons from Europe. He also argued that given the conventional imbalance in Europe between NATO and Russian forces, including precision weapons, TNW play an important role for Russia.[87]

Due to the lack of official transparency on these weapons, estimates as to the precise numbers in the Russian inventory vary widely from 2,000 to 6,000, with the lower figure concentrated more on deployed weapons, while others are stored. One estimate claimed the ground forces still have access to more than 1,100 tactical warheads with more than 2,200 available for naval deployment. By 2007, GUMO reported that all tactical weapons reductions among those assigned to the ground forces had been completed.[88] In late 2003, senior Russian military officials suggested that such weapons were needed to counter possible development of new types of U.S. weapons, and in late 2008, CGS Makarov said these were required as long as the European continent was unstable and so heavily armed. Sergei Karaganov, on the basis of available reports commented: "According to unofficial information (we usually do not provide official information), Russia has 5,400 of these warheads, 2,000 are in a combat-ready state, and the majority of them are in Europe."[89]

Hawkish members of the Russian security elite tend to unite around the idea that it is too early to begin to discuss the tactical nuclear issue. On March 5, 2010, addressing a nonproliferation conference in Moscow dedicated to the 40th anniversary of the Nuclear Non-Proliferation Treaty (NPT), Army-General Yuri Baluyevsky, Deputy-Secretary of the Russian Security Council and former CGS, said that such talks could begin, but only after the United States withdrew such weapons from Europe, stressing the United States is unique in being only country that has TNW on the territories of other states. Baluyevsky stressed that "American tactical nuclear armaments in Europe are strategic for Russia because their delivery vehicles have a small distance to cover."[90] Baluyevsky also reacted negatively to the shift in U.S. nuclear doctrine, saying that it was rooted in the growing capability of its high-precision strike systems, and echoed the concern of other Russian military officials about placing conventional warheads on strategic delivery systems.[91] In October 2009, Lieutenant-General Andrei Shvaichenko, Commander of the RVSN, expressed deep concern that international security might be damaged by the formation of the U.S. Global Strike Command. He said that as conceived, strikes could be launched carrying a nuclear or conventional payload, and he noted that no detection system was capable of distinguishing the type of warhead after its launch. The state targeted by such a strike would need to evaluate the degree of threat and appropriate retaliatory measures to be taken, he said. "In the short time span involved, the response will be quite predictable, which could push mankind to the brink of a nuclear catastrophe," the general explained.[92]

Other aspects of Moscow's attitude towards the issue of reducing TNW appear entirely unrealistic. In early April 2010, Lieutenant-General Yevgeny Buzhinsky, the former Head of the Defense Ministry's International Legal Department, said that Russia could begin such discussions only after first achieving conventional parity with the United States, including in relation to high-precision weapons.

> We should not start negotiations on the reduction of tactical nuclear armaments as long as we have disparity in conventional armaments, especially high-precision ones. Under these circumstances, tactical nuclear armaments are means of deterrence and any reductions will inevitably damage Russian security.[93]

Clearly, given the ongoing problems facing the Russian defense industry combined with the technology lag between its research and development compared to the United States, as well as the woefully inadequate level of modern equipment and weapons in the Russian TOE, such parity will prove impossible to achieve. But his assertion underscores a far deeper anxiety relating to long-term Russian conventional forces weaknesses that will prove to be a significant barrier among the security elites in placing the tactical nuclear reduction issue on the table. Buzhinsky went further than many experts. Referring to the precondition that the United States unilaterally withdraws its TNW from Europe prior to entering US-Russian talks, he added that all related infrastructure in Europe must be dismantled in order to rule out redeployment later.

Following the signing of the New START, Sergey Rogov, the Director of the Russian Academy of Sciences, United States, and Canada Institute, was interviewed in the defense ministry publication, *Krasnaya Zvezda*, on April 7, 2010. Like other Russian experts, Rogov broadly welcomed the new START and outlined a number of its features that suited Russian policy concerns. However, he went on to realistically assess the START breakthrough by highlighting a number of its weaknesses. His starting point was to explain that a balance of forces is not restricted to strategic nuclear arms and that the new treaty continues to preserve U.S. and NATO superiority over Russia in nuclear and conventional terms. Then he noted that the treaty fails to address Moscow's concern that precision weapons being developed by the United States are not limited by the new START, which he highlighted as anomalous since such weapons systems as part of the global strike program might pose a threat to Russian strategic facilities. Moreover, since the number of Russian missiles capable of carrying a large quantity of warheads will be stood down in the future owing to aging, Rogov argued that the United States will maintain its superiority in return potential, though not at the same level as under the Strategic Offensive Reductions Treaty (SORT). Continued work on BMD, while not representing an immediate issue for Moscow, will pose a potential problem in 15-20 years, which Rogov suggested demands the development of Russian countermeasures. Finally, he said that bilateral nuclear treaties must give way to a wider multilateral framework that takes account of the growth in the number of nuclear states.[94]

Tactical Nuclear Reduction Talks as a Risk to Russian Military Reform.

Sergey Karaganov, the Chairman of the Presidium of the Council on Foreign and Defense Policy, in an article published in *Rossiyskaya Gazeta* on April 23, 2010, argued strongly against Russia entering such negotiations on the basis that they would serve to undermine Serdyukov's military reform. Placing TNW on the agenda, in his view, would strengthen the hand of those opposed to the radical conventional reform underway in Russia, which he said was geared toward shifting these forces away from their traditional fixation on NATO toward enhancing their capabilities to deal with "more plausible threats and challenges." Karaganov continued:

> Withdrawal of American TNW (token arsenals as they are) from Europe will weaken the U.S.-Europe link. A good deal of Europeans—and particularly in the so-called New European countries—will start clamoring for better defense from the mythical Russian leviathan.[95]

While noting that he also assumed a unilateral American withdrawal as a precursor to joining this process, he emphatically characterized it as a highly dangerous step leading to strategic confusion and what Karaganov viewed as opening Pandora's Box: "Euphoric over the Prague treaty signing, so called experts insist on tactical nuclear arms reduction talks. Left to their own devices, they will open this Pandora's Box in no time at all."[96] This was not the first time he used the Pandora's Box argument, but here he was clearly signaling that the delicate balance that exists within the Russian defense and security elite over the current military reform would be upset by playing the tactical nuclear card, a balance reflected in the compromise that led to the new military doctrine in February 2010 and one that appeared vulnerable as discussions continued in Moscow on the future shape of the manning system in the armed forces. Should this unpredictable process be unleashed, the likely key indicator that the opponents of military reform have gained the upper hand would be signaled by an increase in the term of conscript service from 1 year back to 2 years, representing political and psychological defeat for Serdyukov's reform.

The bedrock of Karaganov's argument, however, is rooted in the traditionally sacrosanct position of nuclear weapons in Russian security strategy, which underlies his utter opposition to what he sees as the senseless and idealistic call for global zero in nuclear arms reduction advocated by the Obama administration. His assessment of Russia's geopolitical position is bleak: with its modernization impaired by corruption. Russian security is guaranteed by its nuclear capability, which is also the main source of its political economic weight in the world. In this context, Karaganov believes that any move toward abandoning these weapons would prove suicidal for the Russian state. The *only* purpose arms control talks serve for Moscow, he claimed, is to build trust and transparency between the world powers, "This is all Russia needs arms control talks for."[97]

Karaganov's influential work in this area cannot be separated from wider strategic issues and areas of divergence within the complex and evolving U.S.-Russian bilateral relationship. These include the precise nature and trajectory of the reset and how this is interpreted both in Washington and Moscow as well as among Alliance members, future BMD plans, Medvedev's European security treaty initiative, and how the global zero concept is viewed by the Russian security elite. Karaganov has expressed skepticism over the meaning and objective content in the reset policy, openly questioned the administration's plans to deploy BMD components in Bulgaria and Romania by 2015, and has fiercely criticized global zero both in terms of the centrality of nuclear deterrence in Russian security policy and the contradictory posture adopted by its architects.[98]

Karaganov's critique of global zero stemmed from his overview of how the concept was first outlined in January 2007 by the former U.S. Secretaries of State Henry Kissinger and George Schultz, former Senate Armed Services Committee Chairman Sam Nunn, and former Secretary of Defense, William Perry. Despite initially supporting what he regarded more as an aspiration than a policy, Karaganov soon revised his stance, saying that mankind continued to need the nuclear Sword of Damocles.[99] The movement had in effect been launched, and the aspiration was announced by U.S. President Barack Obama in Prague in April 2009 and broadly welcomed by Medvedev and Putin. However, he then objected that in an article in January 2010, the four same authors called for increased spending to increase the reliability and effectiveness of the U.S. nuclear arsenal. In his view, this shift reflected an acknowledgement that the U.S. nuclear capability had been underfinanced in recent years, as well as an admission that the nuclear proliferation genie had appeared. In typically Russian style, he delighted in the semblance of hypocrisy, suggested U.S. power faced a strategic crisis following its experience in Iraq and Afghanistan, and made clear that if anyone expected the Kremlin to pursue global zero, they must be thinking centuries ahead.[100] Washington's strategic thinking was, in his assessment, becoming increasingly confused, ignoring that India, Pakistan, North Korea, and Israel had all joined the nuclear club. Rather than considering how to deal with the new geostrategic situation, the Americans preferred to philosophize such weapons out of existence, Karaganov argued while noting the massive imbalance in favor of the United States that global zero would achieve based on American technological advances in the use of high-precision conventional weapons. NATO's intervention in the Balkans in 1999 and U.S. intervention in Iraq combined with the various attempts to site components of BMD in Central and Eastern Europe all featured in his assertion that a new European security treaty is required, perhaps more than one, and eventually a political-military alliance between Moscow and Washington or Russian membership in NATO.[101] Finally, on the issue of TNW and their possible reduction he highlighted the glaring blunder in the appeal made by the Polish and Swedish Foreign Ministers, Radek Sikorski and Carl Bildt respectively, in their article in February 2010 which called on Russia to remove TNW from the Kola Peninsula and Kaliningrad Oblast, even though none were stationed in the latter. He ridiculed the whole concept, pointing out that withdrawing these weapons from European Russia would hardly help Moscow in its relations with Beijing.[102]

Europeanizing the Debate.

Within a short period, a response to the call for tactical nuclear reduction in Europe made by Sikorski and Bildt was the subject of a scathing demolition in *Krasnaya Zvezda*. Their proposal that Russia should withdraw its TNW from Kaliningrad was highlighted as not only politically incorrect, since a similar appeal was not directed towards the United States, but entirely flawed in as much as these weapons are not based there. The Kola Peninsula was treated differently, and here the author argued that such an appeal could only be considered if the United States eliminated its naval bases in San Diego or Norfolk. It further asserted that the United States, by basing these weapons on the territories of European allies, had violated the first and second articles of the NPT, and stressed that such articles must be followed without exception. The list of flaws in the Sikorski and Bildt hypotheses was extensive, and placed high value on the sovereign right of any state to freely deploy its armed forces in any way, place, or time on its territory. The proposal was described as ill-conceived and unfounded, as the author then proceeded to outline a plausible compromise:

> Before the beginning of official discussions on this theme, Washington and Moscow must take the same starting position in the negotiations. [The United States must agree] to withdraw all of its TNW from the European continent and bring them back to its own territory. That is, it must do what Russia did 15 years ago."[103]

During the 46th International Security Policy Conference in Munich, Germany, in February 2010, Russian Deputy Prime Minister Sergei Ivanov, who led a 30-person strong Russian delegation, said that it was likely that following the signing of the follow-on START, Washington and Moscow would come under pressure to negotiate joint reduction of their tactical nuclear stockpiles. Ivanov expressed a similar position to that adopted in the *Krasnaya Zvezda* article: "But it should not be forgotten that our country has been dealing with this problem since the 1990s. We voluntarily reduced this arsenal, concentrated it on our own territory, removed it from the field, and warehoused it in special storage facilities." In other words, Moscow has already assumed the moral high ground.[104]

Such themes were revisited in a March 2010 article by Viktor Ruchkin in *Krasnaya Zvezda*, emphasizing how Russia had withdrawn nuclear weapons from the territories of Belarus, Kazakhstan, and Ukraine following the collapse of the Soviet Union. In this thesis, the onus was on the United States to reciprocate and follow this Russian model. "It is perfectly clear that the United States must unilaterally and unconditionally withdraw its TNW from Europe. That would realize the aspirations of the Europeans, who view those TNW as a threat to their security, and it would also correspond to the declared intentions of Washington to free the planet of nuclear weapons," Ruchkin asserted. Nothing could be simpler: Washington must learn from the virtuous conduct of Russian nuclear policy.[105] The same author claimed that, far from intending to withdraw these weapons from Europe, Washington instead planned to extend their service lives and modernize them. He provided various figures on the numbers of combat ready U.S. TNW based in Belgium, Germany, Great Britain, Holland, Italy, and Turkey which appeared incongruous in the context of the withdrawal of Russian weapons from former Soviet Republics.

Consequently, for a range of reasons, Moscow views the tactical nuclear issue as mostly a process it would like, at least initially, to observe as unfolding between the United States and its European allies, fearing that, unless handled sensitively, it may exacerbate East European and Baltic clamor for greater defense against Russia, or provide an opportunity to further divide the United States and its allies in Europe. Reluctantly dragged into bilateral talks aimed at joint reduction of these weapons, Moscow would seek to prolong such discussions, at least until the organizational phase of its conventional reform is complete (2012 at the earliest), and thereafter would attempt to form linkages to other issues ranging from BMD and CFE to its advocating a new European security treaty.

Indeed, some Russian commentators portrayed the domestic German political dimension at play in pushing for the elimination of U.S. nuclear weapons on German territory. Originally proposed in the fall of 2009 by German Foreign Minister Guido Westerwelle, the leader of the Free Democratic Party in the ruling coalition, who demanded such withdrawal in a separate paragraph in the coalition treaty with Angela Merkel's Christian Democrats. Addressing the Munich Security Conference in February 2010, Westerwelle confirmed his intention to pursue the elimination of the U.S. nuclear arsenal in Germany by 2013 (the end of the ruling coalition's period in office). It was also noted that the Free Democratic Party is ideologically opposed to nuclear energy in any form and advocate withdrawing German troops from Afghanistan and that Merkel most likely agreed to compromise on the issue of nuclear weapons in order to preserve the German presence in Afghanistan.[106]

While Russian analysts recognized that START III represented a key element within the reset policy and, more importantly, the only forum within which Moscow can hold discussions with Washington on an equal footing, this translated neither into confidence in extending such discussions to include TNW, nor an appetite to hold such talks in perpetuity. Fyodor Lukyankov, for instance, rightly characterized the April 8, 2010, signing of START III as a political-military compromise allowing both sides to claim success without undermining the claims by either side, though he also placed the treaty in the category of the last of the Cold War model agreements, pursued by Washington as an instrument rather than for its intrinsic value or merit. That process, underway since the 1960s, had drawn to a close. A similar approach was unworkable in the realm of TNW, since it could "bring about the absurd remilitarization of the political debate in Europe, but will do nothing to create a stable security system there."[107]

Policy Implications.

As the obsessional phrase in the Russian security lexicon has evolved from "star-wars," to "missile defense," so it is likely that we are already witnessing that progression to include over the course of the next decade "U.S. global strike," and if compromise is reached on BMD or Russian concerns are allayed, the more pronounced the global strike phrase will become. This reflects sensitivity within the Russian security elite about future strategic parity, the potential for conventional capabilities in the hands of the U.S. Global Strike Command to strike anywhere globally, coupled with an acute awareness of the crisis in the domestic defense industry and possible downward spiral for the Russian economy.

A "straight" horse trading over TNW would most likely fail. Its potential appears more rooted in the policy being linked to a range of other issues as part of strategic engagement with Russia, but this would need to include an offer of assistance with conventional defense reform to assuage concerns on the part of some NATO members.

Thus far, Serdyukov's reform agenda has been implemented rapidly and with significant achievements. These are mostly administrative achievements, such as the transition to the permanent readiness brigades. Yet, the challenges ahead are far deeper, and are more connected with the value of the Russian state: its people. More than the introduction of any new weapons or equipment, the future of the Russian armed forces will center on whether the state can harness and develop a new generation of Russian officers, and for each individual that will entail serving as an example, delegating authority, bringing the best out of his subordinates, encouraging a culture of initiative and problem solving: in short *leadership*.

Russia is only in the early stages of conventional defense reform, a process likely to endure for many years, not least in terms of the transition towards network-centric warfare capabilities. It is clear that many critical issues are still in the melting pot, and are unlikely to witness any speedy resolution. Consequently, this domestic defense reform, coupled with the China factor, makes it unlikely that TNW reduction currently presents a realistic option. Serdyukov and Makarov, probably in an effort to shore up support for the reform, have undoubtedly exaggerated its success to date and perhaps there will be a need, at some point deemed as politically safe, to admit that major tasks still lie ahead demanding more time. In this sensitive context, any attempt to place TNW reduction on the agenda risks unraveling that reform, possibly damaging the reset in U.S.-Russian relations, and missing potential defense cooperation opportunities based on the collateral damage to the current conventional defense reform: from a Russian perspective it may represent the correct policy but at the wrong time.

ENDNOTES - CHAPTER 2

1. Aspects of the following analysis of the long-term challenges facing Russian defense reform is based on the author's presentation found in "Russian Defense Reform: Contradictions, Challenges and Reconceptualization," Prague, Czech Republic: Institute of International Relations, May 27, 2010.

2. Dale Herspring and Roger N. McDermott, "Serdyukov Promotes Systemic Russian Military Reform," *Orbis,* Spring 2010.

3. Daniyal Ayzenshtadt and Yelizaveta Surnacheva, "The Abkhaz-Israeli Reform of the Russian Armed Forces," November 19, 2008, available from *www.gazeta.ru.*

4. Viktor Baranets, "The Army Will Be Getting the Latest Weapons and Lodgings and Will Be Rid of Hazing: Dmitry Medvedev Has Formulated Five Principles of Development of the Armed Forces," *Komsomolskaya Pravda,* October 1, 2008.

5. Yuriy Gavrilov, "General's Reduction: They Will Reduce the Armed Forces and Change Their Look," *Rossiyskaya Gazeta,* October 15, 2008; Mikhail Barabanov, "Reform of the Combat Spirit," *Kommersant-Vlast,* October 20, 2008; "The Army Needs to be Protected from Dilettantes," October 22, 2008, available from *www.utro.ru,* Юрий Трифонов, "В рамках реформирования Вооруженных Сил Российской Федерации. Генералов станет меньше, лейтенантов – больше," *Военно-промышленный курьер,* № 42 (258), октября 22-28, 2008 года, available from *www.archive. vpk-news.ru/article.asp?pr_sign=archive.2008.258.articles.army_02;* Yuri Trifonov, "V ramkah reformirovaniya Vooruzhennih Sil Rossiiskoi Federacii. Generalov stanet men'she, leitenantov – bol'she," *Voenno Promyshlennyy Kuryer,* Vol. 42, No. 258, October 22-28, 2008.

6. Baranets, "The Army Will Be Getting the Latest Weapons."

7. Nikolay Poroskov, "Military Arrangements," *Vremya Novostey*, October 8, 2008.

8. Gavrilov, "General's Reduction," *Ibid*.

9. *Ibid*.

10. Interview with Serdyukov, *Rossiya*, No. 24, March 6, 2010.

11. "CINC Ground Troops Press Conference on New Brigades, Armament Plans," *Rossiyskaya Gazeta*, February 26, 2010.

12. *Ibid*.

13. Вадим Соловьев, "Военная реформа 2009–2012 годов, " *Независимое Военное Обозрение*, декабря 12, 2008 года, available from *nvo.ng.ru/forces/2008-12-12/1_reform.html*; Vadim Solov'ev, "Voennaya reforma 2009-2012 godov," *Nezavisimoye Voyennoye Obozreniye*, December 12, 2008.

14. "Around 30 Percent of Russian Air Force Officers to be Dismissed During Reform," *Interfax*, February 11, 2009.

15. Иван Николаевич Воробьев, Валерий Александрович Киселев, "Переход Сухопутных войск на бригадную структуру как этап повышения их маневроспособности," *Военная Мысль*, Номер 2, 2010; Ivan N. Vorobyev and Valeriy A. Kiselev, "Perehod Suhoputnih voisk na brigadnuu strukturu kak etap povisheniya ih manevrosposobnosti," *Voennaya Mysl*, No. 2, 2010; Major-General (Ret.) Ivan Vorobyev and Colonel Valeriy Aleksandrovich Kiselev, "Ground Troops Transition to Brigade Structure as a Phase of Improving Their Maneuverability," *Voyennaya Mysl*, No. 2, 2010.

16. "The Black Sea Fleet is Being Demoted," *Moskovskiy Komosmolets*, February 11, 2009.

17. "Admirals Suffer Fear of the Sea, Navy Main Command Cannot be Moved from Moscow to the Baltic," *Kommersant*, April 22, 2009.

18. Виктор Юзбашев, "Генералы пошли к офицерам. Минобороны начинает разъяснительно-пропагандистскую кампанию," *Независимое Военное Обозрение*, ноября 28, 2008 года, available from *nvo.ng.ru/forces/2008-11-28/1_generaly.html*; Viktor Yuzbashev, "Generali poshli k oficeram. Minoborony nachinaet raz'yasnitelno-propagandistskuu kampaniu, *Nezavisimoye Voyennoye Oborzreniye*, November 28, 2008.

19. "Blow to Rear Services," November 26, 2009, available from *www.gazeta.ru*.

20. Тыл на пути преобразований," *Красная звезда*, 18 ноября 2008 года, available from *www.redstar.ru/2008/11/18_11/2_01. html*; "Til na puti preobrazovanii," *Krasnaya Zvezda*, November 18, 2008.

21. Viktor Baranets, "Chief of General Staff Nikolay Makarov: 'Having Commanded Paper Regiments, Lost Their Bearings in Real War'," *Komsomolskaya Pravda*, December 18, 2008.

22. "Russia to Close 22 Military Hospitals, Cut Over 10,000 Medical Officer Posts," Interfax, May 27, 2009; "Military Reform 2009-2013, *Nezavisimoye Voyennoye Obozreniye*, January 1, 2009; "Defense Ministry to Close Officer Jobs in Military Media," *Interfax-AVN online*, December 3, 2009.

23. "Cuts in Russian Military Higher Educational Establishments Will Start in 2009," *Interfax*, December 23, 2008.

24. "Russian CGS quizzed about Military Reform," *Interfax*, June 7, 2009.

25. Russia: Text of Medvedev Speech to Defense Board, March 6, 2010, available from *www.kremlin.ru*.

26. Roger N. McDermott, "The Reform of Russia's Conventional Armed Forces: Problems, Challenges and Policy Implications," (forthcoming).

27. *Ibid.*

28. "Putin Chairs Meeting in Voronezh to discuss Re-equipping the Russian Armed Forces," *Interfax,* January 19, 2010; Перов Е.А, Переверзев А.В. "О перспективной цифровой системе связи Вооруженных Сил Российской Федерации," *Военная Мысль,* номер 3, март 2008, стр. 7-11; E. A. Perov, A.V. Pereverzev, "O perspectivnoi cifrovoi sisteme svyazi Vooruzhennih Sil Rossiiskoi Federacii," *Voennaya Mysl,* No. 3, March 2008; Александр Кондратьев, "Новые возможности для нового облика," *Военно-промышленный курьер,* номер 45, ноября 18-24, 2009 года; Aleksandr Kondratyev, "Novie vozmozhnesti dlya novogo oblika," *Voyenno-Promyshlennyy Kuryer,* No. 45, November 18-24, 2009.

29. Иван Карев, "Связь дорогого стоит. Цена комплекта средств управления для бригады – 8 миллиардов рублей," *Военно-промышленный курьер,* номер 3, января 27 – февраля 2, 2010 года; available from *www.vpk-news.ru/3-319/qq/10379*; Ivan Karev, "Svyaz dorogogo stoit. Cena komplekta sredstv upravleniya dlya brigadi – 8 milliardov rublei," *Voyenno-Promyshlennyy Kuryer,* No. 3, January 27-February 2, 2010.

30. Denis Telmanov, "Russian Army Transformed into 85 Mobile Brigades: General Staff to Offer Net-Centric Warfare to Military Students," *Gazeta,* February 22, 2010.

31. Василий Михайлович Буренок, "Базис сетецентрических войн – опережение, интеллект, инновации," *Независимое Военное Обозрение,* Апреля 2, 2010, available from *nvo.ng.ru/concepts/2010-04-02/1_bazis.html*; Vasilii M. Burenok, "Bazis setecentricheskih voyn – operezhenie, intellect, innovacii," *Nezavisimoye Voyennoye Obozreniye,* April 2, 2010/ Vasiliy Burenok, "Basis for Network-Centric Wars: Anticipation, Intellect, Innovations," *Nezavisimoye Voyennoye Obozreniye,* April 2, 2010.

32. *Ibid.*

33. Author's emphasis.

34. Burenok, "Basis for Network-Centric Wars."

35. Виталий Шлыков, "Блицкриг Анатолия Сердюкова. Почему современные вооруженные силы невозможны без гражданского Министерства обороны," *Военно-промышленный*

курьер, номер 4, февраля 3-9, 2010, available from *www.vpk-news.ru/4-320/2009-05-02-13-24-27/10988*; Vitalii Shlykov, "Blitzkig Anatoliya Serdyukova. Pochemu sovremennie vooruzhennie sili nevozmogni bez graddanskogo Ministerstva oboroni," *Voyenno Promyshlennyy Kuryer*, No. 4, February 3-9, 2010; Vitaliy Shlykov, "Blitzkrieg of Anatoliy Serdyukov," *Voyenno Promyshlennyy Kuryer*, February 19, 2010.

36. Among the recommendations made in the SVOP report, which have not been adopted by Serdyukov are resubordinating the GRU from the General Staff to the defense ministry, insisting that all officers have a first degree before commencing officer training, further transforming the defense industries, and reforming the security structures. See *Voyennoye stroitelstvo i moderinzatsiya Vooruzhennykh sil russiy* (The Development and Modernization of the Russian Armed Forces), Moscow, Russia: SVOP, April, 2004, available from *www.svop.ru/live/materials.asp?m_id=8481&r_id=9303*.

37. Author's emphasis. See Shlykov, "Blitzkrieg of Anatoliy Serdyukov."

38. *Ibid*.

39. "Russian Defense Ministry Rules Out Need for Special Army Police," *Interfax*, April 6, 2010.

40. "CINC Ground Troops Press Conference on New Brigades, Armament Plans," *Rossiyskaya Gazeta*, February 26, 2010.

41. "Will Have to Serve Without Contract," *Izvestiya*, February 26, 2010.

42. "Military Board," *Ekho Moskvy*, February 20, 2010.

43. Vorobyev was born in 1922. During World War II, he served as a cadet, was promoted to major, and commanded a rifle battalion. He was awarded the Svechin prize of the Academy of Military Sciences in 2000 for his series of works on tactics. He is the author of more than 200 works on tactics and operational art, and is a professor at the armed force combined arms academy. Vorobyev and Kiselev, "Ground Troops Transition to Brigade Structure."

44. *Ibid.*

45. *Ibid.*

46. *Voyennaya Doktrina Rossiyskoy Federatsii* (*Military Doctrine of the Russian Federation*), February 5, 2010, available from *www. scrf.gov.ru/documents/33.html.*

47. *Quadrennial Defense Review 2010*, available from *www.defense.gov/qdr/*; 46th Munich Security Conference, February 2010, available from *www.securityconference.de/Conference-2010.muenchn ersicherheit.0.html?&L=1.*

48. Mikhail Tsypkin, "What's New in Russia's New Military Doctrine?" *Radio Free Europe/Radio Liberty,* February 27, 2010.

49. Interview with General Leonid Ivashov by V. Tetekin, *Segodnya,* February 25, 2010.

50. Aleksey Nikolskiy, "New Words for Old Threats. New Version of Military Doctrine Does Not Differ Fundamentally From 2000 Document—Something That Elicited Negative Response From NATO," *Vedomosti,* February 15, 2010.

51. *Military Doctrine of the Russian Federation.*

52. *Ibid.*

53. *Ibid.*

54. *Ibid.*

55. Aleksandr Khramchikhin, "Comparison of New Military Doctrine with the Military Doctrine of 2000," *Voyenno-Promyshlennyy Kuryer,* February 18, 2010.

56. *Military Doctrine of the Russian Federation.*

57. Reporting in *ITAR-TASS, Interfax,* and *Gazeta,* December 8-10, 2008; Interview with Army-General Gareev, *Nezavisimoye Voyennoye Obozreniye,* December 12, 2008; "Russian Defense Min-

ister, General Staff at Odds Over Reform, Doctrine," *Moskovsky Komsomolets,* February 15, 2007; "Partial Text of Army-General Gareev's Report on New Russian Military Doctrine," *Voenno-Promyshlenny Kuriyer,* January 24, 2007.

58. Viktor Myasnikov, "Serious Discussion of the New Doctrine Impends: the Academy of Military Sciences Will Be Gathering for its Annual Conference in January," *Nezavisimoye Voyennoye Obozreniye,* January 9, 2007; Vadim Solovyev, "There Are More Enemies and the Enemies Have Become More Aggressive," *Nezavisimaya Gazeta,* February 10, 2007.

59. *Military Doctrine of the Russian Federation.*

60. Patrushev Interview, *Interfax,* October 13, 2009; Security Council's Patrushev Interviewed on Military Doctrine, *Izvestiya,* October 14, 2009.

61. *Ibid.*

62. Available from *www.lenta.ru*, October 15, 2009.

63. Author interviews with Central Asian diplomats, December 2009.

64. "Pundit Says Patrushev Remarks Signal Lowered Nuclear Threshold, *Russkaya Liniya,* St. Petersburg, October 14, 2009.

65. *Rosbalt,* October 14, 2009, available from *www.rosbalt.ru/2009/10/14/680419.html.*

66. "Patrushev: New Military Doctrine to Stipulate Preemptive Nuclear Strikes," October 14, 2009, available from *www.segodnya.ru.*

67. "New Military Doctrine Unlikely to Provide for Preventive Strikes," *Vedomosti,* October 9, 2009; "Kremlin 'Source' Outlines New National Security Strategy," April 29, 2009, available from *www.gazeta.ru.*

68. "Russian Defense Minister Reports to Duma on Military Reform," *Zvezda Television,* February 11, 2009; "CGS Makarov

Visits Abu Dhabi Arms Show, Talks of New Military Doctrine," *Nezavisimaya Gazeta,* February 25, 2009.

69. *Krasnaya Zvezda,* May 14, 2009, available from *www.red-star.ru/2009/05/14 – 05/1 – 05.html.*

70. "Russian Security Council Discusses Future Military Doctrine," *ITAR-TASS,* August 5, 2009.

71. Roger N. McDermott, "The Restructuring of the Modern Russian Army," *Journal of Slavic Military Studies,* Vol. 22, No. 4, 2009.

72. Vitaliy, Shlykov, "Serdyukov's Blitzkrieg," *Rossiya v Globalnoy Politike,* No. 6, November-December 2009.

73. Mikhail Rastopshin, "Voyennaya Mysl' Versus the General Staff," *Nezavisimoye Voyennoye Obozreniye,* March 31, 2010; Yuriy Borodin, "Brigade Fires Without a Miss," *Krasnaya Zvezda,* November 23, 2009; Yuriy Borodin, "Proficiency Test," *Krasnaya Zvezda,* November 23, 2009; Vladimir Semenchenko:, "What the Inspection Revealed," *Voyenno-Promyshlennyy Kuryer,* November 20, 2009; Aleksandr Sargin and Denis Telmanov, "An Army of Units That Are Rated 'Satisfactory'," *Gazeta,* November 12, 2009; "Russian Military Units' Readiness Time Cut to One Hour-Makarov," *ITAR-TASS,* November 17, 2009.

74. Jacob, W. Kipp, "Mistral Procurement Divides Russian Defense Leadership," *Eurasia Daily Monitor,* Vol. 6, Issue 225, December 8, 2009.

75. Gennadiy Miranovich, "Military Science: Assignment for Tomorrow," *Krasnaya Zvezda,* December 21, 2009.

76. *Ibid.*

77. Emphasis by author.

78. "Ex-Security Official: Russia Should Keep Improving Strategic Forces," *Interfax,* April 9, 2010.

79. *Military Doctrine of the Russian Federation.*

80. *Ibid.*

81. Aleksandr Konovalov, "Take Tender Care of the Hawks," *Ogonek,* February 25, 2010; Roger N. McDermott, "New Russian Military Doctrine Opposes NATO Enlargement,"*Eurasia Daily Monitor,* Vol. 7, Issue 27, February 9, 2010; Jacob. W. Kipp, "Medvedev Approves New Russian Military Doctrine,"*Eurasia Daily Monitor,* Vol. 7, Issue 26, February 8, 2010.

82. "The Role of TNW on Multipurpose Submarines Set to Grow," *RIA Novosti,* August 23, 2009.

83. Aleksandr Artemyev, "Washington Goes for Tactical Reduction," February 6, 2010, available from *www.gazeta.ru.*

84. Andrey Terekhov, "The United States May Withdraw Its TNW from Europe," *Nezavisimaya Gazeta,* April 28, 2010.

85. Dvorkin is a recognized authority on these issues. He was one of the authors of all major documents related to the Strategic Rocket Forces (SRF). He was an expert involved in preparing SALT II, the INF Treaty, START I, and START II. He made a significant contribution to Soviet and Russian strategic arms reduction talks, and from 1962 to 2001 he worked in the 4th Central Research Institute of the Soviet and Russian Defense Ministries, heading the institute in 1993-2001.

86. *Ibid.*

87. "Chief Of Russia's General Staff to Visit US Over Nukes, Missile Defenses," *Interfax-AVN Online,* April 21, 2010.

88. Miles Pomper, William Potter, and Nikolai Sokov, *Survival: Global Politics and Strategy,* Vol. 52, No. 1, February–March 2010, pp. 75–96.

89. Joshua Handler, "The 1991-1992 PNI's and the Elimination, Storage and Security of TNW," in Brian Alexander and Alistair Millar, eds., *TNW,* Washington DC: Brassey's Inc., 2003; Robert S. Norris and Hans M. Kristensen, "Russian Nuclear Forces, 2010," *Bulletin of the Atomic Scientists,* January/February 2010, p. 79; "US

Nuclear Development Concerns Russia," *Interfax*, November 26, 2003; "Russian Military Chief Defends Nonstrategic Nukes," *Interfax*, December 17, 2008; Andrea Gabbitas, "Non-strategic Nuclear Weapons: Problems of Definition," in Jeffrey A. Larsen and Kurt J. Klingenberger, eds., *Controlling Non-Strategic Nuclear Weapons: Obstacles and Opportunities*, Washington, DC: U.S. Air Force, Institute for National Security Studies, July 2000; Robert S. Norris and Hans M. Kristensen, "Nuclear Notebook: Russian Nuclear Forces, 2009," *Bulletin of the Atomic Scientists*, May/June 2009; William J. Perry, Chairman and James R. Schlesinger, Vice Chairman, *America's Strategic Posture*, The Final Report of the Congressional Commission on the Strategic Posture of the United States, Washington, DC, April 2009, available from *www.usip.org/files/America's_Strategic_Posture_Auth_Ed.pdf*; Commentary by Sergey Karaganov, "The Echo of the Past War or Strategic Confusion," *Rossiyskaya Gazeta*, March 17, 2010.

90. "Too Early To Discuss Reduction Of Tactical Nuclear Armaments-Expert," *ITAR-TASS*, March 5, 2010.

91. "US Lowering Role of Nuclear Weapons in Doctrine Because of Superiority in Conventional Arms," *Interfax-AVN Online*, April 19, 2010.

92. "Conventional Warheads on Strategic Carriers Are Threat to International Security-RVSN Commander," *Interfax*, October 12, 2009; "Creation of Global Strike Command in US Air Force 'a Threat'-Russian Air Force Commander-in-Chief," *Interfax*, August 11, 2009.

93. "Conventional Arms Parity Needed To Discuss TNW," *ITAR-TASS*, April 6, 2010.

94. Interview with Sergey Rogov by Aleksandr Frolov, "The Treaty Has More Pluses Than Minuses," *Krasnaya Zvezda*, April 7, 2010.

95. Sergei Karaganov, "Nuclear Free World is a Dangerous Concept That Ought to be Abandoned," *Rossiyskaya Gazeta*, April 23, 2010.

96. *Ibid.*

97. *Ibid.*

98. Karaganov, "The Echo of the Past War,"

99. For more detail on the place of nuclear deterrence in Russian strategic thought and the high value placed on these weapons by the *Siloviki*, see Mikhail Tsypkin, "Russian Politics, Policy-Making and American Missile Defence," *International Affairs*, Vol. 85, No. 4, 2009, pp. 781–799.

100. Karaganov, "The Echo of the Past War or Strategic Confusion"; Kissinger, Schultz, Nunn, and Perry articles, available from *online.wsj.com/public/article_print/SB120036422673589947.html*, *online.wsj.com/article/SB100014240527487041528045746283442827 35008.html*; Roger N. McDermott, "Russian Analysts Question the Viability of the 'Reset'," *Eurasia Daily Monitor*, Vol. 7, Issue 61, March 30, 2010.

101. Karaganov, "The Echo of the Past War or Strategic Confusion."

102. Radek Sikorski and Carl Bildt, "Next, the Tactical Nukes," *The New York Times*, February 1, 2010.

103. Vladimir Kozin, "TNW: Ill-Conceived Messages from the Foreign Ministers of Poland and Sweden," *Krasnaya Zvezda*, February 21, 2010.

104. Yuriy Gavrilov, "Getting to Zero: Russia and the United States Are Prepared To Fight Together for the Complete Elimination of Nuclear Weapons," *Rossiyskaya Gazeta*, February 13, 2010.

105. Viktor Ruchkin, "Old Bombs and New Problems," *Krasnaya Zvezda*, March 16, 2010.

106. Fedor Lukyanov, "Last Treaty: Russia and United States Have Exhausted Potential for Two-Way Nuclear Disarmament," *Vremya Novostey*, March 30, 2010; Karaganov, "The Echo of the Past War or Strategic Confusion."

107. Lukyankov, "The Last Treaty."

CHAPTER 3

NUCLEAR WEAPONS IN RUSSIAN STRATEGY AND DOCTRINE

Andrei Shoumikhin

INTRODUCTION

The Russian Federation (RF) remains in possession of the world's largest nuclear arsenal. Despite the elimination of some key foundations of superpower rivalry, most notably the intense ideological schism between Communism and Western-type democracies that sparked and fueled the Cold War, the RF Strategic Nuclear Forces (SNF) continue to target the United States and its allies. While the significant disequilibrium in economic, technological, military, power projection, and other capabilities between the United States and the RF continues to expand, Russia remains the only global power presenting an existential threat to the United States.

It is not the weapons, but the people possessing them who kill. Detailed information about the composition, combat readiness, and procedures of RF SNF is important.[1] However, understanding the nature of the Russian political regime, the mentality of Russian leaders, and the underpinnings of Russian nuclear strategy as reflected in Russian doctrinal documents may help assess whether or not that country will ever resort to the ultimate weapon of destruction.

Soviet and Russian military and nuclear doctrines reflect the leadership's threat assessments, perceptions of the strengths and weaknesses of the military, national goals and tasks for the military organization of the state, and other factors. To the extent they are not used for propaganda or disinformation purposes, they may provide insights into disagreements and competitiveness within policymaking elites. Doctrines usually comprise classified components and are accompanied by declaratory and interpretive statements that clarify or, for that matter, complicate the understanding of their intent and purpose.

This chapter deals with the evolution of Russian thinking and policy on nuclear-related issues. It also seeks to understand motivations of the Russian leadership in its continued reliance on nuclear weapons and maintaining an adversarial posture towards other nuclear powers, especially the United States. Past and current doctrinal documents are studied to provide the background of evolving nuclear weapons programs, military-political relations with the United States, perceived defense and security threats, and requirements.[2]

Chronologically and substantively, the main emphasis is on the independence period of Russia from December 1991 to the present. However, a reference to the Soviet period is appropriate. After all, most of the strategic weapon systems Russia possesses today were created during the Soviet period. Moreover, while Russian leaders invariably underline substantive differences between the Soviet regime and the new socio-economic and political environment in contemporary Russia, there are still many similarities between current Russian and former Soviet thinking and behavior. To a large extent, the RF finds itself in a geopolitical situation resembling that of the Soviet Union. Despite considerable changes in the structure and composition of the bureaucracies responsible for the development and implementation of Russian military and foreign policy, many political appointees and professionals currently in charge of this policy have strong backgrounds in the Soviet system.[3]

SOVIET EXPERIENCE: NUCLEAR WEAPONS AND ARMS CONTROL IN THE PURSUIT OF PARITY

Starting in the early-1950s, the Soviet leadership, driven by the need to buy time to bridge the technological gap in nuclear weapons and delivery systems with the United States, put a huge effort into disarmament negotiations and debates at the United Nations (UN). They regarded these efforts as a vital means of slowing down, if not reversing, the U.S. progress in developing advanced weapon systems while the Union of Soviet Socialist Republics (USSR) accelerated its own weapons of mass destruction (WMD) programs. Nuclear disarmament, or rather the politics of nuclear disarmament, had also become a central component of the "peaceful competition of opposite social systems" promoted by the communist regime.

Fiery demagogue Nikita Khrushchev put his unique stamp on nuclear disarmament at the UN by proposing in 1959 a patently unrealistic, but ideologically enticing, plan of "general and complete disarmament" that would start with the nuclear-missile arsenals of the Soviet Union and the United States. From that time on, the Soviets often began negotiating processes by launching initiatives that had little or no chance of acceptance by the opposite side but could score big in the "war of ideas," particularly among the "progressive world public opinion," e.g., the antiwar and antinuclear groups in the West. Additional advantages of this methodology were to draw opponents into protracted bargaining and to eventually reach compromise by demonstrating flexibility while lowering the original excessive demands.[4]

Khrushchev's bold peace initiatives were clearly predicated on the rapid progress of the Soviet nuclear and missile programs. As the result of intense efforts, the Soviets had by October 1957 already put into orbit the first artificial satellite with a clear implication that Soviet missiles were now able to hit U.S. territory by flying through space.

Even during periods of relative relaxation of tensions in U.S.-USSR relations, Soviet perspectives on bilateral arms control were heavily tinted by ideological preconceptions. The Soviets invariably believed that the American side sought unilateral advantages for themselves. Soviet Foreign Minister Andrei Gromyko recalled in his memoirs:

> For Carter, as all other American Presidents—his predecessors, the paramount goal had always consisted in limiting the Soviet nuclear potential, while keeping the main U.S. strike forces intact. Only with great effort, and under the influence of the irrefutable arguments and the constructive line of the USSR that enjoyed wide support in the world, he would deviate from his position aimed at achieving unilateral advantages for the United States.[5]

A real breakthrough for the Soviets in the pursuit of equilibrium in strategic relations with the United States began to emerge by the late-1960s when the United States took note of Soviet efforts to develop a strategic antiballistic missile (ABM) system that eventually became the foundation for the Moscow ABM system.[6] The United States apparently became concerned with the prospect of an arms race in ABM systems.[7]

In June 1967, U.S. President Lyndon Johnson raised the ABM issue in his meeting with Soviet Premier Aleksey Kosygin in Glasborough, NJ. Johnson said he could delay a decision to deploy a U.S. defense system if he could announce that talks with the Soviet Union on the subject would start shortly. Kosygin repeated his personal view: "Defense is moral, attack is immoral," and reiterated the Russian Politburo's position that ABM systems could only be discussed together with setting limits for offensive weapons.[8]

However, Soviet progress in ABM systems and progress by both sides in testing multiple independently targetable reentry vehicles (MIRVs) finally convinced the Politburo that it was time to start talks. In October 1969, U.S. President Richard Nixon was informed that Moscow was prepared to start official negotiations on the subject. Nixon agreed and talks opened on November 17, 1969, in Helsinki, Finland.

It took another 2 1/2 years to prepare the relevant treaties for signature. The ABM Treaty was signed in Moscow on May 26, 1972, the same day as the first Strategic Arms Limitation Treaty (SALT-1). The Brezhnev leadership announced that the ABM and SALT talks and agreements signified that both superpowers had reached parity in their strategic capabilities, even though by the time both agreements were ready for signing (1971), the Soviet Union had 2,163 strategic warheads deployed, and the United States possessed 4,632 warheads.[9] SALT-1 did not stop the nuclear arms race: by 1981, the Soviets increased their nuclear arsenals nearly fourfold to a total of 8,043 warheads, while the United States more than doubled its own numbers to 10,022.[10]

It should also be understood that the Soviet leadership at no time entertained plans to build a national

103

ABM system. According to information that became available long after the initial bilateral debates, negotiations and agreements on the offensive-defensive linkage, feasibility studies ordered by the Soviets at the time resulted in a definite conclusion that such a system would not only be prohibitively expensive but would also be totally ineffective and could be easily penetrated in a massive nuclear attack.[11]

Therefore Moscow decided at an early stage that it would not waste resources on constructing such a system. To be absolutely certain that the United States would under no circumstances achieve a technological breakthrough in defensive systems where the Soviets anticipated failure, thereby gaining strategic superiority over the USSR, they agreed to conclude the Anti-Ballistic Missile Treaty (ABMT). The complete reversal of the Kremlin's initial skeptical attitude towards regulating strategic defensive systems was based on pragmatic calculations. Establishing a moratorium on developing strategic defensive systems that lasted until the early 2000s may be considered a serious Soviet achievement in arms control.

With the conclusion in May 1972 of the ABM Treaty and SALT-1, the paradigm of "Mutual Assured Destruction" (MAD) became dominant in U.S.-Soviet strategic relations.[12] Negotiations on subsequent major arms limitation and arms reduction treaties (SALT-2, Strategic Arms Reduction Treaty [START] I and START II) were conducted with the background of continued reliance on mutual vulnerability to retaliation.

The Russians proclaimed the ABMT "the cornerstone of strategic stability" in bilateral relations and the foundation of geopolitical "parity" between the superpowers.[13] Diplomatic experiences of the early-

1970s had long-term effects on later Soviet and current Russian thinking. They suggested to the Kremlin that:

- Arms control is an extremely valuable means of equalizing capabilities of nuclear adversaries if one of them lags in levels of armaments and technological prowess.
- Success in negotiations is possible as the result of subtle and deceptive moves, as in the game of chess.
- The linkage between strategic offensive and defensive systems is quintessential in preventing unilateral advantages and creating balance in strategic relations.

Soviet nuclear strategy and doctrine were evolving together with the changing balance of strategic forces and progress in arms control negotiations:

> Since the second half of the 1960s, the leadership of the Armed Forces and the state experienced a transformation of views on the possible nature of the world war. The Soviet military doctrine began to take into account the possible initial stage of a military conflict with the sole use of conventional weapons. There began to emerge doubts about the possibility of gaining victory after a massive exchange of nuclear strikes. Since this time, the Soviet leadership began to seek the conclusion of treaties with the U.S. on banning or limiting strategic nuclear weapons. . . . Beginning in the early-1970s, the main concept of developing Soviet strategic weapons was the concept that could be described as "strategic sufficiency." It defined the quantitative and qualitative composition of carriers, their distribution among the Strategic Missile Troops, the Navy and the Air Force, with due account of potential use under different conditions. They established scientifically the optimal ratio of the number of carriers and warheads

for them. It also took into account the process of strategic arms limitations that had already begun between the Soviet Union and the United States.[14]

According to one Western view, by the late-1980s, the Soviets had a fairly elaborate nuclear-use doctrine that included the following elements:

- Preemption (first strike).
- Quantitative superiority (a requisite for preemption and necessary because the war may last for some time, even though the initial hours are decisive).
- Counterforce targeting.
- Combined-arms operations to supplement nuclear strikes.
- Defense, which has been almost totally neglected by the United States under its concept of mutual deterrence.[15]

However, the Soviet leadership insisted publicly that it would not be the first to use nuclear weapons. The first official declaration to this effect was made by Leonid Brezhnev at the Second Special Session of the UN General Assembly on June 15, 1982.[16]

MIKHAIL GORBACHEV'S "NEW THINKING"

Soon after his advent to power in early 1985, Mikhail Gorbachev, the youngest General Secretary in the history of the USSR, announced his own vision and proposals on the in-depth curbing of nuclear armaments. In September 1985, he offered to reduce strategic offensive weapons to 6,000 warheads on each side, while concurrently prohibiting the deployment of offensive weapons in outer space, including weapons aimed at satellites.[17] Clearly, despite his reformist rhetoric, on strategic nuclear matters Gorbachev continued to abide by the concept of MAD and the traditional Soviet position on the offensive-defensive linkage.

Gorbachev's proposals were specifically aimed against the U.S. Strategic Defense Initiative (SDI) announced by the Ronald Reagan administration in January 1984. Together with American counterproposals, they were discussed at the Geneva, Switzerland (November 1985) and Reykjavik, Iceland (October 1986) bilateral summits. In negotiations, while Gorbachev agreed in principle with Reagan's proposal to reduce by half the numbers of strategic offensive weapons, he also emphasized that this would not be possible if the United States went ahead with creating a strategic defense shield. He argued that in this case, the Soviet Union would have to concentrate on developing its strategic strike capacity in order to neutralize the "space shield."[18]

In effect, Gorbachev was the first to offer the antiballistic missile defense (BMD) rationalization that is currently used by leaders of the RF. For example, he doubted the American suggestion to share ABM technology with the Soviet Union once it was ready for use. He told the Americans that "the creation of a shield . . . would allow a first strike without retaliation." He also said that the Soviet Union had already developed a response to SDI that would be "effective, far less expensive and ready for use in less time."[19] In still another effort to reconfirm the rigid linkage of strategic offensive and defense weapons, Gorbachev declared that the SDI stood in the way of a 50 percent cut in strategic arms and insisted that the U.S. administration should do something about it if the administration wanted to reduce the nuclear stockpiles.[20]

Academician of the Russian Academy of Sciences Andrei Kokoshin, who at the time of the Reagan-Gorbachev summits worked as Deputy Director of the U.S. and Canada Studies Institute, was a member of the Gorbachev-appointed interagency group to study Soviet asymmetrical responses to the United States. The SDI program confirmed years later that the Kremlin had indeed agreed on a variety of efficient and cost-effective counteractions to the U.S. strategic defenses if and when they would turn into reality.[21] This more or less rejects the argument of those Russian analysts who claim that the Soviets overreacted in a massive way to the U.S. SDI and that it was enormous appropriations for fighting the "terrifying" American program that finally broke the backbone of the Soviet economy.[22]

Gorbachev continued to press for spectacular new agreements with the United States. By December 1987 when the Soviet leader arrived in Washington for his new summit with Reagan, both sides were prepared to sign a treaty banning intermediate range missiles in Europe (the Intermediate Range Nuclear Forces [INF] Treaty). However, during that summit Gorbachev again did not fail to refer to the U.S. SDI as a stumbling block and reaffirmed the link between offensive and defense weapons.

Finally, a preliminary compromise was reached. Both sides would commit themselves to the ABM Treaty as signed in 1972. Research and development (R&D) and testing would not be contrary to the Treaty. The Soviet Union and the United States would not withdraw from the Treaty for a specified period of time yet to be determined.[23] During his May 1988 visit to Moscow, Reagan confirmed that understanding. This cleared the way for further discussions on reducing strategic armaments and eventually resulted in the signing of START I in Moscow on July 31, 1991.

However, in the course of START I preparation, that part of the 1987 understanding that dealt with the ABM Treaty "was somehow lost on the way."[24] On June 13, 1991, the Soviet Union made a unilateral statement to the effect that a U.S. withdrawal from the Treaty could present a *force majeure* leading to the possible Soviet withdrawal from START I.[25]

Even more importantly, no mention was made in START I itself of its linkage with the 1972 Treaty. This omission was brought to Gorbachev's attention, and he promised to make an oral statement at the signing to the effect that if the ABM Treaty was abrogated, the Soviet Union would not consider itself tied by START I. But for reasons unknown, he failed to do so. Allegedly, as claimed by one of his aides, he did not want to spoil the "festive atmosphere." Actually, in the Russian expert opinion, "this was another of those significant errors Gorbachev made in his last years in office."[26]

Gorbachev's critics in Russia widely accuse him of having consistently given in to American pressures in arms control negotiations. Allegedly, Gorbachev was so carried away by his personal ideas of *perestroika* and détente with the West, and enamored by summitry with Western leaders, that he was prepared to compromise on more important Soviet interests, such as agreeing to stop construction of the large Soviet phased-array radar near the Siberian city of Krasnoyarsk, while turning a blind eye to similar American installations in Thule, Greenland, and Fylingdales, United Kingdom (UK).[27]

Gorbachev's handling of other issues, including conditions for the reunification of Germany, Soviet troop withdrawals from Eastern Europe, elimination of short and medium-range missiles under the INF Treaty, and promises to get rid of tactical nuclear weapons all reverberate today in the Russian disappointments and attempts at revising former agreements and understandings.

THE BORIS YELTSIN REGIME

While Mikhail Gorbachev's ouster from power and the disbandment of the 75-year-old communist regime was generally received in Russia without huge regrets, the effects of the ensuing disintegration of the imperial Soviet state left a deep imprint on the lives of millions of Russian citizens. Without underrating the novelty and magnitude of the problems faced by the government of Boris Yeltsin — the first President of the new Russian state — and minimizing certain achievements in their resolution, it is clear that, by and large, throughout the Yeltsin rule, Russian society continued to slide into moral degradation, structural disintegration, and economic morass.

On top of the significantly diminished territory, population, economy, resources, military, and power projection capabilities, the society continued to be plagued by traditional Russian woes: bureaucratic dictates, mismanagement, and corruption, as well as public apathy and despondency epitomized by alcoholism and addiction. Uncontrolled redistribution, i.e., plunder of what was left of the unwieldy albeit bountiful Soviet inheritance, was accompanied by rampant criminality. By the late-1990s, Russia looked like a failed state on its way to disintegration and collapse.

Internationally, the RF earned a dubious nickname of "Upper Volta with nuclear weapons."[28] Frequent claims at the early stages of the Yeltsin regime that Russia seeks adherence to the "club of civilized Western nations," were not backed up by serious efforts at internal evolution to comply with international standards of democratic governance.

The Yeltsin government was unable to define coherently and explain to the public the goals and orientation of Russian foreign, military, and nuclear policies. Despite a flurry of international exchanges between Russian officials and foreign dignitaries, the Russians remained ultimately confused whether the RF was "with" or "against" the United States and the North Atlantic Treaty Organization (NATO) on most global and regional issues. It appears that Yeltsin himself thought that the Russian nuclear potential was an "automatic guarantee" of Russian security and a barrier to others' alleged anti-Russian policies.[29]

While the Yeltsin government supported denuclearization of other former Soviet Republics and actually helped in this process, e.g., under the "Cooperative Threat Reduction Program,"[30] it continued to rely heavily on nuclear weapons and nuclear deterrence strategies. Moreover, it was under the Yeltsin regime that Russia started a movement away from the non-first-use of nuclear weapons in its military doctrine. The process was typical for Yeltsin's erratic style of policymaking when lots of people in his immediate entourage competed for the right to define and represent Russian interests to the outside world.

On December 21, 1991, at a meeting in Alma-Aty, Kazakhstan, where leaders of former Soviet republics joined the declaration on the creation of the Community of Independent States (CIS), the heads of Russia, Ukraine, Belarus, and Kazakhstan—states with the still-deployed Soviet nuclear weapons—signed an Agreement on Joint Measures Regarding Nuclear Weapons. Article 2 of the Agreement stated that its member-states "reconfirm the obligation on the non-first-use of nuclear weapons."[31] Supreme Soviets of Russia, Belarus, and Kyrgyzstan (that actually never signed the Agreement) ratified it on December 25, 1991, June 10, 1993, and March 6, 1992, respectively. According to the Vienna Convention on the Law of International Treaties, Russia was supposed to abide by this Agreement, unless it reconsidered the decision on its ratification.

However, the Yeltsin government soon started drifting away from the non-first-use obligation. Yeltsin's decree No. 1833 on "Main Clauses of the RF Military Doctrine" of November 2, 1993, was never published officially. However, according to publicly available sources familiar with the document,[32] it failed to make any reference to the non-first-use obligation.[33]

In February 1997, then-Secretary of the RF Security Council Ivan Rybkin declared in an interview to the government *Rossiiskaya Gazeta* that the Soviet obligation not to use nuclear weapons first was a mistake and that Russia was prepared "in case of a direct challenge" to use these weapons.[34] At the time, the President's Office tried to distance itself from Rybkin's "personal opinion." However, a short while later, this personal opinion became part and parcel of the official Russian military doctrine.

Despite this and other policy vacillations and inconsistencies, throughout his rule, Boris Yeltsin tried to appear accommodating and "progressive" on military-political relations with West and eager to compromise on arms control. However, internal political bickering between Yeltsin and the leaders of the State Duma prevented the government from assuring ratification of the key arms control agreement negotiated with the United States — the Strategic Arms Reduction Treaty II (START II).[35] By the time of his voluntary resignation on December 31, 1999, Russian foreign and internal policies appeared to be heading into an impasse. In effect, the RF was standing on the brink of chaos and imminent national disintegration.

THE VLADIMIR PUTIN PRESIDENCY

In sharp contrast, Yeltsin's hand-picked successor, originally a little-known apparatchik, Vladimir V. Putin[36] could become not only a widely popular Russian leader, but actually a symbol of Russian economic and political revival.[37] Putin worked consistently to create a new nation-wide ruling elite based strongly on personal devotions and vassal-type dependencies. The construction of a rigid "vertical of power"[38] and the use of blunt force in subduing regional secessionism, while criticized as "overly authoritarian,"[39] strengthened the central authority and eliminated much of the centrifugal tendencies in Russian regions. Confining Islamic radicalism and terrorist activities predominantly to southern Russia created a sense of relative security in populous hinterland regions.

Under Mr. Putin, a considerable effort was devoted to filling in the "ideological void" created by the disappearance of communist ideology and the Soviet propaganda apparatus.[40] In the search for the new "national idea,"[41] wide use was made of traditional tools of social mobilization in Russia — nationalism, religion and patriotism.[42] While there is no single distinct, let alone dominant ideology in Russia so far, it is not exactly true that "Russian strategic policymakers have no ideology."[43] The Russian ruling elite is driven by strong "Great Russian" instincts and mentality. Another important component of the emerging system of prevailing values and concepts in Russia is the rejection of the geopolitical model that has at its center the conglomerate of advanced Western powers headed by the United States. In the current Russian political vernacular this aspect of the emerging official ideology and strategy is usually identified as opposition to "unipolarity" and American global dictate.

Putin's grand strategy called for mobilizing all available internal resources to restore Russia's political, economic and military grandeur. Nuclear weapons and arms control diplomacy were called upon to play crucial roles in the program of national revival. By late 2002, Putin reversed all plans promoted by the government of his predecessor to reorganize and downsize the Strategic Missile Troops (SMT). Expanding U.S. BMD programs were the strongest argument in favor of preserving the status of the SMT and extending the service lives of aging heavy ICBMs, expressly to counter the alleged U.S. BMD threat to the Russian deterrence potential. Any doubts the Russian military-political leadership could have had previously about the value and importance of the Russian offensive missile-nuclear capability vanished completely.

Ultimately, Vladimir Putin argued that stopping the decay of Russian military power was among the main achievements of his 8-year presidency. In 2006, Vladimir Putin reported to the Russian legislature:

The situation in the armed forces today has changed dramatically. We have created a modern structure for the armed forces and the different units are now receiving modern, new arms and equipment, arms and equipment that will form the basis of our defense through to 2020. . . . Naval shipbuilding has got underway again and we are now building new vessels of practically all types. The Russian Navy will soon commission two new nuclear submarines carrying strategic weapons. They will be equipped with the new "Bulava" missile system, which together with the "Topol-M" system will form the backbone of our strategic deterrent force. I emphasize that these are the first nuclear submarines to be completed in modern Russia. We had not built a single vessel of this type since 1990.[44]

In effect, it was under Vladimir Putin that the Russian missile-nuclear potential became the symbol of Russia's survival as a nation-state and the absolute guarantee of its security. In the Russian President's words, "When looking at today's international situation and the prospects for its development, Russia is compelled to realize that nuclear deterrence is a key element in guaranteeing the country's security."[45]

During his presidency, he consistently alluded to the Russian nuclear potential as the foundation of Russia's special role in geopolitics. Above all, in the eyes of the Russian leadership, a robust nuclear potential created preconditions for "strategic parity" with the United States. The Russian logic was simple:

Russia and the United States are the biggest nuclear powers. Our economy might be smaller, but Russia's nuclear potential is still comparable to that of the United States... Also important is that we have the years of experience, the technology and the production potential, the technological chains and the specialists. Russia is a great nuclear power. No one disputes or doubts this. And the United States and Russia definitely have a shared interest in ensuring security on this planet.[46]

The Putin government offered full support to the Strategic Nuclear Forces and parts of the military-industrial complex (MIC) responsible for the development, maintenance and modernization of the country's missile-nuclear shield. In a typical statement dated June 9, 2006, at an important meeting with heads of enterprises belonging to MIC, the second Russian President declared:

> Our country's nuclear potential is of vital importance for our national security interests. The reliability of our 'nuclear shield' and the state of our nuclear weapons complex are a crucial component of Russia's world power status. I do stress that our work to develop our nuclear arsenal must go hand in hand with the most stringent demands on reliability and security of operation and, of course, with strict compliance with all non-proliferation regimes. In this respect Russia's position is firm and unchanging.[47]

The idea of using nuclear weapons in limited war was also gaining momentum under Vladimir Putin's presidency. Senior Russian generals started talking about using them in exercises and in limited war already in the late-1990s.[48] The new version of the RF Military Doctrine of April 21, 2000, developed under Boris Yeltsin but signed by Vladimir Putin in his capacity of Interim President, elaborated the provisions pertaining to the limited use of nuclear weapons that were set out four months earlier in the "National Security Concept" and in this regard marked a qualitatively new stage in the development of Russian nuclear doctrine.[49] In particular, it stated:

The Russian Federation reserves the right to use nuclear weapons in response to the use of nuclear or other types of weapons of mass destruction against it and (or) its allies, as well as in response to a large-scale aggression involving the use of conventional weapons in situations critical to the national security of the Russian Federation. The Russian Federation will not use nuclear weapons against states-members of the Treaty on the Non-Proliferation of Nuclear Weapons that do not possess nuclear weapons, except in case of an aggression against the Russian Federation, the Armed Forces of the Russian Federation or other troops, its allies or against a state with which it has agreements in the area of security, committed or supported by such a state that does not possess nuclear weapons, jointly or in the presence of allied obligations with a state-possessor of nuclear weapons.[50]

Besides the "RF Military Doctrine," the Putin government approved other doctrinal and strategy documents that reserved a special place for the strategic weapons in assuring Russian security, including the Federal Law "On Defense,"[51] the "National Security Doctrine,"[52] the "Foreign Policy Doctrine,"[53] as well as policy statements by high government officials, e.g., annual "Presidential Addresses to the Federal Assembly," etc. While these documents did not identify the "potential adversaries" of Russia by name, it was obvious that the United States and NATO powers were at the top of the list of the "threat factors" for Russia.[54]

Bellicose statements on Russian readiness to use nuclear weapons continued throughout Vladimir Putin's presidency. In February 2007 then-Defense Minister Sergei Ivanov told the Duma that, "As regards the use of nuclear weapons in case of aggression, of course [we will use them in this case]. What else were

117

they built for?"[55] He did not mention any of the caveats associated with official Russian nuclear use doctrine.

A few days later Colonel-General Nikolay Solovtsov, Commander of the Strategic Missile Troops, made nuclear threats against Poland and the Czech Republic if they were to allow U.S. missile deployment.[56] Despite U.S. protests against such inflammatory tactics, then-Commander of the RF General Staff Army General Yurii Baluyevskii in April 2007 once again threatened to target U.S. missile defense facilities in Europe: "If we see that these facilities pose a threat to Russia, these targets will be included in the lists of our planners—strategic, nuclear, or others. The latter is a technicality."[57]

The Putin government's decision to put nuclear weapons and arms control in the center of its military and foreign policy agenda was apparently taken with several important goals in mind. Firstly, by associating arms control failures with the weakness of Russia's global power and statue, Moscow was creating justifications for intensified efforts at internal militarization in general and modernization of the Russian strategic forces in particular.

Secondly, by playing the arms control "card," Vladimir Putin was subtly distancing himself from the preceding Boris Yeltsin administration, which was associated in the Russian mind with many troubles of their country in the 1990s. Thirdly, emphasis on nuclear-related issues was Vladimir Putin's way of signaling to the United States and other nuclear powers that Moscow would not sit idle while others augment their own capabilities.[58] In a way, the Russians were offering a choice between a new race in advanced weapon systems and return to binding restraints and limitations in developing and introducing these systems.[59]

In the latter case, they expected opponents, the United States in particular, to recognize that Russia deserves a "special place" in geopolitics by virtue of its military and economic potential, size, history, and culture.[60]

In an obvious demonstration of his readiness to deflate tensions and fulfill Russia's arms control obligations, shortly after his formal election to the presidential post, Vladimir Putin moved to expedite ratification of the START II Treaty. On April 14, 2000, Putin could master the majority of votes in the State Duma in support of the Treaty. In assuring the ratification that eluded his predecessor for many years, the new Russian President was motivated as much by the desire to bring the Russian legislature under his control as by the need to avoid the image of a "weakling" in the eyes of Washington.

However, Vladimir Putin and people around him were evidently well aware of the serious misgivings of the Russian military about START II. Almost from the moment it was signed by Presidents Bill Clinton and Boris Yeltsin on January 3, 1993, many in the Russian political elite and the expert community argued against its ratification because allegedly it worked against Russian interests and represented a "huge concession" to the United States.

Moscow was also well aware that parallel to efforts at making START II effective, the United States was considering changes to or abrogation of the ABM Treaty in order to implement its BMD programs. Clearly, it was with Putin's acquiescence that the State Duma added a provision to its START II ratification document stating that Russia would not be tied by this or other arms control agreements if the ABM Treaty was violated by the United States According to Russian experts, "Thus, the link that Gorbachev failed to

119

insist upon in 1991 was re-established nine years later by Russia" under Vladimir Putin.[61]

The START II Treaty had never entered into force. Besides linking the fate of the Treaty to U.S. adherence to the ABMT, the Russian legislative decision on ratification made its implementation contingent on the U.S. Senate ratifying a September 1997 addendum to the treaty that included "Agreed Statements on ABM-TMD Demarcation."[62] Neither of these occurred because of U.S. Senate opposition, where a faction objected to any action supportive of the ABMT. On June 14, 2002, one day after the United States formally withdrew from the ABMT, Russia announced its withdrawal from START II.

However, Russian "firmness" was of dubious political and practical value. In effect, failure to prevent the demise of the ABMT was apparently a good lesson for the Putin government. It demonstrated that no amount of rhetoric and verbal threats can affect actions of a stronger and determined opponent. The Russians realized that dragging their feet with START II ratification, refusal to accept earlier compromise proposals on BMD modification to accommodate particular U.S. interests in developing limited ABM capabilities, and, generally speaking, lack of flexibility and failure to use windows of opportunity in fluid diplomatic exchanges had resulted in the ultimate loss for the weaker side.

To the credit of the Putin government and Vladimir Putin personally, they refused the temptation to react hysterically and stir up still another massive accusatory campaign against the United States in response to the actual U.S. moves to withdraw from the ABMT (the U.S. announcement on the withdrawal was issued on December 13, 2001, and the Treaty ceased to exist on June 13, 2002.)[63]

As seen by a Russian expert:

> In mid-2001 Putin suddenly softened the linkage [between strategic offensive and defensive weapons] . . . eventually permitting George W. Bush to scrap the ABM Treaty without worrying about an adequate Russian response. By doing so, Putin also undermined the arguments of the opposition in the United States to Bush's decision that claimed that scrapping the Treaty would lead to a new armaments race.[64]

Similar *realpolitik* calculations apparently played a mitigating role in defining Russia's reaction to the initial NATO enlargement.[65] Obviously, Vladimir Putin was personally responsible for preventing outbursts of indignation and promises of counteractions that could not be supported by actual demonstrations of Russian power and could do more harm than good to the Russian reputation in Europe and beyond.

Moscow saw a relative "compensation" for ceding ground on the ABMT and taking an accommodating stand on global issues in the U.S. agreement to negotiate and conclude the "Strategic Offensive Reductions Treaty" (SORT), also referred to as the "Moscow Treaty. [66] The Kremlin presented the signing of the Treaty on May 24, 2002 as its "big success" despite the Treaty's alleged deficiencies, such as lack of explicit elaborate verification and other implementing arrangements, on the analogy with START, and the possibility of "uploading" warheads removed from their carriers for storage and not elimination at some point in the future.[67]

As the Soviets before them, the Russians saw arms control negotiations and agreements creating a quintessential paradigm for "equalizing" Russian and U.S. roles in such key areas of international diplomacy as WMD nonproliferation, global and regional security systems, etc.[68] Director of the Russian Institute for Strategic Studies Yevgenii Kozhokhin described Russian "self-interest" in arms control in connection with the signing of SORT and other bilateral agreements in Moscow in May 2002:

> Russia does not conceal its vested interest in the agreements that have been signed. It looks like Moscow is primarily motivated by the desire to enshrine in the agreement equality in the relations with the U.S. and, if possible, to maintain at least a seeming parity in strategic arms. A factor of no less importance is Russia's hope that it will be able to put an emphasis on the principle of interdependence between strategic offensive and defensive weapons. These must be the reasons why Moscow insisted on a legally binding character of the future agreement. From Russia's point of view, no other document could help it achieve these goals.[69]

SORT was particularly welcome for Moscow, especially since it came at a time when the structure of traditional arms control was shattered by the disappearance of the ABMT of 1972, which was long considered by the Russians to represent the cornerstone of the entire bilateral strategic arms control.[70]

By consenting to a significantly less structured arms control and the abandonment of the direct qualitative and quantitative parity in offensive and defensive capabilities, the Kremlin appeared to have not only accepted the unavoidable, but also untied its own hands in pursuing modernization of nuclear forces in line with internal economic and political exigencies.

The Russians took advantage of the relatively improved strategic relations with the United States to facilitate the elimination of weapon systems that were either too old, or too costly to maintain for purposes of "sufficient" deterrence while concentrating on the development and production of modern and more effective systems. They also sought to promote bilateral and multilateral cooperation with the West in areas where Moscow lacked resources and/or advanced technologies, e.g. Ballistic Missile Defense (BMD).

A key Russian diplomatic initiative, intended as an alternative to the U.S. global BMD system, was the offer to create a "European ABM system." The Euro-ABM was supposed to be built with the help of Russian tactical ABM technologies that could allegedly protect the European continent, including the European part of the RF, against non-strategic ballistic missiles[71] Moreover, the Russian government proposed to participate in developing "strategic" ABM systems in cooperation with the United States on the basis of "equality of rights" and under an "appropriate legal framework."[72]

THE MEDVEDEV-PUTIN DUUMVIRATE

The elevation of Dmitrii Medvedev to the pinnacle of the Russian political hierarchy did not and apparently could not make any major changes to the Russian nuclear strategy, especially the reliance on nuclear weapons. Medvedev was hand-picked by Vladimir Putin as his successor. Both share power in a duumvirate arrangement. Disagreements between the two are limited to secondary matters.

As a symbolic gesture addressed to the Russian people and the rest of the world, on May 15, 2008, hardly a week after his formal inauguration as the RF President (May 7, 2008), Dmitrii Medvedev visited the field positions of the 54th missile division of the Strategic Missile Troops at the Teikovo Missile Complex (Ivanovo Region). On the occasion, the presidential press service announced proudly:

> The 54th missile division is the first formation in charge of the new, refitted mobile land-based missile system Topol-M. In 2006 the first missile battalion armed with such weapons came into active service. In December of last year a second Topol-M missile battalion with three launchers was put into service at the Teikovo Missile Complex. The Topol-M missile complex represents the latest achievements of science and technology. The take-off weight of the missiles is 47 tons, their military payload is 1200 kilograms, and their flight range 10,000 kilometers.[73]

Medvedev's first year in power was marked by the worst crisis in Russia's relations with Georgia. The August 2008, war between the two former Soviet republics was ostensibly handled primarily by Medvedev as the new Russian Commander-in-Chief even though it is evident that Mr. Putin participated fully in war planning and eventual resolution of the conflict.[74]

While criticizing the United States for "unilateralism" and foreign "adventurism" the Russian leaders sought cooperation with the United States on many evolving negative global phenomena—from fluctuating market conditions to the rise of radicalism, international terrorism, proliferation of WMD, etc. In effect, despite its displeasure with the Republican Administration, the Medvedev government demonstrated eagerness to involve Russia in global cooperative ventures led by the United States, e.g., the Group of 8 (G-8) and the Group of Twenty (G-20).

With the coming to power in the United States of the Democratic Administration, both Medvedev and

Putin saw added opportunities for promoting Russian strategic interests and, in particular, the Russian arms control agenda. Moscow took advantage of Washington's intention (many think idealistic and eventually detrimental to better U.S. interests)[75] to significantly reduce and eventually eliminate all nuclear weapons, in order to expedite negotiations on the new bilateral strategic arms reduction treaty (START III).

The Kremlin praised the signing of the treaty on April 8, 2010 to replace both SORT and START I (that had actually expired in December 2009) as a symbol of "continued strategic parity."[76] Pro-government experts hailed the new treaty as extremely beneficial for the RF. As stated by the Director of the U.S. and Canada Institute of the RF Academy of Sciences, Sergei Rogov:

> We will not have to reduce anything prematurely. In effect, the ceilings established by the new START Treaty do not force us to reduce currently available strategic offensive forces, in contrast to previous treaties that banned or limited our heavy missiles as well as our mobile MIRVed ICBMs. These limitations have disappeared, and the Treaty allows us to conduct the modernization of our strategic forces since the old Soviet weapons have long exhausted their life-terms. From now on, each side defines the composition and structure of its strategic forces independently. Russia now has the capability — previously denied to us — to deploy new MIRVed ICBMs as well as new sea-based systems. In effect, only budgetary allocations and the potential of our industry will define how many Topol-M and RS-24 missiles — that would apparently, together with the Bulava, form the foundation of Russia's strategic offensive weapons — we would be able to build. It may not be excluded that before the Treaty expires and unless Russia and the U.S. conclude new agreements on further reductions, as championed by

Obama, there will appear a new type of Russian heavy ICBMs. Only the United States will have to conduct reductions, albeit not very dramatic ones.[77]

However a less enthusiastic perspective was offered by analysts without links to the Russian officialdom. For example, Major General (Ret.) Vladimir Dvorkin warned that numerical reductions of nuclear weapons between the two leading nuclear powers do not solve numerous global security problems — from nuclear terrorism to regional nuclear conflagrations. In the case of Russia, diminished nuclear deterrence potential raises uneasy questions about the weakness of Russian conventional forces, vulnerability to attack with precision weapons; medium- and shorter-range missiles no longer possessed by Russia and the United States; and the need to take into account the nuclear arsenals of U.S. allies, China and other existing and emerging possessors of nuclear weapons.[78]

Some government critics came to regard the new START as a "conspiracy" to eventually deprive Russia of its nuclear deterrence entirely. The signing of the treaty gave rise to numerous publications in Russia on the "fallacy" of unilateral nuclear disarmament.[79]

Parallel to the arms control activity, Medvedev, who prides himself on legal expertise and adherence to "international legality," engaged in preparation of numerous internal Russian doctrinal documents, including an update of the RF Military Doctrine and Foreign Policy Concept. In effect, the work on the revision of the 2000 RF Military Doctrine started long before Medvedev's coming to power. For years, Moscow periodically and apparently purposefully circulated rumors on the imminence of the document and its forthcoming major novelty, particularly related to the expanded uses of nuclear weapons. As early as October 2003 the military top brass, President Vladimir Putin, administration officials, ministers, security chiefs, Duma deputies, and journalists gathered in the Defense Ministry to hear Defense Minister Sergei Ivanov present a document titled the "Public Part of the Military Doctrine."[80]

News on the preparation of a new version of the Russian Military Doctrine that was supposed to "concretize" Russian threat perceptions and strategy began to circulate with particular intensity around mid-2006, at a time when U.S.-Russia relations were at their lowest ebb in years.[81] According to media reports, the new document was intended not only to directly identify the United States and NATO as Russia's key "potential adversaries," but also equate threats from Western sources to the threat of terrorism.[82]

On January 20, 2007, at the "Military-and-Scientific Conference" of the Academy of Military Sciences, the leadership of the RF Armed Forces formally reviewed the structure and the content of the new version of the Doctrine. According to the report of the conference proceedings by the Academy's President, Army General Makhmud Gareev, nuclear issues occupied a special place in the discussions.[83] The Doctrine was reported to stress the reemergence of the "existential nuclear threat" to the RF. As emphasized by General Gareev, "nuclear weapons of all states that possess them are ultimately aimed at Russia." In particular, as seen by the Russian military, "NATO is engaged in creation of powerful groupings of armed forces that are dramatically changing the military balance" in Europe and globally.[84] Not surprisingly, in light of such dire assessments, the proposed new military doctrinal document was expected to call for "augmenting the [Russian] nuclear potential" in the future.[85]

Justifications for modernization of the Russian strategic triad were sought and found in American declarations of intentions, statements, and announced programs, such as the decision to resume the production of plutonium parts for nuclear bombs[86] and develop new types of efficient low-yield warheads.[87] Alarmist Russian media reports accompanied the appearance of practically any official U.S. policy statement dealing with the issue of nuclear weapons.[88]

For many years leading to the emergence of a new version of the RF Military Doctrine, Moscow tried to fight off politically and diplomatically the expanding U.S. BMD program and, in particular, U.S. plans to deploy a third BMD site to deal with the growing threat of Iranian missiles in Poland and the Czech Republic. The Medvedev government picked up the task of opposing the third-site idea with enthusiasm. In his first Annual Address to the Federal Assembly in November 2008, he threatened to move *Iskander* missiles capable of carrying nuclear warheads into the Kaliningrad area and provide other responses if and when the United States deploys third site elements into Eastern Europe.[89] Other asymmetrical countermeasures were also mentioned with a clear intention to forewarn the United States and threaten U.S. European allies. For example, former RF Air Force Commander Petr Deikin suggested adding nuclear X-55 cruise missiles and the most recent non-nuclear version, X-555 (both may be carried on Tu-95M and Tu-160 strategic bombers), to augment the political impact of *Iskander* deployments.[90]

Expediting work on a "tougher" version of the RF Military Doctrine that would emphasize wider potential use of nuclear weapons became an additional measure in the Russian arsenal of "asymmetric measures" to counter the U.S. BMD and other perceived American technological advances. In early August 2008, Russian media sources commented briefly on a document allegedly prepared by the RF Defense Ministry titled "Draft Concept of the Development of RF Armed Forces Until 2030." The official status of the document was unclear. In all probability, it represented a trial balloon by the Russian military establishment intended to check expert and public reactions in Russia and abroad to potential changes to the existing RF Military Doctrine.[91]

In December 2008, Russian media sources carried a brief official statement attributed to Army-General Yuri Baluyevsky, then-deputy secretary of the Russian Security Council (formerly head of the Russian General Staff), announcing that the "Security Council, together with the Defense Ministry, other interested bodies of state power, and both chambers of the parliament commenced the preparation of the new military doctrine of Russia."[92] Baluyevsky was quoted saying:

> I was charged to head the working groups of the RF Security Council to prepare the draft of a new wording of the country's military doctrine that would respond to contemporary challenges and threats, and the existing changes in the geopolitical and military-political situation in the world, including the growing role of military power in politics… The new version of the military doctrine should become the response to the most topical problems of assuring Russian military security, including the legal foundations for the legitimate use ("*pravoprimemenie*") of nuclear weapons as an instrument of strategic deterrence.[93]

Along with Medvedev's threats of forward missile deployments, reviving the idea of a "tougher" revision of the Military Doctrine was obviously intended to coincide with the U.S. election campaign. This was Moscow's way of sending a message to the future U.S. Administration on prospects of bilateral strategic relations.

Russian observers also linked the flurry of statements on the imminent appearance of the new RF Military Doctrine to the new effort by Defense Minister Anatolii Serdyukov at reforming RF Armed Forces undertaken under Dmitrii Medvedev. From the very beginning, the reform met with considerable skepticism and criticism by various military and civilian authorities.[94] It clearly affected the interests of powerful groups in the military-political establishment besides thousands in the Officer and General Corps.

Announcing the resumption of work on the RF Military Doctrine, and especially the appointment of Yuri Baluyevsky to chair the Editorial Commission to define the Doctrine's basic parameters and substance, may have represented a concession to the conservatives who began to regard the Serdyukov reform as an attempt to undermine Russia's ability to engage actively in geopolitics and, especially, to use military might in the promotion of Russian interests abroad.[95]

Long before his forced transfer to the RF Security Council from the post of General Staff Commander, Baluyevsky campaigned for turning the original 2000 RF Military Doctrine into an aggressive tool justifying the use of nuclear weapons not only for retaliation purposes but as a practical tool for defeating aggression against Russia with the use of superior conventional forces, and even for preemption and suppression of activities inimical to Russia's interests outside its borders, for example those by terrorists and radicals.[96] Baluyevsky also consistently spoke in favor of offering an "adequate asymmetrical response to American and NATO provocations." In particular, he argued in support of targeting the proposed elements of the U.S. third BMD site in Eastern Europe by Russian tactical and strategic means including nuclear.[97]

In 2009, the current Secretary of the Security Council and former Director of the Federal Security Service, Nikolai Patrushev, sent up still another apparent trial balloon dealing with expanded uses of nuclear weapons for preemption and prevention in the RF Military Doctrine revision. While asserting that Moscow's main goal was to preserve its nuclear power status, he claimed the Doctrine will change conditions for the deployment of nuclear weapons to allow their use "not only in global but also regional and even local conflicts." According to Patrushev,

> The conditions for the use of nuclear weapons to repel aggression with the use of conventional weaponry in large-scale, but also in regional and even in a local war have been corrected. Moreover, in situations critical for national security, the inflicting of a preventive nuclear strike upon an aggressor is not excluded.[98]

The new RF Military Doctrine was finally approved by President Dmitrii Medvedev by virtue of his Decree No. 146 of February 5, 2010. At the same time, Medvedev signed "The Foundations of State Policy in the Area of Nuclear Deterrence until 2020," which was not made public. Opinions differed on the significance of this version of the Doctrine, particularly on the meaning of clauses related to nuclear weapons use. In the opinion of some Russian experts, "it made one more step away from Russia's obligation not to be first in the use of nuclear weapons."[99] A Western observer notes in this connection:

131

There are reasons to assert that the Doctrine sanctions the use by Russia of nuclear weapons in preventive (preemptive) strikes. In its time, this clause stirred a lot of hullabaloo and criticism in the West. Currently, this clause has been removed from the text of the Doctrine. However, was it removed as such? I do not think so. It is probable that the "Foundations of State Policy in the Area of Nuclear Deterrence to 2020" comprise stipulations on preventive (preemptive) strikes."[100]

Other experts maintained that "the new Military Doctrine appears to reduce, at least somewhat, the role of nuclear weapons in Russia's national security policy."[101] In effect, the 2010 RF Military Doctrine states:

The Russian Federation reserves the right to use nuclear weapons in response to the use against it and (or) its allies of nuclear and other types of weapons of mass destruction, as well as in the case of an aggression against the Russian Federation with the use of conventional weapons when the very existence of the state is placed under threat.

Doctrine-writing under Medvedev was marked by major contradictions. A characteristic example is the RF "Foreign Policy Concept" adopted by Dmitrii Medvedev on June 12, 2008. The Concept was promoted by the Kremlin as a demonstration of Russia's resolve "to position itself on the international arena as a civilized, rule-of-law state." It professed Russia's trust in "international law as the most stable foundation in relations among states," and the reliance on the UN to ensure international peace.[102]

Events of the Russian-Georgian war that took place shortly after the publication of the Concept apparently forced Medvedev and the Russian political elite to reconsider its key postulates. Already on September 6, 2008, at the meeting of the RF State Council, the Russian President announced "the discussion of Russia's new foreign policy strategy," i.e., the renewed work on revising the Concept, to proceed together with activities aimed at "national security consolidation."[103]

On May 12, 2009, in his decree No. 537, Dmitrii Medvedev approved still another Russian doctrinal document—"The Strategy of National Security of the Russian Federation to 2020" (NSS). In a sense, it replaced the ill-fated Foreign Policy Concept signed into law less than a year before.[104] The document reiterated that the United States and NATO present threats to Russian military security:

> Threats to (Russian) military security include: policies of a number of leading foreign countries aimed at attainment of overwhelming dominance in the military sphere, primarily in strategic nuclear forces, by means of developing precision, information and other high-tech means of military warfare; strategic weapon systems with non-nuclear warheads; formation, in a unilateral fashion, of the global system of anti-missile defense and militarization of the outer space, which may lead to a new loop in the arms race, as well as proliferation of nuclear, chemical and biological technologies, production of mass destruction weapons or their components and means of delivery. The state of the military security of the Russian Federation and its allies is being further negatively affected by the departure from international agreements in the area of the limitation and reduction of weapons, as well as by actions aimed at the disruption of the stability of the systems of state and military command, missile early warning, space control, the functioning of strategic nuclear forces, installations of nuclear warhead storage, nuclear energy, nuclear and chemical industries, and other potentially hazardous installations.[105]

Measures to deal with the above "threats" were, however, rather cautious and ambiguous. Besides pursuing the reform of the RF Armed Forces to give it "a totally new image," the NSS called for improving strategic deterrence and national defense. "Strategic deterrence" was defined as implying "the development and systemic implementation of a complex of interrelated political, diplomatic, military, economic, information and other measures aimed at forestalling or reducing the threat of destructive actions by the aggressor state (coalition of states)."[106] It was further clarified:

> Strategic deterrence is conducted with the use of the economic capabilities of the state, including the resource support of the national security forces by means of developing the system of military-patriotic education of RF citizens, as well as the military infrastructure and the system of managing the military organization of the state."[107]

As far as "national defense" is concerned, the NSS stipulated:

> The RF assures national defense on the basis of the principles of rational sufficiency and effectiveness, including by methods and means of non-military reaction, mechanisms of public diplomacy, peacekeeping and international military cooperation. Military security is assured by means of developing and improving the military organization of the state and the defense potential, as well as by earmarking for these purposes of sufficient financial, material and other resources.[108]

The "Strategy of National Security of the Russian Federation to 2020" struck many observers in Russia as a fairly eclectic, poorly organized and poorly edited document.[109]

CONCLUSION: PERCEPTIONS AND REALITIES DEFINING RUSSIAN DOCTRINES

Barring unpredictable major changes at the top of the Russian ruling elite or dramatic transformations in the internal Russian situation and/or Russia's international environment, Russian doctrinal thinking will continue to be affected by the following circumstances, considerations, and perceptions that contributed to the emergence recent Russian strategic documents.

Paranoiac Threat Assessments.

Despite repeated calls for strategic partnership between Russia and the West, and limited progress in select areas, such as arms control, as well as some cooperation in areas where Russian and U.S. interests and policies converge, the ruling political elite in Moscow remains deeply suspicious of American intentions and policies. The Russians usually see American advances, especially in the geopolitical and military-technological areas, as intrinsically inimical to Russian interests. In a typical alarmist assessment by Colonel General Andrei Nikolaev, Chairman of the State Duma Defense Committee:

> The gap between good intentions on establishing world peace and the real policy on the use of force is not diminishing but expanding. Tendency to militarizing the international life is becoming more and more awesome. . . . In recent years some progress was achieved in the sphere of reducing and limiting weapons. However, that process mostly involved qualitative parameters of the "man-killing industry", while quantitative transformations in the area of the

creation of new weapon systems and particularly new methods of conducting contemporary warfare remain without attention and critical analysis. High precision weapons, arms based on new physical principles, new methods of using space for the conduct of war... have no legal or moral limits. It is difficult to talk about international legal limitations for the new race in super new weapons when the international law is subjected to the revision by states (the U.S., Britain) that should be guarantors of international stability... Today, the U.S. and NATO have occupied such strategic boundaries in Europe and the Central Asian region that they could not even dream about before. Military structures, created for purposes of the Cold War are not only being preserved but are also expanding... Indeed, today, there exists perhaps no clear threat for Russia. But what will happen tomorrow when the balance of forces changes dramatically? In case of need, NATO may create any military scenario that suits its interests... like in the Balkans."[110]

The prevailing Russian opinion is that the United States seeks to establish its dominance in both offensive and defensive strategic weapons. Current U.S. championship of total nuclear abolition is also generally suspect despite Moscow's eagerness to pay lip service to the abstract ideal of the non-nuclear world. "Nuclear zero" proposals are often seen as a thinly veiled attempt to disarm Russia by neutralizing its nuclear potential. A widely held view among Russian experts is that their country would not be able to compete with the United States and other Western powers and probably even China in advanced non-nuclear systems, and may eventually become victim of pressures and blackmail if left without nuclear weapons:

Today, nuclear weapons are a factor of deterrence. However, take a closer look: the Americans are already developing the theory of strategic non-nuclear deterrence... Actual use of nuclear weapons... puts an end to any deterrence because it results in irreversible processes. In contrast, strategic high-precision non-nuclear weapons may be used both for deterrence and punishment. This is why in America. . . . they are now seriously looking at strategic non-nuclear deterrence that offers significantly more flexible capabilities for use and punishment of any aggressor specifically for purposes of deterrence.[111]

Importantly, since the collapse of the bipolar world, Russian policymakers no longer base their military and foreign policy decisions only on the analysis of the state of relations with the United States and NATO. Currently, Russian leaders recognize the existence and growth of multiple sources of threats and challenges to their country in proximity to Russian borders and across the world. It is highly doubtful that, even if bilateral U.S.-Russian relations miraculously evolved into a strategic partnership in the near future, Moscow would be prepared to give up nuclear weapons as an ultimate guarantee of Russian security.

In view of the persistently negative Russian threat assessments, it is highly questionable that the Russian military-political leadership would make drastic changes to their country's doctrines and strategies in the foreseeable future, let alone relinquish instruments of power painstakingly restored in recent years, particularly the Strategic Nuclear Forces. A more probable development would be the inclusion into Russian doctrinal documents of certain abstract statements on benign Russian intentions that would be attractive to the general public but totally unbinding for policymakers. In effect, this is exactly the way Soviet policies were presented to the outside world as compendiums of grand declarations that often had no link to real intentions and actions of the political elite.

Reliance on MAD.

Russian politicians and experts remain nostalgic of the strategic balance paradigm based on MAD and would like to go back to similar arrangements in current U.S.-RF strategic relations. Many of them would actually like the bilateral strategic balance to remain the foundation of global stability. As explained Major General (Ret.) Vladimir Belous:

> During the Cold War there emerged an approximate balance between both sides in strategic offensive weapons that contributed naturally to strategic stability and the concept of nuclear deterrence based on the central model of mutual assured destruction (MAD) that has never lost its topicality... The process of globalization and 'restructuring' of the world order creates strong premonitions since neither a unipolar, nor a multi-polar system would be able to assure the desired global stability. The unipolar model cannot do that because of the extreme egocentrism of the single state at its center, and the multi-polar one because of the interaction of the mostly antagonistic conglomerate of vectors of geopolitical and geo-strategic interests of many countries. Under these conditions, the role of the nuclear policies, especially of the U.S. and Russia that inherited huge arsenals of nuclear weapons and traditional views on their military uses from the time of the Cold War, is clearly growing.[112]

Under both Presidents Putin and Medvedev, the concept of MAD continued to form the de-facto basis of Russian views on bilateral relations with the United States in the nuclear sphere despite the formal termination of the Cold War and the disappearance of the main document that used to codify MAD-type relationship — the ABMT. In the view of many Russian experts:

> Despite the changes in the world, in U.S.-Russian relations and the policies of both countries, in their doctrines and operational plans for the use of strategic nuclear forces, both Russia and the U.S.A. continue to proceed from the concept of mutual nuclear deterrence[113].

Russia will most probably continue sticking to its opposition to BMD and the need to restore formal linkages between strategic offensive and defensive systems in line with the "classical" model of MAD.[114] However, expert demands in favor of developing Russia's own BMD,[115] as well as other hi-tech systems, such as non-nuclear strategic missiles are growing.[116] It may not be excluded that the military-political leadership will sooner or later recognize the validity of these demands. Russia's interest in cooperation with the United States and other technological powers in developing such systems may grow in the future and lead to changes in adamant Russian views on offensive-defensive linkages.

Search for Strategic Parity.

The Russian psyche was traumatized by the collapse of the Soviet Union. By and large, the new Russian policymaking elite that progressively acquired a distinct nationalistic orientation, refuses to abide by the global status-quo that reserves only secondary roles for Russia in world affairs. The nuclear area is virtually the only area where Russia had retained approximate equality of capabilities with the United States.

It is with this quasi-parity in nuclear potentials in mind, and emboldened by the progress in reconstructing Russia's economic and military potential as the result of favorably changing global prices for energy raw materials, that in early 2007 the Kremlin stepped up efforts to reclaim greater political equality with Washington in global and regional affairs. In a landmark presentation at the "Munich Conference on Security Policy" (February 10, 2007), President Vladimir Putin declared Russian rejection of American unilateralism in international affairs.[117]

The RF President accused the United States of "overstepping its national borders in every way" and essentially declared Moscow's determination to oppose Washington's "unilateral and frequently illegitimate actions."[118] Mr. Putin reiterated Russia's intensely negative reactions to NATO's advancement towards its borders, U.S. BMD-related deployments in Eastern Europe, and "space militarization" and reasserted that his government is prepared to provide "asymmetric responses" to these perceived "threats to Russian security."[119] Importantly, Dmitrii Medvedev, while slightly toning down the anti-American rhetoric of his predecessor in his public statements, essentially continued the critique of American global policies after becoming the RF President.[120]

Liberal Russian politicians and experts were thrilled to hear from the new U.S. Administration that it plans "to stop the development of new nuclear weapons; work with Russia to take U.S. and Russian ballistic missiles off hair trigger alert; and seek dramatic reductions in U.S. and Russian stockpiles of nuclear weapons and material."[121] In line with these goals and the promise "to extend a hand if others are willing to unclench their fist,"[122] both sides rushed to renew strategic arms control negotiations on a follow-on agreement to START I[123] and broader areas of cooperation to reduce the number of nuclear weapons and prevent further proliferation in accordance with joint statements issued by President Obama and Russian President Dmitrii Medvedev in London on April 1, 2009.[124]

The signing of the new START agreement brought many in Moscow to near-euphoria. In Russian eyes, it vindicated Russian adherence to MAD and the linkage between strategic offensive and defensive weapons, and carried a promise of limiting the U.S. global BMD effort, especially as far as deployments close to Russian borders are concerned. The Kremlin will most probably be able to assure the treaty's ratification in the State Duma where it enjoys a comfortable majority (both countries need to proceed to the ratification simultaneously). The situation in the United States, where many question the basic MAD-oriented premise of the treaty, the ultimate value it may have for U.S. security, and the direction it gives to U.S. nuclear strategy, may be very different.[125] In case START ratification stalls or the treaty fails to enter into force altogether, the Russian Federation may experience an upsurge in anti-Americanism. This is bound to be reflected at some stage in Russia rewriting its military and foreign policy guidelines. Even if the treaty is ratified, Russia may change its attitude towards it depending on the on-going U.S. BMD programs in Europe and other regions in accordance with Moscow's clarifying statement on missile defense at the signing of START.[126]

Internal Russian Evolution.

Russia's military and foreign policies depend on internal political, economic, and security stability. At this point, the Medvedev-Putin duumvirate appears to be in control of the situation in the country. However, it faces mounting challenges:

- Russia failed to evolve into an open democracy-based society. An authoritarian regime may hold the country together for a relatively long time, especially if it indulges in populism and has resources to maintain a reasonably reliable repressive apparatus, docile legislature and mass media. However, as the Soviet and other similar experiences demonstrate, collapse of this type of a regime usually comes precipitously and acquires devastating proportions. Regime changes that took place in some former Soviet republics serve as pertinent examples.
- The global and internal Russian economic crises forced the government to make adjustments to ambitious plans of expansion and growth in many areas, including defense modernization. Resources previously available from such sources as exports of oil and gas and were in part used to maintain stability, are dwindling. The gap between the haves and the have-nots in Russia is expanding rapidly, fueling public discontent.
- The authorities are largely incapable of eradicating massive corruption and criminality, as well as the flight of capital from Russia that could otherwise be used for development.[127]
- Frenetic attempts to streamline, restructure and improve the performance of the government apparatus have been ineffective.

- Reforms of the army, law-enforcement and judicial systems that traditionally provide stability and security for the regime are failing.
- According to some worst-case predictions, Russia may soon be unable to effectively defend itself with conventional forces. Under this scenario, the emphasis on nuclear weapons' use will undoubtedly grow.
- Serious deterioration or eventual collapse of law-and-order in the country may again raise the vital question of security and safety of nuclear and other sensitive materials and installations, and potential WMD proliferation from Russian sources.
- The seemingly amicable relationship between two top Russian leaders may deteriorate or break down, especially if the duumvirate comes under serious pressures from opponents, rivals, and an unhappy and irate public, including the military and other people in uniform.

These and many other so far unforeseen developments may change the Russian scene. Any major transformations in Russia are bound to modify that country's policies, stated strategic goals and doctrines.

ENDNOTES - CHAPTER 3

1. On May 12, 2010, The Russian Federation (RF) Foreign Ministry announced it is "considering the possibility of publicizing data on its nuclear weapons" following similar moves by the United States and Great Britain and in the spirit of the new arms control treaty signed by U.S. President Barack Obama and RF President Dmitrii Medvedev in Prague, the Czech Republic, on May 8, 2010. See "Russia May Divulge Data on Its Nuclear Arsenal," *RIA Novosti*, May 12, 2010, in Russian, available from

army.lv/ru/yadernoe-oruzhie/901/24532. It has not been indicated, however, whether Moscow intends to include the numbers and types of tactical nuclear weapons in its possession if and when this information is released.

2. For a more detailed assessment of these issues, see Andrei Shoumikhin, "Goals and Methods of Russian Arms Control Policy: Implications for U.S. Security," *National Institute for Public Policy,* August 2008, available from *nipp.org/Publication/Downloads/ Publication%20Archive%20PDF/Russian%20Arms%20Control%20 web.pdf.*

3. The Kremlin relies on various institutional mechanisms in defining the Russian military, including nuclear and foreign policy. They include the Russian Security Council, the presidential administration, appropriate legislative and technical bodies of the Federal Assembly—the Russian two-chamber parliament consisting of the State Duma and the Council of Federation, such as the committees and commissions on defense, national security, and international affairs; as well as professional apparatuses of government ministries and other bodies, particularly the Foreign Ministry of the Russian Federation, the Defense Ministry, and the Ministry of Atomic Energy. Relatively speaking, there is currently a greater variety of sources for military and foreign policymaking than under the Soviet system. The ongoing, albeit slow, process of the formation of civil society in Russia, including greater freedom of speech and expression allowed various academic and educational institutions, public organizations, think-tanks, expert associations, individual specialists, and representatives of mass media to speak freely on foreign and military matters, particularly arms control policy and negotiation; the military reform; and civilian control of the armed forces. The Council on Foreign and Defense Policy (see *www.svop.ru*); Center for Arms Control, Energy and Environmental Studies at the Moscow Institute of Physics and Technology (see *www.armscontrol.ru/*); The Russian Center for Policy Studies (see *www.pircenter.org*); and the Institute for Political and Military Analysis (see *www.ipma.ru*).

4. See Andrei Shoumikhin, "Change and Continuity in Russian Arms Control," *Comparative Strategy,* Vol. 28, Issue 2, 2009, pp. 140-153.

5. Andrei A. Gromyko, "To Be Remembered," Vol. II, Moscow, Russia: *Politizdat*, 1990, p. 221.

6. The Russians pride themselves on being the first in the world to test a prototype ballistic missile interceptor on March 4, 1961, at the Sary-Shagan testing ground near Lake Balkhash. (See "The Birth of System 'A'," *Voenno-Promyshlennyi Kurier*, Vol. 33, No. 149, August 5, 2006, in Russian, available from *www.vpk-news.ru/article.asp?pr_sign=archive.2006.149.articles.army_03)*. The warhead used was a conventional one and intercepted a ballistic missile of the R-12 type that was moving at the speed of 3 km per second. See Stanislav Menshikov, "Missile Defense: A Russian Perspective," *ECAAR-Russia Paper*, July 21, 2002, available from *www.fastcenter.ru/ecaar/UNdraft.PDF)*.

7. See Anatolii Dobrynin, *Highly Confidential. Ambassador in Washington under Six U.S. Presidents, 1962-1986*, Moscow, Russia: Avtor Publishers, 1997, in Russian, p. 133.

8. *Ibid.*, pp. 150-152.

9. Menshikov.

10. See "Missile Defense and the ABM Treaty, A Status Report," Fact Sheet, Stockholm, Sweden: Stockholm International Peace Research Institute, June 2001, available from *editors.sipri.se/pubs/Factsheet/Missile_defence.pdf*.

11. Pavel Podvig, ed., *Russian Strategic Nuclear Forces*, (With contributions from Oleg Bukharin, Timur Kadyshev, Eugene Miasnikov, Pavel Podvig, Igor Sutyagin, Maxim Tarasenko, and Boris Zhelezov), Cambridge, MA: MIT Press, 2001, pp. 620-622.

12. See R. M. Dyachkov, "The History of the Conclusion of the Treaty on Limiting Antiballistic Missile Defense of 1972," *IX International Conference "Lomonosov-2002,"* available from *www.hist.msu.ru/Science/LMNS2002/23.htm*.

13. See A. A. Gromyko, A. A. Bessmertnykh, P. Zhilin, G. M. Kornienko, and V.F. Petrovskii, eds., *The Struggle of the USSR against Nuclear Danger, Arms Race and for Disarmament. Documents and Materials*, Moscow, Russia: *Politizdat*, 1987, in Russian.

14. See "Concepts of SNF Development of the USSR in 40s-90s," *Arms.ru*, in Russian, available from *www.arms.ru/nuclear/1.htm*.

15. Richard Pipes, "Why the Soviet Union Thinks It Could Fight and Win a Nuclear War," reprinted from *Commentary*, 1977, available from *www.etpv.org/bills_page/nuclear.html*.

16. "Address by the General Secretary of the CC of CPSU, Chairman of the Presidium of the USSR Supreme Soviet to the Second Special Session of the UN," June 15, 1982, in Russian, available from *www.nasledie.ru/politvne/18_6/oonb.htm*.

17. Dobrynin, pp. 598-599.

18. *Ibid.*, pp. 623- 629.

19. Mikhail Gorbachev, "Memoirs," New York: Double-day,1996, pp. 406-408.

20. Gorbachev.

21. See Andrei Kokoshin, "The Competition of 'Asymmetrical Responses' Began in the 80s," *Nezavisimoe Voennoe Obozrenie*, July 7, 2007, in Russian.

22. Maksim Kalashnikov, "The Empire's Broken Sword," available from *www.e-lib.info/book.php?id=1121022183&p=0*.

23. Gorbachev, pp. 445, 451.

24. *Ibid.*, Menshikov.

25. Podvig, ed., "Russian Strategic Nuclear Forces," p. 655.

26. Dobrynin, p. 661.

27. *Ibid.*, Menshikov.

28. Aleksandr Golts, "Why Russia Has Let Its Nuclear Arsenal Go for Soap and Sausage," *Komsomolskaya Pravda*, September 5, 1995, available from *www.fas.org/news/russia/1995/sov95175.htm*.

29. "Yeltsin Rattles Nuclear Sabre after Criticism over Chechnya," *Disarmament Diplomacy*, Issue No. 42, December 1999, available from *www.acronym.org.uk/textonly/dd/dd42/42sabre.htm*.

30. See Ashton B. Carter, "U.S. Assistance to the New Independent States of the Former Soviet Union (FSU) in Dismantling Their Weapons of Mass Destruction," Congressional Hearings, "Special Weapons: Nuclear, Chemical, Biological and Missile," *House Foreign Affairs Committee*, September 21, 1993, available from *www.fas.org/spp/starwars/congress/1993_h/930921-ash.htm*.

31. *The First-Strike Doctrine, Scilla.ru*, June, 13, 2010, available from *www.scilla.ru/content/view/3533/2/*.

32. See "There Will Be No RAKs without MAKs," *Rossiiskaya Gazeta*, March 11, 1999, available from *www.buran.ru/htm/11-3-99. htm*.

33. Decree No. 1833 was submitted for the consideration of the RF Federal Assembly (parliament) elected on December 12, 1993, however, the latter refused to consider it for reasons of continued confrontation between the executive and legislative branches in Russia.

34. See "Rybkin Reasserts Moscow's Right To Use Nuclear Weapons," *Radiostantsiya Ekho Moskvy*, May 13, 1997, *GlobalSecurity.org*, available from *www.globalsecurity.org/wmd/library/news/russia/1997/drsov05131997000591.htm*.

35. The Treaty was signed on January 3, 1993, by President George Bush, Sr., and President Boris Yeltsin. It codified the "Joint Understanding" arrived at by the two Presidents at the Washington summit on June 17, 1992. The U.S. Senate gave its advice and consent to ratification of START II on January 26, 1996. Ratification of the Treaty in the Russian Duma proved elusive for Yeltsin in view of the strong opposition of the Russian legislature. See Eugene Myasnikov, "Problems of START-2 Treaty Ratification in Russia. Is START-3 Possible?" *Nezavisimaya Gazeta*, September 12, 1996, in Russian.

36. See Andre de Nesnera, "Who Is Putin?" *GlobalSecurity. org,* available from *www.globalsecurity.org/wmd/library/news/russia /2000/000128-rus1.htm.*

37. See "The Insider's Guide to Vladimir Putin," October 26, 2006, *CNN International,* available from *edition.cnn.com/2006/ WORLD/europe/10/25/insider.putin/.*

38. See "Vladimir Putin Lines Up the Parties Under the Vertical of Power," *Newsru.com,* April 15, 2005, in Russian, available from *www.moscow2000.ru/news/view2.asp?Id=13767&IdType=2;* "The Russian Opposition Is Unhappy with the Power 'Vertical' Built by Putin," *Information-Analytic Portal of the Union State,* July 9, 2006, in Russian, available from *www.soyuz.by/second.aspx?document=21 540&uid=4&page=4&type=Qualifie*r.

39. "The Russian Opposition Is Unhappy with the Power 'Vertical' Built by Putin."

40. See "Sergei Kortunov, "On the Quality of the National Elite," *Intelligent,* January 23, 2006, in Russian, available from *www.c-society.ru/wind.php?ID=244495&soch=1.*

41. See V. S. Elistratov, "The National Language and National Idea," *Gramota.ru,* in Russian, available from *www.gramota.ru/ mag_rub.html?id=54;* "The Russian National Idea," *Vostok14.ru.* in Russian, available from *www.vostok14.ru/?page=idea.*

42. See Vladimir Putin, "Speech at the Benediction Ceremony of the Cross-and-Banner Procession," *President of Russia Official Web Portal,* in Russian, available from *www.kremlin.ru/ap-pears/2003/07/31/1518_type63374_49692.shtml.*

43. Dmitri Trenin, "Russia's Threat Perception and Strategic Posture," *Russian Security Strategy under Putin: U.S. and Russian Perspectives,* Carlisle, PA: Strategic Studies Institute, U.S. Army War College, November 2007, p. 35.

44. Vladimir Putin, "Annual Address to the Federal Assembly of the Russian Federation," *President of Russia Official Web Portal,* May 10, 2006, available from *www.kremlin.ru/eng/speech-es/2006/05/10/1823_type70029type82912_105566.shtml.*

45. Vladimir Putin, "Opening Address at Meeting on Developing Russia's Nuclear Weapons Complex," *President of Russia Official Web Portal*, March 30, 2006, available from *www.kremlin.ru/eng/speeches/2006/03/30/2300_type82913_104010.shtml*.

46. Vladimir Putin, Interview with Al Jazeera Television Channel, October 16, 2003, President of Russia Official Web Portal, available from *www.kremlin.ru/eng/text/speeches/2003/10/16/1648_54238.shtml*.

47. "Opening Remarks at Meeting with Heads of the Russian Nuclear Weapons and Nuclear Energy Complexes," *Novo-Ogaryovo*, June 9, 2006, President of Russia Official Web Portal, available from *www.kremlin.ru/eng/text/speeches/2006/06/09/1952_type82912type82913_106757.shtml*.

48. Vladimir Sokirko, "Top-ol, Top-ol!!" *Moskovskii Komsomolets*, December 23, 1999, OSC Doc. FTS19991222001392; "CINC Yakovlev Interviewed on 40th Anniversary of RVSN," *Nezavisimoe Voennoye Obozrenie,* December 17, 1999, OSC Doc. CEP19991229000022.

49. Nikolai Sokov, "Russia's 2000 Military Doctrine," October 1999 (revised July 2004), *NTI.org*, available from *www.nti.org/db/nisprofs/over/doctrine.htm*.

50. See "The Military Doctrine of the Russian Federation," Adopted by the Decree of the President of the Russian Federation No. 706, April 21, 2000, in Russian, available from www.rg.ru/oficial/doc/ykazi/doc_war.htm.

51. See "The Law of the Russian Federation on Defense," adopted by the State Duma on April 24, 1996, and approved by the Federation Council on May 15, 1996, in Russian, available from *www.hro.org/docs/rlex/defence/index.htm*.

52. See "The National Security Concept of the Russian Federation," adopted by the Decree of the President of the Russian Federation No. 1300,f December 17, 1997, in the "Edited Version of the Presidential Decree No. 24 of January 10, 2000," in Russian, available from *www.iss.niiit.ru/doktrins/doktr01.htm*.

53. See Robert Legvold, "Russia's Unformed Foreign Policy," *Foreign Affairs*, September/October 2001, available from *www.foreignaffairs.org/20010901faessay5570/robert-legvold/russia-s-unformed-foreign-policy.html*.

54. Alexei Arbatov and Vladimir Dvorkin, eds., *Nuclear Deterrence and Non-Proliferation*, Members of Working Group: Pavel Kamennov, Elina Kirichenko and Vladimir Pyryev, Moscow, Russia: Carnegie Moscow Center, 2006, p. 4, available from *www.carnegie.ru/en/pubs/books/9735arbatov_eng_blok.pdf*.

55. "Russia Reserves the Right to Preemptive Strikes," *Moscow Agentstvo Voennykh Nosostei*, February 7, 2007, Open Source Center (OSC) Doc.CEP200707950213.

56. "General Says Russia May Target Missile Defense Sites in Eastern Europe," *Channel One Television,* February 19, 2007, OSC Doc. CEP20070219950390.

57. "Baluyevskii Says U.S. European Missile Defense Poses Threat to Russia," *WebDigest.ru*, May 3, 2007, OSC Doc. CEP2007054358001.

58. See Andrei Yashlavskii and Inga Kumskova, "Moscow Flexes Its Muscles," *Moskovskii Komsomolets*, March 1, 2007, OSC Doc. CEP20070301021003.

59. Vladimir Putin, "Speech and the Following Discussion at the Munich Conference on Security Policy," February 10, 2007, *President of Russia Official Web Portal*, available from *www.kremlin.ru/eng/speeches/2007/02/10/0138_type82914type84779_118135.shtml*.

60. See Nikolai Zyatkov, "Where Is the Smell of Gunpowder Coming From?" *Argumenty i Fakty*, February 19, 2007, OSC Doc. CEP20070224950135.

61. Menshikov.

62. See Amy F. Woolf, "Anti-Ballistic Missile Treaty Demarcation and Succession Agreements: Background and Issues," *CRS Report to Congress*, April 27, 2000, available from *www.cnie.org/nle/crsreports/international/inter-68.cfm*.

63. Putin's short statement in response to the American withdrawal announcement made the following points: "The U.S. has the legitimate right to abandon the Treaty in accordance with its provisions; though an American 'mistake' the withdrawal decision does not create immediate threats to Russian security; abandonment of the ABM Treaty leads to the emergence of a legal vacuum in the elaborate system of agreements in the sphere of disarmament and the nonproliferation; that 'vacuum' should be filled up by rapid elaboration of a 'new framework' of strategic mutual relations; under that 'framework' considerable reductions of offensive weapons should take place (preferably to the level of 1,500-2,200 warheads for each side)." See Vadim Markushin, "Bad News for the World Community," *Krasnaya Zvezda*, December 15, 2001, in Russian.

64. Menshikov.

65. "Russian Reaction to NATO's Enlargement," *Analitik*, March 4, 2004, in Russian, available from *analitik.org.ua/ukr/current-comment/ext/407412da4f691/pagedoc1095_25/*.

66. "The SOR Treaty calls for the reduction of the strategic nuclear warheads of both Russia and the United States by the end of 2012 to 1,700-2,200, i.e., approximately by three times compared to the level provided by the START 1 Treaty. START 1 itself is to remain in force until December 5, 2009, and may then be extended. The SOR Treaty ensures continuity in disarmament and arms control in the conditions when the ABM Treaty has ceased to be operative, the question of the entry of the START II Treaty into force has fallen away, and other disarmament agreements are undergoing serious trials. The new Treaty was called upon to assist substantially the strengthening of the nonproliferation regime as well." See "Statement by Alexander Konuzin, Deputy Permanent Representative of Russia to the United Nations, at the Session of the UN Commission on Disarmament Held on April 1, 2003." SORT was ratified by the Duma on May 14, 2003 by votes of 294 deputies with 134 voting against and none abstaining.

67. See Nikolai Sokov, "The Russian Nuclear Arms Control Agenda After SORT," *Arms Control Today*, April 2003, available from *www.armscontrol.org/act/2003_04/sokov_apr03.asp*.

68. While keeping a competitive posture on strategic weapons, Russia is prepared to play a partnership role with the United States in curbing WMD proliferation and other areas where both nations face similar challenges and threats. For example, in July 2006, Presidents of both countries launched the joint Global Initiative to Combat Nuclear Terrorism aimed "to prevent the acquisition, transport, or use by terrorists of nuclear materials and radioactive substances or improvised explosive devices using such materials, as well as hostile actions against nuclear facilities." "Joint Statement by U.S. President George Bush and Russian Federation President Vladimir Putin announcing the Global Initiative to Combat Nuclear Terrorism," St. Petersburg, Russia, July 15, 2006, *President of Russia Official Web Portal*, available from *www.kremlin.ru/eng/text/docs/2006/07/108727.shtml*.

69. Yevgenii Kozhokhin, "U.S.-Russian Relations: Facts and Mutual Expectations," *IAIR Publication*, December 2002, in Russian, available from *www.ipmi.ru/html_en/publication_en/m_en/06_%20_1_december_2002_en.htm*.

70. According to Nikolai Sokov: "Coupled with the end of the ABM Treaty and START 2, SORT marks the end of traditional arms control. Further reductions are unlikely in the near future because, after SORT is implemented, the United States and Russia will have reached what they feel is the optimal (or close to the optimal) level of strategic arsenals that they need: 2,200 deployed warheads for the United States and 1,500 for Russia. One possible additional step is codification of the ongoing reduction of Russian nonstrategic nuclear weapons, but its chances are remote. More importantly, managing first-strike capability, which was the key motive of traditional arms control, is no longer urgent following the end of the Cold War." See Nikolai Sokov, "The Russian Nuclear Arms Control Agenda After SORT," *Arms Control Today*, April, 2003.

71. "Sergei Ivanov: Russia is for the Creation of Europe's Non-Strategic Anti-Missile Defense System," *Itar-Tass*, August 30, 2005 in Russian.

72. *Itar-Tass*, August 6, 2005, in Russian.

73. "Visit to Ivanovo, Kostroma, and Yaroslavl Regions." Teikovo (Ivanovo Region), Kostroma, Yaroslavl, *President of Russia Official Web Portal*, May 15, 2008, available from *www.kremlin.ru/eng/events/chronicle/2008/05/200822.shtml*.

74. According to Russian President Dmitrii Medvedev, "The United States of America actively helped Georgia to erect its military machine, pumped money and weapons into it. Unfortunately, at some stage they gave Mr. Saakashvili a carte blanche for any actions, including military ones. All this materialized in the aggression that was launched on the night of 7-8 August." See "Russian President Attacks Georgian Leader, USA in TV Interview," *Vesti TV*, September 2, 2008, OSC Doc. CEP20080902950547.

75. See Andrei Shoumikhin and Baker Spring, *Strategic Nuclear Arms Control for the Protect and Defend Strategy*, Global Security, available from *www.globalsecurity.org/wmd/library/news/russia/1997/drsov05131997000591.htm*, Washington, DC: Heritage Foundation, May 4, 2009, available from *www.heritage.org/research/reports/2009/05/strategic-nuclear-arms-control-for-the-protect-and-defend-strategy*.

76. See "Russian-US Treaty on Reduction and Limitation of Strategic Offensive Arms Has Been Signed. Joint News Conference with US President Barack Obama," April 8, 2010, Prague, The Czech Republic, *President of Russia Official Web Portal*, available from *eng.kremlin.ru/news/271*.

77. Sergei Rogov, "Attempt Number 6: the Balance of Achievements and Concessions. Only the United States Will Have to Reduce Its Strategic Forces," *Nezavisimoe Voennoe Obozrenie*, April 9, 2010, in Russian, available from *nvo.ng.ru/concepts/2010-04-09/1_snv.html*.

78. Vladimir Dvorkin, "START on the Balance of Strategic Stability. The Time Has Come to Rethink Notions Such As Strategic Stability and Nuclear Deterrence," *Nezavisimoe Voennoe Obozrenie*, April 16, 2010, in Russian, available from *nvo.ng.ru/concepts/2010-04-16/1_snv.html*.

79. See Sergei Brezkun (Kremlev), "The World That Ran Away from the Bomb and Was Exploded Afterwards," *Foundation of Strategic Culture*, February 2, 2010, in Russian, available from *www.fondsk.ru/article.php?id=2746*.

80. See "Russian Military Doctrine," *GlobalSecurity.org*, available from *www.globalsecurity.org/military/world/russia/doctrine.htm*.

81. See Yurii Kirshin, "Generals Blueprint New Military Doctrine," *Nezavisimaya Gazeta*, August 28, 2006, in Russian.

82. See "The Draft New RF Military Doctrine: U.S. Equated to Terrorists," *Agentura.ru*, September 19, 2006, in Russian, available from *www.agentura.ru/?p=14&col=1&id=1158642000*.

83. See Makhmut Gareev, "New Conditions—New Military Doctrine," *Nezavisimoe Voennoe Obozrenie*, February 2, 2007 in Russian.

84. *Ibid.*

85. *Ibid.*

86. Yevgenia Borisova, "U.S. Restarts Its Nuclear Machine," *Moscow Times*, April 24, 2003.

87. "The U.S. Develops a Super Bomb," *Utro.ru*, May 19, 2003, in Russian; Vasilii Sergeev, "Nuclear Bombs Become Smaller," *Gazeta.Ru*, May 21, 2003, in Russian.

88. Alla Yaroshinskaya, "Is the World Moving Towards the Nuclear War?" *Rosbalt.ru*, March 23, 2006, in Russian.

89. See "Medvedev Sent a Revolutionary Message: He Responded to the U.S. BMD and Increased the Term of Presidency to 6 Years," *NEWs.ru*, November 5, 2008, available from *www.newsru.com/russia/05nov2008/poslanie1.html*.

154

90. Vladimir Ivanov, "Iskanders Alone Are Not Enough. It Is Proposed to Use Strategic Aviation to Act against the American BMD in Europe," *Nezavisimoe Voennoe Obozrenie*, November 21, 2008, in Russian, available from *nvo.ng.ru/armament/2008-11-21/8_iskander.html*.

91. See "The Military Doctrine of the Russian Federation," Adopted by the Decree of the President of the Russian Federation No. 706 of April 21, 2000, in Russian, available from *www.rg.ru/oficial/doc/ykazi/doc_war.htm*.

92. "They Prepare a New Military Doctrine in Russia— "Response to Problems," *Russianews.ru,* December 12, 2008, in Russian, available from *russianews.ru/news/20211/*.

93. *Ibid*.

94. See Aleksandr Khramchikhin, "The Institute of Political and Military Analysis Raises Alarm. The Reformed Russian Army Will Be Able to Fight against Only One Adversary," December 12, 2008, *Nezavisimoe Voennoe Obozrenie*, in Russian, available from *nvo.ng.ru/forces/2008-12-26/5_analiz.html*; Mikhail Rastopshin, "'Military Thought' against the General Staff. It Is Impossible to Achieve Permanent Readiness for All New-Look Troops," *Nezavisimoe Voennoe Obozrenie*, March 12, 2010, in Russian, available from *nvo.ng.ru/forces/2010-03-12/1_genshtab.html?mthree=3*.

95. Olga Bozhieva, "Russia Prepares an Anti-Military Doctrine," *Moskovskii Komsomolets*, December 11, 2008, in Russian, available from *www.mk.ru/blogs/MK/2008/12/11/russia/385672/*.

96. See for example: "Head of the General Staff: the RF Develops a New Military Doctrine and Plans Military Measures against the U.S. BMD," *Newsru.com*, May 7, 2007, in Russian, available from *www.newsru.com/russia/07may2007/baluevskij.html*.

97. *Ibid*.

98. "Patrushev Interview," *Interfax*, October 13, 2009; "Security Council's Patrushev Interviewed on Military Doctrine," *Izvestiya*, October 14, 2009.

99. "The First-Strike Doctrine," *Scilla.ru*, June, 13, 2010, available from *www.scilla.ru/content/view/3533/2/*.

100. Marcel de Haas, "Doctrinal Stipulations and Political Realities. What Should Be the Western Response to the New Doctrine?" *Nezavisimaya Gazeta*, February 2, 2010, in Russian, available from *www.ng.ru/realty/2010-02-26/1_doktrina.html*.

101. Nikolai Sokov, "The New, 2010 Russian Military Doctrine: The Nuclear Angle," *CNS Feature Stories*, February 5, 2010, available from *cns.miis.edu/stories/100205_russian_nuclear_doctrine.htm*.

102. Olga Mefodyeva:, "Policy Without Double Standards. Russian Foreign Policy Concept Seen in Context of Medvedev Speech to Ambassadors," *Politcom.ru*, July 17, 2008, OSC Doc. CEP20080718379002.

103. "State Council to Discuss New Foreign Policy Strategy," *Itar-Tass*, September 6, 2008, OSC Doc. CEP20080906950051.

104. "The Strategy of National Security of the Russian Federation to 2020." in Russian, available from *www.nsnbr.ru/strategiya_nb_rf.html*.

105. *Ibid.*

106. *Ibid.*

107 . *Ibid.*

108. *Ibid.*

109. See Andrei Konurov, "The Strategy of National Security: the Word and the Deed," Moscow, Russia: Strategic Culture Foundation, May 18, 2009, available from *www.fondsk. ru/article.php?id=2152*; Pavel Felgenhauer, "Russia's Defense Modernization Without a Doctrine," *Jamestown Eurasia Daily Monitor*, March 26, 2009, available from *search.yahoo.com/ search?p=http%3A%2F%2Fwww.ocnus.net%2Fartman2%2Fpub*

*lish%2FDefence_Arms_13%2FRussia_s_Defense_Modernization_
Without_a_Doctrine.shtm&ei=utf-8&fr=b1ie7.*

110. Andrei Nikolaev, "Old Strategy Refurbished," *Nezavisimaya Gazeta*, April 12, 2003, in Russian.

111. Vladimir Slipchenko, "What Kind of War Should Russia Be Prepared to Wage," *Polit.ru*, November 23, 2004, available
from *www.flb.ru/info/32983.html*.

112. V.S. Belous, "Deterrence and the Concept of First Use of
Nuclear Weapons," *Personal Web Page*, available from *www.c-soci-
ety.ru/wind.php?ID=240498&soch=1*.

113. See V.V. Prozorov, "Nuclear Deterrence in the Theory
of the Application of Strategic Missile Forces," Part I: *Theoretical
Aspects of the Activity of SMF Groups in Implementing Nuclear Deterrence*, Moscow, Russia, 1999.

114. Vladimir Ivanov, "The American Anti-Missile Circle — the
Pentagon Presented the Plan on Developing BMD Systems," *Nezavisimoe Voennoe Obozrenie*, February 26, 2010, in Russian, available from *nvo.ng.ru/concepts/2010-02-26/1_anti-usa.html?mthree=2*.

115. Yulii Estenko, "The Capital's Hole-Ridden Umbrella. The
Country Lacks Newest AD/ABM Systems," *Nezavisimoe Voennoe
Obozrenie*, February 26, 2010, in Russian, available from *nvo.ng.ru/
forces/2010-02-26/1_pro.html?mthree=1*.

116. See Leonid Orlenko, "National Security and Modernization of the Army. To Increase Russia's Security We Need Accelerated Rearmament of the Army with Newest Non-Nuclear Weapons," *Nezavisimoe Voennoe Obozrenie*, June 11, 2010, in Russian,
available from *nvo.ng.ru/forces/2010-06-11/1_safety.html*; Vasilii
Burenok, "The Basis for Net-Centric Wars — Acceleration, Intellect, Innovations," *Nezavisimoe Voennoe Obozrenie*, April 2, 2010,
in Russian, available from *nvo.ng.ru/concepts/2010-04-02/1_bazis.
html?mthree=4*; Mikhail Rastopshin, "'Military Thought' against
the General Staff. It Is Impossible to Achieve Permanent Readiness
for All New-Look Troops," *Nezavisimoe Voennoe Obozrenie*, March
12, 2010, in Russian, available from *nvo.ng.ru/forces/2010-03-12/1_
genshtab.html?mthree=3*.

117. Vladimir Putin, "Speech and the Following Discussion at the Munich Conference on Security Policy," February 10, 2007, *President of Russia Official Web Portal*, available from *www.kremlin.ru/eng/speeches/2007/02/10/0138_type82914type84779_118135.shtml*.

118. *Ibid.*

119. *Ibid.*

120. Tatyana Stanovaya, "Medvev Set the Tone of Russian-American Relations," *Politcom.ru*, June 9, 2008, OSC Doc. CEP20080610015002.

121. "The Agenda: Foreign Policy," Washington, DC: The White House, March 19, 2009, available at *www.whitehouse.gov/agenda/foreign_policy/*.

122. President Barack Obama's Inaugural Address, January 21, 2009, Washington, DC: The White House, *The White House Blog*, available from *www.whitehouse.gov/blog/inaugural-address/*.

123. "Treaty on the Reduction and Limitation of Strategic Offensive Arms, with Annexes, Protocols, and Memorandum of Understanding," *Treaties in Force*, Washington, DC: Department of State, 2007, p. 5, at *www.state.gov/documents/organization/83043.pdf*.

124. "Joint Statement by Dmitrii A. Medvedev, President of the Russian Federation, and Barack Obama, President of the United States of America, Regarding Negotiations on Further Reductions in Strategic Offensive Arm," Washington, DC: The White House, April 1, 2009, available from *www.whitehouse.gov/the_press_office/Joint-Statement-by-Dmitriy-A-Medvedev-and-Barack-Obama*; and "Joint Statement by President Dmitriy Medvedev of the Russian Federation and President Barack Obama of the United States of America, Washington, DC: The White House, April 1, 2009, available from *www.whitehouse.gov/the_press_office/Joint-Statement-by-President-Dmitriy-Medvedev-of-the-Russian-Federation-and-President-Barack-Obama-of-the-United-States-of-America*.

125. See Keith B. Payne, "Disarmament Danger," *National Review*, April 7, 2010, available from *article.nationalreview.com/430551/disarmament-danger/keith-b-payne*; Kim R. Holmes, "New START Negotiations: Show Us the Records!" Washington, DC: Heritage Foundation, May 26, 2010, available from *www.heritage.org/Research/Commentary/2010/05/New-START-negotiations-Show-us-the-records*.

126. See "Statement by the Russian Federation on Missile Defense," April 8, 2010, *President of Russia Official Web Portal,* available from *eng.news.kremlin.ru/ref_notes/4*.

127. Anti-government opposition provides scathing critical data on the internal situation in Russia. One of the latest publications of the opposition "Solidarity" movement is a brochure by Boris Nemtsov and Vladimir Milov, "Putin. Results. 10 Years," available from *www.putin-itogi.ru/*

CHAPTER 4

RUSSIA'S SECURITY RELATIONS WITH THE UNITED STATES: FUTURES PLANNED AND UNPLANNED

Pavel K. Baev

INTRODUCTION

In the last 5 years, the pattern of security relations between Russia and the West has changed twice: first towards confrontation resembling a new Cold War, and then towards cooperation maturing to a strategic partnership. The real amplitude of this swing is significantly less than often presented in the media commentary. The deterioration of relations, which reached its nadir in the second half of 2008 following the Russian-Georgian war, was tempered by a mutual desire to minimize damage, while cooperation remains hampered by lack of trust. Even so, the shift from a quasi-Cold War to a partial reset has been remarkably swift; it is essential to point out in this context that Russia-U.S. relations have experienced greater volatility than the more stable relations between Russia and the key European states. It is also useful to establish that the escalation of tensions was primarily of Russia's making, starting with President Vladimir Putin's memorable Munich speech in February 2007, while the breakthrough towards rapprochement was initiated by the U.S. administration of President Barack Obama. The Prague Treaty on reducing strategic arsenals signed in April 2010 is the main achievement in resetting the relations on the cooperative track.

The positive shift in relations coincided with the lowest phase of the economic crisis, which originated in the U.S. financial market but has hit Russia with greater force than any of the 20 largest economies in the world. The impact on mainstream political and security thinking has also been the most profound in Moscow, and not only because of the depth of economic contraction but also due to the sudden overturning of the prevalent worldview. Indeed, during Putin's second presidential term, the perception of fast-strengthening Russia that would reclaim its natural position among several great powers in the emerging world system, which would no longer be shaped by U.S. domination, became a political axiom for the Russian elites. The extent of Russia's economic vulnerability and political weakness revealed by the crisis is not yet fully understood by the disoriented policymakers, so the current thinking comes out as an incoherent mix of residual assertive ambitions, more sober assessments of power balances, and growing concerns about the country's further trajectory.

This chapter does not try to sort out these puzzles, but aims at identifying key inconsistencies in the evolving security perceptions and plans while also seeking to evaluate the gaps between these perceptions and real shifts in Russia's security posture, offering a few propositions about possible development of the latter. It starts by presenting the general picture of Russia-U.S. relations as painted and imagined by the present leadership in Moscow and then moves to analyzing the military-security scenarios and options, narrowing down on specific issues of missiles defense and the Intermediate-Range Nuclear Forces (INF) Treaty. The last section attempts to outline possible changes in the nature of Russia's relations with the United States, the

North Atlantic Treaty Organization (NATO), and the European Union (EU).

THE MULTI-POLAR WORLD ACCORDING TO PUTIN

The vision of a multipolar world constitutes the main mental framework in which Russian-U.S. relations are conceptualized, even if it represents a mix of several ill-compatible ideas rather than a coherent concept. The perception of several global power centers competing for influence is geopolitical in nature, and the conviction that their behavior is determined by pursuit of national interests could be characterized as neo-realist, while there is also a distinctly neo-liberal commitment to upholding international law and a preference for strengthening the regulatory authority of international institutions, primarily the United Nations (UN). In rhetoric, much attention is given to new-age security challenges, from nuclear proliferation to terrorism to climate change, but in real terms, it is the traditional interstate power-play that is seen as the main source of security threats and dangers.[1]

The U.S. hegemony in the world system is believed to be temporary and fast declining to be replaced by a more natural arrangement with five to seven great powers interacting free from fixed alliances but forming flexible coalitions in key regions of the world. It is logical in this worldview to expect determined and even desperate U.S. efforts aimed at prolonging its privileged position as the dominant hyper-power, so the emphasis on multilateralism in the new U.S. *National Security Strategy* is seen as a means to this end, while unilateralism is the prevalent style of behavior. For that matter, the reassurances in this document

163

and in other public statements that the United States would want Russia to be strong and self-confident are interpreted in Moscow merely as diplomatic courtesy or transparent deception. The experience of the 1990s, and in particular the Kosovo war, is accepted as proof positive of U.S. intentions to exploit Russia's weaknesses. These intentions are not seen as driven by preferences of particular presidents but constitute a fundamental strategic line towards marginalization of Russia as a potential rising power.[2]

The assessment of NATO aims and perspectives is rather different, despite the extremely hostile attitude in 2007-08 towards its supposed enlargement to Georgia and Ukraine. The Alliance is generally perceived as a relic of the Cold War destined to drift to irrelevance with the weakening of U.S. leadership.[3] The war in Afghanistan, believed to be unwinnable, is expected to push the allies apart, accelerating the fundamental trend of consolidation of the EU as an independent power pole. At the same time, Western Europe is typically portrayed as a declining and incoherent global actor, which is unable to develop sufficient hard power capabilities for projecting its influence.

This somewhat condescending view illustrates an important evolution in Russian security thinking: At the start of the 2000s, it was heavily tilted towards military-strategic matters, but at the start of 2010s, it has become distinctly economized. Vladimir Putin has never had a strong military background, but at the start of his presidency, his worldview was shaped by the heavy impact of the Kosovo war and the imperative to secure a victory in the second Chechen war. During his second term, however, the spectacular growth of oil and gas revenues caused a corresponding shift of political attention, so that Russia was reconceptualized as an energy super-power.[4] Dmitri Medvedev has very little understanding of, and less interest in, the traditional hard security agenda, so the emphasis on economic globalization and competition has become even more pronounced during his presidency. His personal impact on shaping the mainstream political perceptions may be limited, but the drastic contraction of the oil and gas revenues in 2009-10 has added convincing power to his discourse of modernization, so energy export is now depicted as humiliating dependency rather than as a major source of power.

There are several serious problems with this pseudo-pragmatic worldview, but perhaps the central one is Russia's doubtful ability to establish itself as an independent and influential pole in the envisaged multipolar world.[5] In this respect, the implications of the rise of China are particularly poorly examined beyond the rather thin official guideline on developing strategic partnership. The very real and historically sound proposition that a multipolar world would bring a more tough and less restrained competition between great powers, which could put Russia at greater risk of confrontation with revisionist predators, is typically neglected.[6] There is a pronounced preoccupation with (if not fixation upon) relations with the United States that are supposed to deliver evidence of Russia's status as nearly equal. The economic dimension in these relations is, nevertheless, quite underdeveloped, particularly in the energy interactions, which are generally at odds with the main thrust of Russian foreign policy. This weakness of the economic foundation causes greater volatility in this key fixed *dyad* compared with the more stable but highly complex Russia-EU relations. Overall, acting as a main protagonist of the cause for dismantling the unfair U.S.-centric world order, Moscow remains poorly prepared for the challenges of Hobbesian futures.

THREATS ARE MANY, BUT DEFENSES ARE FEW

Envisioning the turbulent advent of a multipolar world, the Russian leadership adopts a very broad interpretation of security, enunciating doctrines not only of information security but also of climate security and even food security. Each of these doctrines identifies numerous threats and risks, and the aggregate list is provided in the *National Security Strategy to 2020*, approved in May 2009. The document establishes that a qualitatively new geopolitical situation is emerging in which "interstate tensions caused by uneven development resulting from globalization" are growing (Article 8), but states that in Russia "the foundations for guaranteed prevention of external and internal threats to national security are created" (Article 1).[7] It would have been logical to expect that in the area of military security, the rather vague but unmistakably U.S.-focused threats defined in this document (". . . policy of some leading states aimed at acquiring decisive military superiority, first of all in strategic nuclear forces . . .," Article 30) would be elaborated in the Military Doctrine approved in February 2010. In fact, this document defines threats in the most abstract terms (for instance, the first one is ". . . sharp aggravation of military-political situation [international relations] and emergence of conditions for the use of military force," Article 10), and is no more specific in describing "external military dangers" (for instance, ". . . attempts to destabilize situation in some states or regions and to undermine strategic stability," Article 8).[8]

This great variety of poorly specified threats and risks that are not prioritized in any meaningful way makes it impossible to figure out the key parameters of real threat assessments on the basis of a bunch of recently adopted official documents. It should also be noted that the Russian strategic tradition does not include such common analytical exercises as scenario-building (or, for that matter, game-type modeling), so planning for crisis situations typically is linear with no alternatives for possible asymmetric responses of an adversary. In real-life crises, such inflexible leadership often results in confusion over unintended consequences, but in strategic forecasting, it makes it very problematic to suggest how Moscow would react if one thing leads to another. The only way to construct a sequence of rational choices is to derive intentions from available capabilities, assuming that the deciders are not misinformed about the latter. In this respect, the determined execution of reform of conventional armed forces could provide some clues about the security challenges and conflict situations that are seen as highly probable by the current Russian leadership.[9]

The wisdom of launching such a radical military *perestroika* at the start of a devastating and protracted economic crisis is questionable, and the reform is definitely generating greater pain and necessitating higher expenditures than budgeted, while its provisional results are far from the expectations.[10] One of the unannounced but logically deducible guidelines is that Russia is no longer expecting or preparing for a large-scale conventional war against NATO in the Western theater. Indeed, one of the first targets of the reform was disbandment of hundreds of skeleton units in the Ground Forces and the Air Force, which amounts to scrapping of the old Soviet infrastructure of mass mobilization.[11] It is possible to speculate that Defense Minister Anatoly Serdyukov, who has never pretended to have a grasp of high strategic matters, opted for this goal as one of the easiest in implementation, since those empty shells of regiments performed no useful role. However, even if abandoning a strategic model (dating back to World War I) was not intentional, the swift implementation of the disbandment order means that under no circumstances would Russia be able to deploy even a dozen of cadre divisions by calling reservists. This also means that no minimally meaningful conventional defense could be built in the Far East in case of a confrontation with China.[12]

One implicit reflection on this shift in the Military Doctrine is the proposition that:

> Despite the diminishing probability of launching a large-scale war against the Russian Federation with conventional and nuclear weapons, in several directions military dangers for the Russian Federation are increasing (Article 7).

This guideline remains open to interpretation, but it is possible to suggest that a June 22-type conventional offensive from NATO is now perceived as a negligible threat, not least due to unwinnable but inescapable engagements in Afghanistan and Iraq. What is assessed as a real and high-impact threat (demonstrated in the NATO war against Yugoslavia in 1999) is a series of surgical strikes with long-range high-precision weapon systems against which Russia has no effective defense and cannot respond in kind.[13]

The only conceivable, even if unthinkable, option for countering such a threat is escalation to the nuclear level, and this option needs to be credible in order to prevent the execution of punishing strikes. This credibility cannot be created by declaring readiness to cross the nuclear threshold, which would be politically inappropriate, so the Military Doctrine takes a very cautious stance on the issue of "first use," which is reserved for the situation of "threat to the very existence of the state" (Article 22).[14] The strategic arsenal is supposed to counterbalance the U.S. nuclear triad, as well as the nuclear capabilities of France and the United Kingdom (UK), so the main means for upholding this deterrence of conventional noncontact aggression is sub-strategic (or tactical) nuclear weapons. Complete lack of information about these weapons is creating a high degree of uncertainty for the potential adversary, and there is practically no guidance for or debate about the character of their instrumentalization.[15] Moscow remains highly reluctant to engage in any talks on possible reduction of these weapons, which should necessarily start with establishing greater transparency.

It is possible to hypothesize that tactical nuclear weapons are seen as the major instrument for securing Russia's ability to dominate the escalation of several local conflicts around its borders.[16] In principle, the on-going military reform is aimed at creating mobile "permanent readiness" brigades that should be capable of performing interventions of sufficient forcefulness. In reality, however, the cuts in the officer corps and failure to build a corps of professional (or at least serving on contract) noncommissioned officers (NCOs) has led to a sustained decline in the combat readiness of the new look Ground Forces.[17] This creates a high-risk situation for the near future where Russia could find itself so badly trounced in a fast-moving small-to-medium scale hostility that delivering a nuclear strike would become a practical solution.

Since the collapse of the Union of Soviet Socialist Republics (USSR), it has been the Caucasus that registered the highest level of instability with a great variety of violent conflicts overlapping and resulting in nonsustainable deadlocks. Russia performed a number of interventions of different scale, but in 2007-08 the end of the second Chechen war left it with significant and usable free military capacity, which was put to use against Georgia in August 2008.[18] Despite the spectacular victory, that war has left a highly controversial legacy, as Russia is tempted on the one hand to replay the easy walkover and bring the conflict to a final solution, but on the other hand, has much diminished military capabilities. What might make this conflict prone to nuclear escalation is a possibility of U.S. involvement, which Moscow would be desperate to pre-empt.

Another potential seat of conflict that attracts priority attention of Russian policymakers is Ukraine, which is seen as deeply divided and even artificial state. With the election of Viktor Yanukovich as the president in February 2010 and his remarkably swift consolidation of control over the unruly Ukrainian political process, Moscow has become more confident in building brotherly relations with the most important of its neighbors.[19] Nevertheless, the prospect of a new political spasm, similar to the orange revolution of November-December 2004 (which remains a looming specter for Putin's coterie), is perceived as fairly high, particularly as the devastating economic crisis generates massive discontent. Such a replay of the West-sponsored coup against pro-Russian elites could result in a split, or indeed multiple splits, of the failed Ukraine, which would open a door for NATO intervention. The weakness of Russia's conventional forces would make nuclear capabilities the only way to prevent this politically unacceptable intervention, but this non-strategic deterrence could fail, and the Kremlin could refuse to accept that its bluff has been called.

MUCH ADO ABOUT MISSILE DEFENSE
AND NOTHING ADO ABOUT THE INF

The plan for deploying some assets of the U.S. anti-missile defense system in East-Central Europe attracted intense attention of the Russian leadership, which, in retrospect, appears to have been disproportional. The *National Security Strategy* asserts that "The capacity for preserving global and regional stability will significantly decline with the deployment in Europe of global system of anti-missile defense of United States of America" (Article 12); and the Military Doctrine defines "creation and deployment of strategic anti-missile systems undermining global stability and violating the existing balance of forces in nuclear-missile sphere" as one of "external military dangers" (Article 8).[20] With the signing of the Prague Treaty on reduction of strategic offensive weapons, the campaign against (rather than debates about) the U.S. missile defense system in the Russian media and expert community has sharply subsided, but the issue could make a fast comeback if NATO turns down Russian wishes to be inside the defensive perimeter, or if a breakthrough in U.S. research and development in this area happens.

It appears probable that the Russian leadership did fall into a self-made trap of making a claim too far and then escalating the rhetoric to justify its mistake while at the same time trying some backpedaling to avoid the need to act on this rhetoric. The underlying reason for that self-defeating over-focusing is the lack of competence on strategic matters in the Kremlin, which was aggravated by the severe purges of the top brass and mistrust in the few available sources of independent expertise. The level of understanding of the problem is illustrated by Putin's explication:

> As everyone knows, our American partners are building a global missile-defense system, and we aren't. But missile defense and strategic offensive weapons are closely interrelated issues. A balance of forces was what kept aggression at bay and preserved peace during the Cold War. The missile and air defense systems and offensive weapons systems contribute equally to this balance. If we do not develop a missile defense system, the risk arises that our partners will feel entirely secure and protected against our offensive weapons systems. If the balance I mentioned is disrupted, they will feel able to act with impunity, increasing the level of aggression in politics and, incidentally, in the economy. In order to maintain the balance without planning to develop a missile defense system, which is very expensive and of unclear effect, we should develop offensive strike systems. But there is a catch. In order for this balance to be maintained, if we want to exchange information, then our partners should give us information about their ballistic missile defense system and in return we would give them information about our offensive weapons.[21]

Fortunately, this demand was dropped without any damage done to the real talks in Geneva, but Moscow is still bound by the self-imposed commitment to withdraw from the Prague Treaty if the U.S. strategic defense system becomes moderately effective. It is possible to find two distinct directions in Russia's struggle against this destabilizing system:

a) preventing the United States from building a position of strategic invincibility, and b) separating bilateral strategic matters from multilateral security arrangements in Europe. The main problem with President George W. Bush's plan for deploying 10 interceptor-missiles in Poland and a long-range radar in the Czech Republic was exactly that it brought these two directions together. The cancellation of this plan by President Barack Obama has undermined the solid Russian *Nyet*-position, and now Moscow has to construct is opposition more accurately.

In the big strategic picture, there is hardly much doubt that at some point in the mid-term, effective defense against ballistic missiles would become technically possible, and the United States would then proceed with determination to building a protective shield.[22] This new invulnerability is certain to destroy the traditional balance of offensive capabilities, so Russia had to reserve for itself the right to withdraw from the Prague Treaty.[23] The problem with this logically consistent position is two-fold. First, even abandoning the commitment to reduce the strategic arsenal, Russia would hardly be able to increase it, as many of its weapon systems are approaching the end of safe service life, while the replacements are coming in small numbers (and the future of the Bulava submarine-launched ballistic missiles [SLBMs] remains in doubt). Second, there has been much upbeat reporting about Russia's own anti-missile systems, in particular the prospective S-500, which is supposed to be a major upgrade from the currently deploying S-400 and capable of even hitting targets on low space orbits. When the United States makes the decision for full deployment of the missile defense system, Russia should thus be able to answer in kind — even if in fact, the technology behind its modern air-space defenses is antiquated beyond any updates.[24]

As far as the anti-missile shield for Europe is concerned, Russia remains very reluctant to engage in a meaningful cooperation with NATO, where in principle its new early warning radar in Armavir (as well as the very old radar in Gabala, Azerbaijan) and its tactical S-300 surface-to-air missiles could be valuable assets. Its main concern, in the words of Dmitri Rogozin, the ambassador to NATO, is "who will give the order on combat use of the system." Furthermore, behind the claim to be accepted as an equal partner in developing the architecture of the anti-missile system, it is not difficult to see the intention to make it unusable against Russia.[25] The key feature of the new U.S. plan that gradually takes shape (and its major difference from the plan advanced by the previous U.S. administration) is that the multi-element defense would be aimed not against ICBMs but against missiles of intermediate range, which Russia does not have according to the INF Treaty (1987).

Debates in Moscow about the pros and cons of withdrawing from this treaty reached a peak in 2007, as Putin proceeded with suspending Russia's participation in the Conventional Forces in Europe (CFE) Treaty and hinted that "it would be difficult" to maintain a commitment not to deploy two classes of missiles (500-1,000 kilometers (km) and 1,000-5,500 km), while other states keep building their arsenals. A key point in these debates was, however, that Russia could inflict serious damage to its strategic interests by a politically motivated dismantling of this crucial pillar of the much weakened nuclear arms control regime.[26]

In the near future, with the Prague Treaty in force, Moscow would hardly feel much temptation to abandon the INF Treaty, particularly since the production line at its only missile plant in Votkinsk is busy with the orders from strategic forces. The only possible controversy involves the Iskander-M (SS-26 Stone) mobile tactical missile currently deployed in replacement of the Tochka (SS-21 Scarab B); its range is officially reported at 400 km, but may in fact exceed 500 km — so the missile is capable of performing effectively the tasks of the Oka (SS-23) missile destroyed in 1988-90. This controversy could be focused on the Kaliningrad exclave, but its strategic vulnerability cannot be reduced by deploying the Iskander-M missiles there (as Medvedev briefly ordered in early 2009), so it is plausible that Moscow could agree on a self-imposed commitment to withdraw all nuclear weapons from this region. Much would depend upon NATO's position on the U.S. nuclear assets in Europe, which at present are practically unusable.

THINGS THAT MIGHT GO WRONG

This evaluation of evolving Russian perceptions of strategic relations with the United States and Europe cannot lead to an informed conclusion about their further evolution because they not only remain seriously incoherent, but primarily because their connection with reality is rather ambivalent. The mix of rising-power ambitions and declining-power fears requires psychological diagnostics rather than rational choice analysis, but there is nevertheless a common denominator in this pragmatic-schizophrenic worldview. The present Russian leadership takes for an absolute imperative the preservation of its monopolistic control over the political system, even if the experimental and somewhat unnatural construct of Putin-Medvedev duumvirate might be modified or abandoned as soon as 2012. This fundamental posit is, in fact, a rather questionable proposition as the economic foundation of Putinism — the steadily expanding petro-revenues — is shaken by the global crisis and cannot support the functioning of bureaucratic pyramid.

The crisis of the political super-structure of a petro-state could take various turns determining a wide spectrum of possible shifts in the nature of Russia's security relations with the United States and NATO, but before examining the breaks of the current trajectory, it is essential to establish where it leads. The primary goal of preserving the existing political order logically makes Russia a status quo power deeply reluctant to experiment with testing the limits of security arrangements, imperfect as they are. It might seem that the August 2008 war with Georgia was exactly this kind of experiment, and indeed in its aftermath there were plentiful speculations that Russia would behave as a revisionist power.[27] It has become clear by now, however, that even in that war Russia settled for a symbolic victory, which makes it easy for the EU and NATO to resume business as usual.

Clinging to status quo in a fast-changing environment is a vulnerable position, and Moscow finds itself again and again overtaken by events that do not fit into the correct picture of the multipolar world. One such fast-moving intrigue focuses on Iran, and Moscow was quite content with the pattern of some cooperation with Washington and some strengthening of the good-neighbor ties with Tehran that has been sustained since the mid-1990s but is coming to an unavoidable end. Russia takes its privileges as a member of the nuclear club very seriously and would have certainly preferred Iran not to have nuclear weapons. At the same time, a nuclear-armed Iran is not seen as a grave security threat, merely as an undesirable development, which might be preventable (hence the readiness to support some "smart" sanctions) but falls far short of the category of "unacceptable."[28] A far greater security challenge from the Russian perspective is the risk of a unilateral U.S./Israel military action against Iran, which could trigger a chain of asymmetrical responses and, no less important, would signify a disregard for Russian disapproval.

A similar unsustainable stance is maintained by Moscow towards the U.S. and NATO operation in Afghanistan, which is seen both as a neutralization of the direct threat from the Taliban to Central Asia and as a massive drain on Western resources. The Russian leadership shares the view propagated by the top brass that the war is unwinnable, but it certainly does not want to be seen as a spoiler of an international effort, and so is prepared to provide cost-free support, such as granting transit rights.[29] The best option, as far as Moscow is concerned, would be for the United States and NATO to remain involved in sorting out the Afghan disaster for years to come, and thus remain unable to engage in any other conflict situations, with the possible exception of the Balkans. This option, however, is expiring, and Russia — as its response to the state failure in Kyrgyzstan shows — is not prepared to take on additional responsibilities for guaranteeing security in Central Asia and has diminishing military capabilities for such interventions.

Forced Western retreats from Afghanistan and Iraq are seen in Moscow as logically following from the multipolar dynamics, but there is as little planning for such disastrous outcomes as there is in Washington and Brussels, where a victory of sorts is still believed to be non-negotiable. Putin believes that a humbled hyper-power would learn a lesson, but he might yet discover that an isolationist post-Obama America would also be determinedly unilateralist and inclined to project its unsurpassable military power in the form of punishing strikes. Corrupted by absolute power as he is, Putin still understands perfectly clearly that Russia cannot afford any real confrontation with the West or the United States because the economic consequences would be too hurtful. In fact, in the situation of protracted recession, Russia needs as much cooperation with the EU and the United States as it can get, and this essentially means that the imperative of preserving control over the political system would push Putin towards greater amity with the West whatever his personal idiosyncrasies may be.[30]

The issue is not whether the current leadership might decide that it could better advance its goals by turning again to a quasi-Cold War stance (the mobilization potential of such a maneuver is very limited) but how stable is this leadership. Putin may orchestrate his return to the natural position at the top of the pyramid in 2012, but this comeback would not render this issue irrelevant. The system of Putinism is deeply rotten and may collapse in a no less spectacular way than the USSR did in 1991.[31] Unlike Gorbachev, Putin is a ruthless political animal and any sign of opposition has been meticulously exterminated, but his court is riddled with clan squabbles that are exacerbated by the shrinking of petro-revenues.

It may be a fascinating occupation to monitor the discord between different factions of *siloviki* (a much over-estimated political body) or to uncover the feuds inside *Gazprom* exploited by the rising Timchenko-Kovalchuk business empire, but it is hardly possible to figure out which combination of courtiers might stage a coup against the national leader.[32] It is clear, however, that undiluted mercantilist interests are the main driver of this lively competition, so no alternative to the tight business integration with the EU—and by extension to the security policy of rapprochement and de-facto disarmament—is shaping up. Three propositions on the current state of this Byzantine policy-spinning can be advanced on the basis of scant evidence and gut feeling. The first one is that at the end of Medvedev's presidency, he is hardly considered by the key clans as a possible successor to the domineering Putin. The second proposition is that Putin no longer relies upon—or commands loyalty from—the special services, including the Russian Federal Security Service (FSB), the successor to the KGB. Finally, several rounds of purges have left the top brass disorganized and disheartened, so political ambitions in this traditionally influential caste have all but disappeared, while discontent is widespread.

What follows from this unsubstantiated reasoning is that a probable attempt to rescue the self-serving predatory regime by replacing Putin would not resolve any of the underlying faults, but might trigger a strong and unexpected political reaction not dissimilar to that in the USSR after the August 1991 putsch. The possibility that a more democratic and pro-Western government would emerge out of this turbulence appears rather slim. Leaving aside various catastrophic options (which are by no means improbable), it is possible to suggest that the most probable outcome is a populist patriotic regime that would set forth a program for rescuing Russia from failure by strengthening the state and expropriating the stolen property and capital.

Such a hard-driven Russia might turn out to be a difficult neighbor (except for China), but its behavior would in a decisive measure depend upon the economic and political dynamics in the West. A moderately functional NATO under a reconstituted and sensible U.S. leadership has nothing to worry about from this troubled and struggling not-so-great power. European security would look very different if an EU pulled apart by centrifugal forces cannot rely on support from an isolationist United States. The Baltic states in particular could be exposed to pressure from Russia, but this might not be seen as a serious security challenge in Washington or even in Brussels. Russia cannot achieve any absolute increase in power, and specifically military power, and cannot strongly influence its security environment, which can, nevertheless, change in such a way that Russia would find itself with a significant relative gain in power — and would be tempted to use it.

ENDNOTES - CHAPTER 4

1. The term is introduced in the Military Doctrine, which was approved after delays in February 2010, and defined as a "state of international or internal affairs characterized by a combination of factors that under certain conditions could lead to emergence of military threat." The list of these external military dangers is opened by "The desire to grant global functions to the military capacity of NATO, which could be executed in violation of norms of international law, to deploy the military infrastructure of NATO member-states closer to the borders of the Russian Federation, including by enlargement of the bloc." The above is the author's translation; original in Russian available from *news.kremlin.ru/ref_notes/461*.

2. These views are extensively analyzed in Stephen F. Cohen, *Soviet Fates and Lost Alternatives*, New York: Columbia University Press, 2009, see particularly Chapter 7, "Who lost the post-Soviet peace?" pp. 162-198.

3. A key proponent of this view is Sergei Karaganov, "Strategic Havoc," *Russia in Global Affairs*, January-March 2010, available from *eng.globalaffairs.ru/numbers/30/1329.html*.

4. For the author's more elaborate analysis of that evolution, see Pavel Baev, *Russian Energy Policy and Military Power*, London, UK: Routledge, 2008.

5. See Fedor Lukyanov, "Russian dilemmas in a multipolar world," *Journal of International Affairs*, Vol. 63, No. 2, Spring-Summer 2010, pp. 19-32.

6. This risk is emphasized in Vladislav Inozemtsev, "Dreams about a multi-polar world," *Nezavisimaya gazeta*, September 18, 2008, in Russian.

7. It is interesting to note that some threats in this document are described in very definite terms ("Global informational struggle will increase"), while others are presented in a more circumspect way ("In competition for resources, attempts at resolving the emerging problems with military force cannot be ruled out. . . ."). Author's translation, the Russian text is available from *www.scrf.gov.ru/documents/99.html*.

8. Some threats appear to be invented specifically for making diplomatic protestations, for instance "Demonstration of military power in the course of exercises on territory of states bordering the Russian Federation or its allies with provocative aims." One useful overview is Keir Giles, "The Military Doctrine of the Russian Federation 2010," *Research Review*, Rome, Italy: NATO Defense College, February 2010, available from *www.ndc.nato.int/research/series.php?icode=9*.

9. One insightful evaluation of this reform is Vitaly Shlykov, "The secrets of Serdyukov's blitzkrieg," *Russia in Global Affairs*, January-March 2010, available from *eng.globalaffairs.ru/numbers/30/1331.html*.

10. A more detailed analysis of this transformation is found in Pavel Baev, "Military reform against heavy odds," Anders Åslund, Sergei Guriev, and Andrew Kuchins, eds., *Russia After the Global Economic Crisis*, Washington, DC: Peterson Institute for International Economics, 2010.

11. Expert discussion of this issue is in "Current problems and logic of the military reform," *Nezavisimoe voennoe obozrenie*, May 14, 2009, in Russian. See also Aleksandr Hramchihin, "All in all — 85 permanent readiness brigades," *Nezavisimoe voennoe obozrenie*, October 16, 2009, in Russian.

12. For a critical analysis of the Vostok-2010 exercises in July 2010, see Aleksandr Hramchihin, "Inadequate *Vostok*," *Nezavisimoe voennoe obozrenie*, July 23, 2010, in Russian.

13. On the dismal state of Russian air defense system, which currently can intercept at best 20 percent of aircraft or missiles targeting Moscow, see Oleg Vladykin, "Holes in space defense," *Nezavisimoe voennoe obozrenie*, May 21, 2010, in Russian.

14. *Voyennaya Doktrina Rossiyskoy Federatsii (Military Doctrine of the Russian Federation)*, February 5, 2010, available from *www. scrf.gov.ru/documents/33.html*.

15. One useful analysis of this issue is Aleksei Arbatov, "Tactical nuclear weapons — problems and prospects," *Voenno-promyshlennyi kuryer*, May 5, 2010, in Russian, available from *www. carnegie.ru/publications/?fa=40747*.

16. Thus, Nikolai Patrushev, the Secretary of the Security Council, revealed that "conditions for use of nuclear weapons for repelling aggression with the use of conventional weapons are corrected not only for a large-scale but also for a regional or even a local war." He further clarified that "in situations critical for national security, the possibility of a preemptive (preventive) nuclear strike on the aggressor is not ruled out." The Military Doctrine does not contain such propositions, but he was in charge of revising several earlier drafts. See Vladimir Mamontov, "Russia is changing, and its military doctrine is changing also," interview with Nikolai Patrushev, *Izvestiya*, October 14, 2009, in Russian.

17. See Sergei Zhuravlev, "On combat readiness: The 1,000,000-strong army cannot fight," *Nezavisimoe voennoe obozrenie*, April 2, 2010, in Russian.

18. My more detailed evaluation can be found in Pavel Baev, "Russia in the Caucasus: Exploiting the victory for building a position of strength," Bo Huldt *et al.*, eds., *Russia on Our Minds: Strategic Yearbook 2008-2009*, Stockholm, Sweden: National Defense University, 2010.

19. See Aleksandr Karavaev, "Russian-Ukrainian symbiosis," *Nezavisimaya gazeta*, June 2, 2010, in Russian; Gleb Pavlovsky, "Pax Medvedica," *Russkii zhurnal*, May 4, 2010, available from *www.russ.ru/Mirovaya-povestka/Pax-Medvedica*.

20. *Natsional'naya Strategiya Bezopasnosti Rossii, do 2020 Goda*, Moscow, Russia: Security Council of the Russian Federation, May 12, 2009, available in Russian from *www.scrf.gov.ru*, available in English from *FBIS SOV*, May 15, 2009, in translation from the Security Council website; *Voyennaya Doctrina Rossiyskoy Federatsii* (*Military Doctrine of the Russian Federation*).

21. The official translation of the conversation with journalists on December 29, 2009, available from *premier.gov.ru/eng/visits/ru/8759/events/8815/*. One sharp comment is Aleksandr Golts, "Putin derails the talks?" *Ezhednevny zhurnal*, December 30, 2009, *ej.ru/?a=note&id=9772*.

22. One good assessment of this prospect is Viktor Mihailov and Vladimir Stepanov, "Key directions of the new US administration in anti-missile defense," *Security Index*, Vol. 16, No. 2, Summer 2010, pp. 115-119.

23. On the link between strategic offense and defense, see Viktor Litovkin, "Russia and US have to have a serious talk on the balance of strategic arms," *Nezavisimoe voennoe obozrenie*, May 21, 2010, in Russian.

24. See Vladykin; on the problems with research and development of the S-400 Triumph surface-to-air missile complexes, see "'Triumph' without a triumph," Information memo, December 16, 2009, available from *pro-spe-ro.livejournal.com/260.html*. A solid

analysis can be found in Aleksei Arbatov, "Strategic surrealism of dubious concept," *Nezavisimoe voennoe obozrenie*, March 5, 2010, in Russian.

25. See Dmitri Rogozin, "NATO faces the choice," *Nezavisimaya gazeta*, May 17, 2010, in Russian. See also Vladimir Ivanov, "NATO builds an anti-missile shield," *Nezavisimoe voennoe obozrenie*, May 21, 2010, in Russian.

26. See Aleksei Arbatov, "An unnecessary and dangerous step," *Nezavisimoe voennoe obozrenie*, March 2, 2007, in Russian. It should be noted that Rose Gottemoeller, then the Director of Carnegie Moscow Center, made an important contribution to those debates. See "Treaties on the brink of failure," *Nezavisimaya gazeta*, October 22, 2007, in Russian.

27. An influential work elaborating this idea is Ronald D. Asmus, *A Little War that Shook the World*, New York: Palgrave McMillan, 2010. The author has also put forward a challenging thesis about "Finlandization" of Eastern Europe. See *Transatlantic Take*, May 27, 2010, available from *blog.gmfus.org/2010/05/27/the-specter-of-finlandization/*. His conclusion that "we need a new strategy of enlargement" appears positively pro-active, but the obvious unfeasibility of this plan makes it necessary to re-examine the point of departure.

28. See Dmitri Trenin, "Russia, Iran and uranium," *Inosmi.ru*, June 11, 2010, available from *www.carnegie.ru/publications/?fa=40982*; Alexander Pikayev, "Why Russia supported sanctions against Iran?" *CNS Report*, June 2010, available from *cns.miis.edu/stories/100623_russia_iran_pikayev.htm*.

29. A good sample of Russian attitude is Boris Gromov and Dmitri Rogozin, "Russian advice on Afghanistan," *New York Times*, January 11, 2010. A more nuanced analysis is Dmitri Trenin and Aleksei Malashenko, *Afghanistan: a View from Moscow*, Moscow, Russia: Carnegie Center, April 2010.

30. On Putin's meeting with the 10 pseudo-spies caught in the United States, see Dmitri Sidorov, "The Motherland starts again," *Novaya gazeta*, July 28, 2010, in Russian.

31. Mikhail Gorbachev has recently argued about the risks of the split between the regime and the society; see Pavel Baev, "Gorbachev warns of explosive problems with Medvedev's "modernization," *Eurasia Daily Monitor,* July 26, 2010, available from *www. jamestown.org/programs/edm/archivesedm/2010/.*

32. A good source on the petro-politics is the bi-weekly bulletin, "Political risks in the Russian oil-&-gas complex," produced by the National Energy Security Fund, available from *www.energystate.ru/eng/.*

CHAPTER 5

NUCLEAR WEAPONS IN RUSSIAN NATIONAL SECURITY STRATEGY

Nikolai Sokov

Speaking on November 11, 2009, during a visit to the oldest Russian nuclear weapons laboratory at Sarov, Patriarch Kirill, head of Russian Orthodox Church, endorsed nuclear weapons and nuclear deterrence. Calling the closure of the St. Seraphim monastery at the place of the nuclear lab by Soviet authorities a "sinful act," he also congratulated the lab employees who, "at the home of St. Seraphim [developed] a weapon of deterrence that prevented World War III." "We must strive for a world without nuclear weapons," he emphasized, "but in a manner that does not hurt our country."[1]

This statement, which stands in stark contrast to the position advocated by the majority of church leaders in the West, is in tune with the dominant view among the Russian public. Nuclear weapons are widely regarded as a symbol and a guarantee of Russia's influence, independence, and security—the ultimate unbeatable card in global power politics. The world is regarded as a dangerous place, full of potential or actual enemies that would attack or subjugate Russia any moment if it is unable to crush the attacker; the United States and the North Atlantic Treaty Organization (NATO) as a whole (and, more rarely, China) top the list of threats.

Self-reliance and especially reliance on the nation's own military power has deep roots in the Russian psyche. Even a casual visitor to many Russian

Internet forums will find participants fondly quoting Alexander III, a late 19th century Russian tsar known as "Peacemaker" (Russia did not wage major wars during his reign) that Russia had only two reliable allies — its Army and its Navy. Many now add the third ally — Strategic Rocket Forces.

The government readily supports this sentiment. Both President Dmitry Medvedev and Prime Minister Vladimir Putin make frequent statements about their attention to nuclear forces. The Duma readily approves budgets for Strategic Forces. Road-mobile intercontinental ballistic missiles (ICBMs) roll through the Red Square during holiday parades. Certainly, this means that Moscow is and will remain constrained when it comes to concessions in arms control negotiations — nuclear weapons are not a card that could be readily traded.

The Russian government publicly supports the goal of a nuclear-free world, but that goal is regarded so long-term that it becomes impractical. When Putin recently signed a law on funding for upgrades to facilities and equipment for a nuclear weapons complex (primarily to ensure reliability of weapons), he mentioned that the country would need them for the next "30-40-50 years."[2]

The profile of nuclear weapons is further increased by the wide (and perhaps even unbridgeable) gap between Russia and the United States/NATO in modern technology. This gap prevents Moscow from shifting emphasis from nuclear to conventional assets and further strengthens long-term reliance on nuclear weapons in national security policy.

At the same time — and in apparent contrast to public posturing — funding for maintenance and modernization remains limited. Production of new delivery vehicles is apparently below the optimal level (the lowest cost per unit) and research and development (R&D) programs remain underfunded or, at best, funded at bare minimum. Effectively, the government can be said to take a "minimalist" attitude toward its nuclear capability. While this pattern began during the time of relative financial scarcity, it continued through the more financially favorable period almost without change and remains the same today. There is no indication that Moscow plans to radically increase funding for either production or modernization of its nuclear arsenal. The question remains open whether limited funding reflects a relatively skeptical view of the possible role of nuclear weapons in Russia's security. This chapter will address the following issues relevant to the understanding of the future of the Russian nuclear capability:

- The role of nuclear weapons in security policy. While the public profile of nuclear weapons is enormous, of greater relevance are the missions assigned to nuclear weapons and their evolution in the last 20 years. Of special interest are the roles, if any, of tactical (nonstrategic) nuclear weapons, which are increasingly visible in international debates.
- Modernization programs. What are the reasons for the apparent gap between the high public profile of nuclear weapons and the relatively limited funding? How are modernization programs related to nuclear missions?
- What are the prospects for transition from nuclear to conventional capability? This has been a stated goal of the Russian government, but can Russia actually implement it? This section will also tackle debates about abrogation of the

189

Intermediate-Range Nuclear Forces (INF) Treaty: While that agreement provided for reduction of nuclear weapons, it is has apparently become part of a policy aimed at enhancing conventional capability.

- What is the impact of U.S. missile defense plans on the Russian nuclear posture, and how has it changed in the last year or so? Is there any prospect for cooperation with the United States and NATO on missile defense and what are the limits of that cooperation?

Key conclusions can be summarized as follows:

1. During the last 10-15 years, Russian nuclear policy has experienced approximately the same evolution as that of other nuclear weapons states (NWS) — gradual increase in the perceived role of these weapons, emergence of new missions, and then, toward the end of this decade, gradual reduction of their role. In Russia, the decrease of the role of nuclear weapons has been somewhat less pronounced than in other NWS.

2. Nuclear weapons have two missions. One is traditional strategic deterrence — prevention of a large-scale aggression against Russia. The other, which is considered more pertinent under present circumstances, is deterrence of a more limited conventional attack by a powerful country or an alliance (a clear reference to the United States and NATO), which cannot be repelled with Russian conventional forces alone. Recently, the perceived urgency of the latter mission has somewhat receded, but it remains on the books.

3. Russia seeks to gradually shift emphasis from nuclear to long-range high-precision conventional assets. It has been at least 15-20 years behind the United States and its allies, however, and the verdict is still

out as to whether it will be able to cover that gap. It is clear that efforts will continue, in particular because nuclear weapons are increasingly seen as unusable and thus not very relevant for security policy.

4. Nuclear posture has seen rather radical changes in the first half of this decade following a fundamental revision of long-term plans in 2000 and then a series of partial revisions to new policy. Currently, Russia seems to be moving toward a posture that can be characterized as a balanced dyad—a relatively equal (60 to 40 percent) distribution of nuclear warheads between the land and the sea legs. The air leg remains part of the nuclear triad, but only formally—the main mission of long-range aircraft is increasingly conventional and, furthermore, its nuclear assets are subject to the least modernization.

5. The Russian nuclear force remains old—the bulk of delivery systems are still those produced in the Soviet Union. The rate of production and deployment of new weapons is below what production capability can sustain. More importantly, production capability gradually decreases as well, and the Russian government does not appear interested in sustaining ability to expand production. This strongly suggests that the overall size of the nuclear force will gradually decline and that delivery vehicles will carry the maximum load of warheads.

6. Contrary to common perception, short-range nuclear assets (nonstrategic nuclear weapons [NSNW]) do not appear to play a significant role in Russia's security policy, and there are no discernible missions assigned to them with the exception of naval assets. Continued Russian resistance to arms control measures with regard to NSNW is primarily explained by the alignment of domestic politics.

7. The current trends will make Russia interested in further reductions of nuclear weapons, perhaps to the level of around 1,000 strategic warheads. It seems that Russia will probably want to pause at about that point. Reaching new agreements will not be easy, however, due to the multiplicity of divisive issues that have emerged in the last 20 years and especially during this decade. Post-New Strategic Arms Reduction Treaty (START) negotiations are likely to be difficult and time-consuming.

8. The urgency of the missile defense issue has receded rather considerably in the last year, although public statements do not reflect that. The greatest concern is not about the current or the short-term American capability, but rather about the capability that might emerge by the end of this decade. This leaves considerable margin of opportunity to further discuss this issue and perhaps develop a set of predictability and transparency measures that might help alleviate the controversy. Cooperation in missile defense remains possible and could be the "real" long-term answer.

9. On the surface, the trajectory of Russian strategy is similar to what the United States has been doing in the last 2 decades—emphasis is gradually shifting toward long-range high-precision conventional capability, Russia actively develops missile defense capability, etc. This similarity is misleading, however, and will hardly make arms control negotiations any easier because there is an important asymmetry between the two countries. Whereas the United States, for reasons of its geographical location, needs strategic capability in both conventional and defense assets, Russia emphasizes theater-range assets. Consequently, it will remain highly suspicious about U.S. plans to the extent

that they could theoretically affect the credibility of strategic deterrence that is regarded as the foundation of the existing international system.

RUSSIAN VIEWS ON THE ROLE OF NUCLEAR WEAPONS

Nuclear weapons have three partially overlapping roles in Russian national security policy, which can be described as status symbol, existential deterrence, and plans for use of nuclear weapons under certain specific contingencies, first and foremost to deter large-scale use of conventional forces against Russia by the United States and NATO.

1. The role of nuclear weapons as a symbol of status is quite straightforward, although rather difficult to define in clear-cut, unambiguous terms. Status as a recognized nuclear weapons state, along with a permanent seat on the United Nations Security Council (UNSC), coupled with the right of veto, are the most visible and perhaps the only remaining vestiges of great-power ambitions. Partially, this self-image satisfies the nostalgia—particularly widely spread among the public—for the Soviet Union's number two place in the Cold War international system.

More importantly, nuclear status fits very well with the forward-looking conceptualization of the emerging post-post-Cold War (to borrow Colin Powell's term) international system as multipolar, in which Russia sees itself as one of the centers of power and influence. It should be noted, however, that the term (multipolarity) is seriously misused in Russia.[3] In fact, Russian leaders, when they talk about multipolarity, appear to mean a "concert"—a system similar to the 1815 Vienna Congress arrangements. They see the future international system as based on a consensus of key players—countries with the greatest economic and military power. In that conceptualization, Russia is accorded the place of one of the pillars of the emerging system—a state with special rights and responsibilities. Although Moscow recognizes—and welcomes—the rise of new centers of power beyond the five permanent members of the UNSC (such as India, Germany, Japan, Brazil, etc.), it is also keen on preserving certain special privileges. For example, Foreign Minister Sergey Lavrov recently described India as a potential new permanent member of the UNSC, but cautioned that only "old" permanent UNSC members should have the right of veto.[4]

The prospect of nuclear disarmament puts Russian leaders into a rather awkward situation. On the one hand, they cannot question the legal (under Article VI of the Nuclear Non-Proliferation Treaty [NPT]) or the moral obligation to disarm. On the other hand, elimination of nuclear weapons would deprive Russia of one of its key status symbols. Speaking in February 2008 at the Conference on Disarmament in Geneva, Lavrov endorsed the nuclear disarmament initiatives of George Schultz, William Perry, Henry Kissinger, and Sam Nunn, but in a rather half-hearted manner and referred to it as a very long-term prospect.[5] In December 2008, at a meeting with the Association of European Businesses in Russia, Lavrov characterized nuclear disarmament as an "uncertain" goal whose solution is hampered by multiple "unresolved issues."[6] The apparent contradiction is resolved, it seems, by postponing the final solution into a distant future.

2. "Existential deterrence" refers to a general, vague notion that no rational country or alliance, including the United States and NATO, will attack Russia be-

cause Russia can respond with nuclear weapons. This is a guarantee against a threat that, for all intents and purposes, does not exist. As a result, nuclear weapons are often portrayed as a "just-in-case" deterrence for the unlikely situation when, some time in the indefinite future, the United States or another powerful country or coalition becomes hostile to Russia.

At a deeper psychological level, reliance on nuclear deterrence reflects uncertainty about the unpredictable international environment and the lack of confidence in Russia's power and influence. Nuclear weapons played a similar role during the Cold War— a prop for a country that more or less acutely sensed that the enemy, the United States and the Western community in general, were too powerful. The trauma of the 1990s, when Russia suddenly found itself weak and vulnerable, reinforced the psychological need for the ultimate security guarantee. The need for that prop should disappear if the place of Russia in the emerging international system becomes clearer and, especially if the country becomes more deeply integrated into the global economy.

The latter process has been developing quite well where relations between Russia and the European Union (EU) are concerned: even today not only are many EU states (in particular the "Old Europe") reluctant to enter into a conflict with Russia, but Moscow is equally reluctant to enter into a conflict with them. The U.S.-Russian relationship, unfortunately, does not have a solid economic foundation yet, and consequently political and security relations lack stability. The need for stronger interdependence is further reinforced by the belief of Russian leaders (particularly strong among the Putin and Medvedev generation) that economic interdependence is central to cooperation and war prevention: this belief was borrowed from American political science literature during their formative years in the 1970s and 1980s.

Another complicating factor is the weakness of economic and political levers of influence in the international arena, which serves to enhance the perceived importance of military instruments. Although Russia could potentially use its position as an exporter of oil and gas, this is, in reality, a double-edged sword: an attempt to use it could harm the most important source of revenue for the government and private (semi-private) business and vastly strengthen the desire of its customers to diversify energy sources (thereby eliminating Russian influence as well as profit). Instead, Moscow is trying to build a reputation as a reliable supplier and has been reluctant to even hint at interruption of exports. The fact that dependence on Russian oil and gas exports does not affect the rather cold, sometimes even hostile, attitude of Eastern European countries (such as Poland) toward Russia suggests that the utility of this dependence as a political lever is, at best, very limited. Seen through Russian eyes, Russian exports actually depend on other countries — on Ukraine, which provides the main transit route, and on Central Asia, which is an important source of natural gas that is re-exported to Europe. Instead of using oil and gas exports as a lever, Moscow has to fight to hold on to its market against alternative routes (across the Caspian Sea and South Caucasus). Several crises in relations with Ukraine, when transit to Europe was interrupted or nearly interrupted (all of these cases were blamed on Russia), created an acute sense of dependence in Russia and a desire to build alternative routes of its own through the Baltic Sea and the Balkans. Strong objections by Poland, the Baltic states, and Nordic countries to that alternative have only served to reinforce the feeling of vulnerability.

3. As long as nuclear weapons and the research and industrial infrastructure supporting them continue to exist, political and military planning for their use must take place. Planning for nuclear use involves development of scenario-specific missions that pit nuclear assets against real or perceived threats. These missions provide formal rationales for continued maintenance of nuclear capabilities, for distribution of targets, for posture planning, as well as for research and development. The underlying assumption of this type of planning is the belief that certain threats are difficult or even impossible to counter with other, non-nuclear assets or that non-nuclear assets are less reliable or effective.

At the center of nuclear planning in today's Russia is concern about U.S. and NATO conventional superiority. Although a large-scale war with Russia is widely regarded as improbable, the threat of superior conventional force could, according to the prevalent logic, be used to extract political or economic concessions. A long series of limited wars (the Gulf War of 1991, the use of force in Bosnia, the war in Kosovo, and the 2003 war in Iraq) have demonstrated, in the view of Russian policymakers and elite, that (1) American conventional power vastly surpasses anything that Russia has or might hope to have in the foreseeable future, both in technological level and in sheer numbers, and (2) that the United States is prone to use that force with few second thoughts. The continuing weakness of Russian conventional forces vis-à-vis U.S. and combined NATO power as well as the close proximity of NATO forces to Russian territory (making limited use of force both more feasible and more effective) have led Russian military planners to rely on nuclear weapons for the purposes of de-escalation—the threat of a limited nuclear strike in response to a conventional attack that cannot be repelled by conventional forces is supposed to deter the attack in the first place.

A relatively recent new concern is deployment of U.S. missile defense, which eventually could, in theory, intercept a Russian nuclear second strike and thus undermine both the existential deterrence capability and the de-escalation mission. Deployment of missile defense leads Russian military planners to suspect that the United States intends to make the world safe for conventional war and only serves to enhance the perceived value of nuclear weapons for Russia.

Finally, there is the emerging issue of China, which Russians rarely discuss in the open. While the two countries are close partners or a broad range of issues, have solved outstanding problems (border issues in particular), and their economic relationship continues to develop, many in Russia are concerned that the partnership might not survive continued growth of China's economic, political, and military power. Nuclear weapons are regarded as "just-in-case" protection against the risk that China becomes a foe or at least attempts to transform Russia into a subordinate power.

Evolution of Russian views on the role of nuclear weapons can be traced through Military Doctrines adopted in the last 17 years. Military Doctrine is a primarily political document that defines the broad contours of defense policy and outlines of military postures as well as provides a link between overall national security policy and, more narrowly, defense policy. The term "doctrine" is somewhat misleading, because its meaning in Russian and English are not the same. It should be more properly translated as "strategy" or "guidance." This caveat should be kept in mind during any discussion of Russian defense policy.

1993-99.

The end of the Cold War and the diminished relevance of strategic nuclear deterrence were reflected in the first Military Doctrine approved by Boris Yeltsin in November 1993 ("Main Provisions of the Military Doctrine"[7]), which assigned nuclear weapons only to that "old" mission and thus codified their relatively low tangibility in Russia's national security policy. The only innovation of that document was a provision that allowed for first use of nuclear weapons (until then, the official Soviet policy, which was set in the 1970s and confirmed in 1982, allowed for the use of nuclear weapons only in response to a nuclear attack). While this new plank attracted close attention both in Russia and in the West, of greater relevance was the fact that nuclear use was only conceptualized in response to a large-scale attack that threatened the sovereignty and the very survival of the country, i.e., a mission whose probability was officially assessed as low.

The official view of nuclear weapons remained unchanged despite a flurry of proposals in 1996-97 to increase reliance on nuclear weapons in response to the first phase of NATO enlargement. The 1997 National Security Concept retained the plank reserving "the right to use all forces and means at its disposal, including nuclear weapons, in case an armed aggression that creates a threat to the very existence of the Russian Federation as an independent sovereign state."[8] This was effectively a "just-in-case" mission against a conflict that was virtually ruled out.

In a review of an unpublished early draft of a new Military Doctrine produced in 1997, two officers of the General Staff noted that "some 'specialists' . . . attempted to introduce into the documents language that would toughen nuclear policy," but said that these proposals were rejected by the interagency working group charged with drafting the document. It was decided, they said, to retain the 1993 language, "which passed the test of time and was supported by the Russian Ministry of Foreign Affairs."[9]

At that time, the Russian government adopted a series of documents that confirmed earlier policy and laid out development and deployment plans based on the assumption that the sole mission of nuclear weapons was deterrence of a large-scale attack. In line with this policy, several decrees signed by Boris Yeltsin in 1997 and 1998[10] foresaw deep reductions of the Russian nuclear arsenal.

THE ROLE OF STRATEGIC DETERRENCE IN RUSSIAN SECURITY STRATEGY

The mission of strategic deterrence has remained largely unchanged from Soviet times to the present day. It is based on the traditional notion of mutual vulnerability — deterrence through ability to inflict unacceptable damage in a response strike.

The main mode of operation has also remained the same — strike on warning. It should be noted that this mode has always been a forced choice, and since at least the late 1960s, the Soviet Union tried to develop assured second-strike capability by enhancing survivability of weapons systems. Nevertheless, efforts to develop relevant systems succeeded only in the 1980s — mobile ICBMs (SS-25 Topol and SS-24) as well as reduced-noise submarines. In post-Soviet Russia reliance on strike on warning even enhanced due to a number of reasons: (1) the deep economic crisis, which forced drastic reduction of funding, (2) the breakup of the Soviet Union, which left many relatively modern weapons outside Russia, reduced deployment options, and undermined the production capability limiting ability to develop and produce weapons systems, and (3) the deterioration of early warning capability due to the loss of several key radars.

Traditional strategic deterrence is regarded as a skeleton of international security — the underlying structure that keeps the system stable. Speaking at the London Institute of International and Strategic Studies, Sergey Ivanov (at that time still Minister of Defense) called strategic deterrence the foundation of global stability.[11] Similar views have been expressed by almost every official and unofficial source in Russia.

Strategic deterrence is primarily aimed at the United States and, to a smaller extent, its allies. China is present in the background — Russian officials just do not speak about the need to deter China, and relatively few nongovernmental experts are prepared to discuss this mission. The reasons why the United States remains the focus are:

- The United States has demonstrated the willingness to use force, including for humanitarian interventions.
- A U.S. decision to use force cannot be overruled by the UN or its allies.
- It is commonly believed that a large-scale attack (regional conflict) can only be successful if the United States leads it.

- It is assumed that if Russia can deter the United States, it can deter any other state or a coalition of states. The United States, in effect, serves as a benchmark.
- Finally, many among the Russian elite, and especially among the military, still view the United States with unease and suspicion. Only a few years ago, one could hear talk about the intent of undisclosed countries (some directly mentioned the United States) to partition Russia.

One element of strategic deterrence conceptualization that has experienced considerable change in the post-Soviet period is the criterion, "how much is enough," to deter the potential adversary. During the Soviet period (including late 1980s), the goal was assured delivery of 500 warheads to U.S. territory; in the 1990s, the figure apparently decreased to 150-200; recently one can hear an even lower figure—assured delivery of about 50 warheads. The reduction of this all-important criterion is consistent with the acknowledgment in the 1993 and subsequent Military Doctrines of very low probability of a global war, and reflects a fundamental change in the international system after the end of the Cold War. In addition, the lower criterion reduces pressure for creating an assured second-strike capability as well as requirements for nuclear posture and modernization programs. Basically, it means that Russia can be reasonably relaxed with regard to the future of its strategic arsenal and can afford limiting spending and resources necessary to maintain and modernize its strategic force.

Adherence to traditional views on strategic deterrence dictates Russia's negative or, at least, very cautious attitude toward missile defense. At its core, Russian strategy still rests on the theorems of the late 1960-early 1970s embodied in the Anti-Ballistic Missile (ABM) Treaty: (1) offensive and defensive weapons are inextricably linked, (2) robust defense can vastly complicate the calculation of strategic stability (i.e., it becomes difficult to predict how many warheads will reach the adversary in a response strike), and (3) uncontrolled missile defense developments can irreparably upset strategic stability and will result in an arms race. Russia's preferred response has traditionally been in the area of offensive weapons, which are more cost-effective, although in the 1980s, the Soviet Union actively explored strategic missile defense options, i.e., simultaneously pursued both symmetric and asymmetric response. For Russia, symmetric response (development of its own advance strategic missile defense system) has been out of the reach for financial and technological reasons. As a result, it has pursued both political options (through arms control negotiations, mobilization of international community, close cooperation with China, etc.) and the defense penetration capability of new strategic delivery systems.

2000-10.

The *2000 Military Doctrine* rather radically changed the role of nuclear weapons in Russia's national security strategy by introducing a new mission — that of limited nuclear use in response to a limited conventional attack, i.e., one that did not threaten the survival and sovereignty of Russia, but still was beyond the capability of Russian conventional forces. According to the new document, in addition to "the use of nuclear weapons or other weapons of mass destruction" against Russia or its allies, nuclear weapons could also be used "in response to large-scale aggression involving conventional weapons in situations that are critical for the national security of the Russian Federation and its allies."[12]

The new document divided all possible armed conflicts into four categories:

1. "armed conflict"—a predominantly domestic conflict, in which insurgents have outside support (effectively, the war in Chechnya, whose resumption was already obvious by the time of the adoption of the new Doctrine in the spring of 2000);

2. "limited war"—a war with one foreign states with limited goals (a recent example is the war with Georgia in 2008);

3. "regional war"—a war with a powerful state or a coalition, which Russian forces cannot win or terminate on favorable conditions. Russian military publications of the period believed that regional war could be a direct result of escalation of "armed conflict" (for example, as a result of outside interference into the war in Chechnya[13]); and,

4. "global war"—a war against a coalition of powerful states in which sovereignty and very survival of Russia are at stake.

That is, compared to the 1993-97 documents, which assigned nuclear weapons only to the fourth type of conflicts, the 2000 document expanded nuclear missions to the third type. This was a direct result of the war in Kosovo, whose impact on Russian national security of the period is difficult to overestimate. Paradoxically, until 1999 Moscow seemed to believe that the right of veto in the UNSC made it immune to the use of force. Kosovo, as well as the 2003 war in Iraq a few years later, demonstrated that the United States and NATO could use force without UNSC authorization. At the same time, since U.S. and NATO stakes in a Kosovo-size conflict with Russia were expected to be relatively low (at least, not central to U.S. interests), threat of even limited nuclear use was expected to become a sufficiently strong deterrence.

The decision to enhance reliance on nuclear weapons in a departure from all documents adopted in the 1990s was apparently made while the war in Kosovo was still underway — at a meeting of the Russian Federation Security Council in April 1999, the first chaired by Vladimir Putin in the capacity of the council's secretary.[14] The key tenets of the new approach were tested in May 1999 during large-scale maneuvers called "West-99." The new role of nuclear weapons was formalized in the January 2000 *National Security Concept* and the April 2000 *Military Doctrine*.[15] The White Paper, a document adopted in the fall of 2003,[16] added the final touches.

While the obvious, and perhaps initially, the only targets of the new mission were the United States and NATO, subsequently Russian military leaders unveiled that the same provisions applied also to "developing countries, some of which have large, well-armed militaries."[17] This represented a thinly veiled reference to China; perhaps also to some other countries (for example, Iran).

The new mission, which came to be known as de-escalation of conventional conflicts, is similar to NATO's flexible deterrence of the 1960s. A possible scenario was clearly reflected in the "West-99" exercises: a large-scale conventional attack ("West-99" actually simulated an attack by a NATO force exactly the same as the one used in the war in Kosovo), relatively brief resistance by Russian conventional forces, then a limited nuclear strike, after which the opponent was expected to back down because its stakes were not worthy of resulting destruction and losses.

Central to the concept of de-escalation was the notion of calibrated damage (*zadannyi ushcherb*), defined in the 2003 *White Paper* as "damage, which is subjectively unacceptable to the enemy and which exceeds the benefits the aggressor expects to gain as a result of the use of military force."[18] This notion is more flexible than the more common notion of "unacceptable damage" and, in addition to promising to deny benefits from aggression, also conveys a message that damage would be commensurate to the level of conflict rather than devastating. Calibrated damage gave the opponent a choice to back down without escalation to the strategic level.

Even limited strikes were supposed to reach far-away targets: according to the 2003 *While Paper*, in all wars in the 1990s and early 2000s (Balkans, Kosovo, Afghanistan, and Iraq) American victory was ensured by ability to involve out-of-theater assets. Consequently, counterstrategy, whether nuclear or conventional, had to emphasize the ability to defeat targets at large distances.

Accordingly, the *White Paper* postulated "the utmost necessity of having the capability to strike military assets of the enemy (long-range high-precision weapons, long-range Air Force) outside the immediate area of conflict. To achieve this, [we] need both our own long-range high-precision strike capability and other assets that enable [us] to transfer hostilities directly to enemy territory."[19]

Targets for limited nuclear use with calibrated damage could be gleaned from a series of large-scale exercises since 1999. All of them were military targets involved in a potential attack against Russia and the number of warheads involved in simulated strikes was small (fewer than 10):

- Airbases as well as command, communications, and support facilities in European NATO countries and in at least one case in Japan. New members of NATO are clearly considered first candidates for basing countries for launching an attack against Russia;
- Unknown targets in the continental United States (most likely bases from which B-52s and B-2s would fly missions against Russia);
- Aircraft carrier groups in the Pacific Ocean and the Baltic Sea. Similar operations were simulated at least one in the Indian Ocean and Mediterranean; and,
- U.S. bases on Diego Garcia and Guam.

An integral part of making sure that threat of limited nuclear strike is credible is demonstrated ability to escalate to the strategic level (the level of large-scale nuclear exchange).[20] This condition necessitated the maintenance of credible strategic nuclear deterrence capability, giving additional prominence to the "traditional" mission and strategic weapons modernization programs.

The decision tree underlying the de-escalation scenario is pictured in Figure 5-1. The 2003 *White Paper* also cautioned that nuclear deterrence of regional conflicts requires capable modern conventional forces: "only in that case will the threat of nuclear use in response to an attack be credible."[21] This principle closely mirrors one of the seminal documents in U.S. nuclear policy from the 1950s, NSC-68. This is only logical: reliance

on nuclear weapons alone is simply not sustainable because threat of nuclear use is not sufficiently credible
except in a relatively narrow range of circumstances.

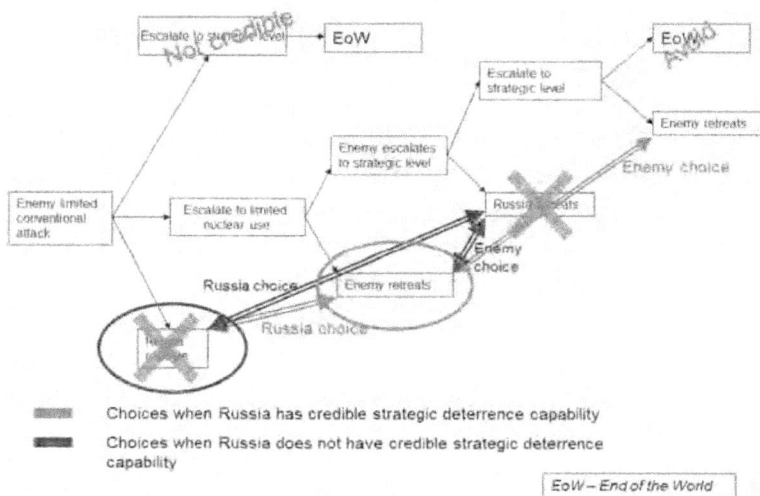

Figure 5-1. Decision Tree.

It should be noted, however, that Russia's 2000
National Security Concept regarded reliance on limited
nuclear use as a temporary fix until Russia builds up
its conventional capability, especially its precision-
guided weapons. A more modern conventional capability together with modern reconnaissance and
targeting assets was supposed to enable Russia to
successfully deter, or, if deterrence fails, fight regional
conflicts. Thus, at least in theory, the limited-use missions should eventually fade away. That thinking remains valid today: in 2009, then-Commander of the
Strategic Rocket Forces (SRF) Nikolai Solovtsov said
that reliance on nuclear weapons in the near future is
intended to buy time while Russia conducts military
reform and upgrades its conventional capability.[22]

2010 AND INTO THE FUTURE

The new, third Russian Military Doctrine, which ushered in yet another turn in the role of nuclear weapons, was revealed in February 2010.[23] Work on that document was launched by a special conference convened at the Russian Academy of Military Sciences in January 2007. Speakers at that meeting, including then-Chief of General Staff Yuri Baluyevskii, agreed that nuclear weapons would still play a central role in Russia's security, but the overall tone suggested that the nuclear component of the 2000 Doctrine would remain unchanged; attention focused instead on the upcoming reforms and modernization of general-purpose forces.[24]

Quite unexpectedly, however, the nuclear section of the draft became a contested issue in the months preceding its release and was perhaps one of the reasons for multiple delays (it was initially scheduled to be released in the fall of 2009). In an interview in October 2009, Secretary of the Security Council Nikolai Patrushev indicated that the future document might assign nuclear weapons to yet one more type of war — "local conflicts."[25] This would have represented a massive expansion of the role of nuclear weapons: whereas the 1993 Doctrine assigned them to "global wars," and the 2000 one added "regional wars," the further expansion described by Patrushev would have assigned them to conflicts similar to the 2008 war with Georgia.

In the end, however, the trend set by the new Doctrine was opposite to what Patrushev described. Instead of further expanding the role of nuclear weapons, it somewhat reduced it by tightening conditions under which these weapons could be used. Specifically, whereas the 2000 Doctrine foresaw the resorting to nuclear weapons "in situations critical for [the] national security" of Russia, the 2010 version allows for their use in situations when "the very existence of [Russia] is under threat."[26] At least in this regard, the new Doctrine returned to the principles of the 1993 and 1997 strategies.

Otherwise, the new document seemed to closely follow the line set in 2000. The role of nuclear weapons, according to the new Doctrine, is "prevention of nuclear military conflict or any other military conflict." They are regarded as "an important factor in the prevention of nuclear conflicts and military conflicts that use conventional assets (large-scale and regional wars)." The new document also clearly indicates that a conventional regional war could escalate to the nuclear level. In a slight change from 2000, the latter provision is formulated in broader terms — this is now not only seen as a means of deterring or dissuading states that might attack Russia with conventional armed forces, but also an expression of concern that similar escalation might take place elsewhere.[27] That is, that the mission of de-escalation remains on the books. The new Doctrine mandates the maintenance of nuclear capability "at the level of sufficiency," which means ability to inflict calibrated damage, same as the previous guidance. An interesting feature of the 2010 Doctrine is the emphasis on *strategic* deterrence capability. The choice of terms seems to indicate that Russia does not assign a visible role to substrategic (or tactical) nuclear weapons.

Overall, the 2010 Doctrine devotes less attention to the nuclear component of Armed Forces than the previous one. At the most superficial level, there are fewer paragraphs about the use of nuclear weapons and nuclear posture than in the 2000 document. The doctrine places considerably more emphasis on conventional forces and in particular on high-precision assets, communications, command, and control systems, and other elements in which Russia has been traditionally behind other major military powers.

Overall, the change in the role of nuclear weapons appears to be positive, but limited: the missions remained the same as before, albeit the criterion for nuclear use was somewhat tightened. The direction of the trend is similar to that in the United States under the new administration, but the degree of change is noticeably smaller. Notwithstanding the fact that the new strategy will remain in force for at least several years, one can hardly expect a significant downgrading of the status of nuclear weapons in the foreseeable future. They continue to enjoy elite and public support as a symbol of Russian power and independence and thus any government that might consider further downgrading of that component of Russian armed forces is likely to encounter stiff resistance. Furthermore, modernization of Russian conventional forces proceeds at a very slow pace. In the foreseeable future, concern about conventional forces of the United States and NATO and, increasingly, of China will remain high, necessitating continued reliance on nuclear capability.

THE TACTICAL NUCLEAR WEAPONS PARADOX

Tactical (non-strategic) nuclear weapons (TNW) enjoy a special and highly controversial place in Russia's nuclear policy. They gained visibility in the mid-1990s during debates about possible response to NATO's first round of enlargement. They are still often conceptualized as a counterweight to NATO conventional superiority, but this view primarily resides with conservative nongovernmental experts while the government and (with one exception noted below) uniformed military remains silent about possible missions for these assets. Instead, all political-military guidance documents issues in the last 15 years have not mentioned them. Moreover, the 2003 *White Paper* referenced above specifically insisted that in case of large-scale (regional or global) war Russia needed long-range capability to strike out-of-theater assets of the adversary. Thus TNW apparently do not have a mission to speak of.

The only exception to that general rule is the Russian Navy. Russian naval commanders admit that they simply cannot confront the U.S. Navy — in case of a direct clash between Russia and the United States — without reliance on nonstrategic nuclear assets. Accordingly, crews of surface ships and submarines have reportedly trained to mate warheads to submarine launched cruise missiles (SLCMs) and launch them.[28] In fact, Vice-Admiral Oleg Burtsev, deputy chief of the Navy's Main Staff, declared recently that the role of tactical nuclear weapons on attack nuclear submarines would increase. "The range of tactical nuclear weapons is growing, as is their accuracy. They do not need to deliver high-yield warheads, instead it is possible to make a transition to low-yield nuclear warheads that could be installed on the existing types of cruise missiles," he asserted.[29] Paradoxically, nuclear warheads for short-range naval systems are supposed to be in the status of nondeployed under the presidential nuclear initiatives (PNIs), unlike those for the Air

Force, whose leaders rarely if ever mention tactical nuclear weapons.

Indicative of the attitude toward the possible role of TNW was the rejection by the Russian government and the military of proposals to deploy short-range nuclear-capable assets in response to the U.S.-planned missile defense assets in Poland in 2008—at the time when George W. Bush plans were regarded as a serious and immediate threat to Russia. The General Staff was quick at dismissing rumors (apparently, originating in Lithuania) that Russia would equip surface ships and submarines of the Baltic Fleet with tactical nuclear weapons.[30] Similarly, a September 2008 high-level meeting in Kaliningrad oblast, involving representatives from the Ministries of Defense and Foreign Affairs at the level of deputy minister, General Staff, Administration of the President, as well as security services, rejected the proposal to deploy nuclear weapons in the exclave.[31] Chairman of the Duma Defense Committee retired General Viktor Zavarzin explained that preference was given instead to high-precision conventional assets.[32] Proposals about deployment of tactical nuclear weapons in Belarus were similarly not taken to heart. Russian ambassador to Minsk Aleksandr Surikov announced that Russia would not return nuclear weapons to Belarus but would consider deployment of tactical conventional Iskander missiles and short-range aircraft with precision-guided weapons.[33]

Short-range weapons are also often said to have another role—that of deterring Chinese conventional forces.[34] The logic is similar to the common beliefs about the role of TNW vis-à-vis NATO: if the opponent has superior conventional forces, Russian needs to rely on nuclear weapons. The Western and the Eastern theaters differ by the nature of challenge — techno-logical in the West and numerical in the East.

This logic appears questionable, however. The Russian-Chinese border is primarily a land border, but, if public statements of Russian officials are to be believed, Russia no longer has land-based short-range nuclear weapons. Also, there are few valuable targets on the Chinese side of the border and, if TNW were used to repel a hypothetical Chinese offensive, nucle-ar weapons would be used on the Russian side of that border in densely populated and economically devel-oped areas. Indeed, confidential interviews with high-level Russian military indicate that nuclear weapons assigned to deterrence of China are strategic and air-launched intermediate-range, i.e., weapons capable of reaching political, military, and economic targets deep inside China. That is, the logic here is similar to the one used in the Military Doctrine for deterrence of the United States and NATO: the emphasis is on long-range assets.

Thus, logically speaking, Russia could, without changing its present-day nuclear strategy, reduce the entire short-range category of nuclear weapons. Yet, it refuses to do that. Instead, Moscow consistently, stubbornly, and very forcefully resists attempts of the United States and its NATO allies to launch almost any kind of arms control measures with regard to its TNW. Thus, up until now U.S. and Russian TNW are still subject to only one arms control regime — uni-lateral parallel statements of George H.W. Bush and Mikhail Gorbachev made in 1991 known as PNIs (in 1992 Boris Yeltsin confirmed Gorbachev's statement in the name of Russia). It only remains to regret that the Soviet proposal, made in the fall of 1991 shortly after PNIs, to launch negotiations on a legally binding and verifiable treaty on TNW was at that time rejected by Washington.

Moreover, since 2004 Russia no longer recognizes PNIs as even politically binding. The last time Moscow formally reported on the implementation of PNIs was at the NPT PrepCom in April 2004, when the Russian representative mentioned that his country had "almost completed implementation" of its "initiatives" except for warheads assigned to Ground Forces, and that the pace of elimination was constrained by the technological capacity and available funding.[35] Six months later, an official representative of the Russian Foreign Ministry declared Russia was not bound by the PNIs, which were characterized as a goodwill gesture rather than an obligation.[36]

That said, PNIs have apparently been implemented, even though Russia does not publicly recognize that. In a report distributed at the 2005 NPT Review Conference, Russia declared that it had reduced its TNW arsenal to one-fourth of what it was in 1991.[37] The following year, the Chief of the 12th *Glavnoye Upravleniye Ministerstvo Oborony* (GUMO, the Main Directorate of the Ministry of Defense responsible for handling nuclear weapons), confirmed that information and even asserted that reductions exceeded the original promise (he asserted that the 1991 statements foresaw a 64 percent reduction while Russia had reduced its TNW arsenal by 75 percent).[38] Speaking in 2007, the new Chief of the 12th GUMO, General Vladimir Verkhovtsev, confirmed the 75 percent figure and added that the promised elimination of TNW warheads assigned to Ground Forces had been completed.[39]

The exact number of Russian TNW is unknown because parties to the PNIs are not required to exchange it. It is commonly believed that Russia has about 2,000 warheads for delivery vehicles that are not subject to START treaties—about double what the United States is assumed to have.[40] Breaking down that uncertain number into categories is even more challenging. According to the Natural Resources Defense Council (NRDC), the Air Force has 650 warheads, the Navy 700, and Air Defense and Missile Defense (nowadays united in the Aerospace Forces) 700.[41] Russian nongovernmental experts use the same figures, but the method of calculation used by NRDC leaves many uncertainties.[42]

It is safe to assume that the overall size of the stockpile is going down. Russia continued to dismantle warheads with expired service life (warranty), and only some of those are refurbished. The rate of dismantlement and refurbishment is limited by the available industrial capacity. There is no saying at what point the decline will stop and the stockpile become stabilized. That time is probably near.

A solution to the paradox of TNW—assets that Russia apparently does not need, but continues to hold on to—can be found in domestic politics rather than in strategic planning. The Russian government attitude toward TNW appears to represent a complex mix of domestic and bureaucratic politics, (mis)perceptions, and idiosyncrasies. Its main elements could be summarized in the following way:

- *"No More Unreciprocated Concessions."* Resistance to arms control measures with regard to TNW appears to reflect the deep-seated rejection of Gorbachev and early Yeltsin propensity to make wide-ranging concessions that Edward Shevardnadze used to call "concessions to common sense." Russian numerical superiority is regarded as an advantage that could be traded for something tangible and should not be given away. Western attempts to persuade Russia to act on TNW (which by default means asymmetric reductions) tend to be regarded with suspicion without serious thought about the reasons for these proposals. Instead, such attempts are seen as proof that these weapons are truly valuable.

- *Inertia.* The longer the same position is maintained, the more entrenched it becomes. A position that has been in place for over a decade can be changed either when the leadership changes (as happened when Gorbachev assumed the highest office in the Soviet Union) or when the external environment changes. Neither condition is present today.

- *"Capabilities-Based Planning."* The Russian elite, including the military leadership, acutely feels the uncertainty of the international environment. The main threat is still associated with the United States and its allies, but other potential threats are emerging and the Russian military is reluctant to part with any assets. In 2005-07, similar arguments were made in favor of the withdrawal from the INF Treaty.

- *Parochial Group Politics.* As noted above, the Navy is interested in keeping TNW as a "just-in-case" option.[43] In contrast, the Air Force appears much less interested in TNW except for weapons assigned to Tu-22M3 medium bombers. Other groups probably have even less interest in TNW, but are unlikely to invest political resources to get rid of these weapons. Similarly, the Foreign Ministry, another important player, has many other more pressing items on its agenda. Since no parochial group is seriously interested in changing the existing position, the Navy's interest wins by default.

- *Arms Control Challenges.* Russian ambivalence with regard to TNW might also reflect the challenges of crafting a verifiable treaty. The traditional approach, according to which nuclear weapons are accounted for and reduced indirectly through accounting and reduction of nuclear-capable delivery vehicles, is inapplicable to TNW. New accounting rules require much more intrusive verification at several categories of nuclear-related facilities that have never been subject to inspections — storage sites for nuclear weapons, dismantlement facilities, etc. While such procedures are, in principle, not unthinkable, it would take serious investment of political resources to overcome entrenched resistance and political opposition.

Russia's response to all Western proposals has remained the same for years — any discussion is only possible after the United States withdraws its TNW from Europe. An interesting aspect of that condition is that Moscow apparently does not have a plan as to what it might do if the United States, indeed, complies with it. One can find a range of rather contradictory opinions on how Russian nonstrategic nuclear weapons (NSNW) could be leveraged, but these come from any quarter except from high-level officials. By all indications, the sole purpose of the current Russian position is to deflect U.S. and European pressure.

While American TNW in Europe are few, they provide a convenient justification for rejection of any initiatives aimed at reducing the Russian TNW arsenal. Effectively, Russia has calculated that NATO would be unable to part with U.S. TNW. So far this calculation has proven solid and, given the outcome of internal NATO debates in the spring of 2010, will continue to succeed at least in the near future.

That said, recently some in the Russian military apparently began to entertain more forward-looking views on the future of the nonstrategic nuclear force. While complete elimination is hardly on the books and withdrawal of the small U.S. force from Europe is not challenged, some thought has been given to designing additional options. In fact, there is reason to believe that in 2009 some in the military establishment favored the inclusion of TNW into the New START negotiations—a proposal that was rejected by military leadership. There is also expectation that the United States would insist on tackling TNW in the next stage of nuclear arms reduction talks and that Russia should prepare a position of its own. While these are clearly minority views, the new developments represent a welcome sign that the stone wall might be cracking.

MODERNIZATION OF RUSSIAN STRATEGIC NUCLEAR ARSENAL

Russian modernization programs are reasonably well known, and for the purposes of this chapter require only an overview of key trends. These can be summarized as follows.

All three legs of the triad undergo modernization. These programs are driven by the expiration of warranty periods of systems inherited from the Soviet Union (i.e., the intended length of service of the weapon)—even though the warranty or length of service time is regularly extended, this cannot continue indefinitely. The rate of replacement is low and new ballistic missiles, both land- and sea-based, carry fewer warheads than Soviet ones. This means that the arsenal undergoes gradual reduction. The strategic arsenal will probably stabilize by the end of this decade at about 800-1,200 warheads.

It is hardly surprising that Russia chose to deploy a new generation of delivery vehicles instead of restarting production of existing types. Behind this decision is the Soviet tradition of uninterrupted modernization, which, in turn, was determined by the structure of the Soviet design and production complex.[44] It should be noted, however, that the majority of new types of strategic weapons were still developed in the Soviet Union.

Technologically and conceptually, current strategic modernization programs represent linear continuation of Soviet programs. In this sense, the emerging Russian strategic nuclear posture is very traditional. SRF will probably account for the bulk of all deployed warheads (around 50-60 percent). The earlier plans to radically change the structure of the triad and shift the emphasis to the Navy, which were developed in 2000 and approved by then-President Vladimir Putin, have been abandoned. Russia has continued the Soviet line toward reduction of vulnerability and maintenance of high degree of readiness for launch—according to the SRF, almost all ICBMs could be launched within 1 minute.[45]

The air-based leg of the triad is gradually shifting to a new tangent, however—to conventional strike capability. Eventually its role in the triad will probably be primarily symbolic, and for all intents and purposes the Russian strategic arsenal will become a dyad.

The pace and the success rate for each leg of the triad are different. Modernization of the land-based, ICBM force began in the 1990s and progresses slowly but surely. Introduction of new types of weapons systems into the sea-based leg has encountered major delays and its future remains uncertain. Modernization of the air leg has been postponed—Russia plans to rely on existing aircraft in the foreseeable future and only weapons for use by strategic bombers are being gradually modernized with an emphasis on conventional assets.

ICBM FORCE

The ICBM force modernization has been both conservative and most successful. It its center is Topol-M, a new ICBM designed in the last years of the Soviet Union. The project was partially revised in the 1990s to adapt to the new industrial base (a large part of relevant enterprises remained outside Russia). In the 2000s, the same ICBM was further redesigned to carry several warheads and was designated RS-24, or Yars. Beginning of deployment was postponed until after the expiration of START I.

The rate of ICBM production is low—less than 10 missiles each year; increase of production is unlikely. After 10 years, only six regiments (60 missiles) of silo-based ICBMs have been deployed and only two regiments (18 missiles) of road-mobile ICBMs. In the meantime, the SRF has been extending service lives of existing types of delivery vehicles—to 31 years for SS-18 and to 23 years for Topol (SS-25) and SS-19.[46]

The low rate of missile production might be surprising, given the impressive Soviet capability to turn out large numbers of new weapons—in the 1980s production of Topol (SS-25) was reportedly at 50 per year. Speaking in late 2007, at the time of relative financial plenty, First Vice-Premier and former Minister of Defense Sergey Ivanov sought to make it clear that the government consciously chose "butter" versus "guns." "We believe," he stated, "that we do not need 30 *Topol-M*s a year.[47] Of course, we would not mind having them, but this would mean that we would need to cut social programs, housing programs, and other things." He added that the annual deployment of six to seven new missiles is sufficient for the SRF.[48] At the same time, Ivanov emphasized that "military capability, especially nuclear capability, should be sufficient if we want to be at a [safe] level or even merely independent. No one likes the weak, no one listens to them, everyone abuses them, and when we have parity, others talk to us differently."[49]

There are other explanations for the low rate of production. One is the breakup of the traditional Soviet networks: many Soviet-era enterprises that contributed to production of components remained outside Russia. It is known that the number of only first-order suppliers for Topol-M is around 200; recreating these networks from scratch is difficult, expensive, time-consuming, and probably outright impossible. Another possible explanation is that Russia sought to reserve some unused production capacity for the new submarine-launched ballistic missile (SLBM) Bulava.

Nonetheless, the SRF confidently promises that by 2016 about 80 percent of all ICBMs will be new, i.e., deployed in the post-Soviet period.[50] Reduction under New START and perhaps under the next agreement could certainly contribute to that goal, but it nevertheless appears wishful thinking without a significant increase of funding.

Even more remote is the plan to develop a new liquid-fuel multiple independent reentry vehicled (MIRVed) ICBM to replace the Soviet SS-18 (the new ICBM will hardly classify as "heavy" under START I definitions, but its throw-weight will likely be significantly greater than that of Topol-M, probably at the level of SS-19).[51] Development of the new ICBM is supposed to be completed by 2016, but the goal does not appear realistic. More likely, same as talk about the revival of the rail-mobile ICBM, it reflects the wishes of the military rather than definitive plans.

That said, liquid-fuel missiles have, in the eyes of the military, certain advantages that explain why this line of missiles is still alive in Russia unlike in the United States. Traditionally, Soviet liquid fuel has been more efficient than Soviet solid fuel, allowing for greater throw-weight for the same weight of missile. Liquid-fuel missiles have helped Russia retain an impressive strategic arsenal after two decades of financial, economic, and political turmoil: a large number of these systems that had been produced in the Soviet Union remained in "dry storage," i.e., were kept without fuel. During the post-Soviet period, the military could simply take them from storage, fuel, and deploy. This cannot be done with solid-fuel missiles, whose length of service time period begins at the moment of production.

Recently the SRF was criticized by the government for being insufficiently ambitious. Reportedly, chief of the Government's Department for the Support of the Military-Industrial Commission, Sergey Khutortsov, declared that the SRF was bogged down in small-scale programs and does not have an ambitious long-term goal around which its future should be built, unlike the Navy or the Air Force. The new liquid-fuel

MIRVed ICBM and even the rail-mobile ICBM did not classify as sufficiently ambitious, he said.[52]

The SRF proudly advertizes the defense-penetration properties of its new ICBMs[53] but conveniently fails to mention that this capability was part of a Soviet-era design. In particular, Topol-M features reduced boost phase (about one-third of that of SS-18), which was intended to reduce the effectiveness of space-based interceptors; today this capability is probably less relevant. Topol-M can also carry a maneuverable warhead known as Igla. There is no public authoritative confirmation that Igla is actually being deployed following a very small number of successful tests. Overall, the anti-missile defense capability of new Russian ICBMs should not be overestimated.

SLBM FORCE

Modernization of the sea leg of the triad has encountered major technological and political failures. The initial plan was apparently fairly logical: retain the more modern *Delta III* and *IV* submersible submarine ballistic nuclear (SSBNs), and eventually only the latter, with replacement missiles, develop replacement missiles for *Typhoon* SSBNs, and build new SSBNs to carry the same missiles as *Typhoons*. This plan quickly fell apart. The replacement for SS-N-20, known as Bark, was canceled after three failed test flights. Although the failures had been attributed to production shortcomings and one *Typhoon*-class SSBN had been converted for further tests of the Bark,[54] the contract for the new solid-fuel SLBM was nevertheless given to the Moscow Institute of Thermal Technology (MITT), the same that developed Topol and Topol-M ICBMs. Design of the new SSBN had to be radically altered:

construction of the first submarine in the new class was put on hold until new designs could be drawn to accommodate a radically different missile. The *Typhoon*-class SSBN converted for Bark was converted once again to serve as a testing pad for the new missile. This decision, made in the late 1990s, was widely attributed to parochial fights, and in particular to the close relationship between the Director of MITT Yuri Solomonov and the then-Defense Minister Igor Sergeev, previously the Commander of the SRF.

MITT planned to make the new SLBM, code-named Bulava, an example of a new approach to development of missiles—relatively fast, relatively cheap, with fewer test flights, and large-scale use of computer simulation. The new missile was supposed to become a major departure from Soviet traditions of SLBM design and be much lighter and smaller than Soviet solid-fuel SLBMs. The plan failed utterly—to date, seven out of 12 test flights have failed, and those by rather relaxed official criteria; the majority of non-governmental experts classify only one or two tests as successful.

By the end of 2009 the government and the Ministry of Defense lost patience. Solomonov had to resign from the position of the head of MITT and a special commission was established to investigate the cause of failures concluded that the missile's design was faulty.[55] Resumption of tests was initially scheduled for early summer 2010, but then was postponed until late fall.[56] Solomonov, however, continues to insist that failures were caused by substandard components supplied by the industry, which no longer can maintain high quality.[57]

In the meantime, the new SSBN program continued in spite of delays with the missile. The first submarine in the new class, *Yuri Dolgoruki*, has been commissioned, two more are being built, and the keel of the fourth was laid in January 2010. It was also decided to retain one more *Typhoon* SSBN and convert it for Bulava. Eventually this might mean that, given the low production capability, Russia will have serious problems producing the necessary number of SLBMs to equip all submarines (16 per each new *Borey*-class SSBN and 20 per each *Typhoon*; future *Borey* SSBNs are expected to carry 20 missiles each).

The sorry state of modernization of the Navy increasingly causes displeasure of the top echelons of the government—last year First Deputy Prime Minister Sergey Ivanov revealed that the Navy consumes 40 percent of the total defense budget, more than the SRF, Air Force, and Space Forces combined, and that the bulk of that spending goes to the nuclear submarine force.[58] Implicit in the tone of his remarks was recognition that the yield from that investment remains unsatisfactory.

In the meantime, the sea leg of the Russian triad consists of *Delta III* and *IV* SSBNs. These submarines were given an overhaul to extend their service lives. The Makeev design bureau, which had lost the contract for a new SLBM, produced a modernized version of SS-N-23. In the coming decade, *Delta IIIs* will be probably phased out and only slightly newer *Delta IVs* will remain in service. Thus, early completion of the Bulava program remains a must—without it, Russia risks losing the sea leg completely by the end of this or the beginning of the next decade.

It might be interesting to contemplate the Russian strategic triad without the naval component. Proposals to phase out SSBNs were quite popular in the late 1990s-early 2000s, when investment into modernization of that leg was still minimal. In that case, Russia might seek much deeper cuts in nuclear arsenals than otherwise likely and the mission of strategic deterrence would be supported by the SRF while de-escalation would still be entrusted to the Air Force. In the end, transition from a triad to a dyad might be a good choice, but it appears unlikely for political reasons and also because too much money has already been spent on Bulava—it is difficult to imagine a political or military leader who would be willing to accept responsibility for the failure.

AIR FORCE

The Air Force never played a major role in the Soviet nuclear posture; its share in the strategic arsenal was limited to about 5 percent of deployed warheads. This choice is easy to explain by the traditional drawbacks of Soviet aircraft-building (especially in engines and navigational equipment) as well as the long distances heavy bombers had to cover to reach the United States, meaning a very long gap between decision to launch and delivery as well as very limited payload. The situation began to change somewhat in the 1980s after the Soviet Union succeeded in development of long-range air-launched cruise missiles (ALCMs). Posture plans drawn in the late 1980s foresaw some (albeit still limited) increase in the share of warheads carried on heavy bombers.

In the post-Soviet time, the Air Force remained at the back burner during the larger part of the 1990s until Ukraine agreed to sell some heavy bombers to Russia instead of eliminating them under START I. This allowed increasing the number of heavy bombers to a level that had at least some military sense. In the 2000s, the Air Force became the leading asset to support the new mission, that of de-escalation.[59]

Nuclear-capable aircraft (heavy bombers Tu-160 and Tu-95MS as well as medium Tu-22M3) have remained at the back burner of modernization efforts: existing heavy bombers are expected to last until at least the end of this decade, so there is no rush, in contrast to the ICBM and SLBM forces, which must be replaced as a matter of urgency. Instead, Russia has concentrated on upgrading the electronics and avionics of these aircraft; some heavy bombers designed to carry ALCMs are being converted to carry gravity bombs.

Modernization of nuclear weapons has been very limited. Russia is working on a new-generation (reportedly supersonic) ALCM, Kh-101, and its conventional version, Kh-102. Work on that program has been exceedingly slow—it began in the 1990s and the last mention of it is in 2000. After that, mentions of that program ceased until recently, when it surfaced only once and almost by accident. Obviously, the program is highly classified, but work continues, which is hardly surprising because at the moment the only long-range nuclear asset is a hopelessly outdated Kh-55. There is also a plan to give high precision capability to gravity bombs using the emerging Global Navigation Satellite System (GLONASS).

Eventually aircraft have to be replaced, of course. Among the existing types, the Tu-22Ms will probably be phased out completely. Some suggest that Su-34 could take up its roles, but it is unclear whether a decision has been made yet, which probably indicates that Russian military does not foresee many nuclear missions at Su-34 ranges.

Long-range plans of the Air Force are built around a brand new bomber, which will reportedly fall some-

228

where between Tu-22M3 and heavy bombers in range and load and is expected to be cheaper than the heavy bombers.[60] Its main missions are reported to be in Eurasia and perhaps also the northern part of Africa. One wonders whether the new aircraft will actually fall under the traditional START I definition of a heavy bomber. The beginning of test flights is scheduled for 2015-16 and production could begin around 2020. These dates are certainly subject to revision, which is hardly surprising given the tradition of delays of all modernization programs: in fact, first reports about the new bomber appeared more than 10 years ago, but the Ministry of Defense concluded a formal contract with Tupolev design bureau for a new aircraft only in August 2009.

Information about modernization of the air leg of the strategic triad is scarce, but is the information available leads to three conclusions. First, the Air Force is likely to lose a role in strategic deterrence, even though formally and for arms control purposes it will remain part of strategic arsenal. Second, the Air Force will maintain and perhaps even enhance a nuclear role at the theater level. This role will not require large capability and the number of long-range aircraft will remain relatively small. Third, long-range aircraft will increasingly support conventional long-range missions. In this, Russia follows the trends of the U.S. Air Force with about 15-20 years lag. More about this aspect of Air Force modernization will be discussed in the relevant section of this chapter.

MISSILE DEFENSE IN U.S.-RUSSIAN RELATIONSHIP

American missile defense plans are an old issue in U.S.-Russian relations. They date back to Reagan's *Strategic Defense Initiative* (SDI); tensions declined in the early 1990s, but began to build up again toward the end of that decade and reached the peak during the last decade as a result of U.S. withdrawal from the ABM Treaty and the subsequent announcement of the intention to deploy 10 interceptors in Poland and a radar in Czech Republic. The announcement in September 2009 of a change in missile defense plans for Europe helped to significantly alleviate the acrimony, but did not remove it completely.

Thus conflict has continued for almost 3 decades. A truly curious element of the picture is that strategic missile defense still does not exist. So far, it has all been about intentions and the projected capability of the future system.

Another curious element is that there is actually very little to be said about the nature and the dynamic of that conflict. The fault lines are simple and straightforward; they have not changed in many years.

The Russian view of missile defense is informed by the traditional view of strategic deterrence built around mutual vulnerability. Underlying Russian opposition is fear that the United States could acquire the ability to deny Russia ability to respond to an attack; this concern was shaped in the 1980s by SDI plans. Even though the likelihood of a large-scale nuclear war is practically nonexistent, there is fear that such a capability could be used as a leverage to extract concessions and exert political pressure. In other words, it goes straight to the heart of the view that nuclear weapons guarantee Russia's security and sovereignty. Hence, opposition to missile defense amounts to more than just a straightforward military calculation. The issue has become emotionally charged and suspicions now matter more than cool-headed assessment.

Virulent, often hysterical Russian opposition to the George W. Bush plans to build a limited strategic defense capability in Europe has demonstrated two underlying and intertwining trends that make conflict almost inevitable.

The first trend is the multiple capabilities of a system designed to protect the United States against Iranian or North Korean missiles. The same assets could theoretically intercept Russian missiles as well, and that residual capability conveniently feeds into the concern about the credibility of strategic deterrence.

Almost no one in Russia believed the official justification provided by the Bush administration because, according to Russian military's estimates, Iran will not acquire missiles with strategic range for many years. Hence, Russians tried to imagine the "real" purpose of the planned missile defense and, not surprisingly, concluded it was intended against Russia — worst-case planning and suspicions still to a large extent rule the day in Moscow. Washington's assurances that the system would be limited were not taken seriously — the planned deployment was regarded as a "foot in the door," with the first 10 interceptors supplemented by dozens more at a later stage.

A further complication was the manner and style of Russian rhetoric, which almost always failed to clearly convey the true nature of concern — it was not about the system the Bush administration planned, but rather about its possible expansion in the future. Russian statements were usually devoted to short-range plans. Concern about future capability was further enhanced by the insistence of the White House that the plan was open-ended and refusal to set any limits, whether formally or informally. The open-ended nature of the proposed system further strengthened Russian belief that the "true" plans were much more ominous than those announced publicly.

Only relatively rarely did Russians clearly distinguish between immediate American plans and possible future expansion. Speaking in February 2007, Chief of the Air Force Vladimir Mikhailov said that he regarded "very calmly" the planned missile defenses in Eastern Europe.[61] Former Chief of Staff of Strategic Rocket Forces Viktor Yesin opined that the main threat of missile defense came from "undefined architecture." "Will there be 10 interceptors or a thousand? It's 10 now, but no one can guarantee there will not be more." He anticipated that eventually the United States would also deploy missile defense assets in Japan, Great Britain, or Norway.[62] Deputy Chief of the Main Directorate of International Cooperation at the Ministry of Defense Yevgenii Buzhinskii said that current small-scale deployment plans were but elements of a broader vision—a global network of missile defense around Russia's borders.[63]

This leads to the second and perhaps the most important feature of the conflict over missile defense—it has been about the lack of predictability. In the absence of reasonably clear-cut, definitive long-term plans, Russian thinking has been unavoidably informed by worst-case scenarios. **The most important lesson that could be drawn from the conflicts of the last decade over missile defense is simple, but perhaps difficult to implement—the need for predictability. U.S. efforts to maintain transparency through provision**

of information about plans turned out to be insufficient.

It is no wonder that the lowest point in U.S.-Russian interaction on missile defense was the end of 2007 and 2008. In October 2007, a two-by-two meeting (between foreign and defense ministers of the two countries) seemed to have achieved a preliminary agreement on a set of confidence building measures intended to alleviate Russian concerns. Neither side was fully satisfied with it, but about a week after that meeting Vladimir Putin (at that time still president of Russia) indicated that Moscow regarded that tentative deal as a foundation for possible future agreement.[64] When the United States transmitted its proposals on missile defense in writing a month later (delay was ascribed to protracted bureaucratic in-fighting in Washington), however, Russian officials promptly rejected them, accusing the United States of retracting the compromises discussed during the Gates-Rice visit and returning the negotiations to square one.[65] After that, Moscow came to regard dialogue with the United States on missile defense as impossible.

Against that background, the September 2009 announcement about a revision of plans for defense of Europe was seen as positive news. While principled opposition to missile defense did not disappear, the new architecture was at least logically explainable. It was clearly intended to defend Europe from *existing* Iranian missiles and at the same time in the near future will not have capability to intercept Russian ICBMs.

Acknowledgment by the United States in the New START treaty of a relationship between offensive and defensive weapons also contributed to a calmer tone of interaction on missile defense. New START did not resolve the issue from the Russian perspective but was

233

a positive first step toward a final solution. Effectively, it bought time for a more constructive engagement, and this is probably the maximum that could be done at the current stage.

Nevertheless, the issue did not fade away completely. While current plans are not a source of serious concern, possible future capabilities still are. Chief of General Staff Nikolai Makarov declared that U.S. missile defense in its current shape and capability is not a concern for Russia, but long-term plans to develop strategic missile defense could become a threat.[66] According to Vladimir Dvorkin, "the crisis between Russia and the United States over missile defense has been postponed [by the signing of New START], but it could return in an even more acute shape after the sea-based missile defense system built around SM-3 interceptors and their ground-launched analogues acquire strategic capability by 2020."[67] That is, while the first irritant — multiple capabilities — has been removed, the other and more important one, predictability, still needs to be addressed.

A complicating feature that has emerged during the last decade was the emergence of close cooperation between Russia and China in opposition to U.S. missile defense plans. Both countries share many of the same concerns and have jointly acted in almost every conceivable international forum to oppose and derail American plans. A turning point in that cooperation was 2005, when Foreign Minister Sergey Lavrov declared that Russia and China *both* face the *same* threat from U.S. missile defense plans. As a result, Russia's ability to find accommodation with the United States, launch cooperative programs, etc., is now limited because it could be seen by China as a betrayal.

Quite paradoxically, another, equally persistent theme in the Russian approach to U.S. missile defense programs has been proposals for cooperation. In the early 1990s, these proposals were built around a notion that Russia could contribute technologies developed during decades of R&D in missile defense. These included programs launched in the 1980s — although the Soviet Union vehemently opposed SDI and advertized "asymmetric" responses to it (i.e., through enhancement of offensive weapons capability), it simultaneously pursued a wide range of its own defense programs, a "symmetric" response. These were not particularly advanced and mostly remained at the stage of research, but their scale was quite impressive — they consumed more than half (about 52 percent) of all spending on strategic weapons.

Since the late 1990s, Russia sought to showcase a defense system against tactical missiles, S-300, as well as another system, S-400 (at that time still in the pipeline), which was intended to counter intermediate-range missiles. Indeed, the 1997 New York Protocols, which drew a line between strategic and nonstrategic defenses (i.e., those that were banned or allowed under the 1972 ABM Treaty), were carefully crafted by Russia to protect S-400. The highest point of these initiatives was a proposal made in early 2001, which foresaw a relatively well-developed plan for the defense of Europe consisting of a combination of S-300 and S-400; this proposal was overlooked by the United States, which, under the new administration, was moving toward abrogation of the ABM Treaty.

It is important to understand the Russian definition of cooperation. It assumed that Moscow would supply weapons systems (and get paid for them), be an integral part of decisionmaking on the architecture of the defense system (and have the right to veto elements of the system that could be used to track and/or intercept Russian missiles), and be part of operating the system (including the right to prevent launches of interceptors against Russian missiles). The definition of cooperation used by the George W. Bush administration was different. The most important practical contribution that was expected from Russia was data from the radar it operated—from Gabala in Azerbaijan and later from the new radar in Armavir. That is, Russian participation would have to be passive. This mode did not satisfy Moscow, and it was not prepared to supply data to an American-operated system, only to a joint one.

Proposals about a joint missile defense resumed under the Obama administration and have recently become a central point in Russian official and unofficial statements on missile defense. President Dmitri Medvedev declared recently, in response to NATO overtures on cooperation in missile defense, that Russia would be interested in a joint system with NATO if the proposal was serious.[68] Former Chief of Staff of the SRF Viktor Yesin opined that the United States and Russia could create a joint defense system to protect Europe against Iranian missiles and mentioned that such a system could be configured to intercept Iranian missiles with speeds up to 7 kilometers (km)/second (that is, it would be classified as nonstrategic under the 1997 New York Protocols) and use data not only from American radars, but also from radars at Gabala and Armavir. According to Yesin, such a system could be created after 2015.[69] Similarly, Vladimir Dvorkin wrote that a joint system building on simulations conducted between the United States and NATO during the last decade is the only way to resolve the continuing controversy over missile defense. In his view, however, the system does not need to be fully integrated and instead could be built on dividing responsibility for different sectors. [70]

The proposed Russian contribution is still S-300 and S-400 systems, which are now in a more advanced stage than they used to be 10 years ago. In fact, the S-400 entered test deployment in 2007 and is expected to go into mass production later this year or in 2011, following long delays with development of a new interceptor. Moreover, Russia is conducting R&D on a still more advanced system, S-500 Triumphator, which is supposed to be ready for production in 2015 (given multiple-year delays with S-400, this official timeline does not sound very realistic, though). With S-500, Russia could reach the parameters proposed by Yesin (7 km/second for incoming missiles; S-400 can only intercept missiles with less than 5 km/second speed).

All in all, solution to the issue of missile defense remains elusive. Perhaps the biggest challenge is lack of any clarity with regard to a final solution; thus, it is difficult to decide which way dialogue should steer. The Russian preference seems to be for a new ABM treaty of some sort that would regulate missile defense to guarantee mutual vulnerability of the United States and Russia. Such a solution is hardly feasible in the near future. Furthermore, the Russian position on missile defense is limited by its close cooperation with China, whose criteria for a new international regime in missile defense are likely to be even more restrictive than those of Russia. While a new politically or legally binding regime on missile defense seems improbable, it is nevertheless still advisable to discuss it, perhaps unofficially, to enhance predictability and promote better understanding of the positions of all parties.

In the absence of a final solution, a series of small-scale partial agreements on various elements of the relationship in the missile defense area seems more feasible. These could address confidence building measures and enhance transparency and predictability. That is, conflicts seem unavoidable, but they can be regulated and kept in check. There appears to be two ways of tackling differences, neither fully acceptable to the United States or Russia for reasons of domestic politics.

The first option is **enhanced predictability**. All the loud, sometimes shrill, statements notwithstanding, Russia has never been concerned about short-term American plans; even the George W. Bush administration's system was not regarded as an immediate threat. Concern has been primarily about future capability, which has so far remained undefined. Interaction in the last decade has demonstrated that simple information about plans is not sufficient because plans can change; other ways to enhance predictability should be considered together with enhanced consultations. An ultimate predictability mechanism is a new full-scale treaty on missile defense, but other, more limited options should be considered.

The second option favored by Russia is a **fully integrated missile defense system**. A strong cooperative program in that area could change the lineup of domestic parochial groups in Russia in favor of a more moderate attitude toward American plans, but such a joint system would give Russia a role in decisionmaking on all aspects of building and operating it. That degree of involvement and especially the right of veto over the use of the system, whether formal or de facto, is likely to be unacceptable to Washington, too.

A positive element in all the conflicts and debates over a possible missile defense system, which has not attracted sufficient attention, is that Russia is actually prepared to contribute to the defense of Europe and potentially of the United States from Iran as long as it is accepted as a full partner. This could finally and unequivocally put Moscow into the Western camp with regard to Iran and end the Russian attempts to straddle the fence when it comes to Russian-Iranian relations. Interestingly, the military and the defense industry seem to favor that solution and, for a change, the Foreign Ministry takes a more conservative approach.

In the end, there is probably no prospect of a final solution to the issue of missile defense. In all likelihood, controversy and conflict will continue in the foreseeable future. The parties will continue to muddle through, 1 year after another with ups and downs and perhaps with some partial, small-scale agreements on various aspects of the issue.

LONG-RANGE CONVENTIONAL CAPABILITY

Russian opposition to the emerging U.S. Global Strike is well-known. Multiple concerns voiced by Russian officials and uniformed military fall into three categories.

First, high-precision conventional weapons could be used in a disarming first strike against the Russian nuclear arsenal. This was a major concern in the 1990s, but its urgency has been gradually declining. Among the military, there is still concern about the ability of high-precision conventional weapons to destroy soft targets, particularly road-mobile ICBMs, but even that is not considered a high-priority threat, at least not at the moment. By and large, this concern is now limited to conservative quarters. It should be noted however, that decline of this concern rests, to a large extent, on continued reliance on nuclear weapons. Even well-known liberal expert Aleksei Arbatov emphasized recently that "as long as Russia has a reliable nuclear deterrence capability, the scenario of a massive and extended conventional air and missile U.S. strikes using high-precision conventional weapons remains an artificial threat."[71] Without it, Russia could have been much more concerned about U.S. conventional strike capability.

Second, in a large-scale conflict conventional assets can do many of the same things as nuclear weapons, but are more usable. To some extent, this is not so much a concern as envy — where the United States could utilize conventional assets Russia is still limited to nuclear options. The recent *Nuclear Posture Review* was assessed by Russian experts from precisely that angle — the United States no longer needs nuclear weapons for its security and can (or will in the near future) support almost all missions with conventional assets.[72]

Third, and finally, it is difficult to distinguish a long-range delivery vehicle with a conventional warhead from the same vehicle equipped with a nuclear warhead. Since trajectories toward the majority of likely targets cross Russian territory or closely skirt it, they could be interpreted by the early warning system as an attack.[73] This concern appears real and needs to be addressed — the Russian military are clearly not going to be satisfied with U.S. notifications in case of a launch and will want the ability to verify it independently. Very limited (nonexistent for all practical purposes) Russian capability to detect single launches from submarines is likely to complicate the matter even further. Paradoxically, ICBMs armed with conventional warheads might be a better option for Global Strike because Russian inspectors could verify the type of warheads on designated ICBMs during re-entry vehicle (RV) inspections under New START (on the other hand, to reach the majority of targets in Eurasia, the ICBM must fly over Russian territory, which can be a cause for concern as well).

Even as Russian politicians, military, and non-governmental experts continue to criticize American plans for Global Strike, they simultaneously advocate acquisition of similar capability by Russia. As a well-known Russia expert, Aleksandr Khramchikhin, noted, "strategic weapons are not a panacea for defense against attack against Russia."[74] It is worth recalling that the 2000 *National Security Concept* and subsequent documents called reliance on nuclear weapons a temporary fix until Russia acquires a modern conventional capability.

Efforts toward that goal were started in the 1980s, but progress is slow. Nonetheless, it enjoys greater attention than modernization of the nuclear capability. Programs include long- and short-range precision guided air- and ground-launched missiles as well as new communication, command, and control assets, a Russian analogue to global positioning satellites (GPS) and GLONASS, which should enable precision strikes.

In the early 2000s Russia began production of the Kh-555 conventional ALCM (a version of the nuclear Kh-55); in the 1990s, it also started to work on a brand-new Kh-101/102 ALCM: the 101 variant for a nuclear warhead and 102 for conventional. This R&D program has apparently been exceedingly slow and secretive—

it was fairly often reported in the media in the 1990s, but then all information about it disappeared from open sources until 2009, when it was mentioned only once and apparently inadvertently. The Air Force has also begun conversion of some Tu-160 heavy bombers from cruise missiles to conventional gravity bombs.

In the 1990s, Russia also developed a new tactical missile, Iskander; its production began in the mid-2000s. Initially Iskander-E was reported to have the range of 280 km,[75] but subsequently its range was reportedly increased to more than 400 km—about the same as the SS-23 Oka, which was eliminated under the 1987 INF Treaty. Later, a cruise missile was also developed for the Iskander launcher. The decision, announced in 2008, to deploy five brigades (probably 60 launchers with two missiles each) of Iskanders in Kaliningrad oblast—officially in response to an American plan to deploy missile defense assets in Poland and the Czech Republic[76]—perhaps signaled a move in the shifting emphasis from nuclear to conventional capability vis-à-vis NATO. Moscow had to cancel these plans in 2009 after revision of the U.S. missile defense program, but this probably shows only that the pretext was wrong—a change of U.S. plans was apparently not expected. If deployment of Iskanders was indeed part of a move toward greater reliance on conventional assets, the idea will be revived in a new context.

An important element of the emerging conventional capability is multipurpose (attack) submarines. Russia is building new types of nuclear powered submarines (SSNs) and diesel-powered submarines—Project 885 Yasen (the first SSN, *Severodvinsk*, should be commissioned this or next year), Project 677 Lada (construction of the first submarine was completed in

2005, two more are close to completion). These and other submarines are equipped with dual-capable cruise missiles, both those intended against other ships and against land targets. As mentioned above, the Navy seeks to maintain its nuclear capability, especially vis-à-vis U.S. Navy, but conventional assets play an increasingly visible role in the long-term plans.

The pace of conventional rearmament is set to increase following the "5-day war," the conflict between Russia and Georgia in August 2008. Russia won this conflict largely due to the sheer size of the army it sent to battle. Speaking in September 2008, Dmitri Medvedev declared:

> We must achieve superiority in the air, in high-precision strikes against land and sea targets, in quick relocation of troops. . . . By 2020, we must solve the problem of . . . comprehensive equipment of forces with new models of arms and reconnaissance assets.[77]

More than 2 decades of work on GLONASS, which should allow precision guidance for conventional weapons, is gradually coming to completion as well. It currently features 21 satellites allowing coverage of Russia's own territory, with two or three satellites for each location; launch of six additional satellites is planned for 2010. The system is still inferior to GPS—the accuracy of its coordinates in Russian territory is reported to be six meters, several times worse than for GPS, but on the other hand its characteristics are gradually improving—in 2009 it was 10 meters.[78] One of the main drawbacks of Soviet satellites that necessitates frequent replacement of satellites in orbit—short life span—is also slowly improving. A new satellite was introduced several years ago, and in 2010 Russia plans to launch the first satellites that will last 7 or more years. Given multiple delays and the Russian propensity to overestimate the ability to deliver new products, GLONASS will probably reach full functionality only in the second half of the coming decade.

While Russian efforts to acquire long-range conventional capability seem to mirror what the United States has been doing for over 20 years, there is an important asymmetry that could complicate finding a common language. In contrast to Global Strike, which emphasizes strategic ranges because potential targets are located in southern Eurasia (Middle East, South Asia, etc.), Russia is developing a theater-level conventional capability. Ironically, American and Russian targets, if not the same, at least overlap, but Russia is simply closer to these targets. Furthermore, assets the United States needs to strike in the areas of ongoing and potential conflicts could also be used against Russia, which will remain a source of unending concern for Moscow, whereas Russian theater-range assets will not be able to strike the United States. Thus, Russian military and civilian experts will continue to voice concern about Global Strike. This concern could be alleviated somewhat through a set of confidence building measures, but hardly removed completely, at least not in the foreseeable future.

WITHDRAWAL FROM THE INF

The 1987 INF Treaty has never been particularly liked by the Russian military. It is closely associated with major concessions on part of the Soviet Union, which had to eliminate many more missiles in that class than the United States. Characteristically, the security benefits the Soviet Union obtained from that deal (removal of American missiles with very short flight-time) is practically never mentioned — the emphasis is almost always on the numbers of weapons subject to elimination. Particularly painful for the military is the agreement by Mikhail Gorbachev to include SS-23 Oka missiles into the treaty: the range of that missile is widely believed (not without reason) to be below 500 km and thus it should not have been subject to the INF Treaty, or so many still believe. In other words, the INF Treaty is often regarded as a symbol of betrayal and unwarranted concessions. This perception has strongly affected many other arms control issues, including Russian resistance to Western proposals with regard to reduction of nonstrategic nuclear weapons.

Nevertheless, the INF Treaty was not only implemented, but Russia continues to uphold it. Until relatively recently, there was no reason to believe that constant grumbling would translate into proposals to abrogate it. Such proposals did emerge, however, in the middle of 2000s.

When the United States withdrew from the ABM Treaty in 2002, many in Russia regarded this as an example that could be emulated — namely, that it is acceptable to withdraw from treaties once they are no longer regarded as serving national interest. U.S. withdrawal from the ABM Treaty certainly undermined the argument about sanctity of international agreements, especially among the Russian military. Central to the argument about abrogation of the INF was its bilateral nature: "others have 'em." Official statements did not point at specific countries, but public debates mentioned China, North Korea, India, Pakistan, Iran, and Israel.

An important point to bear in mind is that proposals for withdrawal from the INF Treaty were not part of a desire to enhance nuclear capability. Instead, they were part of Russian desire to develop long-range conventional assets. Indeed, for the first time, regret about the ban on intermediate-range missiles was voiced during the second war in Chechnya, when then-Secretary of the Security Council Sergey Ivanov complained that without such assets Russia could not take out Chechen training camps in Afghanistan.

The desire to add intermediate-range missiles to the planned conventional capability was officially spelled out during Ivanov's meeting of U.S. Secretary of Defense Donald Rumsfeld in August 2006 in Alaska. Responding to Rumsfeld's attempt to explain the benefits of the United States equipping some strategic missiles with conventional warheads to make them usable for strikes against terrorists, Ivanov said that conventionally-armed strategic missiles were not the only option for strikes against terrorists and far from the safest:

> Theoretically, one could use long-range cruise missiles with conventional warheads, . . . One could even consider a theoretical possibility of using intermediate range missiles, although the United States and Russia cannot have them, unlike many other countries, which already have such missiles.[79]

Uniformed military were clearly delighted to see their old favorite proposal pitched to the U.S. Secretary of Defense and quickly sought to elaborate it and calm possible American anxieties. An unnamed representative of the Ministry of Defense said that while the abrogation of the ABM Treaty opened a door to a similar step with regard to the INF Treaty, the United States should not be concerned because Russian intermediate-range systems cannot reach U.S. territory except from Chukotka, across the Bering Strait from Alaska, "but they will not be deployed there." Referring specifically to North Korea, he stated that, for Russia, intermediate-range missiles would be far more useful as conventionally armed systems than intercontinental missiles, as proposed by the United States.[80]

Ultimately, however, the rationale for withdrawal from the INF Treaty changed and came to be linked to George W. Bush administration's plans for missile defense in Europe. Early in 2007, Chief of the General Staff Yuri Baluevski declared that Russia was considering whether to withdraw from the INF Treaty, and the final decision was contingent upon U.S. actions with regard to deployment of a missile defense system in proximity to Russia. [81]

The leading role in the push for withdrawal was often attributed to the SRF, which sought to expand its force and give it more relevance within the military establishment. It is noteworthy that Director of the 4th Central Research Institute of the Ministry of Defense (the institute conducts research to support the SRF) Major-General Vladimir Vasilenko, in a departure from the standard Russian perspective, said that intercontinental strategic missiles were preferable to intermediate-range systems as conventional assets because the longer range of the former made them a more versatile asset.[82] The Air Force was a more vocal voice of opposition—its representatives declared that they could support any conventional or nuclear mission at the theater level implying that there was no reason to spend all the political and financial resources to deploy intermediate-range land-based missiles. The Foreign Ministry was another force opposing the abrogation of an important treaty. There was also quite serious—and surprising—opposition in the ranks of retired generals who claimed that the United States could use the abrogation of the INF Treaty once again to deploy Pershing II and ground launched cruise missiles (GLCMs) in Europe; clearly, uniformed military, who are less wedded to Cold War concepts, did not regard that as a likely scenario.

The outcome of the debates that raged in 2005-07 reminded NATO's 1979 "dual-track" decision (it is noteworthy how much contemporary Russian policies are influenced by examples set by past policies of NATO) — Russia would not withdraw from the INF Treaty, but would propose to make it a multilateral agreement. It was tacitly assumed that abrogation was not off the agenda, however, and the issue could be revisited if countries with intermediate-range missile programs do not join. The United States joined the initiative and in 2008 Moscow even tabled a draft multilateral INF Treaty at the Conference on Disarmament in Geneva. Thus the issue has remained on the agenda, and from time to time Moscow reminds other countries about the proposal. The specter of withdrawal from the INF Treaty has not disappeared completely, but is mentioned very rarely. It is possible that it could eventually die out quietly, but a new international crisis (for example, between Russia and Iran) could reignite it once again.

An important variable in any future decisions with regard to the withdrawal from the INF Treaty is funding. While resumption of production of SS-20s or extending the range of Iskander tactical missiles are technologically feasible, the Russian government has consistently limited funding for production of even existing classes of weapons — ICBMs and short-range missiles. It does not appear likely that it will be supporting of an even more expensive programs for intermediate-range missiles. It seems likely that reluctance to allocate funds played an important role in the decision to pursue a diplomatic option and postpone the abrogation decision to an indefinite future.

CONCLUSION

Nuclear weapons retain a high profile in Russian national security strategy and will keep it in the foreseeable future. Contrary to official statements, there is no reason to believe that Russia could agree to a very significant reduction, much less elimination, of its nuclear arsenal. Instead, 10 years ago nuclear weapons were given additional roles — those of deterring and deescalating limited ("regional") conventional wars. They are likely to keep that role as well, at least during the coming decade.

At the same time, Russian leadership clearly understands the limited utility of nuclear weapons and seeks to enhance conventional capability. In this sense, Russia is moving in some of the same directions as the United States — it seeks to develop missile defense and precision-guided long-range conventional assets. According to long-term plans, eventually these efforts should allow Russia to reduce reliance on nuclear weapons. These programs encounter multiple delays, however, and progress much slower than anticipated. Russia will hardly succeed before the end of the coming decade and might never completely close the gap with the United States and NATO. In that case, reliance on nuclear weapons will continue indefinitely.

Certain similarities notwithstanding, differences between the United States and Russia will continue — Moscow is likely to continue seeing U.S. Global Strike and missile defense plans as a potential threat. There exists an important asymmetry: While the United States emphasizes strategic capability (intercontinental-range conventional assets and ability to intercept strategic missiles), Russia seeks intermediate-range capability and will continue to view American programs from the perspective of strategic balance.

Overall, the relationship will remain uneasy, but manageable. The key condition for a stable relationship is predictability — first and foremost careful management of American capabilities that can affect Russian strategic deterrence. This is not impossible, but might be difficult to achieve due to the dynamic of domestic politics in the two countries.

ENDNOTES - CHAPTER 5

1. "Rossii Poka Neobkhodimo Yadernoe Oruzhie — Patriarkh Kirill" ("Russia Still Needs Nuclear Weapons — Patriarch Kirill"), *RIA-Novosti*, November 11, 2009.

2. "Podpisano Dopolnenie k Programme Razvitiya Yaderno-Oruzheinogo Kompleksa," *RIA-Novosti*, June 9, 2010.

3. For an early critique of the Russian concept of "multipolarity," see Nikolai Sokov, "Mnogopoluysnyi Mir v Zerkale Teorii Mezhdunarodnykh Otnoshenii" ("The Multipolar World Reflected in the Mirror of International Relations Theories"), *SShA: Ekonomika, Politika, Ideologiya (Journal of the Institute of USA and Canada Studies, Russian Academy of Sciences)*, No. 7, 1998, pp. 19-27; No. 8, 1998, pp. 19-31. For the latest Russian critique of this concept, see Vladislav Inozemtsev, "Mechty o Mnogopoluysnom Mire" ("*Dreams about a Multipolar World*"), *Nezavisimaya Gazeta*, September 18, 2008; Aleksandr Konovalov, "Mir Ne Dolzhen Byt Mnogopolyarnym" ("*The World Must Not Be Multipolar*"), *Nezavisimaya Gazeta*, September 16, 2008.

4. The transcript of press conference of Minister of Foreign Affairs of the Russian Federation with Russian media, New Delhi, India, October 20, 2008, document 1650-22-10-2008, available from *www.mid.ru/brp_4.nsf/2fee282eb6df40e643256999005e6e8c/168f 10e1ae44dd7dc32574ea0041988a?OpenDocument.*

5. Roman Dobrokhotov, "Obezoruzhivauyshchie Argumenty" ("Disarming Arguments"), *Novye Izvestia*, February 13, 2008.

6. Disarmament was tackled during the Question and Answer part of the meeting and was not addressed in the main speech. See Arkadi Dubnov, "Treugolnaya Diplomatiya" ("Triangular Diplomacy"), *Vremya Novostei*, December 11, 2008.

7. "Osnovnyye polozheniya voyennoy doktriny Rossiyskoy Federatsii," *Rossiyskaya gazeta*, November 18, 1993, pp. 1, 4.

8. Kontseptsiya natsionalnoy bezopasnosti Rossiiskoi Federatsii. Utverzhdena Ukazom Prezidenta RF ot 17 dekabrya 1997 g. No. 1300, *available from 194.226.83.2/documents/decree/1997/_1300-1. html*.

9. Anatoliy Klimenko and Aleksandr Koltuykov, "Osnovnoy dokument voyennogo stroitelstva," *Nezavisimoye voyennoye obozreniye*, February 13, 1998, p. 4.

10. These included a decree of Boris Yeltsin, "On urgent measures toward reforming the Armed Forces of the Russian Federation," July 1997; and two Security Council documents: "The Concept of Development of Nuclear Forces until 2010" and "The Foundations (Concept) of State Policy in the Area of Defense Development until 2005," July-August 1998. These documents are classified, but their general thrust could be gleaned from newspaper publications: "Sovet Bezopasnosti RF Reshil Sokhranit Trekhkomponentnyi Sostav Strategicheskikh Yadernykh Sil," *Interfax daily news bulletin*, No. 4, July 3, 1998; "Russia to be Major Nuclear Power in 3d Millennium—Official," *ITAR-TASS*, July 3, 1998; Ivan Safronov and Ilya Bulavinov, "Boris Yeltsin Podnyal Yadernyi Shchit," *Kommersant-Daily*, July 4, 1998; Yuri Golotuyk, "Yadernoe Razoruzhenie Neizbezhno," *Russkii Telegraph*, July 11, 1998; Yuri Golotuyk, "Moskva Skorrektirovala Svoi Yadernye Argumenty," *Russkii Telegraph*, July 4, 1998; Anatoli Yurkin, "Perspektivy Voennogo Stroitelstva," *Krasnaya Zvezda*, August 5, 1998, p. 1, 3; Oleg Falichev, "Vpervpe So Vremeni Miluykovskikh Reform," *Krasnaya Zvezda*, August 18, 1998, p. 1, 2.

11. Sergei Ivanov's statement at the International Institute of Strategic Studies, is found in "Sergey Ivanov: Terrorizm Iskhodit ot Nesostoyavshikhsya Gosudarstv" ("Sergey Ivanov: Failed States are the Source of Terrorism"), *Strana.ru Information Service*, July 13, 2004.

12. *Voennaya Doktrina Rossiiskoi Federatsii* (*Military Doctrine of the Russian Federation*), April 21, 2000.

13. V. Prozorov, *Yadernoye Sderzhivaniye v Teorii Primeneniya RVSN* (*Nuclear Deterrence in the Theory of Use of the SRF*), Moscow, Russia: Pyotr Veliki Military Academy, 1999, p. 19.

14. For details of this meeting, see Nikolai Sokov, "The April 1999 Russian Federation Security Council Meeting On Nuclear Weapons," NIS Nuclear Profiles Database, Monterey, CA: Center for Nonproliferation Studies, Monterey Institute of International Studies, June 1999, available from *www.nti.org/db/nisprofs/over/rf-secmtg.htm*.

15. National Security Concept of the Russian Federation, January 2000; *Military Doctrine of the Russian Federation*, April 2000.

16. "Aktualnyye Zadachi Razvitiya Vooruzhennykh Sil RF" ("Immediate Tasks of Development of the Armed Forces of the Russian Federation"), October 2, 1003.

17. Yuri Baluevski, Speech at the Academy of Military Sciences, January 2007. The full text of Baluevski's speech was published about 2 weeks after the conference and can be found at the official site of the Ministry of Defense (in Russian), available from *www.mil.ru/847/852/1153/1342/20922/index.shtml*. See also Vadim Solovyov, "Voennaya Reforma Obyavlena Bessrochnoi" ("Military Reform Has Been Declared Unending"), *Nezavisimoe Voennoe Obozrenie*, January 26, 2007.

18. "Aktualnyye Zadachi Razvitiya Vooruzhennykh Sil RF"("Immediate Tasks of Development of the Armed Forces of the Russian Federation"), p. 43.

19. *Ibid.*, p. 24.

20. A. Khryapin and V. Afanasiev, "Kontseptualnye Osnovy Strategicheskogo Sderzhivaniya" ("Conceptual Foundations of Strategic Deterrence"), *Voyennaya Mysl*, January 2005.

21. "Aktualnyye Zadachi Razvitiya Vooruzhennykh Sil RF" ("Immediate Tasks of Development of the Armed Forces of the Russian Federation") p. 30.

22. "Yadernyi Shchit Dast RF Vremya na Formirovanie Novogo Oblika Armii — RVSN," *RIA-Novosti*, June 10, 2009.

23. *Voennaya Doktrina Rossiiskoi Federatsii (Military Doctrine of the Russian Federation)*, February 5, 2010, *available from www.scrf. gov.ru/documents/33.html*.

24. For details, see Nikolai Sokov, "Russian Academy of Military Sciences Debates Role of Nuclear Weapons in Conference on New Military Doctrine," *WMD Insights*, March 2007, *available from www.wmdinsights.com/I13/I13_R2_RussianAcademy.htm*.

25. "Menyaetsya Rossiya, Menyaetsya i ee Voennaya Doktrina" ("As Russia Changes, its Military Doctrine Changes Too"), *Izvestiya*, October 14, 2009.

26. *Voyennaya Doktrina Rossiyskoy Federatsii (Military Doctrine of the Russian Federation)*, February 5, 2010, available from *www. scrf.gov.ru/documents/33.html*.

27. *Ibid.*

28. Interviews by one of the authors with Russian officials, who requested anonymity.

29. "Rol Takticheskogo Yadernogo Oruzhiya na Mnogotselevykh APL Vozrastet — VMF" ("The Role of Tactical Nuclear Weapons on Multipurpose Submarines Set to Grow — the Navy"), *RIA-Novosti*, August 23, 2009, *available from www.rian.ru/defense_safety/20090323/165742858.html*.

30. Mark Franchetti, "Russia's New Nuclear Challenge to Europe," *London Sunday Times*, August 17, 2008.

31. Vadim Smirnov, "Kalinigradskii Platsdarm," September 8, 2008.

32. *RIA-Novosti*, September 4, 2008.

33. Olga Tomashevskaya and Viktor Volodin, "Do Czhekhii I POlshi Letet Nedaleko," *Vremya Novostei*, August 7, 2008.

34. See, for example, Alexei Arbatov, "Deep Cuts and de-Alerting: A Russian Perspective," p. 321.

35. Vystuplenie Glavy Rossiiskoi Delegatsii A.I.Antonova na 3 Sessii Podgotovitelnogo Komiteta Konferentsii po Rassmotreni-yu Deistviya DNYaO (A Statement of the Head of the Russian Delegation A.I. Antonov to the 3rd Session of the Preparatory Committee of the NPT Review Conference), April 28, 2004, Document 927-28-04-2004, available from *www.mid.ru/Ns-dvbr.nsf/10aa 6ac6e80702fc432569ea003612f0/432569d800226387c3256e840046adc 4?OpenDocument.*

36. See Endnote 2.

37. "Prakticheskie Shagi Rossiiskoi Federatsii Oblasti Yader-nogo Razoruzheniya" ("Practical Actions of the Russian Federation in the Area of Nuclear Disarmament"), Report presented at the 7th NPT Review Conference, slide 13, available from *www. mid.ru/ns-dvbr.nsf/10aa6ac6e80702fc432569ea003612f0/526da088ef75 26e3c325700d002f81c7/$FILE/Presentation-Russian.pdf.*

38. "Rossiya Perevypolnila Plany po Sokrashcheniyu Yader-nogo Oruzhiya" ("Russia Has Overfulfilled the Plan for Reduction of Nuclear Weapons"), *RIA-Novosti*, June 22, 2005, *available from www.rian.ru/politics/20050622/40566772.html.*

39. To be sure, some analysts have pointed to statements from a few Russian officials that appear to argue that the weapons assigned to Ground Forces have not been eliminated. One prominent example is Colonel-General Vladimir Zaritski, commander of the Rocket and Artillery Forces, which are part of the Ground Forces (sometimes referred to as General Purpose Forces). In 2003, Zaritski declared that "the main delivery assets for the use of tactical nuclear weapons are in the hands of Rocket and Artillery Forces." (Oleg Falichev, "Bog Voyny v Zapas ne Ukhodit"

("The God of War Does Not Retire"), *Voenno-Promyshlennyi Kurier*, November 19-25, 2003. In subsequent publications, Zaritski did not mention tactical nuclear weapons (TNW) at all or alluded to some nuclear role for the Ground Forces in a general, nonspecific way without identifying missions or assets and referring to earlier late 1990s military manuals or doctrines. See Vladimir Zaritski, "O Razrabotke Novoi Metodiki Planirovania Ognevogo Porazheniya Protivnika v Operatsii i Bouyu" ("Toward Developing New Methods for Planning of Use of Firepower Against Adversary in an Operation and a Close Fighting"), *Voyennaya Mysl*, No. 12, 2006; "Napravleniya Sovershenstvovaniya Form i Sposobov Boevogo Primeneniya RViA v Obshchevoiskovoi Operatsii (Bouyu)" ("Ways to Enhance the Ways and Means of Combat Use of Rocket Forces and Artillery in an Operation (Close Combat) of General Purpose Forces") *Voyennaya Mysl* No. 11, 2006; V. Zaritski, L.Kharkevich, *Obshchaya,Taktika (Foundations of Tactics)*, Tambov, Rusia, 2007. Information supplied by the Chief of the 12th GUMO, the Defense Ministry agency directly responsible for handling of all nuclear weapons, should probably be regarded as more authoritative. The statements by Zaritski could also signify that nuclear weapons are still regarded by a significant sector of the Russian military as desirable both in terms of mission support and status. His attitude seems to be in line with the insistence of Russian Navy officials that they need nuclear weapons to support some of their missions. Although the value of Zaritski's assertion as direct evidence with regard to the status of sub-strategic weapons in Russia should probably be questioned, it certainly testifies to the "nuclear romanticism" of many Russian military leaders.

40. There is no good way to calculate the numbers—the 2,000 figure is most often cited by Western and Russian nongovernmental experts and is often privately confirmed by Russian officials. If, however, one takes as a baseline the number provided by Alexei Arbatov for 1991—21,700 (Alexei Arbatov, "Deep Cuts and de-Alerting: A Russian Perspective," in *The Nuclear Turning Point*, Washington, DC: The Brookings Institution Press, 1999, p. 320), then the 75 percent reduction officially announced by Russia would leave it with 5,400 warheads by 2004—a figure that should be lower as dismantlement continues.

41. Robert Norris and Hans Kristensen, "Nuclear Notebook," *Bulletin of the Atomic Scientists*, May/June 2009, *available from thebulletin.metapress.com/content/h304370t70137734/fulltext.pdf.*

42. The National Resource Defense Council (NRDC) has traditionally calculated both the overall number (2,050) and categories of Russian TNW by counting nuclear-capable delivery vehicles. Unlike strategic weapons, however, the relationship between delivery vehicles and warheads is far from direct where TNW are concerned—it is far from obvious that Russia keeps nuclear warheads for all nuclear-capable delivery vehicles (meaning that the stockpile number is lower than the number of delivery vehicles) or, alternatively, might have several warheads for each delivery vehicle.

43. It is ironic that confidential interviews collected in 1991-92 among U.S. officials attributed the rejection by George H. W. Bush of the Russian proposal to start negotiations on a legally binding and verifiable treaty on TNW to the U.S. Navy, which was reluctant to allow on-site inspections of ships and submarines to confirm the absence of nuclear warheads.

44. For details, see Nikolai Sokov, *Russian Strategic Modernization: Past and Future*, Lanham, MD: Rowman and Littlefield, 2000, chap. 1.

45. "Pochti Vse Puskovye Ustanovki RVSN Nakhodyatsya v Miutnoi Gotovnosti," *RIA-Novosti*, February 11, 2009.

46. "Vtoroi Polk Mobilnykh 'Topol-M' Zastupit na Dezhurstvo do Kontsa Goda," *RIA-Novosti*, November 18, 2009.

47. It is widely assumed that 30 Topol-Ms a year would be the cost-effective level of production—the lowest cost per unit—and has been regularly mentioned by leading figures of the Russian military-industrial complex.

48. "Rossiya ne Budet Narashchivat Proizvodstvo Raket v Ushshcherb Sotsialnym Programmam" ("Russia Will Not Increase Production of Missiles at the Expense of Social Programs"), *RIA-Novosti*, December 7, 2007.

49. "Pervyi Vitse-Premier Sergey Ivanov Zayavil o Neobkhodimosti Pariteta Yadernyih Sil Rossii i SShA" ("First Vice-Premier Sergey Ivanov Declared that Parity of Russian and U.S. Nuclear Forces is Needed"), *RIA-Novosti*, December 7, 2007.

50. For a recent statement to that effect, see, for example, a statement of the new SRF Commander Andrey Shvaichenko: "Udarnaya Gruppirovka RVSN Budet na 80 Protsentov Sostoyat iz Novykh Raket," *RIA-Novosti*, October 12, 2009.

51. "RF Sozdast Novuyu Tyazheluyu Ballisticheskuyu Raketu na Smeny Kompleksu 'Voyevoda'," *RIA-Novosti* December 16, 2009.

52. "Sredstva na RVSN Sostavlyayut Okolo Treti Finansirovaniya Yadernoi Triady," *RIA-Novosti*, December 8, 2009.

53. "Raketnye Kompleksy RVSN Sposobny Preodolevat Noveishuyu PRO SShA," *RIA-Novosti*, September 10, 2009.

54. Yuri Zaitsev, "Ot RSM-40 do 'Sinevy'," *RIA-Novosti*, March 11, 2009.

55. "Prichinoi Neudachnogo Puska 'Bulavy' Yavlyaetsya Konstruktorskaya Oshibka," *RIA-Novosti*, January 12, 2010.

56. Dmitri Litovkin, "'Bulavu' Ispytayut Osenyu," *Izvestia*, May 24, 2010.

57. 'Solomonov Obyasnil Neudachi 'Bulavy'," *Voeno-Promyshlennyi Kurier*, No. 9, 2010.

58. "Lvinaya Dolya Buydgeta MO Idet VMF, v Osnovnom Yadernym Silam—Ivanov," *RIA-Novosti*, June 3, 2009.

59. For an overview of the aspects of major military exercises relevant to the analysis of nuclear doctrine, see Nikolai Sokov, "Significant Military Maneuvers," Part V of *Issue Brief: Russia's Nuclear Doctrine*, August 2004, available from *www.nti.org/e_research/e3_55a.html*.

60. "Dalnaya Aviatsiya: Perspektivy Strategicheskikh Mashin," *RIA-Novosti*, December 23, 2009.

61. "Rossiya Perenapravit Rakety" ("Russia Will Retarget Missiles"), *Vzglyad*, February 19, 2007.

62. *RIA-Novosti*, July 24, 2008

63. *Ibid.*, May 27, 2008; Vadim Udmantsev, "Pautina Vokrug Granits," *VPK*, June 4-10, 2008.

64. Interview Iranskomu Gosteleradio i Informatsionnomu Agentstvu IRNA (An Interview with the Iranian TV, an Information Agency IRNA), October 16, 2007, Official Website of the President of the Russian Federation, available from *president.kremlin. ru/text/appear/2007/10/148471.shtml*.

65. For details, see Nikolai Sokov, "Moscow Rejects U.S. Written Proposals on Missile Defense, Downplays New Iranian Missile Test," *WMD Insights*, February 2008.

66. "PRO SShA v Nyneshnem Sostoyanii 'Ne Volnuet' Rossiiskikh Voennykh—Genstab," *RIA-Novosti*, April 12, 2010.

67. Vladimir Dvorkin, "Otlozhennyi Protivoraketnyi Krizis," *Nezavisimaya Gazeta,* April 20, 2010.

68. "Rossiya Skazhet 'Da' Predlozheniyu NATO po PRO, Esli Predlozhenie Seryoznie," *RIA-Novosti*, April 26, 2010.

69. "Rossiya i SShA Mogut Sozdat Sovmestnuyu PRO v Evrope Protiv Irana," *RIA-Novosti*, September 21, 2009.

70. Vladimir Dvorkin, "Otlozhennyi Protivoraketnyi Krizis," *Nezavisimaya Gazeta*, April 20, 2010.

71. Aleksei Arbatov, "Strategicheskii Surrealizm Somnitelnykh Kontseptsii," *Nezavisimoe Voennoe Obozrenie*, March 5, 2010.

72. Vladimir Ivanov, "Vashington Shagnul v Bezyadernyi Mir," *Nezavisimoe Voennoe Obozrenie*, April 16, 2010; Dmitri Ruyrikov, "...Plus Bystryi Globalnyi Udar," *Voennoe-Promyshlennyi Kurier*, No. 10, 2010.

73. The 1995 "Black Brunt" incident, when a single Norwegian research rocket triggered a false alarm in the Russian strategic command and control system, serves as a reminder that this concern is not pure imagination: as it turned out later, the rocket

closely fit one of first strike scenarios built into the early warning system. For details, see Nikolai Sokov, "Can Norway Trigger a Nuclear War? Notes on the Russian Command and Control System." PONARS Policy Memo No. 24, 1997.

74. Aleksandr Khramshikhin, "Strategicheskie Vooruzheniya ne Panatseya ot Ugrozy Voennogo Napadeniya dlya Rossii," *Voenno-Promyshlennyi Kurier*, No. 11, 2010.

75. The Iskander-E was developed with a range of 280 km to avoid the restrictions of the Missile Technology Control Regime (MTCR) — the multilateral arrangement that seeks to restrict exports of missiles able to carry a 500 km payload to a distance of 300 km or more. The letter "E" in the missile's name denotes the "export" variant. See Nikita Petrov, "Asimmetrichnyi Otvet" ("An Asymmetric Response"), *Strana.Ru*, February 16, 2007; Nikolai Poroskov, "Evropa pod Pritselom" ("Europe in Sights"), *Vremya Novostei*, February 16, 2007.

76. See the Address to the Federal Assembly by President of Russia Dmitri Medvedev on November 5, 2008, *available from president.kremlin.ru/text/appears/2008/11/208749.shtml*.

77. Vera Sitnina, "Voina Mozhet Vspykhnut Vnezapno," *Vremya Novostei*, September 29, 2008.

78. Viktor Myasnikov, "GLONASS Dlya Vsekh," *Nezavisimoe Voennoe Obozrenie*, June 4, 2010.

79. Artur Blinov, "Raketnyi Torg na Alyaske" ("A Missile Trade-off"), *Oborona i Bezopasnost*, August 30, 2006.

80. "Minoborony: Pri Neobkhodimosti Rossiya Mozhet Vyiti iz Dogovora po RSMD" ("Ministry of Defense: If Necessary, Russia Could Withdraw from the INF Treaty"), *RIA Novosti*, August 25, 2006; "Ekspert: Rossiya Mozhet Vyiti Iz Dogovora po RSMD v Odnostoronnem Poryadke" ("Expert: Russia Could Unilaterally Withdraw from the INF Treaty"), Interfax, August 25, 2006.

81. "Rossiya Mozhet Vyiti iz Dogovora po Raketam Srednei Dalnosti" ("Russia Could Withdraw from the Intermediate-Range Missiles Treaty"), *Strana.Ru*, February 15, 2007; Nikita Petrov, "Asimmetrichnyi Otvet" ("An Asymmetric Response"), *Strana.*

Ru, February 16, 2007; Nikolai Poroskov, "Evropa pod Pritselom" ("Europe in Sights"), *Vremya Novostei*, February 16, 2007; Viktor Myasnikov, "Asimmetrichnyi Otvet naiden" ("An Asymmetric Response Has Been Found"), *Nezavisimaya Gazeta*, February 16, 2007; Ilya Azar and Dmitri Vinogradov, "Otvet Srednimi Raketami" ("A Response with Medium Missiles"), *Gazeta.Ru*, February 15, 2007.

82. "SYaS Rossii: Narashchivanie Vozmozhnostei po Preodoleiyu Protivoraketnoi Oborony" ("Russia's Strategic Rocket Forces: Enhancing the Capability to Penetrate Missile Defenses"), *Voenno-Promyshlennyi Krier*, March 8-14, 2006.

CHAPTER 6

CAUGHT BETWEEN SCYLLA AND CHARYBDIS: THE RELATIONSHIP BETWEEN CONVENTIONAL AND NUCLEAR CAPABILITIES IN RUSSIAN MILITARY THOUGHT

Daniel Goure

INTRODUCTION

Russian security policies and military plans are undergoing the most profound set of changes of any period since the collapse of the Soviet Union. In some ways, this is the best of times for the Russian military. Moscow has the fortune of a government in Washington committed to "pushing the reset button" in U.S.-Russian relations. The Obama administration has made it clear that it intends to take Russian interests and opinions seriously in everything from the deployment of missile defenses to the imposing of new United Nations (UN) sanctions on Iran. A new Strategic Arms Reduction Treaty (START) agreement has been signed that allows Russia to make inevitable reductions in its strategic nuclear forces under the guise of the furtherance of strategic parity with the United States. If Russian sources are to be trusted, the U.S. Government committed to limiting its deployments of missile defenses in Europe. The pace of the North Atlantic Treaty Organization's (NATO) eastward expansion has been slowed, possibly halted for good. The Russian Navy's lease on the naval base at Sevastopol was extended for an additional 25 years. All in all, it has been a good year for the Russian military. It might be assumed that Russia has never been in a better position to develop a new security partnership with the West or to feel more secure in general.

Yet, this is the time when the Russian government has chosen to undertake an ambitious, even radical, transformation of its conventional and nuclear forces. The publication of both a new National Security Strategy (NSS) and Military Doctrine provides the policy foundation, albeit somewhat schizophrenic, which justifies, even demands, the creation of military capabilities commensurate with Russia's self-defined status as a major global power. Russian President Dmitry Medvedev has made a commitment to the military for more money and for an array of new weapons systems that is eye-watering in terms of its breadth and cost. Plans have been articulated by the chiefs of the major services intended to address the widely recognized problems of sclerotic command and control structures, obsolete personnel policies, and aging equipment.

The path before Russia's leaders may well be characterized as that between Scylla and Charybdis. As Homer's epic, *The Odyssey*, tells the tale, the challenge is to chart a course between two dangers. The problem is that moving away from one danger causes an increase in the threat posed by the other. In the view of Russian leaders, Moscow cannot be too accommodating and forthcoming, either politically or militarily, without risking the appearance of being too weak. A Russia that is weak will have its interests ignored or even undermined. At the same time, if Russia is too belligerent, it risks a confrontation with states incomparably stronger than it is, thereby revealing how truly weak it is.

The source of Russia's Homeric problem is its determination to assert a position in global affairs

262

completely out of proportion to its economic, political, technological, demographic, or military situation. Moreover, its principal adversary is the most powerful economic and military alliance in human history. Russia must do whatever it can to assert its position as an equal, recognizing that it lacks the means (with the exception, perhaps, of its nuclear arsenal) to enforce its claim of equality. As one observer described Russia's dilemma:

> The Russian Federation is certainly not in an enviable situation when it comes to foreign or security policy. Devoid of significant alliances, with an economic output comparable to that of France, and a standard of living that is far below that in Europe at large, it must find the means to secure a huge territory and overextended borders, end the violent conflicts in the Northern Caucasus, and maintain the strategic nuclear balance with the U.S. At the same time, the Russian leadership is laying claim to act as a hegemon in the post-Soviet space and as a great power on the international stage. The question is whether Russia has the economic, military, and political potential to resolve security issues successfully and to back up its international ambitions. The fundamental problem to be resolved by the country's foreign and security policy is the disparity between aspirations and resources. That dilemma is further aggravated by the international financial crisis and plummeting energy prices, which have hit the Russian economy hard.[1]

Professor Alexei Bogaturov of the Moscow Institute for International Security Studies described the problem as "Medvedev's dilemma." On the one hand, Russia would prefer not to return to a policy of confrontation; on the other hand, the Kremlin cannot just stand by and watch the United States and NATO pursue their policy of military superiority. The Russian solution, reflected in the new NSS, is to pursue a two track policy:

> . . . without interrupting the dialogue with the U.S. on strategic issues, try to concentrate resources in order to create the capacity for a political and diplomatic counterweight to NATO, while taking all necessary steps to prevent the possibility of the neutralization of Russia's ability to effectively confront even theoretically predicted attempts to dictate conditions under the threat of force.[2]

In order to understand the relationship between conventional and nuclear capabilities in Russian military thought, it is necessary to appreciate the extent of the dilemma Russian political and military leaders have created for themselves. The international environment is filled with malevolent forces intent on the diminution of Russia and the undermining of its national interests. These adversaries must be directly and aggressively countered, preferably with nonmilitary means. However, Russia cannot rely entirely on such means, particularly as its adversaries are intent on achieving overwhelming military superiority and undermining the strategic stability achieved through arms control agreements in the late 20th century. To be secure, Russia must develop a modern, largely nonnuclear military while retaining until the day that goal is achieved a nuclear capability that can deter both the conventional and nuclear might of its opponents.

The U.S. Director of National Intelligence observed that Russia continues to rely on its nuclear deterrent and retaliatory capability to counter the perceived threat from the United States and NATO. For the past several years, Moscow has also been strengthening its conventional military force to make it a credible foreign policy instrument, both to signal its political resurgence and to assert its dominance over neighboring states like Georgia. Moscow has actively engaged in foreign military cooperation with countries such as China and Venezuela, in part to remind the United States and others of Russia's global military relevance.[3] This tendency has been reflected in scenes not seen in some 2 decades: Russian subs off the U.S. coast, *Bear* bombers penetrating NATO airspace, and Russian warships repeating the old Soviet-era Caribbean cruise—this time to Venezuela.

Recent military demonstrations cannot hide the fact that Russia's conventional military stands on the precipice of irrelevance. Almost 2 decades of underfunding has resulted in obsolete equipment, inadequate maintenance, poor training, and low morale. In this same period, there has been a revolution in military capabilities centered on the exploitation of information technologies. The result has been an order-of-magnitude improvement in the lethality and operational effectiveness of conventional military forces. This is a revolution in which the Russian military has yet to participate. Whatever may be the Kremlin's ambitions for the Russian military of 2020 and beyond, the decline of the Russian defense industrial base means there is little chance of Russia being able to reach those objectives.

The likelihood that Russia can achieve its goal of a thoroughly modern conventional capability, one able to take on the West in a regional conflict by 2020 is fanciful at best. The Kremlin is left, therefore, with two strategic options. One is to seek to constrain Western and particularly U.S. military advances through pursuit of an aggressive arms control agenda. The other is to try and return to the past, focusing the U.S.-Russian relationship on nuclear issues. In order to do this, Russia must take the necessary steps to maintain and modernize its nuclear arsenals, both strategic and tactical. Unfortunately, on this path lies confrontation.

NEW SECURITY STRATEGY AND DOCTRINES

The publication of a new NSS and Military Doctrine set the stage for Russia's Homeric challenge. These documents set out a formidable set of security challenges confronting Russia. In particular, both documents identify as the most serious threat activities and behaviors by foreign nations and groupings—read NATO—to create a condition of political and military superiority over Russia. In essence, the course between Scylla and Charybdis is that between different modes of competition, not between competition and cooperation.

The new Russian NSS offers something for everyone. The list of potential dangers and challenges is long, broad, and extremely varied. But with respect to military threats, the focus of concern is not with irregular warfare or so-called rogue states, but rather the behavior of the United States and its allies. In particular, the NSS identifies the threat as that posed by the drive of some countries to achieve overwhelming military superiority, to create new types of weapons and the means to engage in new forms of warfare, and the impact on Russian security of attempts to overturn existing international agreements.

The threats of military security are: the policy of a number of leading foreign countries aimed at achieving overwhelming superiority in the military field,

266

especially in the strategic nuclear forces, through the development of high-precision, information and other high-tech means of warfare, strategic weapons in non-nuclear form, the formation of a unilateral global missile defense system and the militarization of Earth's space environment that could lead to a new arms race, as well as the spread of nuclear, chemical, biological technology, the production of weapons of mass destruction or their components and delivery systems.

The negative impact on the military security of the Russian Federation and its allies exacerbated by a departure from international agreements on arms limitation and reduction, as well as actions aimed at violating the stability of systems of government and military control, missile warning, space control, the functioning of strategic nuclear forces, storage sites, nuclear weapons, nuclear energy, nuclear and chemical industries, and other potentially dangerous objects.[4]

This formulation is repeated almost endlessly in Russian political-military documents and articles by security analysts. It reflects the basic reality that the Russian leadership sees its security very much as a function of the ability to neutralize an ever-present threat posed by the West. One example is a report in the *Guardian* on remarks by Russia's Minister of Defense, Anatoly Serdyukov:

Today, Russia's defense minister, Anatoly Serdyukov, said the world situation meant the "likelihood of armed conflicts and their potential danger for Russia" was rising. "The military-political situation is characterized by the U.S. leadership's desire … to expand its military presence and that of its allies in regions adjacent to Russia," he declared.

America was actively trying to steal energy and mineral resources in central Asia and other post-Soviet countries on Russia's borders, he complained, adding that the U.S. was "actively supporting processes aimed at ousting Russia from the area of its traditional interests."[5]

The existential nature of the threat means that it can only be countered by a condition not merely of military parity, but of absolute Western vulnerability.

> Moscow cannot conceive of its security in terms other than those of an adversarial relationship with the United States and NATO. That relationship is based on both global and regional deterrence and what Moscow calls strategic stability – where both sides are locked into the Cold War relationship of mutually assured destruction at the global and regional level. For Russia to be secure, not only must the United States not be able to defend itself against missile threats, neither can Europe, for then Russia cannot intimidate it by the threat of missile strikes. Russia still believes that the condition of its security is the insecurity of its neighbors and partners. Consequently, to secure itself, Russia must have the right to supervise the limits of Europe's defense activity, thereby revising the settlements of 1989-91.[6]

Much of the NSS focuses on the actions to reverse Russia's social, economic, and technological inferiority. Such steps are necessary certainly to improve the welfare of the Russian people. But they are vital also to the Kremlin's goal of establishing Russia as a great power and creating the conditions to support a transformation of the Russian military.

The new Russian Military Doctrine, signed on February 5, 2010, extends the vision of the threat contained in the NSS and brings it close to home. Although it acknowledges that the risk of large-scale conventional/nuclear war has declined, the overall external threat to Russian security has intensified. The list of external military dangers includes:

- The desire to endow the force potential of NATO with global functions carried out in violation of the norms of international law and to move the military infrastructure of NATO member countries closer to the borders of the Russian Federation, including by expanding the bloc;
- The attempts to destabilize the situation in individual states and regions and to undermine strategic stability;
- The deployment (buildup) of troop contingents of foreign states (groups of states) on the territories of states contiguous with the Russian Federation and its allies and also in adjacent waters;
- The creation and deployment of strategic missile defense systems undermining global stability and violating the established correlation of forces in the nuclear-missile sphere, and also the militarization of outer space and the deployment of strategic non-nuclear precision weapon systems;
- Territorial claims against the Russian Federation and its allies and interference in their internal affairs; and,
- The proliferation of weapons of mass destruction, missiles, and missile technologies, and the increase in the number of states possessing nuclear weapons.[7]

The Military Doctrine provides a vision of future conflicts that frankly differs little from writings produced by the Soviet military some 2 decades ago. Future conflicts will involve the massed use of weapons systems based on new physical principles that are comparable to nuclear weapons in effectiveness; the expanded use of air space and outer space; intensified information warfare; reduced warning time based on an adversary's preparation to conduct military operations; and, an increase in the responsiveness of command and control systems. The characteristic features of future military conflicts will be the employment of forces based on speed, maneuverability, and precision targeting. A wide variety of new technologies will be seen on these future battlefields beyond just precision-guided weapons including electromagnetic, laser, and infrasound weaponry; computer controlled systems; drones and autonomous maritime craft; and guided or robotic versions of manned platforms.[8]

There had been indications that the new Military Doctrine would expand further the role of Russian nuclear weapons in future conflicts. In an interview with *Izvestia*, Nikolay Patrushev, the secretary of the Russian Security Council, was quoted saying that in the Military Doctrine, "We have corrected the conditions for use of nuclear weapons to resist aggression with conventional forces not only in large-scale wars, but also in regional or even a local one." Moreover, he went on "There is also a multiple-options provision for use of nuclear weapons depending on the situation and intentions of the potential enemy. . . . In a situation critical for national security, we don't exclude a preventive nuclear strike at the aggressor."[9]

As published, the Military Doctrine does not extend the role of nuclear weapons into the area of local wars. However, given expressions of concern made earlier in that document regarding the potential for future conflicts to involve destabilizing command and control, nuclear weapons sites, and other critical government assets, the point at which a regional war would place the existence of the state at risk, thereby warranting a nuclear response, is ambiguous, at best.

Nuclear weapons will remain an important factor for preventing the outbreak of nuclear military conflicts and military conflicts involving the use of conventional means of attack (a large-scale war or regional war). In the event of the outbreak of a military conflict involving the utilization of conventional means of attack (a large-scale war or regional war) and imperiling the very existence of the state, the possession of nuclear weapons may lead to such a military conflict developing into a nuclear military conflict. The NSS and Military Doctrine put enormous pressure on the Russian military to achieve across-the-board improvements in organization, capabilities, operations, and personnel. It is not clear that the military and its supporting industrial base will be able to meet those challenges.

THE LIMITS OF RUSSIAN CONVENTIONAL FORCE RESTRUCTURING

Russian leaders have long recognized the need for comprehensive structural reforms of the military. Since the early 1990s, several attempts at reform have run afoul of a combination of institutional resistance, a lack of funds, the decline of the Russian defense industrial base, and recruitment and retention problems. The NSS and Military Doctrine both emphasize the importance of a transformation of the Russian military.

> The main task of national defense in the medium term is the transition to a qualitatively new look of the Armed Forces of the Russian Federation to the conservation potential of the strategic nuclear forces by improving the organizational and staff structure and system of territorial-based troops and forces, increasing the number of units of permanent readiness, as well as improve the operational and training, organization of interspecies interaction forces and forces.[10]

President Medvedev personally committed his administration to a complete overhaul of the Russian armed forces.

> A guaranteed nuclear deterrent system for various military and political circumstances must be provided by 2020. . . . We must ensure air superiority, precision strikes on land and sea targets, and the timely deployment of troops. We are planning to launch large-scale production of warships, primarily, nuclear submarines with cruise missiles and multi-purpose attack submarines. . . . We will also build an air and space defense network.[11]

The weakness of Russia's conventional forces has not been a secret to anyone. But the experiences of the Russian-Georgian conflict appear to have given the drive for reform a new impetus. The poor performance of Russian forces was an apparent shock to the Kremlin leadership. The conflict revealed a host of problems ranging from obsolescent equipment, an inability to operate during the night, archaic information systems, a lack of precision strike capabilities, communications failures, poor or nonexistent computer systems, inadequate command and control capabilities, bad training, inflexible or nonexistent logistics, and manpower problems.[12] Equally important, the Georgian experience undermined a mixed conscript-contract Army. As Western militaries had discovered decades earlier, a mixed force of professionals and conscripts was on balance extremely expensive while providing little of value.[13]

The central purpose of the military reforms is to improve the ability of Russia's armed forces to engage successfully in relatively small conflicts along that country's periphery. If these reforms are successful, Russia would be able to place lesser reliance on its nuclear forces except to deter large-scale conflicts.

> The publicly stated goal of the reform is to create a compact army of constant readiness, designed mainly to fight local and regional conflicts. At the same time, Russia will maintain its strategic nuclear forces as a safeguard in the event of a "big war." The country's nuclear capability should guarantee the possibility of inflicting unacceptable damage on any aggressor or coalition of aggressors.[14]

The design of what some are calling Russia's New Model Army was announced by Defense Minister Serdyukov on October 14, 2008. The main elements of the reform were to include the following:

- A cut in the total number of military personnel from 1,130,000 to one million, including a reduction in the total number of officers from 355,000 to just 150,000. The General Staff would be particularly affected, with 13,500 of its 22,000 personnel positions slated for elimination.
- Remaining officers and contract soldiers will see a significant pay increase over the next 4 years.

- Henceforth, all military units will be considered permanent readiness units and will be fully staffed with both officers and enlisted soldiers.
- The existing 140,000 noncommissioned officers (NCOs) will be replaced by 85,000 professional sergeants trained over the next 3 years.
- The four-tiered command structure will be replaced with a three-tiered structure, with the brigade serving as the basic unit.
- The disbandment of 23 divisions and 12 brigades, and the creation of 39 fully manned, combat ready all-arms brigades.
- The military's Main Intelligence Directorate (GRU) will be cut in size and subordinated directly to the civilian defense minister.
- The consolidation of military institutes and medical facilities.[15]

The to-be-formed combat brigades must be equipped with modernized or upgraded equipment. Shrinking the size of the ground forces will result in an excess of equipment. Unfortunately, virtually all of it is aging and even obsolete. Moreover, the Ground Forces lack the equipment and systems in such areas as logistics, intelligence, medical care, and engineering needed to support a proposed mobile, high-readiness force.

Restructuring of the ground forces is only one thread in a complex weave of actions that must be taken in order to create a modern Russian conventional military. Similar initiatives have been declared in the Air Force and Navy. Air Force Commander in Chief, Colonel General Alexander Zelin, announced a series of reforms in his Service including a new command structure, consolidated logistics, and modernized weapons. The number of commands and air bases was to be drastically reduced. Army aviation and air transportation assets were being integrated into the new structure.[16] The new Air Force structure appears to be designed to parallel the reforms in the Ground Forces so as to allow the creation of a truly joint capability.[17]

Organizational reforms will be meaningless unless the Air Force is able to overcome an almost 20-year procurement holiday. No less a figure than First Deputy Defense Minister Army-General Nikolai Makarov recently warned that the Russian Air Force was not procuring sufficient numbers of new modern aircraft and has fewer serviceable aircraft, manned by insufficiently combat-trained pilots, who are incapable of conducting modern-era combat operations.[18]

Former Chief of the Air Force General Anatoly Kornukov painted an even more dismal picture of conditions in the Air Force. According to him, Russia is lagging 25 to 30 years behind the United States in developing prospective air defense weapons because of a meltdown of its defense industries. General Kornukov complained that the nation's air defense capabilities were waning with the S-330 approaching retirement and only two batteries of the new S-400 deployed. In addition, air defense fighters were often grounded due to a lack of engines and spare parts. "Regrettably, our air defense forces only have a limited capability to protect the nation's security."[19]

Colonel General Zelin claims that a major program to upgrade the Air Force's platforms and systems was being undertaken. Central to these was the introduction of a so-called fifth-generation fighter, the TA-50, purchases of advanced fourth-generation aircraft such as the Su-34 and 35, S-400 and S-550 air and missile defense systems, and the KA-52 *Alligator*. In addition, the Air Force is reported to be receiving refurbished versions of older systems, such as the MiG-29s and 31s, and Su-27 and 30 fighter, Tu-22 bomber, and Il-76 transport. One report suggests that by 2020 the Air Force will have upgraded some 1,500 aircraft, while also introducing brand new platforms.[20]

The Russian Navy is facing the end of the projected service lives for virtually all of its deployed platforms. What scarce resources have been made available since the fall of the Soviet Union have gone largely to maintain the ballistic missile submarine (SSBN) Fleet. Even this portion of the Fleet is on shaky ground, with the *Delta*-class SSBNs fast becoming obsolete and the new *Boray* class just entering service. Even then, repeated test failures of the *Bulova* submarine launched ballistic missile (SLBM) raise concerns that one leg of the Russian strategic triad may be at risk. Elsewhere in the Fleet, the number of surface combatants and submarines continues to decline. There are programs to build new submersible nuclear ships (SSNs); submersible, guided missile, nuclear ships (SSGNs); long-range hunter-killer submarines (SSKs); frigates; and corvettes; but these are all progressing slowly. The most significant reform step the Navy took was to propose the creation of five or six carrier task groups built around a new aircraft carrier, the first of which will begin construction in 2012 or 2013.[21]

The sheer magnitude of reforms must give any reasonable observer pause. President Medvedev is reported to have ordered the upgrading of an average of 9-11 percent of the military's weapons and military equipment each year, resulting in an overall modernization level of approximately 70 percent by 2020. According to one Russian source, this means annual deliveries of 35 ballistic missiles, 50 new and 50 upgraded warplanes, 20 to 25 military helicopters, 3-4 sea-going and ocean-going warships, 2 nuclear-powered submarines and 1 diesel-powered submarine.[22]

The current plan requires the Air Force to receive 100 new or refurbished aircraft a year. But even with all of these programs, the overall number of aircraft would decline by nearly 50 percent. In 2008, however, the Air Force received five Su-24M2s, eight Su-27SMs, four Su-25SMs, a couple of upgraded MiG-31Ms, one new and one upgraded Tu-160 strategic bomber, and a single Su-34 fighter, for a total of only 21. The current plan requires the Air Force to receive 100 new or refurbished aircraft a year. But even with all of these programs, the overall number of aircraft would decline by nearly 50 percent.[23]

If anything, the Navy is in the worst condition of all the Services. According to the *Independent Military Review*, Russia's shipbuilding industry cannot sustain the overly ambitious plan proposed by the Ministry of Defense. The Russian shipbuilding industry is "incapable of producing warships in either the quantity or at the level of quality that their navy customer requires."[24] Perhaps reflecting this reality, in June 2009 the Ministry of Defense announced that the widely touted plan to build five or six carrier battle groups had been postponed.[25]

It is clear that Russian military leaders are intent not simply on streamlining their military and making its assets more deployable and employable, but of developing means for neutralizing what they perceive as the most significant threat to Russia's security: the advanced conventional military capabilities being deployed by the United States and, to a lesser extent, NATO and China. Russian defense experts recognize that they have little hope of matching the U.S.

military's conventional capabilities. Russia lacks the technological base or the financial resources for such an arms race. It is extremely unlikely that the Russian military will receive the quantities of new and upgraded platforms and systems it desires. But even if a miracle were to occur, the Russian military would still continue to fall behind the West (and China) which, as Russian threat statements underscore, are investing heavily in a wide range of military technologies including advanced command, control, and communications (C3); information warfare; unmanned systems; hypervelocity platforms; and directed energy weapons.

This led Russia to examine the possibility asymmetric responses. Then President Vladimir Putin described such an approach in 2006.

> We are to keep our eyes open on the plans and development trends of other countries' armed forces, and to know about their future developments. Quantity is not the end, however. . . . Our responses are to be based on intellectual superiority. They will be asymmetrical, and less costly.[26]

What form might such an asymmetric response take? One Russian author suggests that this would involve horizontal escalation against strategic targets in the enemy's territory.

> Combining defensive operations undertaken to beat off aggression and asymmetrical actions relying on the efficiency of modern high-precision conventionally equipped strategic weapons systems, supported by subversive and reconnaissance groups is a persuasive enough factor for the enemy to cease military operations on terms favorable for Russia. This conclusion has a practical significance and relevance in view of

the fact that the economy and infrastructure of any European country has a large number of objectives, some of them potentially dangerous, vital for the survival of its population and government.

Strategically important targets that, if destroyed, lead to unacceptable damage include the top government administration and military control systems; major manufacturing, fuel, and energy enterprises (steel and engineering plants, oil refineries, defense industry enterprises, electric power plants and sub-stations, oil and gas production, accumulation, and storage facilities, life support facilities, and so on); vitally important transportation facilities across the adversary's entire territory (railroad hubs, bridges, strategic ports, airports, tunnels, and so on); potentially dangerous objectives (hydroelectric power dams and hydroelectric power complexes, processing units of chemical plants, nuclear power facilities, storages of strong poisons, and so on).[27]

THE CONTINUING LURE OF NUCLEAR WEAPONS

Russian leadership's sense of their own vulnerability causes them to behave in a certain way on the international stage. Secular demographics and social and economic trends argue that Russia's sense of its own weakness, and hence of vulnerability, will only grow. Moscow is determined to take what little time and few available resources it has to try and leverage itself into a secure position as a co-equal of the world's great and rising powers.

As noted above, the NSS makes clear the Kremlin's view that the U.S. withdrawal from the Anti-Ballistic

279

Missile (ABM) Treaty and refusal to continue the bilateral process of strategic arms negotiations of its predecessors created a threat to the Russian Federation.
From this point, it is easy to conclude that what the
Russian leaders seek is a return to the bygone days of
mutual assured destruction and continuous repetitive
arms control. This relationship serves three functions.
First, it justifies the Kremlin's threat perceptions as
detailed in the NSS and Military Doctrines. Second,
it justifies a continuing reliance on nuclear weapons
in military strategy and obviates the need for reforms
of the scale and scope necessitated by an alternative
strategy. Finally, the very process of negotiations
serves to validate Russian claims of relevance and
status in the international system. As one eminent
analyst of both Soviet and Russian military thought
observed recently:

> The MAD-based U.S.-RF relationship organically pre-
> supposes continued tensions and the need for rigid
> controls over the nuclear weapons of both countries.
> Moscow is interested in maintaining the system of
> continuous strategic negotiations for many reasons.
> These negotiations are marked by the aura of unique-
> ness and unparalleled significance in international
> relations. They symbolize the equal status of the in-
> volved parties. Russians, like the Soviets before them,
> believe that the negotiations together with the accom-
> panying summitry create a powerful background for
> and define the tone of all other bilateral exchanges.
> They also see direct linkages between maintaining the
> bilateral strategic balance and the global security situ-
> ation, including Russia's relations with NATO, the fate
> of the Conventional Forces in Europe Treaty, the role
> of tactical nuclear weapons systems and anti-ballistic
> missile defenses in Europe and other regions, the fu-
> ture of nuclear nonproliferation and nuclear weapons
> testing.[28]

The threat environment fabricated by the Russian government may serve obvious domestic political needs. But it creates an important dilemma for Russia internationally. How can Moscow agree to the elimination of its nuclear weapons when they alone are the essential bulwark against those threats? Additionally, what would be the basis for Russia's claim for a high place and unique status in the world were they not to retain one of the world's largest arsenals of nuclear weapons?

The combination of domestic weakness and a sense of a continuing, even intensifying, external threat leads the Russian leadership to look for areas where they can shore up their situation. The truth is that Russia desperately needs nuclear weapons. It is a power on the international stage almost solely because it possesses nuclear weapons. The collapse of Russia's economy following the end of the Cold War, the parlous state of Russian conventional forces, and the sense of proliferating threats result, in the minds of the Kremlin oligarchs, in a logical argument for increased reliance on nuclear weapons. It is no wonder that under these conditions, Russian leaders in general, and certainly the military, would view nuclear weapons as being the one capability that guaranteed Russia's ability to deter aggression. Indeed, it appears as if strategic nuclear weapons are the only factor that contributes to Russia having any relevance in the evolving international system.

One Western political scientist with extensive experience in Moscow made the connection between the retention of nuclear weapons and Russian political and psychological needs explicit.

As the self-perceived isolated great power in a highly competitive global environment, Russia regards nuclear weapons as the mainstay of both its security posture and status among the major powers of the 21st century. Even though the likelihood of a war with its ex-Cold War adversaries—America, its European allies, and China—is extremely low, nuclear deterrence gives a measure of comfort to the Kremlin that Russia's vital interests will be respected under all circumstances by Washington and Beijing, whose military power and "combined national might," respectively, are now far greater than Russia's.[29]

We should not be confused by Russia's willingness to pursue strategic arms reductions and to sign a new arms limitation treaty with the United States. This is not a sign of a change in Moscow's views of international relations or of an acceptance of the need to move beyond relations based on "old style" measures of national power. The new START Treaty was a matter of absolute necessity for Russia. Absent the new agreement, Russia would have been forced to reduce its strategic nuclear forces unilaterally. In an era in which the two former adversaries no longer view each other as principal threats, why should this be a problem? But for the leaders of the Kremlin, it was imperative that they bring down U.S. strategic forces equally. Any other outcome would be a clear admission of Russian weakness.

Russia's nuclear strategy also does not help. Faced with a decaying conventional military and the perception of external threat, the Russian military doctrine focused on an expanded role for nuclear weapons. Nuclear weapons became the way not to lose a conventional conflict. As a senior U.S. defense official commented:

There are aspects to their nuclear doctrine, their military activities that we find very troubling. If you read recent Russian military doctrine they are going in the other direction, they are actually increasing their reliance on nuclear weapons, the role in nuclear weapons in their strategy.[30]

To make matters worse for Russia, the world is experiencing an ongoing revolution in the means of conventional warfare. As U.S. Secretary of Defense Robert Gates has pointed out in a number of recent speeches, the capabilities that underlie this revolution are proliferating. He has made repeated reference to the so-called anti-access/area denial capabilities being deployed by China, Iran, and even Hezbollah. In response to such dangers, the Secretary, as well as other military leaders and defense experts, advocate accelerating investments in revolutionary capabilities. In many instances, these are precisely the kinds of weapons platforms and systems identified as leading threats in the new Military Doctrine. One senior Russian military leader put the problem this way:

By 2030 . . . foreign countries, particularly the United States, will be able to deliver coordinated, high-precision strikes against any target on the whole territory of Russia.[31]

The Final Report of the Commission on the Strategic Posture of the United States noted that, "Ironically, our edge in conventional capabilities has induced the Russians, now feeling their conventional deficiencies, to increase their reliance on both tactical and strategic nuclear weapons."[32]

In a larger sense, nuclear weapons are an all-purpose instrument with which to address most of the military security challenges of the 21st century.[33] Russian political and military leaders and defense analysts, echoing arguments made by their predecessors in the 1980s, have repeatedly argued that the threat of conventional precision-strike weapons could be countered by the employment of theater nuclear weapons.[34] According to the NSS:

> In the interest of ensuring strategic stability and equitable multilateral cooperation in the international arena Russia during the implementation of this Strategy will make every effort at the least cost level to maintain parity with the United States in the field of strategic offensive weapons under the conditions of deployment of a global missile defense system and realization of the concept of global lightning strike using strategic delivery systems with nuclear and conventional warheads.[35]

ARMS CONTROL, MISSILE DEFENSES, AND STRATEGIC STABILITY

The recent reset in U.S.-Russian relations should not be taken as a sign that all the difficulties between these two countries are a thing of the past. In fact, in many ways recent events may create a false expectation on both sides that it will be easy to bridge remaining differences on matters of security. In fact, the opposite condition may be true.

Were Moscow able to achieve its desired ends with respect to conventional force modernization, there might be a reasonable chance that Russia and the United States could move along a common path towards a stable strategic relationship at very low numbers of nuclear weapons. Unfortunately, Russia and the United States are on divergent strategic paths that are likely to result in greater friction and a more difficult security dialogue in the future. Simply put, the U.S. position is that conventional means, including missile defenses, offers a means for maintaining deterrence and reassuring allies while relying less on nuclear weapons and, possibly, even dissuading some potential proliferators from pursuing a nuclear capability.

But it is precisely the U.S. advantage in advanced conventional weapons and defensive technologies, broadly defined, that poses the greatest near-term threat to the Kremlin's conception of its security needs. The focus on conventional forces reduces the salience of nuclear weapons, certainly as a means of deterrence but also as the political lodestone of great power status. The growing U.S. concern about China's military might is a reaction to that country's investments in advanced conventional capabilities, particularly so-called anti-access and area denial systems and not to the modernization of China's nuclear arsenal.

Some in the West have worried that if the promises held by the revolution in military affairs materialize, even incompletely, they may significantly lower the threshold of military intervention. This is exactly the outcome that Russia is worried about, for it believes that the new capabilities might open the way to a more aggressive interventionist policy of the United States and NATO that might well challenge Russia's interests in various regions and especially in areas close to the Russian borders.[36]

There is virtually no chance that Moscow can meet its objectives for reforming the Russian military by 2020. It will be a monumental challenge for the Kremlin simply to slow the pace of erosion of the Russian military. Technology limitations, industrial decay, re-source constraints, and personnel problems may well force the Russian leaders to seek security in a smaller but modernized nuclear posture.

Another issue that holds the potential to increasingly divide the two countries is that of missile defenses, particularly the proposed deployment of a limited missile defense system in Europe. The Obama administration has confirmed the view of its predecessor that missile defenses are a legitimate, even central, part of the deterrence and reassurance equation. Properly managed in a so-called phased, adaptive strategy, such defenses can provide deterrence of missile threats and reassurance to allies that might otherwise only be attainable by explicit nuclear guarantees.

The Russian government and leading strategic experts were highly critical of the U.S. proposal to deploy a limited ballistic missile defense system in Eastern Europe. A number of officials have gone so far as to warn that Moscow will take offensive counter-measures, some of which would increase the threat to Europe, in the event that the system went forward. On the day President Barack Obama was elected, President Medvedev warned that unless the plan to deploy the missiles in Europe was halted, Russia would deploy additional short-range ballistic and cruise missiles against Eastern Europe.[37]

While it was assumed that Russian opposition to missile defenses in Europe was a function of their deployment in the absence of a formal agreement as well as the nature of the defenses themselves (the original Third Site was an extension of the National Missile Defense system), this may not be the case. Russia has raised concerns about the deployment of a land-based version of the Aegis/Standard Missile system in Europe. Recently, Moscow even objected to the deployment of a U.S. Patriot battery to Poland.

Russia has a two-fold problem with the U.S. pursuit of effective theater defenses. The first is the impact defenses may have on their efforts to deploy superior theater capabilities, both conventional and nuclear. The second is their belief that theater defenses, particularly if "Internetted" and connected to space-based and other mobile sensors, will be a dandy platform for creation of a highly effective strategic defense capability. Such a defense, employed in conjunction with an advanced, precision conventional offense, could provide the basis for a disarming first-strike scenario.

Missile defenses, particularly those in Europe, appear to strike at the very heart of the Russian concept of strategic stability and Moscow's requirement to be able to hold Europe at risk regardless of the balance of forces between Russia and the United States. One analyst sought to answer the question why a defense of only 10 interceptors oriented towards the threat from Iran would so antagonize the Russian government.

> Close examination of Russian policy reveals that these defenses entrench the United States in Eastern Europe's military defense and foreclose Russia's hope of intimidating Central and Eastern Europe or of reestablishing its hegemony there and possibly even in the Commonwealth of Independent States (CIS). If missile defenses exist in Europe, Russian missile threats are greatly diminished, if not negated. Because empire and the creation of a fearsome domestic enemy justify and are the inextricable corollaries of internal autocracy, the end of empire allegedly entails Russia's irrevocable decline as a great power and – the crucial point – generates tremendous pressure for domestic reform.[38]

Russia needs either to build a conventional military commensurate with its sense of itself as a great power and reflecting its concern over the threat posed by the United States and NATO or to drag the focus of the U.S.-Russian strategic relationship back to its erstwhile preoccupation with nuclear weapons and a stable balance of terror. The former is unlikely to happen. The latter strategy is the source of Medvedev's Dilemma referenced above. Russia cannot take the bilateral strategic relationship back to the future without, at a minimum, undermining the Obama administration's goal of moving towards zero or, more problematic still, stimulating a new era of confrontation.

ENDNOTES - CHAPTER 6

1. Henning Schröder, "Russia's National Security Strategy to 2020," *Russian Analytical Digest*, June 18, 2009, p. 6.

2. Alexei Bogaturov, "Do you Want Open Systems? Build a Closed Bloc: Medvedev's Military-Strategic Dilemma," *Nezavisimaya Gazeta*, June 15, 2009.

3. Admiral Dennis Blair, *Annual Threat Assessment of the Intelligence Community for the Senate Select Committee on Intelligence*, Washington, DC: U.S. Congress, February 12, 2009, p. 27.

4. *The National Security of the Russian Federation until 2020* (NSS), Presidential Decree No. 537, Moscow, Russia, May 12, 2009.

5. Luke Harding, "Russia announces new arms race," *The Guardian*, March 17, 2009.

6. Dr. Stephen Blank, "Russia Challenges the Obama Administration," *Op-Ed*, Carlisle, PA: Strategic Studies Institute, U.S. Army War College, December 2008.

7. *Military Doctrine of the Russian Federation*, Moscow, Russia, February 5, 2010, p. 3.

8. *Ibid*, p. 6.

9. "Russia to broaden nuclear strike options," *RT*, October 14, 2009.

10. NSS.

11. President Dmitry Medvedev, cited in "Russia ready for Meaningful Military reform. Again. Really," available from *moscowsshadows.wordpress.com/2008/09/27*.

12. Roger McDermott, *Russia's Armed Forces: The Power of Illusion*, Russie.Nei.Visions No. 37, Brussels, Belgium: French Institute of International Relations, March 2009, pp. 16-18. Also see Roger McDermott, "Russia's 'Lessons' from the Georgia War: Impacts on Military Reform Plans," *CACI Analyst*, November 12, 2008.

13. Andrew Liaropoulos, "The Russian Defense Reform and its Limitations," *Caucasian Review of International Affairs*, Vol. 2, No. 1, Winter 2008, pp. 44-45.

14. "Military reform: Basic guidelines," *RIA Novosti*, February 24, 2010.

15. Dmitriy Gorenburg, "Russia's New Model Army: Radical Reform in the Russian Military," August 14, 2009, available from *russiamil.wordpress.com*.

16. Lieutenant Colonel Andrew Wallace, "Challenges to Russia's Air Force Reform," *The ISCIP Analyst*, Vol. 16, No. 12, April 22, 2010.

17. Roger McDermott, "Stall and Spin in Russian Air Force Reform," *Asia Times Online*, August 22, 2009.

18. David Eschel, "In Spite of Medvedev's Optimism, Russian Military is Facing Severe Crisis," Defense Update online, July 24, 2009, available from *defense-update.com/analysis/russian_military_crisis_240709.html*.

19. Vladimir Isachenkov, "Former Russian Air Force Chief says Air Defenses have Weakened,"Associated Press, May 13, 2010.

20. "The Future of the Russian Air Force: 10 Years On," *RIA Novosti*, available from *en.rian.ru/analysis/20100317/158228523.html*.

21. Milan Vego, "The Russian Navy Revitalized," *Armed Forces Journal*, April 2009.

22. "Russian Military Reform in a Time of Crisis," *RIA Novosti*, March 15, 2010.

23. Alexey Komarov, "Russian Air Force Expects 100 New Aircraft," *Aviation Week*, March 10, 2009.

24. Cited in Reuben F. Johnson, "Russian Navy Facing 'Irreversible Collapse'," *The Weekly Standard*, July 13, 2009.

25. Roger McDermott, "Naval Overhaul Slides off Russia's Agenda," *Asia Times* online, June 26, 2009.

26. V. V. Putin, "Address to the Federal Assembly of the Russian Federation," *Krasnaya Zvezda*, No. 89, May 11, 2006.

27. Colonel S. G. Chekinov and Lieutenant General S. A. Bogdanov, "Asymmetric Actions to Maintain Russia's Military Security," *Military Thought*, No. 1, 2010, p. 8.

28. Andrei Schoumekhin and Baker Spring, "Strategic Nuclear Arms Control for the Protect and Defend Strategy," *Backgrounder*, No. 2266, Washington, DC: The Heritage Foundation, May 4, 2009, pp. 7-8.

29. Dmitri Trenin,"Russian Perspectives on the Global Elimination of Nuclear Weapons," Barry Blechman, ed., *Russian and the United States*, Washington, DC: The Stimson Center, July, 2009, p. 1.

30. Under Secretary of Defense for Policy Michelle Flournoy, "Moscow's Nuclear Doctrine under Fire," *Financial Times*, March 18, 2010, p. 1.

31. Colonel General Alexander Zelin, Chief VVS, cited in *RIA Novosti*, August 11, 2009.

32. Commission on the U.S. Strategic Posture.

33. Stephen Blank, *Russia and Arms Control: Are There Opportunities for the Obama Administration?* Carlisle, PA: Strategic Studies Institute, U.S. Army War College, March 2009, p. xi.

34. Stephen Blank, "Undeterred: The Return of Nuclear War," *Georgetown Journal of International Affairs*, Vol. I, No. 2, Summer/Fall 2000, pp. 55-63.

35. NSS.

36. Pavel Podvig, *Revolution in Military Affairs: Challenge to Russia's Security*, Paper Presented at the VTT Energy Styx Seminar, Helsinki, Finland, September 4, 200.1

37. Stephen J. Blank, "Russia Challenges the Bush Administration," *Op-Ed*, Carlisle, PA: Strategic Studies Institute, U.S. Army War College, December 2008.

38. *Ibid*.

CHAPTER 7

RUSSIA AND NUCLEAR WEAPONS

Stephen J. Blank

Many U.S. analysts in and out of government maintain that nuclear weapons are increasingly irrelevant both politically and militarily. Allegedly at best, they can only deter other nuclear weapons, and in any case conventional capabilities are fast achieving a comparable capability, rendering the military-strategic utility of nuclear weapons increasingly dubious. A huge and growing literature speaks to the "senselessness" of nuclear weapons that are supposedly increasingly devoid of military utility and that they are becoming merely symbols of great power status.[1] Unfortunately, this largely U.S. and European view is not grounded in the "real world" about which these analysts sometimes speak disdainfully. Rather, it is often rooted in the wish to be rid of, delegitimize, or at least minimize the utility of nuclear weapons. Certainly the idea that nuclear weapons perform no discernibly useful military mission is rooted in theoretical exercises not, fortunately, empirical evidence. At the same time, much of this writing suffers from an excessive focus on U.S. policy and strategy and the corresponding neglect of other states' thinking and experience.

Analysis of Russia's nuclear agenda, not to mention nuclear issues in other nuclear powers or proliferators, suggests, as this author noted a decade ago, that even if numbers decline, the range of missions is increasing, as is the overall importance of nuclear weapons for Russia.[2] Moreover, close examination of Russian defense issues, both in their domestic and foreign policy context, suggests that very strong objective and subjective forces are driving Russia toward enhanced reliance upon nuclear weapons, even as their numbers decrease, for a host of critical (as seen by Moscow) political and military missions. These factors exist irrespective of numbers, because no Western analysis known to this author has calculated how many nuclear weapons that Russia actually needs or for what missions (a common failing as well among much writing on U.S. forces). Consequently, regardless of the numbers of nuclear weapons that Russia may have in 2020 or 2030, it is also unlikely that the new arms control treaty will lead Russia to embrace the idea of "global zero" despite many favorable statements by Russian leaders concerning this goal.[3] Indeed, the evidence to date suggests that Moscow will be reluctant to conisder any further reductions in nuclear forces without a sizable reduction in what it considers to be threats to Russian security. Those threats first comprise the U.S./the North Atlantic Treaty Organization (NATO) and China. Beyond that, they also comprise the new nuclear proliferators, and then possibly terrorism. Since the new Russian defense doctrine openly expects the advent of new nuclear powers, the advent of these proliferators, many of whom are concentrated in Russia's neighborhood, will provide added reasons for not reducing the number of nuclear weapons or at least Russia's reliance on them.[4]

This conclusion obviously contradicts the rather rosy expectations of many U.S. analysts that the great powers can safely and unilaterally reduce nuclear weapons without experiencing any adverse consequences. This conclusion might well cause dismay among advocates of global zero. But Russian writing, obviously not without its own shortcomings, remains centered on the real possibility of fighting wars from an inferior strategic position. For example, a recent Russian article describing the need for a fundamentally new universal armored vehicle states that:

> We must not neglect the preservation of the capabilities for the restoration of the combat capability during an exchange of nuclear strikes by the weapons and equipment (VVT) system. **After the employment of weapons of mass destruction, a troop grouping must rapidly take heart, rid itself of radioactive contamination, restore its combat capability, and continue to accomplish the combat missions. If that will not occur, the permissibility of the conduct of a preventive nuclear strike by Russia, which is declared in the new Military Doctrine, simply doesn't make sense.** The 1980s field regulations examined these variants of the developments of events. Today rehearsals of operations to restore combat capability after employment of nuclear weapons are actually not being conducted.[5] (emphasis by author)

Moreover, Russia has incorporated nuclear warfighting scenarios into its exercises in Europe as in Zapad-2009 and in Asia in the Vostok-2010 exercise. In an otherwise unremarkable 2008 interview, General Vladimir Boldyrev, then Commander in Chief of Russia's Ground Troops, described the missions of Russia's tank troops as follows:

> Tank troops are employed primarily on main axes to deliver powerful splitting attacks against the enemy to a great depth. Having great resistance to damage-producing elements of weapons of mass destruction, high firepower, and high mobility and maneuverability, they are capable of exploiting the results of nuclear and fire strikes to the fullest and achieving assigned objectives of a battle or operation in a short time.[6]

Indeed, from Boldyrev's remarks we may discern that he, and presumably his colleagues, fully expect both sides to use nuclear weapons as strike weapons in combat operations. The comments above concerning armored vehicles point in the same direction.[7]

At the same time, an analysis of Russia's current thinking about nuclear issues reveals ongoing and vigorous high-level debates about nuclear weapons. This debate is evidently linked to the domestic struggle for primacy between the factions around Prime Minister Vladimir Putin and President Dmitry Medvedev. In other words, one vital subjective factor that will drive future Russian thinking about nuclear weapons, policies, and strategy is the identity of the chief decision-maker, whatever his title. In a system devoid of checks and balances, any democratic control over the armed forces and where many military men, and maybe civilian elites, still harken for a military leadership like that of Stalin in World War II, the personality, outlook, and thinking of the leader is of much more critical importance than is the case in more structured and accountable polities.[8] This point is even more compelling when we realize that the structure of Russian politics means that this absence of democratic controls in defense policy generates a constant temptation to use military forces to solve political problems.

This debate concerning nuclear weapons is not only visible in the controversies surrounding the recent defense doctrine of February 2010, indeed, it precedes the publication of the doctrine.[9] It involves several questions revolving around nuclear weapons. First, it comprises the question of using nuclear weapons in a preventive or even preemptive mode in smaller or so-called local wars that have hitherto been purely conventional wars. The public debate began in earnest in October 2009 when Nikolai Patrushev, Secretary of Russia's Security Council, told an interviewer that the forthcoming defense doctrine will be amended to allow for the possibility of preventive and preemptive first strikes, including nuclear strikes, even in the context of a purely conventional local war and even at the lower level of operational-tactical, as opposed to strategic, strikes.[10] This triggered a major public debate over those questions that paralleled the private debate among Russia's leaders. Although ultimately the published doctrine omitted to say these things, the citation above about armored vehicles suggests that for many Patrushev's views are nevertheless reflected there.[11] In addition, the doctrine was accompanied by a classified publication on nuclear issues that left foreign observers in the dark about when Russia might or might not go nuclear and for what purposes and missions.

At the same time, a concurrent and related debate became public between Putin and Medvedev as to whether or not Russia needs to build more offensive nuclear weapons than it had originally planned in order to meet the alleged challenge posed by U.S. missile defenses in Eastern Europe. Even as Medvedev was hailing the progress being made in negotiating this treaty, saying that a final version was close at hand, Putin decided to show who was boss and to play to the hawks' gallery. On December 28, 2009, in Vladivostok, he said that:

> The problem is that our American partners are developing missile defenses, and we are not, . . . But the issues of missile defense and offensive weapons are closely interconnected....There could be a danger that having created an umbrella against offensive strike

systems, our partners may come to feel completely safe. After the balance is broken, they will do whatever they want and grow more aggressive. . . . In order to preserve a balance, while we aren't planning to build a missile defense of our own, as it's very expensive and its efficiency is not quite clear yet, we have to develop offensive strike systems.[12]

But at the March 5, 2010, expanded session of the Defense Ministry Collegium, Medvedev made it clear that Russia does not need to increase its offensive nuclear capability any further than was originally planned.[13] Thus the divisions between the two men on this issue are out in the open. But their resolution will take place in a tough context for innovative and nonbelligerent policymaking where strong trends for greater reliance on nuclear weapons, regardless of quantity, will exist.

In the domestic context, the recent admission that the effort to build a professional Army was a failure and that Russia is returning to conscription has profound objective consequences for overall defense policy.[14] Indeed, Russia is even radically cutting the number of contract positions in ways that do not affect (so it says) its combat capability.[15] As regards nuclear issues, this failure means that Russia had to forsake the dream of a professional highly educated and motivated Army capable of fighting a high-tech conventional, and most likely, local war. While there will undoubtedly be pockets of excellence, the ensuing Russian Army will probably be unable to fully optimize the use of high-tech systems and will be plagued by low morale, education, health levels, large-scale draft evasion, and corruption. This outcome suggests that Russia may well have to invoke nuclear forces in many cases to substitute for what would otherwise have been a much more robust high-tech conventional capability and deterrent.

Russian defense industry's concurrent failure to modernize to the point where it can satsify both the government and the armed forces' demands for serial production of reliable high-tech weapons and platforms and system integration capabilities reinforces this likely outcome, and suggests that Russia will only partially realize its plan of a comprehensive modernization of the armed forces by 2020. Here again, rather than modernize the armed forces by 10 percent a year to 2020 as previously planned, Medvedev is now demanding that 30 percent of the armed forces' weaponry be modernized by 2015, a sure sign of continuing failure.[16] What makes this outcome even more likely is the fact that, due to the impact of the current crisis on the backward and overly statist Russian economy, budgetary spending will be constrained at least through 2015 if not 2020.[17] Indeed, the recently approved State Armament Program from 2011-20 spends only 13 trillion rubles to rearm the armed forces, a figure that the Acting Defense Ministry Chief of Armaments, Lieutenant General Oleg Frolov, claims will only allow for modernization of the strategic nuclear forces, air, and air defense forces, leaving the Navy and Army under-financed.[18] Not surprisingly, the military demanded another 23 trillion rubles to modernize the Army through 2020 and to modernize all of the armed forces and their accompanying infrastructure.[19] This pressure already forced the Finance Ministry to make concessions to the miliary, for instance whereas defense spending stood at 2.6 percent of gross domestic product (GDP) in 2010, in 2011-12 it should increase to 2.9 percent of GDP and 3 percent in 2013, after which it will grow to 3.1 percent, leading to increased purchases of weapons and hardware.[20] But this did not appease the armed forces. Even within those constraints, we see rising defense spending as a percentage of the state budget and possibly the overall economy, i.e., signs of structural militarization. Moreover, we can also see rising pressure by the military on the budget. However, the government has gone even further down this road.

Earlier failures in the defense sector are now generating the tendencies toward militarization (albeit at a much lower level than in Soviet times) to compensate for these failures in Putin's Russia and the continuing crisis of the economy and defense sector. As a recent Russian article observed, from 2000-10 defense spending has gone from 141 billion rubles to 2,025 trillion rubles, without leading to an equivalent growth in deliveries as these figures were consumed by rising costs for modernizing old models and for new models as well as losses due to corruption.[21] Richard Weitz has summarized the trajectory of defense spending since 2007.

> In 2007 the Russian government approved a $240 billion rearmament program that will run through 2015. In February 2008 Russia's Ministry of Defense announced that it would further increase the military budget by about 20 percent, allocating approximately one trillion rubles (about $40 billion) to military spending in 2008. Following the August 2008 war in Georgia, the Russian government announced it would increase the defense budget yet again in order to replace the warplanes and other equipment lost in the conflict as well as to accelerate the acquisition of new weapons designed since the Soviet Union's dissolution. This year [2008] the Russian military will spend over $40 billion. The figure for 2009 should exceed $50 billion.[22]

Even though defense spending has been steadily rising and was projected before the economic crisis to rise still faster, the war in Georgia and the visible animosity to America has led the regime to embark on a return to quasi-Stalinist military planning. *Nezavisimaya Gazeta* reported that the Ministry of Defense has already begun working on a 10-year plan for arms procurement and re-equipment from 2011-20 that was to be sent to the Duma for approval in 2010. This program grows out of the failure of the current arms program from 2006-15 that was budgeted at 5 trillion rubles ($155 billion). Typically, that plan proved to be "ineffective and expensive, leading to delays in introducing new armaments."[23] Indeed, "Not a single one of the previous arms programs was fulfilled even at 20 percent of the planned level. Even the existing program, which came about during the years of oil-sale prosperity, is not being fulfilled."[24]

Yet despite this continuing record of failure, it has not only led to ever greater state control of that sector but to neo-Stalinist answers. Even in late 2008 when crisis was apparent, Moscow sought to accelerate the utterly failed 2006-15 plan and compress it to be completed by 2011 when the new plan, which certainly entails even more state control and thus guaranteed suboptimal outcomes, is to begin.[25] Thanks to the economic crisis, the unending inflation in the Russian defense industry and its inability to function in a market economy, the government first had to cut the 2009 defense budget by 15 percent and, despite its denials, cut procurement.[26] By July 2009, funding cuts were hampering the acquisition of manpower for the planned new permanent readiness units, construction of the *Yuri Dolgoruky* class of ballistic nuclear submarines (SSBNs), and funding for the development of foreign naval bases.[27] Yet the defense sector refused to accept this outcome as final.

Debates over defense spending clearly did not end in 2008 or even when they were originally supposed to end in 2009. Thus the Security Council was reportedly supposed to accept the national security strategy at its meeting on February 20, 2009.[28] But that meeting did not occur until March 24, suggesting further objections. Apparently one major reason for the postponement of the appearance of the security strategy was the continuing economic crisis. It clearly had worsened to the point where the overall economy shrunk by 10.1 percent from January-June 2009 and 8.5 percent for the year.[29] By all accounts, this forced the drafters and the Security Council, not to mention those who would have to approve the document, to assert the importance of economic factors as a part of security. Thus in his address to the Security Council on March 24, 2009, Medvedev explicitly said that economic security was a part of national security.[30]

Consequently, a major struggle has broken out within the defense and defense industrial sector over access to resources, and it clearly involves the effort to buy weapons abroad, which has touched off a major debate within these two communities on the virtues of being autarkic or of buying abroad. The two key issues for now are the amount of money to be spent on military modernization and whether or not to buy foreign weapons systems. Frolov and his allies clearly brought substantial pressure to bear upon the government, but they were operating in a climate based on the precedent of rising outlays for procurement. The government is currently operating under the 2006-15 program. It was supposed to cost 5 trillion rubles or $155 billion. The original program for 2011-20 that

Medvedev announced in May 2010 substantially increased that spending to 13 trillion rubles or $420 billion, more than doubling the preceding figure. But, as Frolov said, this would essentially deprive the Army and Navy of funding for procurement that would allow it to make up for a generation of neglect. Instead he advocated an increase of the program to 36 trillion rubles for the entire armed forces or $1.161 trillion over the 2011-20 decade. If this proposal was unacceptable, then at a minimum a program costing 28 trillion rubles or $920 billion would allow the Army to rearm.[31]

Although many Duma deputies, officials, and commentators, including Deputy Prime Minister Sergei Ivanov who formerly supervised defense industry, derided Frolov's demands as wishful thinking, he did in fact prevail. Vladimir Popovkin, Frolov's boss, told audiences at the Farnborough Show that the government would spend 20 trillion rubles or $620 billion more on procurement, less than Frolov asked for, but still a large increase. Under these revised figures, spending on research and development (R&D) and procurement will exceed $50 billion annually. Perhaps more importantly, total Russian defense spending may reach 4-5 percent of GDP, more than any other major power and a sign of creeping structural militarization. Neither can we doubt the high rate of defense spending in the annual budget.[32] Finance Minister Alexei Kudrin recently conceded that budgetary outlays on national defense would rise in 2010 by 13.3 percent, while spending on national security and law enforcement would go up by 8.8 percent. The overall rise in those sectors through 2013 will be 22.1 percent. Since spending on health care, culture, cinematography, and education are also going up by hefty amounts, general state expenditures will supposedly fall by 4.5 percent, allegedly through attrition of bureaucrats by 20 percent through 2013, reducing the rise of administrative costs, and the privatizations mentioned above.[33]

In addition, "Popovkin announced plans to spend this windfall to procure a thousand new helicopters in ten years including heavy Mi-26 helicopters that can carry 25 tons of cargo or more than 100 passengers for short distances."[34] The need for such weapons is quite visible in the North Caucasus, which is on fire. Likewise, Russia will also procure 20 new heavy AN-124 *Ruslan* transport aircraft and 60 new T-50 "fifth generation" stealth jet fighters starting in 2013. Meanwhile, Russia is already deploying new RS-24 intercontinental ballistic missiles (ICBMs).[35] Thus by 2013, Russian defense spending will be 2 trillion rubles more than it is today and rise by 60 percent relative to 2010 figures. These sums will go largely to nuclear, naval, and air forces.[36] Indeed, the budget through 2013 raises procurement by 50 percent above the earlier figures.[37] However, if one takes into account the costs of actually procuring these airplanes, ships, etc., in reality rather little can be built (and costs will rise and inefficiencies, absent reform, will continue to add to these increased costs) and ultimately the deployment of hundreds of airplanes and dozens of ships by 2015 and 2020 is quite unlikely to materialize.[38]

Obviously, lucrative and productive investment will be squeezed in the coming budgets as is already the case. It is most likely that without significant governmental reform these increased outlays will be inefficiently and ineffectively spent and will ultimately increase inflationary pressures. While these procurements plans were stimulated by real threats in the North Caucasus and to the alleged threat presented by

NATO/U.S. and Chinese air and other strike capabilities in terms of both air defense and nuclear systems; they certainly add considerably to the burden on the Russian economy. If the new treaty fails to achieve ratification, as appears quite possible, Russia may decide it needs to undergo even more nuclear and conventional buildups from this level.

Even taking rising defense budgets into account, the inefficiency of much of that spending, the inherent inflationary pressures in the Russian economy, especially in the raw materials sector, the ineptitude of the defense industrial sector, and its vulnerability to the theft of 30-40 percent of the defense budget, which has not decreased despite a vigorous anti-corruption campaign, suggests a corresponding and ongoing structural inability to realize the goals indicated in the plans for modernizing the Russian armed forces by 2015 or by 2020.[39] Moreover, given the constraints on the budget even under increased defense spending, Russia will probably not be able to afford the necessary outlays for this comprehensive technological modernization of the armed forces and will have to utilize nuclear capabilities more than others do. Those capabilities are also under pressure as the Bulava's sorry experience indicates (the Bulava is Russia's new submarine launched ballistic missile [SLBM] and, as of April 2010, it has failed during all of its first 12 tests). So we may likely see Russia assigning to its nuclear forces a broader range of missions than might otherwise be performed by conventional forces.[40]

THE NATIONAL SECURITY CONTEXT

Beyond domestic factors that generate considerable pressure to continue relying on a possibly smaller, albeit somewhat improved nuclear deterrent, the imperatives of both external trends and overall Russian national security policy also strongly incline toward enhanced reliance on nuclear weapons. The three external trends are: U.S. missile defenses initiatives; the rise of China; and, at least in some quarters, an increased concern about missile and nuclear proliferation, a phenomenon that Russia actually expects to increase by 2020 if its new defense doctrine is a reliable guide.[41] But these phenomena are perceived and mediated through a unique cognitive and ideological landscape that underlies and drives Russian national security policy.[42]

Bluntly stated, Moscow approaches its security from the belief that while major war is not likely, smaller wars fought over access to resources, especially energy, around its border are increasing in likelihood. Worse, these wars are approaching Russia's borders. Furthermore, these wars can easily grow into major conflagrations where the use of nuclear weapons could well be contemplated or even implemented.[43] The aforementioned exercises in 2009-10 reflected such possibilities. Indeed, Russian elites believe that if Russia lacked nuclear weapons, NATO would then feel emboldened to intervene in some variant of a Kosovo-like scenario in those conflicts, for example, Georgia in 2008.[44] In other words, it is the possession of nuclear weapons alone that gives Russia the means to declare the Commonweath of Independent States (CIS) off limits to foreign powers, maintain psychological and political equality with the United States, assert Russia's identity as a great power, and most crucially back up that claim with a real force. Russia's nuclear capability ensures Russia's strategic independence as an international actor, but even more to the point, its identity as a truly soveriegn state, i.e., one that makes policy strictly on the basis of its own calculation of national interest, not the actions of other states.

Furthermore, official documents like the new defense doctrine and the 2009 national security concept explictly state that the incidence of major power reliance on force and the bypassing of the United Nations (UN) is rising, making the outbreak of wars more rather than less likely.[45] Thus Defense Minister Anatoly Serdyukov told the Defense Collegium in 2009 that:

> The military-political situation has been characterized by the U.S. leadership's striving to achieve global leadership and by an expansion and buildup of military presence of the United States and its NATO allies in regions contiguous with Russia. The American side's aspirations were directed toward gaining access to raw-material, energy, and other resources of CIS countries. Processes aimed at crowding Russia [out] from the area of its traditional interests were actively supported. International terrorism, religious extremism, and the illegal arms trade seriously influenced the military-political situation. They have been manifested more and more often in countries bordering on Russia. Georgia's attack on South Ossetia was a direct threat to RF national interests and military security. This attempt to settle the conflict by force was aimed first and foremost at destabilizing the situation in the Caucasus. **On the whole the analysis of the military-political situation permits a conclusion about the growing likelihood of armed conflicts and their potential danger to our state** [Author's Emphasis].[46]

Not only did Serdyukov accept this General Staff threat assessment, he intensified it by saying that the likelihood of threats to Russia in the form of wars and military conflicts is increasing. Yet, when he spoke, the share of modern armaments in the armed forces only made up 10 percent of their arsenal. At that time, 2008, only 19 percent of defense spending was earmarked for re-equipping the Army and Navy with that being a third priority behind organizational reform and maintenance of the nuclear forces.[47] So the priority of the nuclear deterrent while Russia undergoes modernization is already evident from here. Neither has that priority changed since 2008 despite the current financial crisis or the increase in nuclear spending discussed above.

Beyond the presupposition of actual military-political conflict with the West and China (the latter being the threat that we dare not speak of), a constant factor in the relationship with the West irrespective of its political temperature at any time is the fact that the nuclear forces of both sides remain frozen in a posture of mutual deterrence that implies a prior adversarial relationship that could easily deteriorate further under any and all circumstances and devolve into that kind of shooting war.[48] This point is critical: The problematic nature of the bilateral relationship, just as was the case during the Cold War—albeit less intensely today—is not due to deterrence. Rather, deterrence is a manifestation of a prior, underlying, comprehensive, and fundamental political antagonism in which Russia has settled upon deterrence as a policy and strategy because that strategy expresses its foundational presupposition of conflict with America and NATO.[49]

The fundamental basis of the rivalry with Washington is political and stems from the nature of the

Russian political system which cannot survive in its present structure without that presupposition of conflict and enemies, and a revisionist demand for equality with the United States so that it is tied down by Russian concerns and interests. From Russia's standpoint, the only way it can have security vis-à-vis the United States and Europe given that presupposition of conflict is if America is shackled to a continuation of the mutual hostage relationship based on mutual deterrence that characterized the Cold War, so that it cannot act unilaterally. At the same time, Europe must be intimidated by the specter of Russian military power which, given present realities, means nuclear weapons. To the degree that both sides are shackled to this mutual hostage relationship, Russia gains a measure of restraint or even of control over U.S. policy. For, as Patrick Morgan has observed, this kind of classic deterrence "cuts through the complexities of needing to have a full understanding of or dialogue with the other side." Instead it enables a state, in this case Russia, to "simplify by *dictating*, the opponent's preferences" [Italics in the original].[50] Thanks to such a mutual hostage relationship, Russian leaders see all other states who wish to attack them or even to exploit internal crises like Chechnya as being deterred. Therefore, nuclear weapons remain a critical component of strategic stability and, as less openly stated, for giving Russia room to act freely in world affairs.[51]

Indeed, Moscow sees its nuclear arsenal as a kind of all-purpose deterrent that has deterred the United States and NATO from intervening in such conflicts as the Chechen wars and Georgia. Nevertheless, its military and political leaders, e.g., Serdyukov, the doctrine which is now official policy, and Colonel-General Nikolai Solovtsov, Commander in Chief of the Strategic Missile (Rocket) Forces in 2008 all charge that threats to Russia are multiplying. Thus Solovtsov argued that:

> Some potential threats to the defense and security of the Russian Federation, including large-scale ones, remain, and in some sectors are intensifying. Moreover, the possibility cannot be ruled out that major armed conflict could arise near Russia's borders, which will affect its security interests, or that there could be a direct military threat to our country's security. This is graphically illustrated by the military aggression unleashed by Georgia overnight from 7 to 8 August against South Ossetia.[52]

While such statements represent the fantasy world of the Russian military where threats are always rising despite the plain evidence of Western demilitarization — and they also omit to mention that Georgia neither attacked Russia nor in fact started the war that was clearly a Russian provocation — his remarks do amply underscore the importance of deterrence and the permanent sense of being threat that drives Russian policy. Hence, the need for deterrence, primarily though not exclusively of the United States, at the price of accepting that Russia too, is deterred from a nuclear strike on the United States (or Europe or China).

In return for accepting that it too is similarly deterred, Russia postulates as one of the fundamental corollaries of its policy and strategy that it must retain a capability to intimidate and destroy Europe with its nuclear and other missiles. This is why the Russians have such reliance upon tactical nuclear weapons (TNW) no matter the cost. Thus while Germany, Poland, and Norway have called on the United States to remove its TNW from Europe, Russian military leaders like Lieutenant General Yevgeny Bushinsky, former head of the Defense Ministry's International Legal Department, argue that Russia should only enter into negotiations on TNW in case of parity in conventional armaments between Russia and the United States, i.e., never.[53] This is because TNW are Moscow's deterrent in a situation of conventional inferiority like the present.[54] Worse yet, the Navy plans to introduce new TNW in the form of nuclear cruise missiles on its submarines.[55] In any case, as Swedish Foreign Minister Carl Bildt has stated regarding Russian threats in the Baltic: "According to the information to which we have access, there are already tactical nuclear weapons in the Kaliningrad area. They are located both at and in the vicinity of units belonging to the Russian fleet,"[56] This means that Russia has effectively violated the Bush-Yeltsin Presidential Nuclear Initiatives of 1991-92, which barred TNW from naval vessels. Finally, Chief of Staff General Nikolai Makarov has publicly stated that Russia will retain its TNW as long as Europe is "packed with armaments" as a guarantee of Russian security and that priority of funding will be directed to Russia's nuclear arsenal.[57]

In other words, believing *a priori* that Europe is the site of a presumptive enemy action against it, Russia demands as a condition of its security that the rest of Europe be insecure. Russia's defense doctrine openly says that the United States and NATO represent the main threats to Russian security and that Washington will continue to seek military supremacy and disregard international law for a generation.[58] Furthermore, unlike the United States, Russia is engaged in a comprehensive modernization and renewal of all of its nuclear weapons, clearly in the belief that it needs to deter America by military means, and maybe even to

311

fight using such weapons. Consequently, there will be enormous opposition to any plans for further reductions or curtailment of this modernization program.

Likewise, Moscow has consistently said that the deployment of U.S. missile defenses in Europe and Asia will disrupt existing balances of strategic forces and undermine global and regional stability.[59] Moscow also tried hard to link the new treaty to the removal or missile defenses from Central and Eastern Europe.[60] In addition, Russia's leaders openly contend that one cannot discuss European security without taking into account the missile defense issue or the Conventional Forces in Europe (CFE) Treaty.[61] Certainly, Russian officials see the weaponization of space, the integration of space and terrestrial capabilities, missile defenses, the Reliable Replacement Weapons (RRW), and the U.S. global strike strategy as a part of a systematic, comprehensive strategy to threaten Russia. As Pavel Podvig has observed:

> One of the consequences of this [U.S. military strategy] is that if the promises held by the revolution in military affairs materialize, even incompletely, they may significantly lower the threshold of military intervention. And this is exactly the outcome that Russia is worried about, for it believes that the new capabilities might open the way to a more aggressive interventionist policy of the United States and NATO that may well challenge Russia's interests in various regions and especially in areas close to the Russian borders.[62]

So in response, Moscow must threaten Europe. Indeed, Foreign Minister Sergei Lavrov repeatedly has invoked the now habitual, but no less mendacious, charge that missile defenses in Europe, systems that allegedly used to be regulated by bilateral agreements

312

to maintain parity are now being introduced close to Russia's borders, thereby rupturing that parity in Europe and elsewhere.[63] During his 2008 trip to Poland, Lavrov went even further, saying that,

> For many decades, the basis for strategic stability and security in the world was parity between Russia and the United States in the sphere of strategic offensive and defensive arms. However, in recent years, the U.S. Administration chose a course towards upsetting that parity and gaining a unilateral advantage in the strategic domain. Essentially it's not just about global missile defense. We also note that the U.S. has been reluctant to stay within the treaties on strategic offensive arms, and that it is pursuing the Prompt Global Strike concept, and developing projects to deploy strike weapons in outer space. This, understandably, will not reinforce the security of Europe or of Poland itself.[64]

Lavrov then went on to say that, under the circumstances, if Poland chose a "special allied relationship" with Washington, then it would have to bear the responsibilities and risks involved, and that Moscow, in principle, opposed having its relations with third parties being a function of Russian-American disputes.[65] Thus Russia's arms control posture also represents its continuing demand for substantive, if not quantitative, parity, as well as for deterrence with the United States in order to prevent Washington from breaking free of the Russian embrace and following policies that Russia deems antithetical to its self interests.[66] Moreover, that parity is calculated not just globally, but in regional balances as well, so that Russia also demands a qualitative or substantive parity with America at various regional levels, most prominently Europe. Russia's demand for restoring parity at both the global and regional levels entails not an unreachable numerical parity, but rather a strategic stability or equilibrium where both sides remain mutually hostage to each other in a deterrent relationship and where the United States cannot break free to pursue its global or regional interests unilaterally.

Several practical strategic consequences flow from this posture. First, under all circumstances, Russia must retain the capability to intimidate Europe with nuclear weapons and hold it hostage to that threat. Therefore, the elite unanimously believes or professes to believe that any U.S. missile defense is a threat, because it presages a network covering Europe that will negate Russia's ability to threaten Europe and counter its first-strike capability, even though Lavrov admitted that the present stage of missile defense developments do not threaten Russia.[67] This is particularly true as the Obama administration's plans envisage extending the adapted phased construction of missile defenses throughout Europe until 2020. [68] The unanimity of the Russian elite puts the new treaty into jeopardy even before it is ratified, because Russian statements about missile defenses mean that if Russia should decide that U.S. missile defense programs exceed Russia's definition of strategic stability within the treaty's limits, and therefore threaten Russia's strategic deterrence forces, then Russia can withdraw unilaterally from the treaty.[69] Thus key members of the Duma, like Speaker Boris Gryzlov, threatened to block ratification if this legally binding linkage is omitted.[70]

Russian demands also relate to the fact that according to former Secretary of State George Shultz and former Secretary of Defense William Perry, the Russians that they have talked with still believe their country is encircled (their word) by hostile or potentially hostile forces in both the east and west. Therefore, they are very loath to any further reduction of nuclear missiles. Indeed, many of them still express the idea of repealing the Intermediate Range Nuclear Forces (INF) Treaty and building INFs and intermediate range ballistic missiles (IRBMs) to counter this threat.[71] As if on cue, Lavrov immediately afterwards called for, as have previous supporters of repeal of the INF treaty, a universal treaty banning intermediate and short-range missiles, a propaganda point if there ever was one, but one aimed also at China, not just the West.[72]

Consequently, Russian demands for nuclear weapons also relate to the fact that Moscow cannot conceive of defending itself against the threats it perceives, mainly from NATO, but also from China, without continuing to build, renew, and modernize nuclear weapons. Its capacity for doing so is visibly open to debate, a fact that creates many dilemmas for Russia's strategic leadership. Certainly its continuing program to build new nuclear missiles and usable nuclear weapons like low-yield and fusion weapons and the RS-24 (Yars) missile shows what it thinks of President Obama's quest for a global zero for nuclear weapons, as does the new doctrine's expectation that there will be more nuclear powers by 2020.[73] Therefore, it regards any U.S. missile defense, whether in Europe or Asia, as being a constant threat to its strategic stability and vital interests.

Second, Russia's military is clearly unwilling to accept the notion of that there is no linkage between offensive and defensive weapons. It claims that the United States reshaped its missile defense posture in Europe in September 2009, "because, according to our clear assessment, this area would definitely create risks for Russia."[74] But since then, this Russian demand to curtail even the new adaptive phased Obama program for missile defenses became the principal obstacle to the successful conclusion of the treaty.[75] It has also become a matter of public controversy within Russian politics. Putin's aforementioned remarks from December 2009 underscore that point.[76] Putin's demands relate both to the domestic power struggle in Russia and the Russian hawks' demand that they be free to build nuclear weapons without constraint. Thus it appeared that Russia's hawks were willing to obstruct the treaty to gain total freedom of action to build offensive weapons against a nonexistent threat.[77] Putin, Defense Minister Serdyukov, and the General Staff all argued for slowing down negotiations to insist on linking offenses to defenses and to maintain the primacy of Putin's line on these issues over Medvedev's apparently less confrontational approach. They did so regardless of the fact that doing so placed chances for U.S. Senate ratification at greater risk.[78]

Indeed, during the final stage of negotiations, Russia demanded that the treaty include a joint statement signed by both sides stating Russia had the right to terminate the treaty should it deem U.S. missile defense programs to be dangerous.[79] This, too, would have doomed the treaty in the U.S. Senate. Russia has also stated in the treaty-related documents its right to unilaterally withdraw from the new agreement if it believes U.S. missile defense deployments upset "strategic stability."[80] Even though this is in no way legally binding, in reply to this revelation:

In a not-yet-released letter obtained exclusively by *The Cable,* Arizona Sens. Jon Kyl and John McCain, and Connecticut Sen. Joseph Lieberman, warn National

Security Advisor James L. Jones, 'Even as a unilateral declaration, a provision like this would put pressure on the United States to limit its systems or their deployment because of Russian threats of withdrawal from the treaty.'[81]

Therefore even a unilateral Russian statement of expressing these views could become grounds for increased Senatorial opposition to the treaty, if not a failure to ratify, as increasingly seems possible. Should the treaty fail to be ratified, that would only further justify the arguments made by Russian hawks. Since the U.S. Government has just stated that it will complete the construction of a pan-European missile defense by 2018, Russia could easily execute its threat to withdraw from the treaty on those grounds.[82]

Nevertheless, despite the risks to the reset policy, the Russian military remains unappeased on this issue. Russian Chief of Staff General Nikolai Makarov warned that:

The factor of parity should be accompanied by the factor of stability, if the U.S. missile defense begins to evolve; it will be aimed primarily at destroying our nuclear missile capabilities. And then the balance of force will be tipped in favor of the United States. . . . With the existing and maintained parity of strategic offensive means, the global missile defense being created by the U.S. will be able to have some impact on the deterrence capabilities of the Russian strategic nuclear force already in the medium term. . . . This may upset the strategic balance of force and lower the threshold for the use of nuclear weapons. Although missile defense is a defensive system, its development will basically boost [the] arms race.[83]

317

Neither is this just rhetoric. As one recent assessment of the obstacles encountered during the negotiations charged, Washington told Moscow that if it did not move forward on the treaty, the administration might take Russia off its priority list and move the issue from the President to some lower level official. Whether or not this conversation occurred, it was described as an ultimatum. This article also points out that current Russian nuclear programs aim to overcome or even neutralize U.S. missile defenses.[84]

The impression is that the Kremlin no longer believes in America's military omnipotence. Russia responded to the ultimatum with a maiden flight of its latest T-50 fighter and the rearmament of its antiaircraft defense system with T-400 Triumph complexes (this may be referring to what we call the S-400 SAM). To all appearances, Triumphs are anti-satellite missiles (ASAT) that are also capable of intercepting and destroying inbound ballistic warheads. Continuation of Bulava missile tests was announced as well. Work on the missile will be brought to its logical end, sooner or later. Specialists are even working on a concept of the future strategic bombers that will replace TU-95s and Tu-160s one day.[85]

When it had to back off from this point due to President Obama's steadfastness in regard to missile defenses, Moscow then demanded that the United States pledge to not do anything unilaterally, evaluate threats jointly with Russia based on corresponding reports from experts of both countries within the framework of the joint threats evaluation mechanism, and make decisions concerning the deployment of theater and eventually global missile defenses against ICBMs exclusively on that basis. Moscow also wants Washington to confirm that it will discuss missile defenses once this treaty is ratified.[86] Therefore, Russia still seeks a veto on U.S. force decisions. When seen in the context of Russian politics and overall defense policy, this is a most instructive episode.

Third, since Moscow rigorously adheres to this mutual hostage concept, it cannot trust the United States, and any U.S. unilateral advance in defenses must be compensated by greater Russian offensive capabilities. The following citations demonstrate this deep-rooted belief in the mutual hostage relationship, deterrence of the enemy, and the action-reaction process regarding armaments among the Russian political and military leadership. First, Lavrov told an interviewer in February 2007 that:

> Our main criterion is ensuring the Russian Federation's security and maintaining strategic stability as much as possible. We have started such consultations [on strategic nuclear weapons] already. I am convinced that we need a substantive discussion on how those lethal weapons could be curbed on the basis of mutual trust and balance of forces and interests. We will insist particularly on this approach. We do not need just the talk that we are no longer enemies and therefore we should not have restrictions for each other. This is not the right approach. It is fraught with an arms race, in fact, because, it is very unlikely that either of us will be ready to lag behind a lot.[87]

Here Lavrov signaled Russia's unwillingness to leave a mutually adversarial relationship with America and its presupposition of mutual hostility as reflected in both sides' nuclear deployments. Similarly, Alexei Arbatov ridiculed the Bush Administration's view, stated by Ambassador Linton Brooks, that because the two sides are no longer adversaries, detailed arms control talks are no longer necessary, as either naiveté or outright hypocrisy.[88]

Since then Deputy Foreign Minister Sergei Ryabkov recently stated that:

> Issues of strategic offensive and defensive arms are inextricably linked. To deny this relationship is meaningless because it is the essence of relations between the countries that have the appropriate potential in both areas. An augmented capacity of one of the parties in the realm of missile defense is automatically echoed in the form of plans and decisions of the other party in the realm of strategic offensive arms. And not even obliquely, but in the most direct way what is happening in the field of missile defense and U.S. relations with its East European allies on this topic has an impact on our START follow-on negotiations. Without recognition of the relationship between strategic and offensive defensive arms, there can be no such treaty, it cannot take place.[89]

Likewise, Deputy Prime Minister Sergei Ivanov told the Munich Security conference in February 2010:

> It is impossible to speak of reducing nuclear potentials in earnest while a state that possesses nuclear weapons is developing and deploying systems of defense against means of delivery of nuclear warheads that other states possess. It is like the sword and shield theory, where both are continuously developing with the characteristics and resources of each of them being kept in mind.[90]

Putin's aforementioned remarks fit right into this outlook.

> The problem is that our American partners are developing missile defenses, and we are not . . . But the issues of missile defense and offensive weapons are closely interconnected. . . . There could be a danger

that having created an umbrella against offensive strike systems, our partners may come to feel completely safe. After the balance is broken, they will do whatever they want and grow more aggressive.[91]

Fourth, given these conditions, the danger (as listed in the new defense doctrine) of NATO enlargement, and the threat of missile defenses coming closer to Russia, Moscow believes that it is being placed under mounting military-political pressure, or at least professes to be so, even though it undoubtedly knows that NATO is hardly an offensive threat and that the U.S. missile defenses cannot threaten its systems.[92] Therefore, it has been ready for at least a decade with its threat of striking first with nuclear weapons, even against conventional strikes, if the threat to its interests is dire enough. Thus in 1999 Colonel General Vladimir Yakovlev, commander in chief of Russia's nuclear forces, stated that: "Russia, for objective reasons, is forced to lower the threshold for using nuclear weapons, extend the nuclear deterrent to smaller-scale conflicts and openly warn potential opponents about this."[93] Since then, there has been no mention of any further alteration of this threshold.

Consequently Russia sees nuclear weapons as warfighting weapons, and both doctrinal statements and exercises confirm this. This process of conventionalizing nuclear weapons, in and of itself, substantially lowers the threshold for nuclear use just as Moscow did in 1999. Since then, others have amplified upon this point. For example, Solovtsov stated that new military uses for nuclear weapons are coming into being. Thus:

The radical changes that have occurred since the end of the Cold War in international relations and the considerable reduction of the threat that a large-scale war, even more so a nuclear one, could be unleashed, have contributed to the fact that in the system of views on the role of nuclear arms both in Russia and the U.S., a political rather than military function has begun to prevail. In relation to this, besides the traditional forms and methods in the combat use of the RVSN [Strategic Rocket Forces], a new notion "special actions" by the groupings of strategic offensive arms has emerged — Such actions mean the RVSN's containment actions, their aim to prevent the escalation of a high-intensity non-nuclear military conflict against the Russian Federation and its allies.[94]

In other words, though there is no threat or a diminishing threat of large-scale war, a new mission for nuclear weapons will be for their use in actions during such a war to control intra-war escalation. It is not surprising that Solovtsov argued for increasing the forces under his command, but it also is the case that such dialectical reasoning makes no sense unless one postulates an *a priori* hostility between East and West and grants Russia the right of deterrence that it has unilaterally arrogated to itself over other states who have never publicly accepted it. Indeed, the new calls for renovating the nuclear forces and having a solution guaranteeing nuclear deterrence in all cases has now become policy even if America deploys its global defense system and moves to a defense dominant world.[95]

Makarov's aforementioned statement concerning retention of TNW could take place in potential European contingencies, i.e., in the Baltic or in a war with China.[96] In Vostok-2010, the exercise concluded with a simulated TNW strike against the People's Liberation

Army (PLA).[97] Similarly, proof of the intended use of nuclear weapons in Europe appeared in the Russian combined arms exercises entitled Ladoga and Zapad 2009, which were divided in two to avoid CFE treaty monitoring and which prominently featured nuclear strikes against a so-called Polish-Lithuanian offensive against Belarus which was defended by both native and Russian forces. Given the manifestations here of an old fashioned Soviet tank offensive but using newer arms, the presence of nuclear strikes, and the new command, control, communications, and intelligence (C3I) organizations developed by Russia with its reforms since 2006 (and presumably information warfare operations), it is hardly surprising that Baltic littoral states feel threatened and demand more security.

Beyond that, Russia is building new nuclear missiles whose main attribute is their ability to evade U.S. missile defenses and as part of the new prioritization of its nuclear forces will deploy over 70 strategic missiles, over 30 short-range Iskander missiles, and a large number of booster rockets and aircraft.[98] Moscow will also spend $35.3 billion on serial production of all weapons in 2009-11 (1 trillion rubles) and virtually doubled the number of strategic missile launches to 13 in 2009.[99] This procurement policy represents both a quantum leap in Russian capabilities if it can be accomplished. But more importantly, it also would constitute a major step in a new action-reaction cycle of procurements based on the old Cold War paradigm. Indeed, these dynamics could lead to a new arms race, especially if Russia insists that any new treaty should first eliminate the missile defenses in Eastern Europe as a condition of its acceptance and consummation.

The remarks by Patrushev in October 2009 that triggered the debate are fully consonant with the military's viewpoint. Patrushev told an interviewer that the forthcoming defense doctrine will be amended to allow for the possibility of preventive and preemptive first strikes, including nuclear strikes, even in the context of a purely conventional local war and even at the lower level of operational-tactical, as opposed to strategic, strikes.[100] Soon afterward Lieutenant General Andrey Shvaichenko, Commander in Chief of Russia's Strategic Rocket Forces (SRF)/(RVSN), stated on December 16, 2009, that:

> In a conventional war, the RVSN and the strategic nuclear forces ensure that the opponent is forced to cease hostilities on advantageous conditions for Russia by means of multiple preventive strikes against the aggressors' most important facilities. . . . Regional instability in immediate proximity to the borders of Russia and the CIS countries does not make it possible to completely rule out the risk that our country may be pulled into military conflicts of various intensity and scale.[101]

Here Shvaichenko went beyond the previous line that nuclear weapons may be used to defend Russia's vital interests in a first-strike mode if the vital interests of the country are at risk or deemed to be at risk as stated in the 2000 military doctrine.[102] That posture translated into a peacetime strategy of using Russia's nuclear forces as a deterrent against any aggression launched against either Russia or its CIS neighbors or against Russia if it made war upon those states as in Georgia's case in 2008.[103] In other words, the nuclear warning's strategic political purpose is to demarcate a theater of both military and peacetime operations wherein Russia would have relative if not full freedom of action to operate as it saw fit, free from foreign interference. In political terms, it not only represents a "no go" sign for potential enemies, it also is an attempt to intimidate NATO allies by making them targets of Russian nuclear strikes if they try to invoke Article V of the Washington Treaty should Russia move on the Baltic States or undertake similar kinds of attacks.

In those remarks, we see a hidden or at least an unnoticed mission for Russia's nuclear weapons. They serve to demarcate its sphere of influence by setting up a "no go" zone for foreign military entities, because the Russian elite almost unanimously believes that without such weapons, the whole of the CIS would be open to NATO intervention in a crisis. Thus, if Russia is to have a sphere of influence in the region, it must extend its deterrence umbrella throughout that sphere to make its claim credible and with that its claim to great or even superpower status.

Neither is Russia's professed readiness to use nuclear weapons confined to land-based systems. Vice-Admiral Oleg Burtsev, the Navy's Deputy Chief of Staff, told *RIA Novosti* that: "Probably, tactical nuclear weapons will play a key role in the future," and that the Navy may fit new, less powerful nuclear warheads to the existing types of cruise missiles. "There is no longer any need to equip missiles with powerful nuclear warheads," Burtsev said. "We can install low-yield warheads [possibly fusion weapons?] on existing cruise missiles."[104] This is clearly something that creates an unacceptable threat to European security.[105] Certainly, we cannot assume this to be mere rhetoric, for as Bildt has told us, Russia has already deployed TNW on its Baltic Fleet ships.[106] In apparent confirmation of Bildt's remarks, the following episode from 2006 is informative.

In responding to a question from Putin on the number of nuclear submarines currently deployed worldwide, Ivanov stated: 'At this moment. . .we have eight nuclear submarines deployed. Of them, five are strategic submarines and three are multipurpose submarines, but all of them are deployed with nuclear weapons. The ships have different missions – intercontinental, that is, and multipurpose, but on board of each of them are nuclear weapons.' Since general purpose (attack) submarines do not carry SLBMs, Ivanov's comments appeared to indicate that these vessels, which prior to the Presidential Nuclear Initiatives had carried tactical, nuclear-armed cruise missiles and nuclear-armed torpedoes, were again carrying weapons in either or both of these categories.[107]

The worst aspect of these deployments and plans as stated here is that they point to the General Staff's and the government's strategy as being one of supposedly limited nuclear war. Key officials confirmed this interpretation, conceding that limited nuclear war is Russia's officially acknowledged strategy against many different kinds of contingencies.[108] Ilya Kedrov, in his discussion of armored vehicles above, also showed that he understood the doctrine as affirming this strategy.[109] In September 2008, at a roundtable on nuclear deterrence, General Solovtsov noted that Russia was giving explicit consideration to the concept of "special actions" or "deterring actions of the RVSN aimed at the prevention of escalation of a non-nuclear military conflict of high intensity against Russia." Solovtsov further stated that:

These actions may be taken with a view to convincingly demonstrating to the aggressor [the] high combat potential of Russian nuclear missile weapons, [the] determination of the military-political leadership of

Russia to apply them in order to make the aggressor stop combat actions. . . . In view of its unique properties, the striking power of the Strategic Missile Forces is most efficient and convincing in the de-escalation actions.[110]

This strategy also openly reflects Moscow's bizarre, unsettling, and unprecedented belief that Russia can control escalation and nuclear war by initiating it despite 40 years of Soviet argument that no such control was feasible. Meanwhile, current procurements display a reliance on new, mobile, survivable, and allegedly indefensible nuclear weapons, even as numbers fall. For example, Russia seeks to keep its mobile missile systems of the nuclear forces invisible to foreign reconnaissance systems, while also developing means to suppress those reconnaissance and surveillance systems.[111] Accordingly, as Russian officials regularly proclaim, nuclear procurements are intended to develop missiles against which America has no defense, i.e., mobile missiles, multiple independent reentry vehicles (MIRVs), and fusion, low-yield nuclear weapons that can also be used on the battlefield.

Thus, nuclear weapons are warfighting weapons. Moscow's threats from October 2009 not only follow previous doctrine, they expand on it by openly admitting that limited nuclear war is its option or ace in the hole. If Russia should decide to invade or seize one or more Baltic State, then that would mean it is prepared to wage nuclear war against NATO and the United States to hold onto that acquisition although it would prefer not to, or thinks it could get away with it without having to do so. The idea behind such a "limited nuclear war" is that Russia would seize control of the intra-war escalation process by detonating a first-strike even in a preventive or preemptive mode, and this would supposedly force NATO to negotiate a political solution that allows Russia to hold onto at least some of its gains. Apart from the immensity of Moscow's gamble that NATO will not have the stomach to retaliate against Russian nuclear strikes, which will be carried out to inflict a "preset" amount of damage that Moscow believes will signal its "limited" intent. In essence, Moscow is essentially engaging in a game of nuclear chicken or blackmail. In fact, the real risk here is that the West will not acquiesce but rather that it will retaliate or even escalate, further adding to the inherent unpredictability of any conceivable nuclear war scenario.

A recent article by Vipin Narang analyzing Pakistan's nuclear posture outlined three differing nuclear postures among the nuclear powers, i.e., their operational rather than their rhetorical nuclear doctrine. It is apparent that posture and doctrine generate deterrent power against all potential enemies and can be used to develop different levels of ability to deter varying contingencies, as well as to induce nuclear and other political forms of restraint among adversaries. Russia's nuclear posture which aims to deter both conventional and nuclear threats through varying levels of threatened response or first-strike use of nuclear weapons exemplifies the process.[112] Russia's declared nuclear posture therefore falls into the category of an "Asymmetric Escalation Posture." This posture conforms with numerous statements by Putin *et al.* that Russia's responses to U.S. missile defenses and NATO enlargement will be asymmetric in nature, hence the threat of a nuclear first-strike. This posture has the following characteristics and entails the recommendations that follow the portrayal of those characteristics below.

The asymmetric escalation posture is geared for the rapid and asymmetric first use of nuclear weapons against conventional attacks to deter their outbreak, operationalizing nuclear weapons as usable warfighting instruments. A state with this posture must therefore have sufficient tactical and potentially survivable second-strike strategic weapons to absorb potential retaliation. Although peacetime deployments can be centralized, to credibly deter conventional attacks, an asymmetric escalation must have the ability to disperse and deploy assets extremely quickly and to enable their release on the battlefield through pre-delegative procedures to military end-users in the event of a crisis; [in Russia's case, its mobile missiles typify this first requirement and little or nothing is known in the unclassified literature as to whether it has pre-delegated end-user release] it is thus the most aggressive option available to nuclear states. To credibly threaten first use, this posture must be largely transparent about capabilities, deployment patterns, and conditions of use. The asymmetric escalation posture may have the most significant deterrent effect at all levels of conflict intensity, given the costly signal of credibly threatening early first use of nuclear weapons against even conventional attacks.[113]

It should be clear that in this context what Moscow seeks is to deter as well as to defend. Obviously, Moscow seeks to deter a U.S. nuclear strike in defense of its allies. But beyond that obvious concern is the fact that for Moscow, it is of paramount significance to deter the U.S. concept of global strike which entails both conventional and nuclear strikes from land, sea, and air based platforms and for which, by its own admission, it has no sufficient defense. As the Russian military commentator Petr Belov recently observed, the resort to nuclear weapons indicates that Russia can no longer guarantee a retaliatory response to aggression or defend against a conventional strike. Moreover, he believes that a fierce struggle that could culminate in a war can develop around attempts to seize Russia's natural resources. (This notion is also enshrined as an official view in the 2009 *National Security Concept*).[114] Therefore, to prevent foreign precision-guided munitions from destroying Russia's C3I network, the order may be given to launch these weapons either to pre-empt such attacks or in a preventive mode.[115]

Russia's exercises fully reflect these plans (and not only in the West).[116] The Zapad 2009 and Ladoga exercises, bifurcated in half to avoid foreign inspections, were part of a nation-wide series of exercises in August-October 2009 from the Arctic to the Black Sea and culminated in a simulated nuclear strike on Poland, probably for the reasons given by Belov above.[117] The 2009 exercises built upon Stabilnost' 2008 and earlier exercises that involved the use of nuclear weapons in a first-strike mode. During the period September 28-October 10, 2009, Russia's SRF (RVSN), i.e., their nuclear forces, conducted drills to launch massive nuclear strikes using the Topol-M and Stiletto RS-18 ICBMs to apparently strike "army assets."[118] It is noteworthy because these exercises represented a change from the 2004 exercises where the Russians used TNW in a first-strike mode because they could not otherwise stop a conventional offensive. In other words, now it is equally as likely that they will use ICBMs or SLBMs against the United States or Europe for those purposes rather than TNW.[119] Since Russian leaders acknowledge that large-scale exercises are both a show of strength and a training exercise, the significance of these exercises and their component operations, as well as ongoing nuclear war exercises, is quite evident to all observers.[120]

Finally, we must understand that Russian rhetoric is not just rhetoric but actual policy. Recent deployments of the SS-26 Iskander missile (that comes in both nuclear and conventional formats) in the Leningrad Military District where it could threaten Finland and the Baltic States suggest not just a desire to deter NATO, but also the continuing desire to intimidate Russian neighbors.[121] Should Russia divine a threat in Europe, it reserves the right to place these missiles in Kaliningrad from where it could threaten Poland and even Germany as well.[122]

BEYOND THE DOCTRINE

From an optimistic standpoint, we can say that Medvedev successfully overrode the hawks and signed the treaty.[123] Moreover, he rebuffed both Putin and the military on the idea of an expanded nuclear program. Thus, at the March 5, 2010, expanded session of the Defense Ministry Collegium, Medvedev made it clear that Russia does not need to increase its offensive nuclear capability any further than was originally planned.[124] Clearly this directly contradicted Putin's public remarks in December 2009, underscoring the continuing divisions between Putin and Medvedev and within the Russian military-political elite. Beyond those debates, the fact of Putin's intervention on behalf of the military and his attempt to use them to check Medvedev is no less striking. First, it represents another in a series of ongoing efforts to assert the supremacy of military orientations in Russian national security policy over all other imperatives, while simultaneously representing another attempt to politicize the military in the context of the visible rivalry between Putin and Medvedev as well as their respective entourages. Such trends are dangerous in and of themselves and even more so where nuclear weapons and Russia's most crucial foreign policy relationships are involved.

Second, administration officials have stated that Medvedev told them in private what Putin said in public and that the two were in very close policy coordination and lockstep.[125] Yet the public record, and not just the issue of building more nuclear weapons, clearly belies such contentions underscoring a wide range of disagreements between Medvedev and Putin on a broad range of both domestic and foreign policy issues.[126] While debates over policy and the subsequent pressure on policymakers are the normal state of politics everywhere, the sheer scope of issues in which such discordance is manifest in Russian politics clearly points to ongoing tensions within Russia. What this means for the treaty is that it depends for its survival and endurance on the domestic balance of power in Russia because the Russian military and Putin are already publicly on record indicating that the U.S. missile defense program as it is represents exactly the kind of threat that Makarov and so many before him have invoked as justification for leaving the treaty. Indeed, one could argue as well that the Republican and conservative opposition in the U.S. represent an analogous case of the fragility of the reset policy and the limits to it.

Furthermore, these facts of Russian domestic political life contravene that Obama administration's argument that Russia's statement is essentially for domestic posturing and that every treaty contains a withdrawal clause (as did the Anti-Ballistic Missile (ABM) Treaty when the United States withdrew from it). Every treaty does contain a withdrawal clause, but this Russian statement essentially represents a loaded gun held against the temple of the treaty, given the potential for a reversal of the domestic balance of forces in Russia, since the military has already argued as did Putin that missile defenses in and of themselves represent a threat to vital Russian interests like deterrent capability and its strategic stability. Indeed, the overall Russian reception of this treaty was not enthusiastic, and its critics allege that just as the 1991 Strategic Arms Reduction Treaty (START) was detrimental to Russia, so is this treaty. They particularly emphasize the failure to constrain U.S. missile defenses.[127]

Therefore the doctrine's statements that: "The Russian Federation reserves the right to utilize nuclear weapons in response to the utilization of nuclear and other types of weapons of mass destruction against it and (or) its allies, and also in the event of aggression against the Russian Federation involving the use of conventional weapons when the very existence of the state is under threat," may be less than meets the eye.[128] In fact, this represents only the public formulation of the deeply contested nuclear use issue. As Patrushev forecast, a classified document on nuclear use was signed along with the doctrine, but obviously not released for discussion.[129]

THE ASIA-PACIFIC AND CHINA

Until now we have focused on Europe, but similar dilemmas plague Russian strategists when they look at Asia. Moscow sees Washington as trying to bring its military forces closer to Russian borders in both Europe and Asia. So this is not only a question of NATO enlargement, but also of the enlargement of America's Asian-Pacific alliances.[130] Certainly, from Moscow's

333

standpoint its perception is a valid one and it may also have merit in more objective analyses. For example, David McDonough's analysis of U.S. nuclear deployments in the Pacific Ocean states that:

> The increased deployment of hard-target kill weapons in the Pacific could only aggravate Russian concerns over the survivability of its own nuclear arsenal. These silo-busters would be ideal to destroy the few hundred ICBM silos and Russia's infamously hardened command-and-control facilities as well as help reduce any warning time for Russian strategic forces, given their possible deployment and depressed trajectory. This is critical for a decapitation mission, due to the highly centralized command-and-control structure of the Russian posture, as well as to pre-empt any possible retaliation from the most on-alert Russian strategic forces. The Pacific also has a unique feature in that it is an area where gaps in Russian early-warning radar and the continued deterioration of its early-warning satellite coverage have made it effectively blind to any attack from this theatre. This open-attack corridor would make any increase in Pacific-deployed SLBMs appear especially threatening.[131]

Similarly, already in 2003 when the first reports of the Pentagon's interest in new low-yield and bunker busting nuclear weapons became public, Russian analysts warned that even if such programs were merely in a research stage, they would add to the hostile drift of Russo-American relations.[132] Events since then have only confirmed this assessment and their warning.

A second major concern is the strengthening of the U.S.-Japan alliance in the twin forms of joint missile defenses and the apparent consolidation of a tripartite alliance including Australia and South Korea, if not India. For both Russia and China, one of the negative consequences of the Democratic People's Republic of Korea's (DPRK) nuclear and missile tests has been the strengthened impetus it gave to U.S.-Japan cooperation on missile defense. The issue of missile defense in Asia had been in a kind of abeyance, but the North Korean nuclear tests of 2006, made in defiance of Chinese warnings against nuclearization and testing, intensified and accelerated the Japanese and American collaboration on missile defenses as the justification for them had now been incontrovertibly demonstrated. But such programs always entail checking China, which naturally is considerably annoying to Beijing.[133] Therefore, China continues to criticize U.S.-Japan collaboration on missile defenses publicly.[134] Perhaps this issue was on Chinese President Hu Jintao's mind in September 2007 when he called for greater Russo-Chinese cooperation in Asia-Pacific security.[135]

Russian experts long ago noted that the military balance in the Asia-Pacific was unfavorable to Russia and specifically invoked the specter of Russia losing its nuclear naval potential there.[136] That nuclear naval potential remains precarious as Moscow recently admitted that its submarines conducted a total of three patrols in 2007.[137] In fact, in the Pacific, according to Japanese sources, Moscow is deploying formerly retired ships like the nuclear powered *Admiral Lazarev*, a decommissioned *Kirov* class cruiser, to counter the rise in Chinese power and deter threats ranging from an outbreak of war in Korea to growing Chinese naval and strike power along with U.S. buildups.[138] To overcome these weaknesses and threats, and thanks to Russia's economic resurgence (largely energy-driven, however), then President Vladimir Putin and Defense Minister Sergei Ivanov announced a planned strategic upgrade for the Pacific Fleet, specifically to address this problem and make the Fleet Russia's primary naval strategic component.[139]

This policy reversed the prior naval policy that made Russia's Northern Fleet the strategic bastion for anti-American scenarios during the 1990s, testifying to an enhanced threat perception in Asia despite the recent Russian show of force in the Arctic and calls to incorporate Arctic scenarios into the training and doctrine of Russia's armed forces.[140] Here we should understand that Russia's forces, particularly those in the North and the Far East, may be deployed on a "swing basis," where either the fleet or air forces in one theater moves to support the fleet or air forces in the other. Russia has carried out exercises whereby one fleet moves to the aid of the other under such a concept.[141] Likewise, Russia has rehearsed scenarios for airlifting ground forces from the North to the Pacific in order to overcome the "tyranny of distance" that makes it very difficult for Russia to sustain forces in Northeast Asia. The revival of regular air patrols over the oceans have clearly involved the Pacific-based units of the Long Range Aviation forces as well as some of the air forces based in the North and Arctic who fly in the areas around Alaska.[142] Indeed, nuclear exercises moving forces or targeting weapons from the North to the Pacific or vice versa have also occurred.[143] To the degree that Arctic missions become part of the regular repertoire of the Russian armed forces, they will also to some degree spill over into the North Pacific.

Indeed, Russia's heightened threat perception in Asia resembles its perception of European threats. Just as in regard to the perceived threat of U.S. missile defenses in Europe, Putin proposed that Russia and America share operation of the Gabala and Krasnodar radar and missile defense bases, and by so doing cre-

ate a real strategic partnership that would revolution-
ize world politics, so too in Asia, Moscow wants to
participate in shaping strategic relationships there.[144]
But at the same time, Moscow has warned that if its
concerns are not heeded, it will go its own way. In
Asia that means, at least in regard to missile defenses,
enhanced cooperation with China. As Deputy Foreign
Minister Aleksandr' Losyukov said in 2007:

> We would like to see a non-circuited [i.e., non-exclu-
> sionary, or non-bloc] system. Besides, we might make
> our own contribution to it, too. Then we would have
> no reason to suspect this system is targeted against
> us,—If it is true that the system being created is ex-
> pected to ward off some threats posed by irresponsible
> regimes, then it is not only Europe, the United States
> or Japan that one should have to keep in mind. When
> some other countries' concerns are kept outside such
> a system, they may have the feeling threats against
> them are growing, too. Consequently, the systems to
> be created must accommodate the concerns of other
> countries concerned.[145]

Clearly the other countries to which he refers are
Russia and China. Thus it is not surprising that Russia publicly criticized the U.S.-Japan collaboration on
missile defenses and the linking of Australia to the
U.S.-Japanese alliance about which it had previously
been silent. Here Moscow has adopted China's argument, for certainly the U.S. alliance system is not
primarily targeted on Russia. Such arguing on behalf
of mainly Chinese interests suggests that, as part of
the Sino-Russian partnership, we are beginning to encounter the phenomenon that many Russian analysts
warned about, specifically that Russia ends up following China's line. But this may well be because Russia
perceives that Washington will not grant it the admit-

tedly self-inflated status that it claims for itself either in
Europe or in Asia. Interestingly enough, while China,
according to most analysts, had been seen as desist-
ing from challenging the U.S. missile defense program
by a vigorous program of building nuclear weapons,
Russia seems ready to do so even though the utility of
that program for its overall interests, which normally
focus on getting the West to include it as a major international actor, is decidedly moot.[146]

Russian opposition to an American missile defense
system goes back a decade, and Russia argued against
its appearance in Asia, using every available Asian
security forum to voice its opposition at that time.[147]
By 2005, it also was becoming apparent that the place-
ment of such defenses in the Asia-Pacific as part of the
U.S. alliance system was part of an effort to create a
bloc to isolate Russia.[148] And now, as it increasingly
appears Russian hopes that a peaceful resolution of
the North Korean nuclear problem would undermine
Washington's justification for Asian missile defenses
will be dashed, it may have decided to go on the offensive in Asia just as it has in Europe.[149]

While Western and U.S. scholars and policy, seen
from Moscow's point of view, tend to marginalize
Russia as an actor in Asia, Russia made up its mind
to react.[150] Russia perceives U.S. nuclear policy as part
of an overarching strategy to isolate and threaten it,
and therefore is responding accordingly, asymmetri-
cally as promised. Thus its response includes: partnership, if not alliance, with China; pressure on Japan to
desist from targeting Russia with its missile defenses,
coupled with alternating offers of economic incentives
for partnership in the region; and the nuclearization
of the Pacific Fleet to ensure robust deterrence and a
second-strike capability.

Neither are Russian military analysts or planners unaware of the possibility of Chinese military threats, even though they do not frequently discuss them. These threats are usually debated by people who are critical of the partnership with China or who profess to believe, as is apparently now the case, that they have at least 10 years before China can be a real threat and that China is currently not a real threat to Russia.[151] Even so, at least some writers have pointed out that the rise in China's capabilities could go beyond a conventional threat to Russian assets in Siberia and Russian Asia.

For example, China's "no first use" of nuclear weapons injunction in Chinese military doctrine is coming under pressure from younger officers there.[152] Thus China is now debating retention of its no first use posture regarding nuclear weapons, and such weapons appear to be playing a more prominent role in Chinese strategy than was hitherto believed to be the case. China is building a previously undisclosed nuclear submarine base in the Pacific and a major nuclear base in its interior, moves that suggest consideration of a second strike capability, but that can also put much pressure on Russia's Pacific Fleet and Russian Asia.[153] Indeed, China's new DH-10 cruise missile represents a significant advance in China's own TNW capability, as does the operationalization of several cruise missile brigades. Even if Taiwan is the focus of Chinese military planning, that planning still identifies Russia and the United States (as well as India) as potential enemies, thereby envisaging possible nuclear scenarios against them.[154] If Vostok-2010 is any guide, the simulated launching of TNW and of Tochka-U precision missile strikes against China suggests that the role of TNW in Asia will grow, not decrease.[155]

The following analysis from 2004 took into account both the limited nuclear capability China had at that time and the possibilities that could ensue based on the ongoing development of those forces:

Despite the significant qualitative makeup of the current Chinese nuclear missile potential, its combat capabilities are quite limited; it would hardly be adequate to destroy highly protected command and control posts and could not substantially degrade Russia's ground and sea-based strategic nuclear forces. However, this potential would be capable of substantially degrading the Russian Federation Armed Forces group in the Far Eastern theater of Military Operations and of doing major damage to the population and economy not only in the Far Eastern and Urals regions, but even in the Central Region of European Russia. According to available data, so far China does not have missile systems with MIRVed warheads, but the upsurge in activity related to the building of antimissile defense systems could accelerate its development of that type of weapons system, including antimissile defense countermeasures. It should be noted that the PRC's economic and technological potential is quite adequate for a quantitative and qualitative breakthrough in the area of its strategic offensive weapons development.[156]

Given the aforementioned discoveries of growing Chinese interest in and capabilities for using nuclear weapons that suggest consideration of a second strike capability, which can also put much pressure on Russia's Pacific Fleet and Russian Asia, it is understandable why we see a rethinking of Russia's nuclear strategy in Asia.[157]

Thus, Moscow is already increasingly ambivalent about the INF Treaty of 1987-88. While this part of a heightened ambivalence about most of the Gorbachev-era's arms control treaties are very much tied to the consequences of NATO enlargement, the apprehension about this treaty reflects Russian concerns about China's (and Iran's) missile buildup. As Russian officials from Putin on down have argued, other countries to Russia's south and east are building such missiles, but America and Russia are debarred from doing so. In October 2007:

> Mr. Putin said that Russia would leave the INF treaty unless it was turned into a global agreement to constrain other states, including those 'located in our near vicinity.' He did not identify any country but Iran and North Korea are within the range covered by the treaty. Dmitri Peskov, a Kremlin spokesman, later acknowledged that China, India and Pakistan had medium-range missile capabilities. He insisted that Mr. Putin was concerned about an imbalance of regional security rather than any specific threat.[158]

But these remarks also demonstrates that Moscow cannot publicly reveal or confront its true threat perceptions and consequently blames Washington for its failure to take Russian interests into account. Thus, while Moscow had "privately told Washington it wanted medium range missiles to counter Iranian threats, it publicly argued that the lack of Iranian missiles meant the U.S. did not need a defense system."[159] As part of this debate, General Vladimir Vasilenko raised the issue of Russian withdrawal from the treaty after Sergei Ivanov did so in 2005, though it is difficult to see what Russia would gain by a withdrawal from that treaty.[160] Furthermore, it is by no means clear that Moscow could regenerate production for either IRBMs or ICBMs, because of production difficulties. Therefore, a withdrawal from the treaty could actually further diminish Russian security, not enhance it.[161]

Consequently,[162] Vasilenko also stated that the nature and composition of any future U.S.-NATO missile defense would determine the nature and number of future Russian missile forces and systems. Therefore, he argued in 2005 that:

> Russia should give priority to high-survivable mobile ground and naval missile systems when planning the development of the force in the near and far future. . . . The quality of the strategic nuclear forces of Russia will have to be significantly improved in terms of adding to their capability of penetrating [missile defense] barriers and increasing the survivability of combat elements and enhancing the properties of surveillance and control systems.[163]

Obviously such advocacy represents a transparent demand for new, vast, and unaffordable military programs, similar to the demand for reactivating production of IRBMs regardless of consequences. But in that case, Russia's government and military are, as Nikolai Sokov suggested, postulating an inherent East-West enmity that is only partially and incompletely buttressed by mutual deterrence.[164] Vasilenko's recommended posture makes no sense in today's strategic climate, especially when virtually every Russian military leader repeatedly proclaims, as did Chief of Staff General Yuri Baluyevsky through 2006, that no plan for war with NATO is under consideration and that the main threat to Russia is terrorism, not NATO and not America.[165] But since then, as is apparent to everyone, NATO and America have become enemy number one. Nevertheless, at the same time, that posture also openly warns Beijing and Tehran of Russian suspicions concerning their ambitions and capabilities.

Russia's reaction to Asian military challenges comprises both conventional force reforms and nuclear strategies. Here we restrict ourselves to nuclear issues. The Pacific Fleet will be the main fleet and one of two nuclear fleets, suggesting that the main mission of the fleet is to provide a reliable second-strike deterrent. The mission of the non-nuclear vessels of the fleet is to protect the "boomers" (nuclear armed submarines) and prevent hostile forces from coming within range. In other words, Russia is following a deterrence strategy here just as they are in Europe. Meanwhile, Russia's long-term rearmament program apparently envisions the renewal of the submarine fleet as nuclear propelled multirole submarines, in an effort to save money. Three missions for them will be anti-submarine warfare, anti-aircraft carrier missions (mainly against U.S. carrier battle groups), and attacking surface ships and transports. They will be armed with precision conventional weapons in an effort to be a strategic non-nuclear deterrence force.[166]

The drive to the Arctic also presupposes the use of both Pacific and Northern Fleets, in particular the latter which is also a nuclear armed fleet, as a swing fleet that can challenge enemies from the North Pacific, presumably from bases there. Just as that fleet has a bastion or bastions in the Kola Peninsula, so too does the Pacific Fleet have its major bases which the Northern Fleet or elements thereof may be tasked to help defend. Alternatively, the Northern Fleet and Russian air forces based in the high north will be used to sweep the North Pacific of enemy air and naval assets. Nonetheless and even though the Far East is very much a naval theater, Moscow's main investments through 2010 will evidently go not so much to the Navy as to nuclear weapons (to redress Russia's conventional inferiority vis-à-vis U.S. and Chinese threats) and to air and air defense in order to forestall a Kosovo-like aerial campaign.[167]

At the conventional level, apart from ongoing reinforcement or resupply of the forces with what is hoped to be more advanced conventional weapons and improved training and quality of the manpower (a very dubious assumption given the inability and refusal to build a truly professional Army), reform also entails experiments in new force structures and rapid reaction forces. While conventional forces in the Far East will have no choice but to fight at the end of a precarious supply line in an austere theater, Moscow is trying to develop a functioning mechanism of rapid response and airlift (the idea of the swing fleet also plays here) from Russia's North or interior to threatened sectors of the theater. This program of airlift and rapid air mobility also applies to nuclear forces.[168]

Second, Russia is building an integrated, mobile, and all arms (if not combined arms) force, consisting of land, air, and sea forces capable of dealing with failing state scenarios, insurgencies, terrorism, scenarios involving large-scale criminal activities, and ultimately conventional attack. Third, if, however, the scale of the threat overwhelms or is too large for the conventional forces, doctrine evidently continues to point to the use of nuclear weapons (probably tactical or what Moscow calls non-strategic nuclear weapons [NSNW]) in a first-strike or possibly even preventive mode as stated by Baluyevsky on January 20, 2008:[169]

> We do not intend to attack anyone, but we consider it necessary for all our partners in the world community to clearly understand . . . that to defend the sovereignty and territorial integrity of Russia and its allies, military forces will be used, including preventively, including with the use of nuclear weapons.[170]

Russian commentators noted that he was speaking entirely within the parameters of established Russian doctrine and that he essentially conceded the failure of conventional forces to provide adequate defense and deterrence at the high end of the spectrum of conflict.[171] Beyond that, Baluyevsky invoked the use of nuclear weapons in a first or preventive strike to defend allies. While he probably meant largely the CIS states to which Moscow has extended an unsolicited nuclear umbrella, in the context of Russia's Asia-Pacific territories, his remarks bring us to the political dimensions of Russia's efforts to overcome the strategic challenges it faces there. Here again, we see the inclination to threaten limited nuclear war as part of the deterrence strategy.

China's rise presents Russia with difficult choices, especially given its nuclear naval deficiencies. Russia must take account of the growing internal pressure in China to abandon its no first use policy and China's increased nuclear and apparent second-strike capability, even as it must reduce its nuclear forces.[172] This downward pressure on the Far East's regional arsenal was already apparent in 2004-05, and if Baluyevsky's remarks are to be taken seriously, it is likely that the Northern Fleet's nuclear forces and Russia's NSNW will become more important for consideration of deterrence or first strike in the Asian as well as European theater. As of 2004:

> Currently, about 20% of the deployed Russian strategic nuclear forces remain in the Eastern part of Russia. As strategic forces shrink, the pace of reductions in the region is the fastest. In particular, three of the four divisions of the Russian Strategic Forces that have been disbanded since 2000 were located here. And the

345

reductions will continue. Most likely, the SS-18 base at Uzhur will be closed down after 2010. The future of the SS-25 mobile intercontinental ballistic missiles (ICBMs) is also uncertain, as they are getting older. The submarine base on the Kamchatka peninsula will likely no longer host strategic submarines once the last Delta-III nuclear submarines will be retired. Thus, perhaps, the only place where strategic forces will remain in this part of Russia is Ukrainka, the home of strategic bombers. As deployment of strategic nuclear forces in the Eastern part of Russia is curtailed, non-strategic nuclear weapons in the region may be assigned a stronger role. According to the author's assessment, nearly one third of the 3,300 Russian non-strategic weapons are assigned for deployment with general-purpose forces in the Siberian and Far Eastern military districts. All of these weapons are currently kept at central storage facilities of the 12th Directorate of the Russian Armed Forces. In case of hostilities they can be deployed with surface-to-surface, surface-to-air, air-to-surface, anti-ship, antisubmarine missiles, and other dual-use means of the Ground, Air, and Naval Forces.[173]

However, if nuclear missions grow in importance, that will inhibit any possible North Korean disposition to give up its existing nuclear weapons, not to mention foregoing new nuclear weapons. Similarly, Japan and South Korea will either be further tempted to go nuclear or cling ever more to Washington, who would likely increase its regional military presence under such conditions.[174] Therefore, a purely military and very considerable nuclear strategy leads Russia into a strategic dead end. A political strategy is essential and even paramount in Russia's endeavors to defuse potential security challenges.

CONCLUSIONS

Nuclear weapons issues deserve the most serious, rigorous, and sober thought based on evidence from the actions of governments other than the United States. The foregoing analysis shows that much U.S. writing about the inutility or "senselessness" of nuclear weapons is misplaced, unfounded, and based on a failure to take into account the evidence of other governments' thinking and policies. Russia is by no means the only government whose programs must be seriously considered. Those who argue that nuclear weapons are only good for deterring nuclear attacks might profit by more serious study of Russia, Pakistan, China, and Israel, to cite only a few examples. They might also remember that in 1987 Iraq launched chemical missiles against Iran in defiance of international agreements, and that Iran, not irrationally drew the appropriate conclusions from those attacks.

If we are to make progress towards the noble goal of abolition and enhanced global security, a more rigorous understanding of contemporary international relations, strategy, and politics is needed, not more moralism or wishful thinking. It is clear that, for many states, nuclear weapons serve many useful purposes apart from gaining big power status or retaining it. We cannot make progress here until we realize that, for whatever reason, other nations genuinely feel threatened, and not just psychologically deprived. A sober unsentimental analysis would confirm that point rather than stigmatizing these states as being somehow benighted, as in Paul Warnke's memorable phrase, as "apes on a treadmill." Apart from the policy significance of Russia for the United States, Russia's strategic posture needs to be understood and not just brushed aside.

347

If Russian leaders are to decrease their reliance on nuclear security, they must feel that their security is some manner enhanced, a conclusion that is not readily apparent to them at the present. If we are to convince the Russians of the rightness of reducing their reliance on nuclear weapons, like it or not, we must understand their perspective and take it seriously. Otherwise, as has all too often been the case, we will continue to talk at or past each other. Russia demands that it be taken seriously. While doing so might not and probably should not lead to our approval of their policies or thinking, taking Russian nuclear postures seriously means engaging with their strategy and policies, not dismissing them outright or worse, deprecating our own capabilities on the basis of a hoped-for end that is not grounded in empirical validation. Until such time as we or others can persuade other states that they do not need nuclear weapons to defend themselves against us or anyone else, the mere repetition of the incantation that nuclear weapons serve no useful purpose in utter defiance of the facts is merely an invitation to a disaster.

ENDNOTES - CHAPTER 7

1. Stephen J. Cimbala, "Nuclear Arms control After a Time of Troubles" Mark Galeotti, ed., *The Politics of Security in Modern Russia*, Farnham, Surrey, and Burlington, VT: Ashgate Publishing Company, 2009, pp. 105-122.

2. Stephen Blank, "Undeterred: The Return of Nuclear War," *Georgetown Journal of International Affairs*, Vol. 2, Summer/Fall, 2000, pp. 55-63.

3. Simon Saradzhyan, *Russia's Support For Zero: Tactical Move or Long-term Commitment?* Cambridge, MA: Belfer Center, Harvard University, 2009, available from *belfercenter.ksg.harvard.edu/files/russias-support-for-zero.pdf*.

4. *Military Doctrine of the Russian Federation,* February 5, 2010, *www.kremlin.ru,* Open Source Center, Foreign Broadcast Information Service Central Eurasia (Henceforth *FBIS SOV*), February 9, 2010.

5. Ilya Kedrov, "An Expert Evaluation: A Universal Armored Vehicle; The Infantry Needs a Fundamentally New Combat Vehicle and Not a Taxi to the Forward Edge of the Battle Area," Moscow, Russia, *Voyenno-Promyshlenny Kuryer Online,* in Russian, May 26, 2010, *FBIS SOV,* June 4, 2010.

6. Artem Troitsky, "Interview With CINC Ground Troops General of the Army Vladimir Anatolyevich Boldyrev," Moscow, Russia, *Voyenno-Promyshlennyi Kuryer,* in Russian, October 1, 2008, *FBIS SOV,* October 19, 2008.

7. Kedrov.

8. For an example of this nostalgia for Stalin's leadership structure of 1941-45, see Colonel V. V. Natvichuk and Colonel A. L. Khryapin (Ret.), "A Strategic Deterrence System Under New Conditions," *Military Thought,* No. 1, 2010, pp. 43-49.

9. *Military Doctrine of the Russian Federation.*

10. Interview With Russian Federation Security Council Secretary Nikolai Patrushev, Moscow, Russia, *Izvestiya,* in Russian, October, 14, 2009, *FBIS SOV,* October 14, 2009; David Novak, "Report: Russia To Allow Pre-Emptive Nukes," Associated Press, October 14, 2009.

11. Kedrov.

12. "Putin Says Russia will build weapons to offset planned US missile defences," December 29, 2009, available from *www.guardian.co.uk/world/2009/dec/29/nuclear-weapons-russia.*

13. Speech at an Expanded Meeting of the Defense Ministry Board, March 5, 2010, available from *eng.kremlin.ru/speeches/2010/03/05/2058_type82913_224669.html.*

14. "Failure to build a professional army, return to conscription," Moscow, Russia, *Interfax*, in English, May 26, 2010.

15. *Ibid.*

16. "Share of Modern Weaponry in Russian Military Must Be 30% by 2015-Medvedev," *RIA Novosti*, May 24, available from *2010,en.rian.ru/military_news/20100524/159135253.html*.

17. Maria Antonova, "Kudrin Signals Steep Spending Cuts," *The Moscow Times*, April 7, 2010.

18. Pavel Felgenhauer, "Russia Struggles to Modernize Its Military," *Eurasia Daily Monitor*, June 10, 2010.

19. Moscow, Russia, *Interfax*, in English, June 3, 2010, *FBIS SOV*, June 4, 2010 CEP20100607964184.

20. *Ibid.*; Moscow, Russia, *Inteerfax*, in English, June 2010, *FBIS SOV*, CEP 20100607964287.

21. Vladislav Inozemtsev, "Then Most Modernized," Moscow, Russia, *Vedomosti Online*, in Russian, August 9, 2010, *FBIS SOV*, August 19, 2010.

22. Richard Weitz, "Strategic Posture Review: Russia Resurgent," *World Politics Review*, January-February 2009, pp. 58-59.

23. Martin Sieff, "Russia Reveals New 10-year Arms Plan to Upgrade Armed Forces," *UPI*, January 20, 2009, available from *www.upi.com*.

24. Dmitry Litovkin, "The Army Will Become a Trillionaire," Moscow, Russia, *Izvestiya*, in Russian, January 20, 2009, *FBIS SOV*, January 20, 2009.

25. Sieff.

26. Stephen Blank, "The Political Economy of the Russian Defense Sector," Jan Leijhonhielm and Frederik Westerlund, eds., *Russian Power Structures: Present and Future Roles in Russian Politics*, Stockholm, Sweden: Swedish Defense Research Agency,

2008, pp. 97-128; Stanislav Secrieriu, "Illusion of Power: Russia After the South Caucasus Battle," *CEPS Working Document*, No. 311, February, 2009, p. 5, available from *www.ceps.be* (CEPS stands for Center for European Policy Studies); Alexander Chuykov, "Bulava and Dolgoruky Unveiling," Moscow, Russia, *Argumenty I Fakty*, in Russian, June 18, 2009, *FBIS SOV*, June 18, 2009.

27. Alexander Chuykov, "Bulava and Dolgoruky (Unveiling)," Moscow, Russia, *Argumenty Nedeli Online*, in Russian, June 18, 2009, *FBIS SOV*, June 18, 2009; Alexander Chuykov, "The Crisis Has Caught Up with the Military Bases," Moscow, Russia, *Argumenty Nedeli Online*, in Russian, June 25, 2009, *FBIS SOV*, June 15, 2009; Moscow, Russia, *Prime-TASS Online*, in Russian, June 29, 2009, *FBIS SOV*, June 29, 2009.

28. Roger McDermott, "Russia Flexes Its Military Muscle," January 4, 2009, available from *www.guardian.co.uk*.

29. Catherine Belton, "Russian Economy Plummets 10.1%," *Financial Times*, July 15, 2009, available from *www.ft.com*.

30. Roger McDermott, "Russia's National Security Strategy," *Eurasia Daily Monitor*, May 19, 2009.

31. Pavel Felgenhauer, "Russia Will Spend 20 Trillion Rubles on New Weapons," *Eurasia Daily Monitor*, July 22, 2010.

32. *Ibid.*

33. Moscow, Russia, *Interfax* in Russian, July 28, 2010, *FBIS SOV*, July 28, 2010.

34. Felgenhauer, "Russia Will Spend 20 Trillion Rubles on New Weapons."

35. *Ibid.*

36. "Russia in Counter-Trend: Defense Spending Will Increase by 60% in 2013," available from *www.avionews.clom*; "Russian Defense Spending To Rise By 60% by 2013," *RIA Novosti*, July 30, 2010, available from *en.rian.ru/military_news/201000730/16000003543.html*.

37. Moscow, Russia, *Interfax-AVN Online,* in Russian, August 5, 2010, *FBIS SOV,* August 5, 2010.

38. Vladimir Kalinin, "Realities," Moscow, Russia, *Nezavisimoye Voyennoye Obozreniye*, in Russian, *August 6,* 2010, FBIS *SOV*, August 6, 2010.

39. Remarks by Stephen Blank, Eugene Rumer, Mikhail Tsypkin , and Alexander Golts at the Heritage Foundation Program, "The Russian Military: Modernization and the Future," April 8, 2008, available from *www.heritage.org/press/events/ev040808a.cfm;* Stephen Blank, "Civil-Military Relations and Russian Security," Stephen Blank, ed., *Contemporary Issues in International Security, Russian, European, and American Views*, Carlisle, PA: Strategic Studies Institute, U.S. Army War College, Forthcoming.

40. Julian Cooper, "The 'Security Economy'," Mark Galeotti, ed., *The Politics of Security in Modern Russia*, Farnham, Surrey and Burlington, VT: Ashgate Publishing Company, 2009, pp. 145-169.

41. *Military Doctrine of the Russian Federation.*

42. *Ibid.*

43. *Ibid.*

44. "Russia Could Focus On Tactical Nuclear Weapons For Subs," *RIA Novosti*, March 23, 2009, available from *en.rian.ru/russia/20090323/120688454.html.*

45. *Natsional'naya Strategiya Bezopasnosti Rossii, do 2020 Goda*, Moscow, Russia: Security Council of the Russian Federation, May 12, 2009, available from *www.scrf.gov.ru*, in English, *FBIS SOV,* May 15, 2009; *Military Doctrine of the Russian Federation.*

46. Text of Speeches by President Dmitry Medvedev and Defense Minister Anatoly Serdyukov at a Defense Ministry Collegium, Samara Volga Inform, in Russian, March 17, 2009, *FBIS SOV,* March 17, 2009.

47. *Ibid.*

48. Colin Gray, *House of Cards*, Ithaca, NY: Cornell University Press, 1991; Keith Payne, *Deterrence In the Second Nuclear Age*, Lexington, KY: University Press of Kentucky, 1996; Keith Payne, *Fallacies of Cold War Deterrence and a New Direction*, Lexington, KY: University Press of Kentucky, 2001; Alexei Arbatov and General (Ret.) Vladimir Dvorkin, *Beyond Nuclear Deterrence: Transforming the U.S.-Russian Equation*, Washington, DC: Carnegie Endowment for International Peace, 2006, John F. Steinbruner, Foreword.

49. Patrick M. Morgan, *Deterrence Now*, Cambridge, UK: Cambridge University Press, 2003, pp. 26-32.

50. *Ibid.*, p. 66.

51. Moscow, Russia, *Agentstvo Voyennykh Novostey Internet Version*, in Russian, September 10, 2008, *FBIS SOV*, September 10, 2008.

52. *Ibid.*

53. Moscow, Russia, *ITAR-TASS*, in English, April 6, 2010, *FBIS SOV*, April 6, 2010.

54. *Ibid.*

55. "Russia Could Focus On Tactical Nuclear Weapons For Subs," *RIA Novosti*, March 23, 2009, available from *en.rian.ru/russia/20090323/120688454.html.*

56. "Bildt Plays Down Russian Nuclear Threat," *The Local*, August 18, 2008," available from *www.thelocal.se/13780/20080818*; Mark Franchetti, "Russia's New Nuclear Challenge to Europe," *Times Online*, August 17, 2008, available from *www.timesonline. co.uk/tol/news/worldeurope/article4547883.ece.*

57. "Russian Military Chief Defends Nonstrategic Nukes," *Global Security Newswire*, December 17, 2008, available from *gsn. nti.org.*

58. *Military Doctrine of the Russian Federation.*

59. Open Source Committee, *OSC Analysis*, August 1, 2008, *FBIS SOV,* August 4, 2008.

60. Martin Sieff, "Russians Bet On Dems' Passion For Arms Control," December 19, 2008, available from *www.upi.com*; "US Sen Lugar Hopeful On Renewing Russia Nuclear Arms Treaty," *Agence France-Presse*, December 19, 2008, give the two conflicting impressions as to whether or not Russia is tying those missile defenses to achievement of a strategic nuclear missile treaty.

61. Moscow, Russia, *ITAR-TASS* in English, September 11, 2008, *FBIS SOV,* September 11, 2008.

62. Pavel Podvig, "Revolution in Military Affairs: Challenges to Russia's Security," Paper Presented at the VTT Energy Styx Seminar, Helsinki, Finland, September 4, 2001, available from *www.armsocntol.ru/Podvig/eng/publications/misc/20010904styx.shtm*.

63. Moscow, Russia, *Zvezda Television*, in Russian, September 11, 2008, *FBIS SOV*, September 11, 2008.

64. "Interview with Russian Foreign Minister Sergei Lavrov, Warsaw, Poland, *Gazeta Wyborcza*, September 11, 2008; and Moscow, Russia, *Ministry of Foreign Affairs Internet Version*, in English, September 15, 2008, *FBIS SOV*, September 15, 2008.

65. *Ibid*.

66. Dmitri Solovyov, "Russia Says It Must Have Nuclear Parity With U.S.," *Reuters*, December 7, 2007; Moscow, Russia, *Interfax*, in English, October 1, 2004, *FBIS SOV*, October 1, 2004.

67. Transcript of Remarks and Response to Media Questions by Russian Foreign Minister Sergey Lavrov at Press Conference in Relation to the Upcoming Signing of a Treaty between Russia and the USA on Measures to Further Reduction and Limitation of Strategic Offensive Arms, Moscow, Russia, April 6, 2010, available from *www.mid.ru*.

68. Unclassified Statement of Lieutenant General Patrick J. O'Reilly, USA, Director, Missile Defense Agency, Before the House Armed Services Committee Regarding Missile Defense in Europe, October 1, 2009.

69. Transcript of Remarks and Response to Media Questions by Russian Foreign Minister Sergey Lavrov at Press Conference in Relation to the Upcoming Signing of a Treaty between Russia and the USA on Measures to Further Reduction and Limitation of Strategic Offensive Arms, Moscow, Russia, April 6, 2010, available from *www.mid.ru*; Moscow, Russia, *Ministry of Foreign Affairs of the Russian Federation*, in English, May 24, 2010, *FBIS SOV*, May 24, 2010.

70. Moscow, Russia, *Interfax* , in English, March 16, 2010, *FBIS SOV* March 16, 2010.

71. William J. Perry and George P. Shultz, "How to Build on the Start Treaty," *New York Times*, April 11, 2010, available from *www.nytimes.com*.

72. Moscow, Russia, *ITAR-TASS*, in English, April 6, 2010, *FBIS SOV*, April 6, 2010.

73. *Military Doctrine of the Russian Federation*.

74. "US Does Its Best to Accelerate Drafting of New START-State Department Aide,"Moscow, Russia, *ITAR-TASS* in English, November 14, 2009, *FBIS SOV* November 14, 2009.

75. "Russia Says Arms Control Talks Held Up By US Missile Shield Plan," *Global Security Newswire*, available from *www.nti.org*, February 22, 2010; Moscow, Russia, *Interfax*, in English, February 9, 2010, *FBIS SOV*, February 9, 2010.

76. "Putin Says Russia will build weapons to offset planned US missile defences."

77. Viktor Litovkin, "Strategic Reservations in Geneva, Moscow, and Washington Seek Compromise on START, But on Their Own Terms," Moscow, Russia, *Nezavisimoye Voyennoye Obozreniye*, in Russian, January 22, 22010, *FBIS SOV*, February 10, 2010; Ellen Barry, "Putin Sounds Warning on Arms Talks," *New York Times*, December 30, 2009, available from *www.nytimes.com*; Moscow, Russia, *Ekho Moskvy Agency*, in Russian, December 29, 2009, *FBIS SOV*, December 29, 2009.

78. Open Source Center, "Russians Remain Publicly Optimistic On New START Treaty," January 7, 2010, *FBIS SOV*, January 7, 2010; Russian Deputy Foreign Minister Sergei Ryabkov Interview to the Interfax News Agency," Moscow, Russia, available from *www.mid.ru (Ministry of Foreign Affairs of the Russian Federation)*, in English, February 25, 2010, *FBIS SOV*, February 25, 2010; Andrey Lavrov, "START I Falters Over Missile Defense," Moscow, Russia, *Novaya Politika*, in Russian, February 27, 2010, *FBIS SOV*, March 2, 2010.

79. Yaroslav Vyatkin, "Armed Forces Fight for the Title of World Champion in the Nuclear Heavyweight Class," Moscow, Russia, *Argument I Nedeli Online*, in Russian, March 11, 2010, *FBIS SOV*, March 11, 2010.

80. Josh Rogin, "Stage Set for New Fight Over START Treaty," *The Cable*, February 17, 2010, available from *thecable.foreignpolicy. com/posts/2010/01/17/stage_set+for+new_fight_over_missile_defense*.

81. *Ibid.*

82. "Missile Shield Should Completely Cover Europe by 2018, U.S. Says," *Global Security Newswire*, available from *www.nti.org*, April 16, 2010.

83. Moscow, Russia, *ITAR-TASS*, in English, March 22, 2010, *FBIS SOV*, March 22, 2010.

84. Andrei Uglanov, "What is Behind Washington's Ultimatum?" Moscow, Russia, *Argument Nedeli*, in Russian March 10-17, 2010, *Johnson's Russia List*, March 17, 2010.

85. *Ibid.*

86. "Moscow Pulls the Brake At START Talks," Moscow, Russia, *ITAR-TASS*, March 11, 2010, in English, *FBIS SOV*, March 11, 2010; Peter Baker, "Twists and Turns On Way to Arms Pact With Russia," *New York Times*, March 27, 2010, available from *www.nytimes.com*; Mary Beth Sheridan and Michael D. Shear, "U.S., Russia Agree To Nuclear Arms Control Treaty," *Washington Post*, March 27, 2010, p. A02.

87. "Interview with Foreign Minister Sergei Lavrov," *Rossiyskaya Gazeta*, February 21-28, 2007, available from *www.mid.ru*.

88. Alexai Arbatov, *Russia and the United States – Time To End the Strategic Deadlock*, Moscow, Russia: Carnegie Moscow Center, June 2008, p. 2.

89. Ryabkov, Interview, *FBIS SOV*, February 25, 2010.

90. Moscow, Russia, *Interfax*, in English, February 6, 2010, *FBIS SOV*, February 6, 2010.

91. "Putin Says Russia will build weapons to offset planned US missile defences."

92. Dimitry Rogozhin and Boris Gromov, Open Letter, *New York Times*, March 17, 2010. The Russians fear that the Sm-3 can shoot down the IRBMs.

93. Martin Nesirsky, "Russia Says Threshold Lower for Nuclear Weapons," *Reuters*, December 17, 1999.

94. Troitsky.

95. Moscow, Russia, *Agentstvo Voyennykh Novostey Internet Version*, in English, September 29, 2008, *FBIS SOV*, September 29, 2008.

96. "Russian Military Chief Defends Nonstrategic Nukes," *Global Security Newswire*, December 17, 2008, available from *gsn.nti.org*.

97. Roger McDermott, "Reflections on Vostok 2010: Selling an Image," *World Security Network*, July 20, 2010, available from *www.worldsecuritynetwork.com/showArticle3.cfm?article_id=18355&topicID=54*.

98. Moscow, Russia, *Agentstvo Voyennykh Novostey Internet Version*, in English, September 29, 2008, *FBIS SOV*, September 29, 2008.; "Russia Orders 70 Nuclear Missiles by 2011; Report," *defensenews.com* from *Agence-France Presse* December 22, 2008.

99. "Russia To Allocate $35.3 Billion For Arms Production in 2009-11," *RIA Novosti*, December 12, 2008; "Russian Military Confirms 13 Strategic Missile Launches for 2009," *RIA Novosti*, December 12, 2008.

100. Interview With Russian Federation Security Council Secretary Nikolai Patrushev, Moscow, Russia, *Izvestiya*, in Russian, October, 14, 2009, *FBIS SOV*, October 14, 2009; David Novak, "Report: Russia To Allow Pre-Emptive Nukes," *Associated Press*, October 14, 2009.

101. Moscow, Russia, *Interfax*, in Russian, December 16, 2009, *FBIS SOV*, December 16, 2009.

102. See Russia's last doctrine of 2000, Moscow, Russia, *Nezavisimoye Voyennoye Obozreniye* in Russian, January 14, 2000, *FBIS SOV*, January 14, 2000.

103. *FBIS SOV*, December 16, 2009.

104. "Russia Could Focus On Tactical Nuclear Weapons For Subs," *RIA Novosti*, March 23, 2009, available from *en.rian.ru/russia/20090323/120688454.html*.

105. *Ibid.*

106. "Bildt Plays Down Russian Nuclear Threat," *The Local*, August 18, 2008," available from *www.thelocal.se/13780/20080818*; Mark Franchetti, "Russia's New Nuclear Challenge to Europe," *Times Online*, August 17, 2008, available from *www.timesonline.co.uk/tol/news/worldeurope/article4547883.ece*.

107. "Russia's Newest Submarine-Launched Missile Fails in Tests, But Tests of Other Systems Succeed: Defense Minister Ivanov Raises Questions on Status of Russian Sea-Based Tactical Nuclear Weapons," *WMD Insights*, November 2006.

108. "Bildt Plays Down Russian Nuclear Threat"; Franchetti.

109. Kedrov.

110. "Russia RVSN Military Academy Discussing Strategic Deterrence," *ITAR-TASS*, September 22, 2008, Johnson's Russia List, No. 173, September 22, 2008, available from *ww.worldsecurityinstitute.org*.

111. Moscow, Russia, *Interfax*, in English, December 17, 2009.

112. Vipin Narang, "Posturing For Peace? Pakistan's Nuclear Postures and South Asian Stability," *International Security*, Vol. XXXIV, No. 3, Winter 2009/10, p. 41.

113. *Ibid.*, p. 44.

114. Moscow, Russia, *Ekho Moskvy Radio* in Russian, December 15, 2009, *FBIS SOV*, December 15, 2009; *Natsional'naya Strategiya Bezopasnosti Rossii, do 2020 Goda*, Moscow, Russia, Security Council of the Russian Federation, May 12, 2009, available from *www.scrf.gov.ru*, in English, *FBIS SOV*, May 15, 2009, in a translation from the Security Council website available from *www.scrf.gov.ru*.

115. *FBIS SOV*, December 15, 2009.

116. Stephen Blank,"Russia's Strategic Dilemmas in Asia," *Pacific Focus*, Vol. XXIII, No. 3, December, 2008, pp. 271-293.

117. Matthew Day, "Russia 'Simulates' Nuclear Attack On Poland," November 2, 2009, available from *www.telgraph.co.uk*.

118. Moscow, Russia, *Interfax-AVN* in English, October 12, 2009, *FBIS SOV*, October 12, 2009

119. Viktor Myasnikov, Vladimir Ivanov, and Anton Khodasevich, "Lukashenka Presses Nuclear Button," Moscow, Russia, *Nezavisimaya Gazeta*, in Russian, June 26, 2006, *FBIS SOV*, June 26, 2006.

120. Dmitri Litovkin, "Defense Minister: Any Large-Scale Maneuvers Are a Show of Strength as Well as a Training Exercise," Moscow, Russia, *Izvestiya*, in Russian, November 2, 2005, *FBIS SOV*, November 2, 2005.

121. Jussi Kontinen, "Russia Plans to Deploy Some of its New Missiles Next to Finland," Helsinki, *HS.6*, in Finnish, March 29, 2010, *FBIS SOV*, March 29, 2010.

122. "Russia Says May Yet Deploy Iskander Missiles in Baltic Exclave," *RIA Novosti*, February 19, 2010.

123. Baker; Barry.

124. Speech at an Expanded Meeting of the Defense Ministry Board, March 5, 2010, available from *eng.kremlin.ru/speeches/2010/03/05/2058_type82913_224669.html*.

125. "Russian Leaders Seen in "Lockstep" During the START Talks," *Global Security Newswire*, April 1, 2010, available from *www.nti.org*.

126. Stephen Blank," Presidential Succession: The Achilles Heel of Russian Politics," *Perspectives,* Forthcoming.

127. Phillip P. Pan, "Critics Uneasy About Russian Concessions in Arms Control Deal," *Washington Post*, April 8, 2010, p. A08.

128. *Military Doctrine of the Russian Federation.*

129. Interview With Russian Federation Security Council Secretary Nikolai Patrushev, Moscow, Russia, *Izvestiya*, in Russian; Novak.

130 . Stephen Blank, "Threats to and From Russia: An Assessment," *Journal of Slavic Military Studies*, Forthcoming.

131. David McDonough, "The US Nuclear Shift to the Pacific," *RUSI Journal*, April, 2006, p. 68.

132. Vladimir Dvorkin, *The Russian Debate on the Nonproliferation of Weapons of Mass Destruction and Delivery Vehicles*, Cambridge, MA: Belfer Center for Science and International Affairs, Harvard University, No. 4, 2004, p. 9.

133. Jonathan Pollack, "U.S. Strategies in Asia: A Revisionist Hegemon," Byung-Kook Kim and Anthony Jones, eds., *Power and Security in Northeast Asia: Shifting Strategies,* Boulder, CO: Lynne Rienner Publishers, 2007, pp. 86-87.

134. Moscow, Russia, *Interfax, in English, October 24, 2007, FBIS SOV,* October 24, 2007.

135. Beijing, China, *Xinhua,* in English, September 8, 2007, *FBIS SOV,* September 8, 2007.

136. Moscow, Russia, *Interfax,* in English, September 15, 2003, FBIS *SOV,* September 15, 2003.

137. "Russia 'No Longer Uses' Nuclear Sub Deterrent, "*United Press International,* April 29, 2008.

138. Tokyo, Japan, *Tokyo Shimbun Morning Edition,* in Japanese, May 10, 2010, *FBIS SOV,* May 10, 2010.

139. Open source Center, *OSC Report,* in English, *FBIS SOV,* September 7, 2007.

140. Kristian Atland, "The Introduction, Adoption, and Implementation of Russia's "Northern Strategic Bastion" Concept, 1992-1999," *Journal of Slavic Military Studies,* Vol. X, No. 4, 2007, pp. 499-528; "Russia and Norway's Arctic Challenge," *Jane's Intelligence Digest,* May 20, 2008.

141. Dmitri Litovkin, "We Didn't Send Him For a Star: A Skif Flew From the North Pole to Kanin Nos," Moscow, Russia, *Izvestiya Moscow Edition* in Russian, September 13, 2006, *FBIS SOV,* September 13, 2006.

142. Moscow, Russia, *ITAR-TASS,* in English, May 5, 2008, *FBIS SOV,* May 5, 2008; Yuri Gavrilov, "Long-Range Aviation Inhabits Arctic Skies," Moscow, Russia, *Rossiyskaya Gazeta,* in Russian, May 15, 2008, *FBIS SOV,* May 15, 2008; Moscow, Russia, *IRAR-TASS,* in English, March 20, 2008, *FBIS SOV,* March 20, 2008.

143. Litovkin, "We Didn't Send Him For a Star: A Skif From the North Pole to Kanin Nos"; Moscow, Russia, *Agentstvo Voyennykh Novostey*, April 9, 2008.

144. Moscow, Russia, *ITAR-TASS,* in English, July 4, 2007, FBIS *SOV*, July 4, 2007; Moscow, Russia, *ITAR-TASS*, in English, July 2, 2007, *FBIS SOV*, July 2, 2007; Moscow, Russia, *Agentstvo Voyennykh Novostey*, July 4, 2007, *FBIS SOV*, July 4, 2007.

145. Moscow, Russia, *ITAR-TASS*, in English, October 23, 2007, *FBIS SOV*, October 23, 2007.

146. Minxin Pei, "China's Hedged Acquiescence," Byung-Kook Kim and Anthony Jones, Eds., *Power and Security in Northeast Asia: Shifting Strategies,* Boulder, Colorado: Lynne Rienner Publishers, 2007, p. 115.

147. Esook Yoon and Dong Hyung Lee, "A View From Asia, Vladimir Putin's Korean Opportunity: Russian Interests in the North Korean Nuclear Crises," *Comparative Strategy*, Vol. XXIV, No. 3, 2005, p. 188.

148. Alexander Ignatov, "Russia in the Asia-Pacific, " Rouben Azizian, ed., *Russia and America in the Asia-Pacific*, Honolulu, HI: Asia-Pacific Center for Security Studies, 2007, pp. 9-11.

149. Yoon and Lee, p. 194.

150. Glenn C. Buchan, David Matonic, Calvin Shipbaugh, and Richard Mesic, *Future Roles of U.S. Nuclear Forces: Implications for U.S. Strategy*, Santa Monica, CA: Rand Corporation, 2000, p. 15; Joseph Ferguson, "U.S.-Russia Relations: Awaiting the G-8," *Comparative Connections*, June 2006.

151. Open Source Committee, *OSC Analysis*: "Russia: Foreign Policy Thinkers Undaunted by Rising China," *FBIS SOV*, September 6, 2007.

152. Larry M. Wortzel, *China's Nuclear Forces: Operations, Training, Doctrine, Command, Control, and Campaign Planning*, Carlisle, PA: Strategic Studies Institute, U.S. Army War College, 2007; Richard Spencer, "China To Modernize Nuclear Weapons Capability," *London Daily Telegraph*, May 9, 2008; Baohui Zhang, "The

Taiwan Strait and the Future of China's No-First-Use Nuclear Policy," *Comparative Strategy*, Vol. XXVII, No. 2, March-April, 2008, pp. 164-183.

153. Wortzel; Spencer; Zhang; "Extensive Missile Site in China Revealed by Satellite: Analyst," *Space War*, May 15, 2008; "Extensive Nuclear Missile Deployment Are a Discovered in Central Asia," posted by Hans Kristensen, May 15, 2008, available from *www.fas.org/blog/ssp/2208//05/extensive-nuclear-deployment-area-discovered-in-central-china.*

154. "Power Posturing—China's Tactical Nuclear Stance Comes of Age," *Jane's Intelligence Review*, August 12, 2010, available from *www4.janes.com/subscribe/jir/doc_view.jsp?K2DocKey.*

155. Moscow, Russia, *infox.ru*, in Russian, July 8, 2010, *FBIS SOV*, August 23, 2010; Private conversation with Roger McDermott, August 9, 2010.

156. Aleksandr' Menshikov, "Problems of Russian Antimissile Defense: What It Can and Should Protect Against, And What It Should Not," Moscow, Russia, *Vozdushno-Kosmicheskaya Oborona*, in Russian, August 15, 2004, *FBIS SOV*, August 15, 2004.

157. Wortzel; Spencer; Zhang.

158. Tony Halpin, "Putin Confronts US With Threat To Arms Pact," *Times Online*, October 13, 2007, available from *www.timesonline.co.uk/tol/news/world/europe/article2648440.ece.*

159. Demetri Sevastopulo, Neil Buckley, Daniel Dombey, and Jan Cienski," Russia Threatens To Quit Arms Treaty," *Financial Times*, February 15, 2007, available from *www.ft.com.*

160.Martin Sieff, "Russia Rattles Missile Treaty," *UPI*, March 2, 2006.

161. "The ISCIP Analyst," Vol. XIII, No. 9, March 8, 2007, Boston, MA: Institute for the Study of Conflict, Ideology, and Policy, Boston University, available from *www.bu.edu/iscip.*

162. "Press Conference with Political Analyst Alexei Arbatov and Vice President of the Academy of Geopolitical Problems Leo-

nid Ivashov on Russian Foreign Policy," *RIA Novosti*, February 6, 2007, available from *www.fednews.ru*; Alexei Arbatov, "An Unnecessary and Dangerous Step," *Nezavisimoye Voyennoye Obozreniye*, No. 7, March, 2007, available from *www.america-russia.net/eng/security/143683092*.

163. *Interfax*, February 27, 2006.

164. Nikolai Sokov, "Second Thoughts About a First Strike," *Nonproliferation Review*, Vol. XIV, No. 1, March, 2007, p. 141.

165. Keith C. Smith, *Russian Energy Politics in the Baltics, Poland, and the Ukraine: A New Stealth Imperialism?* Washington, DC: Center for Strategic and International Studies, 2004, p. 13.

166. Moscow, Russia, *Agentstvo Voyennykh Novostey Internet Version*, March 21, 2005, *FBIS SOV*, March 21, 2005.

167. *FBIS SOV*, November 17, 2006.

168. Litovkin, "We Didn't Send Him For a Star: A Skif Flew From the North Pole to Kanin Nos."

169. Steve Gutterman, "Russia Could Use Preemptive Nuclear Strikes," *Associated Press*, January 21, 2008.

170. *Ibid.*

171. *Ibid.*

172. Wortzel; Spencer; Zhang, pp. 164-183.

173. Eugene Myasnikov, "Russian Perceptions and Prospects for Nuclear Weapons Reductions in Northeast Asia," *Inesap Bulletin*, No. 24, 2004, available from *www.inesap.org/bulletin24/art05.htm*.

174. James Clay Moltz and Alexandre Y. Mansourov, eds., *The North Korean Nuclear Program: Security, Strategy and New Perspectives from Russia*, New York, NY: Routledge, 2000.

CHAPTER 8

RUSSIAN TACTICAL NUCLEAR WEAPONS: CURRENT POLICIES AND FUTURE TRENDS

Richard Weitz

From Moscow's perspective, nuclear weapons, including tactical nuclear weapons (TNWs), serve a variety of valuable and often unique security functions that Russian policymakers will not soon surrender. First, they deter other countries from launching a nuclear strike against Russia. Second, having such an enormous nuclear arsenal bolsters Moscow's international status. Third, Russia's nuclear weapons help compensate for weaknesses in Russian conventional forces in two ways—for deterrent purposes (by denying adversaries the presumption that they can guarantee that any conflict with Russia will remain conventional) and, under certain conditions, for actual battlefield operations, by destroying important targets more effectively than conventional weapons.

Fourth, Russian nuclear weapons can achieve both results at a lower financial cost than Moscow would incur by acquiring and sustaining a conventional force equivalent in strength to that of the United States (if this were even possible, notwithstanding the major weaknesses in Russia's military-industrial base). Fifth, Russia's response to the North Atlantic Treaty Organization's (NATO) expanding ballistic missile defense program has been to strengthen its offensive nuclear forces so as to overwhelm any defense system. Russia's large number of TNWs would almost guarantee that at least some nuclear strikes, especially against frontline forces, would evade enemy defenses.

Sixth, Russian policymakers can issue nuclear threats to try to influence the foreign and defense policies of other countries. In recent years, Russian political and military leaders have sought to discourage former Soviet bloc states from joining NATO or hosting U.S. ballistic missile systems on their territory by warning that such actions would make them legitimate targets for Russian nuclear strikes. Finally, TNWs represent one of the few defense dimensions in which Moscow has a clear advantage over NATO militaries. This superiority enhances Russia's bargaining position in certain arms control negotiations. Given the many benefits that the Russian Government derives specifically from its TNWs, Russian officials would likely require major NATO concessions to relinquish, reduce, or otherwise restrict them.

FORCES

There is no agreed definition of what constitutes a "tactical nuclear weapon." Terms such as "nonstrategic," "substrategic," "short-range," "battlefield," and "theater" nuclear weapons are also used. The yield of the weapon's explosive power may no longer be a good indicator, now that many countries are developing low-yield nuclear weapons. Range is therefore more often used as a classifying category, but many nuclear warheads can simply be moved from a short-range launcher to a longer-range one. Yet, relying on nonphysical properties—such as the weapon's intended use—is difficult when some countries, such as Russia, intend to use TNW for both tactical battlefield purposes and strategic ones. Fundamentally, these systems are those nuclear weapons not deployed on "strategic" nuclear delivery vehicles such as land-based Intercontinental Ballistic Missiles (ICBMs), submarine-launched ballistic missiles (SLBMs), and long-range heavy bombers.

All three systems are capable of attacking targets at great distances (at least 5,500 kilometers [km], and often twice as far). The 1987 Intermediate-Range Nuclear Forces (INF) Treaty prohibits Russia and the United States from developing, manufacturing, or deploying ground-launched ballistic and cruise missiles with ranges of 500-5,500 km. The two countries still retain many nuclear weapons with ranges under 500 km. These shorter-range tactical systems can be launched by short-range missiles, dropped from the air as gravity bombs, loaded onto torpedoes or other tactical naval weapons, or otherwise delivered by nonstrategic systems (though neither country appears to have the fabled "nuclear" hand grenade). Another possible criterion for identifying a tactical nuclear weapon, its small yield, offers a less helpful indicator since the constantly improving accuracy of strategic delivery vehicles has meant that their warheads can also have low yields but still destroy their distant targets.

No bilateral treaty limits the number of short-range nuclear weapons in the American and Russian arsenals. The most important measure constraining these weapons occurred in 1991. That fall, U.S. President George H. W. Bush became alarmed that the ongoing disintegration of the Soviet Union, which had been accelerated by the failed August 1991 coup by communist hardliners, was endangering Moscow's control over thousands of Soviet nuclear warheads. Therefore, in late September, Bush announced major reductions in the number of deployed American TNWs, including the elimination of all U.S. ground-launched systems and the removal of all nuclear weapons from

U.S. surface ships and attack submarines, and invited Soviet President Mikhail Gorbachev to reciprocate. Gorbachev made a similar announcement on October 5, pledging to eliminate many TNWs and transfer others from deployment with operational units to central storage facilities. The following January, Boris Yeltsin, President of the new Russian Federation, committed his government to implement Gorbachev's original offer, as well as some other reductions that Yeltsin subsequently added.[1]

Although these 1991-92 Presidential Nuclear Initiatives (PNI) consisted only of parallel and reciprocal measures, they have eliminated more nuclear weapons than any arms control treaty. Under their terms, Russia and the United States have destroyed thousands of their nonstrategic nuclear weapons and removed other nonstrategic nuclear systems from operational deployment, transferring their warheads to secure storage. Yet, the PNIs are not a formal arms control agreement, and they do not entail provisions to verify compliance. Neither Russia nor the United States has allowed monitors from the other country to conduct technical inspections at its TNW storage sites. The two governments also do not exchange data about their remaining nonstrategic weapons, though at some NATO-Russia meetings, they have simply reported the percentage of PNI-applicable warheads, but not their absolute numbers, that they have eliminated.[2]

In 2005 and 2006, however, American officials complained that the Russian Government was not providing sufficient information to substantiate its claims to have made further reductions in its nonstrategic nuclear systems.[3] Some multilateral nuclear arms control agreements do cover TNW, but their provisions are also not well enforced. The Nuclear Non-Proliferation Treaty (NPT) anticipates the eventual elimination of all nuclear weapons. Proposals to reduce and better control Russian and American nonstrategic weapons regularly arise at NPT-related meetings. For example, several delegates to the May 2010 NPT Review Conference advocated making greater efforts to eliminate nonstrategic weapons regardless of their range. Yet, nuclear abolition is seen by the Russian and American Governments as a long-term goal — the horizon appears to be longer in Moscow — requiring stringent conditions. Other arms control agreements — such as those establishing nuclear-free zones or requiring that nuclear weapons states guarantee never to use their nuclear weapons against states not possessing them — restrict the legally permissible use of nuclear weapons, but they lack means to ensure compliance.

The number, status, and other characteristics of the nonstrategic nuclear weapons stockpiles of Russia and the United States are state secrets. Information about the possible nonstrategic nuclear weapons of other countries is also minimal, though all the nuclear weapons of India, Pakistan, and North Korea appear to have ranges below 5,500 km. Although China appears to have some 20 intercontinental-range ballistic missiles capable of reaching targets in North America, the Chinese military has hundreds of nonstrategic nuclear weapons designed for potential use around China's periphery as well as possibly on Chinese territory against an invading land army (a very unlikely contingency at present).

Although the United States had thousands of nonstrategic nuclear systems during the Cold War, analysts believe that the U.S. military now has only some 500 short-range nuclear weapons in its operational arsenal, as well as approximately an equal number in the U.S. inactive stockpile. These TNWs consist of B61-3 and B61-4 nuclear gravity bombs for airplanes (some at U.S. air bases in Europe) and nuclear-armed submarine-launched Tomahawk land-attack cruise missiles (TLAM-N) deployed at secure land facilities in the United States.[4] The Obama administration's *Nuclear Posture Review Report*, published in April 2010, decided to retire the TLAM-N after the Japanese Government indicated that Tokyo no longer saw that particular weapon system—as opposed to other U.S. nuclear and conventional forces—as essential for maintaining the credibility of U.S. extended deterrence guarantees for Japan.[5]

The U.S. Armed Forces have been dramatically reducing their holdings of TNWs because the advent of precision-guided conventional munitions has reduced the number of missions that might require nuclear warheads. In addition, an important role for TNWs—defending NATO allies in Europe from the large conventional militaries of the Soviet bloc—vanished with the end of the Cold War. Furthermore, many U.S. commanders and civilian strategists doubt that the American President or other senior civilian and military leaders would authorize the use of a nuclear weapon except under the most extreme circumstances. The U.S. military has preferred to redirect monetary and other resources to researching and developing conventional weapons whose use is more likely. At present, the main factor sustaining the U.S. TNWs is to meet NATO's formal requirements for such weapons, make U.S. extended nuclear deterrence guarantees appear more credible to countries that might otherwise decide to pursue their own nuclear weapons, and have some nonstrategic assets to trade away in any TNW negotiations with Moscow.

The Soviet and Russian Armed Forces have also decreased their TNWs since the mid-1980s. The INF Treaty required the Soviet Union to eliminate several important medium-range missile systems, while the PNI led to the destruction of many shorter-range systems. During the early 1990s, the withdrawal of the Russian Army from central Europe and the Russian Navy from combat patrols also decreased Russian military interest in nonstrategic nuclear weapons. The severe problems experienced by the Russian defense industry during this period also led the Russian Government to concentrate Russia's limited production resources on higher-priority weapons, such as strategic delivery systems and major conventional weapons systems, though few of either was produced. But toward the end of the decade, Moscow's interest in strengthening Russia's nuclear forces, including those having short ranges, increased. Russian policymakers decided to retain many nonstrategic nuclear weapons because they perceived them as a vital instrument for preventing NATO, which was then expanding its membership and engaging large and unprecedented military operations in the former Yugoslavia, from exploiting its conventional military superiority in a possible war with Russia.

Even today, the Russian defense industry finds it impossible to manufacture the large number of sophisticated precision conventional weapons like those produced by several NATO countries.[6] The Ministry of Defense has also proved unable to transition the Russian military to an entirely professional force of long-term contract soldiers. Instead, it has had to keep using large numbers of unmotivated, poorly trained, but low-cost short-term Russian conscripts.[7] To make up for the weaknesses of Russia's conventional forces, the Russian military has continued to deploy hundreds of nuclear warheads on short-range tactical surface-to-surface and air-to-ground strike missiles as well as systems designed for anti-air and anti-ship defense. The greater destructive power of their nuclear warheads compensates for the higher targeting inaccuracies and lower preparedness of Russian military forces compared with their NATO counterparts. Some Russian military leaders also seem to view Russia's TNWs as helping Russian troops compensate for China's much larger ground forces in the event of a Russia-China war—though this perspective is rarely discussed in public given the official line.[8] Since it could take decades for Russia's defense industrial and military reform programs to achieve success, the Russian military will likely believe it will need to rely on nuclear weapons, including TNWs, for years to come.

Although security tensions between Russia and the United States and its NATO allies have lessened from the time of troubles in the years between 2007 and 2009, Russian leaders still consider nuclear weapons—tactical as well as strategic—an essential tool in their foreign and defense policy portfolio. Despite the recent emphasis on how Russia's oil and gas have replaced the Army and Navy as Russia's two most influential strategic tools, the most important fact about Russia is that, along with the United States, it possesses one of the world's two most powerful nuclear arsenals, with sizeable offensive nuclear forces in all categories of the traditional triad of strategic nuclear delivery vehicles—ICBMs, SLBMs, and long-range strategic bombers. Russia also possesses far more TNWs than any other country.

During a Duma hearing on ratifying the New Strategic Arms Treaty (START) in July 2010, Russian nuclear expert Alexei Arbatov confirmed that Russia had a least 10,000 nuclear warheads in its current arsenal when one includes its large TNW holding.[9] Other Russian sources also confirm that the Russian Armed Forces possess thousands of TNWs.[10] In their latest annual survey of Russian nuclear forces, Robert S. Norris and Hans M. Kristensen calculate that, in late 2009, the Russian military possessed a total of approximately 12,000 nuclear warheads. Some 4,600 nuclear warheads were in Russia's operational arsenal (i.e., ready for rapid use), of which approximately 2,600 were deployed on strategic nuclear delivery vehicles and some 2,000 were "nonstrategic" or TNWs. They conclude that roughly 7,300 nuclear warheads were in a reserve status or awaiting dismantlement.[11] In terms of nonstrategic warheads (i.e., those not designed for use on the triad of strategic delivery vehicles), Norris and Kristensen assess that Russia has some 5,390 TNWs. These consist of 2,000 TNWs (AS-4 air-to-surface missiles and a variety of gravity bombs) for use by tactical aircraft, 1,120 tactical warheads for air defense, and 2,270 nuclear warheads for use by Russian warships. They also estimate that the Russian Army has an indeterminate number of TNWs that might still be usable for ground operations.[12]

The Russian Navy is especially prone to view TNW on Russian surface ships and submarines as an important operational weapon to compensate for the potentially superior numbers and capabilities of Russia's maritime adversaries, above all, that of the U.S. Navy. For example, in 2009, Vice-Admiral Oleg Burtsev, Deputy Chief of the Russian Navy General Staff, claimed that the Navy was making such progress in extending the range and accuracy of its TNWs that: "They do not need to deliver high-yield warheads, instead it is possible to make a transition to low-yield nuclear warheads that could be installed on the existing types of cruise missiles."[13] Burtsev also implied that Russia's new nuclear-power attack submarines, such as the *Severodvinsk*-class ships, would "probably" continue to carry TNW. Norris and Kristensen calculate that the Russian Navy maintains 2,270 operational nonstrategic nuclear warheads, primarily for use on various types of short-range cruise missiles. These include nearly 700 warheads for naval cruise missiles, anti-submarine weapons, anti-air missiles, or anti-ship torpedoes.[14] These TNWs are stored on land at various Russian naval bases. Russian crews regularly rehearse loading these warheads on delivery systems and launching them.[15]

DOCTRINE

On February 5, 2010, the new *Military Doctrine of the Russian Federation* was finally published on the Kremlin website. Despite all the developments of the past decade, including the wars in Afghanistan, Iraq, and Georgia, this latest version generally advocated the same policies as the previous *Military Doctrine* adopted in 2000. Notably, the new draft expresses particular dissatisfaction with NATO, complaining about the growth of the alliance's military infrastructure close to Russia's border as well as its alleged efforts to acquire "global functions in contravention of international law."[16] The current draft identifies four types of military conflicts:

- small-scale armed conflicts;
- local wars such as that between Russia and Georgia in 2008;
- regional wars that can potentially involve many countries;

- large-scale conflicts such as World Wars I and II.

Although U.S. defense officials briefed their Russian colleagues in advance about the content of the recently released U.S. *Quadrennial Defense Review* (QDR), Russian doctrinal writers appear not to have taken the other's declaratory doctrine into account when composing the Russian text. Whereas the current Russian *Military Doctrine* basically describes U.S. actions as threatening Russia, the QDR characterizes Russia as a potential partner with the United States against weapons of mass destruction (WMD) proliferation, terrorism, and ballistic missile threats. We thus have a conceptual asymmetry in which Russian defense planners are preoccupied with hypothetical U.S. and NATO threats while American strategists are seeking Moscow's help in winning the war in Afghanistan as well as countering international terrorists, states, and proliferation concerns.

The 2010 *Military Doctrine* affirms that:

> The Russian Federation reserves the right to use nuclear weapons in response to the use of nuclear and other types of weapons of mass destruction against it and (or) its allies, as well as in response to large-scale aggression utilizing conventional weapons in situations critical to the national security of the Russian Federation.[17]

Similarly, the 2010 *Military Doctrine* affirms Moscow's readiness to employ nuclear weapons only in retaliation for the use of nuclear or other WMD against Russia or its allies. It also allows Russia to initiate the employment of nuclear weapons first when a conventional attack by an aggressor proves so effective that it endangers the Russian state (a provision not in the first 1993 doctrine).

In both documents, the declared purpose of Russian nuclear weapons is to deter other countries from engaging in a military conflict with Russia. Like the United States and the other declared nuclear weapons states, with the notable exception of China, the Russian Government has refused since the release of its November 1993 *Military Doctrine* to declare in public its adherence to an unqualified no nuclear-first-use posture.[18] In principle, Russian officials are prepared to start a nuclear war in an emergency. These declaratory statements still appear operationally relevant, since Russian military forces continue to conduct large-scale exercises with scenarios involving possible nuclear use — though these seem to involve longer-range strategic systems rather than tactical nuclear weapons.[19]

Despite expectations based on earlier statements by the Russian Government, the 2010 doctrine does not expand the range of permissible uses of nuclear weapons to include preventive or preemptive nuclear strikes or explicitly affirm Russia's right to employ nuclear weapons for regional and even local wars against terrorists. Such an expansive posture was offered in several apparent trial balloon statements by senior Russian military and security policymakers in the years before the 2010 *Military Doctrine* was published, including General Yuri Baluyevsky, head of the Russian General Staff and First Deputy Defense Minister.[20] Likewise, Security Council Secretary Nikolai Patrushev made the following statement to the *Rossiyskaya Gazeta* concerning the draft of the new *Military Doctrine* then under consideration: "The conduct of a nuclear strike against an aggressor, including a preemptive strike, is not ruled out in critical situations for national security."[21] At the same time that President Medvedev endorsed the public *Military Doctrine*, however, he also approved a classified document: "The Foundations of State Policy in the Area of Nuclear Deterrence until 2020," which defined in greater detail the conditions under which Russia might employ nuclear weapons. Observers speculate that this document may contain some of the more expansive language about the use of nuclear strikes for purposes of preemption, regional conflicts, or other purposes not explicitly identified in the public *Military Doctrine*.[22]

Other Russian Government security documents confirm that maintaining a strong nuclear force and the option to use it has long been — and will likely remain — a key element of Russian security policy.[23] The statements of Russian officials and defense analysts also support this declaratory policy — Russia must retain and be prepared to use nuclear weapons to defend itself from major conventional as well as nuclear threats. In a January 12, 2006, article entitled, "Military Doctrine: Russia Must Be Strong," published in the Russian *Vedomosti* newspaper, then Defense Minister Sergey Ivanov said Russia's first task for the 2006-10 period was "to sustain and develop strategic deterrent forces at the minimum level needed to guarantee that present and future military threats are deterred."[24] In February 2007, Ivanov stressed to the Russian Duma that, were deterrence to fail, the Russian military was prepared to use these nuclear forces, observing: "What else were they built for?"[25]

Russian Government representatives openly acknowledge that they take U.S. nuclear capabilities into account when structuring their own forces. As Ivanov put it: "Moscow is attentively tracking the developments in the U.S. strategic nuclear forces."[26] In particular, Russian Government representatives insist they will retain sufficient—if not necessarily equal—nuclear weapons capacity to overcome any U.S. attack. Russian leaders also see their nuclear forces as essential for deterring threats by the other nuclear powers—including not only NATO allies, Britain and France, but also China, though the Chinese threat is never mentioned by name. When Russia's new *Military Doctrine* was being revised, one of its main authors, Army-General Makhmut Gareyev, argued that:

> The nuclear weapons of all major nuclear powers are ultimately designed to be used against Russia, whether we want to admit it or not. In this context, the task of curbing a potential aggressor by means of a strategic nuclear deterrent is becoming more important than in the past.[27]

Similarly, "The Strategy of National Security of the Russian Federation to 2020," approved on May 12, 2009, also sees a major threat to Russia's security in how the other countries aim to achieve overwhelming dominance in the military sphere through their development of strategic nuclear forces; precision, information weapons; strategic weapon systems with non-nuclear warheads; global anti-missile defense systems; and by militarizing outer space. It describes nuclear weapons as essential for compensating for any weakness in Russia's conventional forces.[28]

Although the process of modernizing Russian conventional forces was underway at the time the 2009 *National Security Strategy* was written, it was (and still is) moving at a slow pace.[29] For this reason, when looking at U.S. and NATO superiority in advanced conventional military technologies, and China's potential conventional advantages in Central and East

Asia, Russian leaders see resorting to—or at least threatening to employ—nuclear weapons as an essential equalizer. In December 2006, Russian President Vladimir Putin reportedly told Ivanov that Russia's nuclear forces account for 90 percent of the country's security.[30] According to Russian nuclear expert Alexei Arbatov: "Nuclear weapons are for Russian people now much more important than decades ago. . . . They are more important than during the Cold War times as a pillar of national security."[31] This assessment makes sense given that during the Cold War period, Moscow disposed of massive conventional military power in the form of both the Soviet Armed Forces and the military forces of its captive Warsaw Pact allies.

As in Cold War times, however, Russian leaders continue to issue nuclear threats to try to influence the foreign and defense policies of other countries. In recent years, Russian leaders have proclaimed their intent to consider nuclear strikes against former Soviet bloc states that join NATO or establish U.S. ballistic missile systems or military bases on their territory. In addition to whatever Russian security dangers these Russian nuclear threats tried to avert, the threats also aimed to support Moscow's claim that the former Soviet states fall within Russia's special security zone—a type of sphere of influence in which Moscow asserted the right to veto foreign and defense policies of the Commonwealth of Independent States (CIS) countries that Russian leaders might perceive as a challenge to Moscow's vital national interests. Polish Prime Minister Jaroslaw Kaczynski, for instance, characterized Russian threats as an attempt to establish that his country still falls within Moscow's zone of control when international security issues arise: "We are talking about the status of Poland and Russia's hopes that

Poland will once again come under its sphere of influence."[32]

In January 2008, the leaders of Ukraine's new pro-Western coalition government—Prime Minister Yulia Tymoshenko, President Viktor Yushchenko, and Parliament Chairman Arseny Yatsenyuk—submitted a joint letter to NATO Secretary General Jaap de Hoop Scheffer, declaring Ukraine's readiness to accept a Membership Action Plan (MAP) for NATO.[33] Russian leaders quickly underscored their opposition to Ukraine's becoming yet another NATO member on Russia's borders. After meeting with Yushchenko at the Kremlin on February 12, Putin warned that if Ukraine were to join NATO and host U.S. missile defense sites: "It's horrible to say and even horrible to think that, in response to the deployment of such facilities in Ukrainian territory, which cannot theoretically be ruled out, Russia could target its missile systems at Ukraine."[34]

Russian nuclear threats against nearby states showing an interest in hosting U.S. ballistic missile defense (BMD) systems have become even more common in recent years. Starting in 2006, senior Russian Government officials, military officers, and policy analysts offered an escalating range of complaints regarding the planned deployment of U.S. BMD in former Soviet bloc countries. They insisted that, whatever their stated aim, the deployments really sought to intercept Russia's own decreasing ICBM arsenal. They also claimed that, despite the small number of BMD interceptors originally intended for deployment, the United States aimed to establish many more missile defense systems near Russia in coming years, accompanied by additional military facilities close to Russia using the pretext that they were needed to defend the BMD systems.

In response, Russian leaders threatened to retaliate with nuclear weapons to destroy the offending facilities. In September 2006, *Interfax* quoted retired Major General Vladimir Belous as stating that his country's "military doctrine envisages that Russian Armed Forces are allowed to attack installations in foreign countries that threaten its security."[35] That same month, two Russian submarines—one based in the North Pole and the other in the Pacific Ocean—each launched a ballistic missile towards the Kizha missile range in northwest Russia rather than the traditional Kamchatka test range in the Russian Far East. If the Russian Navy sought to attack targets in Poland or other Eastern European countries, they would launch them in that direction.[36] Another Russian defense analyst, Alexander Pikayev, acknowledged that Russia could use tactical nuclear weapons to ensure the elimination of threatening BMD systems in Eastern Europe.[37] In October 2006, Yevgeny Buzhinsky, the head of the international military cooperation department of the Russian Ministry of Defense, told the daily *Izvestia* that the Russian Government would consider NATO's deployment of BMD near Russia's borders as "a real threat to our deterrent forces" and "as an unfriendly gesture on behalf of the United States, some Eastern European nations and NATO as a whole." He cautioned: "Such actions would require taking adequate retaliatory measures of a military and political character."[38]

As U.S. BMD deployment plans continued in the following years, so did Russian threats of nuclear retaliation. Colonel-General Nikolai Solovtsov, the commander of Russia's Strategic Missile Forces, warned in 2008 that should the governments of Poland, the Czech Republic, or other neighboring countries agree to host U.S. BMD facilities, Russia would "have to take appropriate action." He explained that:

> I cannot rule out that should the country's military-political leadership make such a decision, some of our ICBMs could be targeted at missile defense sites in Poland and the Czech Republic, and subsequently at other such facilities.[39]

Similarly, Deputy Chief of the General Staff Colonel General Anatoli Nogovitsyn warned that the Polish decision "cannot go unpunished."[40] He added that it was now "100 percent" certain Poland would be a priority target of the Russian military in a future war with NATO.[41]

In his first state of the nation address before both houses of the Russian parliament, President Dmitry Medvedev said that Russia would, "if necessary," deploy short-range Iskander missile systems in Kaliningrad "to neutralize if necessary the anti-ballistic missile system in Europe."[42] Kaliningrad, a Baltic Sea port which lies between NATO members Lithuania and Poland, hosts a major Russian military base. Medvedev also stated that Russian electronic equipment would jam the U.S. systems and that he had cancelled plans to dismantle three Russian missile regiments deployed in western Russia. The Iskander-M surface-to-surface missile has a declared range of slightly under 500 km (300 miles), which allows it to escape the prohibition in the INF Treaty. If deployed in the Kaliningrad region, the missile could allow Russia to target all of Poland and also territory in eastern Germany and the Czech Republic.[43] Each missile can carry several warheads. The Iskander has been tested with a conventional payload but could carry a nuclear warhead, though the Russian Government has not indicated any such intent. In July 2010, Aleksandr Postnikov, the commander of Russia's Ground Forces, told Ekho Moskvy radio that the Russian military was deploying the Iskander near St. Petersburg. From there, they could hit targets in Estonia, Latvia, and Finland.[44]

STRATEGY AND TACTICS

At a minimum, Russian nuclear forces aim to prevent the United States or any other country from launching a major attack against Russian territory. This requirement is likely to persist for at least the next decade. In late 2006, Putin told Russian military leaders that the country's "deterrent forces should be able to guarantee the neutralization of any potential aggressor, no matter what modern weapons systems he possesses."[45] Russian nuclear planners most likely concentrate their planning and resources on surviving a war with the United States, since such a capability should provide the assets that Russia would need to defeat weaker nuclear adversaries (e.g., Britain, China, or France). Russian strategists most fear an American attempt to decapitate the Russian leadership through a surprise attack involving U.S. nuclear and conventional attacks against Russia's centralized command-and-control networks and against its nuclear forces when they are on their lower peacetime alert status. They worry that American leaders might anticipate crippling the Russian military response by incapacitating Russia's political and military decisionmakers before they could organize a coherent retaliatory strike. Such a hypothetical attack could employ SLBMs with depressed trajectories from *Trident* submarines on patrol near Russia, or stealthy conventional weapons that would exploit weaknesses in Russia's early warning systems. U.S. ballistic missile and air defense systems would then attempt to intercept any Russian nuclear delivery platform that had survived an American first strike and was launched in reprisal.[46]

Should deterrence fail, then Russia's nuclear weapons could perform various strategic warfighting roles. In terms of damage limitation, a massive counterforce strike that overcame the adversary's active and passive defenses might be able to severely weaken the targeted state's ability to retaliate. In addition to compensating for Russian weaknesses in conventional military power, Russian military thinkers perceive their nonstrategic weapons as helping accomplish missions that otherwise might require the use of Russia's more limited supply of effective strategic nuclear weapons, which at present primarily lie in the latest-generation ICBMs due to lagging modernization of the strategic air and Navy deterrents. For example, they could be used to uphold Russian security guarantees offered to some of the former Soviet republics through the Collective Security Treaty (CST), which was signed in Tashkent, Uzbekistan, in 1992 by the members of the CIS.[47] Under CST Article 4, members pledge to render each other "all necessary assistance, including military assistance" in case of external aggression. Following a joint Russian-Belarusian military exercise in June 2006, Belarusian President Alexander Lukashenko said that he could not exclude the use of Russia's TNW in his country's defense.[48] The CST underpins the Russian-dominated Collective Security Treaty Organization (CSTO), which includes Armenia, Kazakhstan, Kyrgyzstan, Tajikistan, and Uzbekistan, as well as Russia and Belarus.

Russian strategists have long considered using limited nuclear strikes to alter the course of a conventional conflict that Russia risked losing. The January 2000 *National Security Concept*, for example, implied that Russia could use nonstrategic nuclear forces to resist a conventional attack without engendering a full-scale nuclear exchange. Russian strategists have also indicated that they might detonate a limited number of nuclear weapons — perhaps just one — to induce an adversary to end ("de-escalate" in Russian terminology) a conventional military conflict with Russia.[49] The selective strike would seek to exploit the inevitable "shock and awe" effect associated with nuclear use to cause the targeted decisionmakers to weigh the risks of nuclear devastation more heavily. This strategy exploits the fear that, after one nuclear explosion, the prospects of further detonations increase substantially. Initiating nuclear use would underscore the seriousness with which the Russian Government viewed the situation and might encourage the other side to de-escalate the conflict and to pressure its allies into making concessions.

A related function of Russia's nuclear forces would be to prevent other countries from escalating a conventional conflict to a nuclear war. In such a scenario, Russia could threaten to retaliate disproportionately should an adversary employ nuclear weapons to try to alter a conventional battle in its favor. Even after one party has initiated a limited nuclear exchange, Russian commanders might attempt to control further intra-war escalation by issuing nuclear threats, showing restraint, or pursuing other "nuclear signaling." The most commonly discussed contingency for a "de-escalation" mission is a NATO decision to intervene against a Russian military ally (e.g., Belarus) or on behalf of a nonmember country (e.g., Georgia) in a conflict with Russia. In its 1993 *Military Doctrine*, the

Russian Government abandoned its declared pledge not to employ nuclear weapons first in a conflict, effectively establishing a justification in Russian doctrine for initiating nuclear use.[50] The statement brought the declared strategic posture of Russia into line with that of the United States, Britain, and France (but not China). These NATO countries have never renounced the right to resort to nuclear weapons first in an emergency.

Actually exploding a nuclear device in a conflict would prove problematic. On the one hand, it could terminate the conflict in Russia's favor. On the other, it could potentially lead to large-scale nuclear use if the other side considered the detonation as a prelude to additional nuclear strikes and subsequently decided to escalate first. Russian officials would probably attempt to underscore the strike's limited nature to minimize the risks of further escalation. In conducting a nuclear strike for a "de-escalation" mission, for instance, Russian commanders could seek to minimize their opponent's civilian and perhaps even military casualties to discourage further nuclear use. For example, they could employ a low-yield tactical nuclear warhead against an adversary's military base, warship, or armored formation operating in a scarcely populated area. Alternately, Russian forces could detonate a high-altitude burst near an adversary's warships with the expectation that the explosion would not produce casualties or nuclear fallout, but would still devastate the fleet's sensors and communications due to its electromagnetic pulse (EMP) and other effects. Since Russia's strategic nuclear forces are needed to deter adversaries from resorting to major nuclear war, detonating a TNW might provide the optimal balance between signaling Moscow's seriousness and avoiding an action that might provoke more escalation than the Russian Government is actually seeking.[51]

Russia's nuclear weapons also play an important role in ensuring Moscow's status as a significant global player. During the 1990s, Russian strategists vigorously debated the importance of maintaining a robust nuclear deterrent.[52] A minority argued that, in the post-Cold War world, nuclear weapons had lost much of their military utility, and hence Russia should concentrate on developing its conventional forces. The majority, however, continued to view Russia's nuclear arsenal as an essential instrument for preserving its status as a great power, especially since the other nuclear powers showed little inclination to relinquish their own arsenals.

The 1968 NPT formally designates Russia as one of the five countries legally permitted to possess nuclear weapons for an indefinite transition period leading to global nuclear disarmament. The long-standing strategic nuclear arms control negotiations between Moscow and Washington help confirm Russia's equality with the United States in an important security dimension. When asked why Russia deserved to be in the G-8, Russian President Vladimir Putin told a January 31, 2006, press conference that:

> the G-8 is a club which addresses global problems and, first and foremost, security problems. Can someone in this hall imagine resolving, shall we say, problems concerning global nuclear security without the participation of the largest nuclear power in the world, the Russian Federation? Of course not.[53]

Later that year, Putin told leading defense sector managers that: "The reliability of our 'nuclear shield' and the state of our nuclear weapons complex are a crucial component of Russia's world power status."[54]

In addition to the traditional function of deterring a nuclear strike against the Russian Federation as well as securing Russia's elite global security status, many Russians see their nuclear forces as a way to negate NATO's advantage in conventional forces. The decisive Western victories in Iraq, Kosovo, and Afghanistan were due to the precision conventional strike capabilities the United States and certain other NATO militaries had acquired in recent decades. Although Russian analysts recognized that these new conventional capabilities further decreased NATO's need to employ nuclear weapons in an operational role, they drew the lesson that Russia needed, if anything, to increase its reliance on having a strong nuclear arsenal to balance the conventional weaknesses of the post-Soviet Russian Army. Moreover, they observed that upgrading Russia's conventional forces to American standards, even if technically possible (a dubious assumption given the frailties of Russia's military-industrial complex) would entail considerably greater expenditures than maintaining even a large nuclear force.

In April 2006, General Baluyevsky told a press conference:

> Strategic parity in a sense of an equal number of missiles, aircraft, and ships — this meaning is going and has already gone into non-existence. We are not going to tighten our belts or take off our last pair of trousers to achieve parity in the number of aircraft and missiles with the United States or all of NATO. . . . [Russia] has and will have nuclear deterrent forces sufficient

to bring to reason anyone who could try to test the strength of our borders or tap our natural resources.[55]

In his May 2006 address to the Federal Assembly, Putin likewise stressed that Russia could not afford to wage a quantitative arms race with the United States, but instead had to rely on less costly, asymmetric means in designing Russia's strategic deterrent.[56]

Yet, Russian leaders are caught in a vicious circle. They hesitate to shift funds away from their nuclear arsenal at a time when Russia's conventional forces lack sufficient strength to counter a NATO conventional military offensive. But by refusing to transfer substantial financial or other resources to the country's conventional forces, Russian decisionmakers cannot wean themselves away from their dependence on nuclear deterrence. By some estimates, up to 40 percent of the Ministry of Defense's annual budget has been devoted to developing the fundamentally troubled Bulava SLBM, around which Russia's next generation of strategic submarines have been designed.[57] Russian force planners could resolve this spending dilemma if they abandoned the need to defend against implausible threats such as an American nuclear attack or a NATO conventional invasion, and instead focused on managing small-scale wars, insurgencies, and terrorist threats within Russia and neighboring states.

Adopting a new force-sizing standard, however, would require a top-level decision by the Russian leadership that the West no longer presented a mortal threat, which the Russian leadership has consistently refused to do.[58] Until now, they have merely added the new challenge of resisting insurgents and terrorists to the traditional requirement of deterring and defeating a U.S.-NATO attack. In his May 2006 address, Putin himself reaffirmed the ambitious force planning goal that Russia's Armed Forces must be "able to simultaneously fight in global, regional and — if necessary — also in several local conflicts."[59] Only a large conventional military backstopped by strategic and tactical nuclear weapons can meet such demanding criteria.

TNW ARMS CONTROL

Many Western arms control advocates favor eliminating TNW because their small size, scattered location, relative mobility, and weaker security and safety features (the older Russian systems are thought to lack advanced electronic locks) render them more at risk for terrorist seizure than the nuclear warheads that are deployed on strategic nuclear delivery vehicles, which are generally some of the most well-guarded military assets in the Russian and American defense communities.[60] These arms control specialists also fear that Russia and the United States are more likely to employ a TNW than a strategic nuclear warhead. In addition to their generally lower yield, their battlefield missions encourage commanders to see them as weapons for warfighting rather than deterrence.[61] In turn, this status might place them under the tactical control of field commanders in certain conditions. A RAND Corporation (RAND) study concluded that some Russian operational commanders can launch ground-based TNW without further central government approval after Russia's civilian national security leaders have authorized their deployment to front-line troops.[62] Pending their elimination, analysts concerned about TNWs seek to bring non-strategic weapons under a more formal and transparent arms control regime than the existing PNIs, which lack a legal basis and do not entail obligatory data exchanges or other verification procedures.[63] The governments of many developing countries also favor eliminating Russian and NATO TNWs, a position they again advocated during the May 2010 NPT Review Conference.

The George W. Bush administration concluded that it would prove too difficult to address TNWs within the context of the Russian-American strategic nuclear arms control talks. The May 2002 Strategic Offensive Reductions Treaty (SORT), like previous Soviet-American and Russian-American arms control agreements, does not address nonstrategic nuclear forces. In subsequently explaining this TNW exclusion before the U.S. Senate, then-Secretary of Defense Donald Rumsfeld explained that the parties decided it would prove too difficult to resolve the many arms control complexities associated with these nonstrategic weapons:

> We might have argued that Russia's proximity to rogue nations allows them to deter these regimes with tactical systems; because they are many thousands of miles away from us; the United States distance from them requires more intercontinental systems possibly than theater systems. This could have resulted in a mind-numbing debate over how many non-strategic systems . . . should equal an intercontinental system, or open the door to a discussion of whether an agreement should include all nuclear warheads regardless of whether they're strategic or tactical.[64]

In early June 2005, Assistant Secretary of State for Arms Control Stephen Rademaker said Russian officials continued to evince "very little interest in talking to us" on further Russian-American non-strategic arms control.[65]

The Obama administration also decided not to press Russia to address nonstrategic nuclear weapons in the negotiations on the New START. When asked about the issue at the April 6, 2009, session of the Carnegie Endowment for International Peace conference on nuclear nonproliferation, chief U.S. New START negotiator Rose Gottemoeller said that, while President Obama was concerned about nonstrategic warheads: "My own view is that the immediate START follow-on negotiations will not be the area where that issue is immediately pursued." Instead, she simply advocated that "we should begin exploring the issues with the Russian Federation and decide how to fit that into the agenda." At the same session, Sergey I. Kislyak, currently the Russian Ambassador to the United States and an influential figure in determining Russia's strategic arms control policies, argued that, while nonstrategic nuclear weapons would need to be eliminated "if you decide to move to the world free of nuclear weapons," for the moment Russia and the United States "have enough work to do now to focus on things that are doable," adding that, "when you go to substrategic, there will be a lot of other things that needs to be entered into the play." Among these issues, Kislyak cited "the imbalances in conventional weapons [and the] appearance of new systems that maybe are non-nuclear, but designed to do the same job."[66]

The provisions of the New START Treaty—the term encompasses the main treaty text, a protocol specifying some additional rights and obligations of the parties, and the technical annexes—will not affect the TNW issue directly but will help define Russian military planning for future nuclear scenarios. Many provisions legally confirm reductions that have already taken place or are in the process of occurring as Russia and the United States continue their decades' long practice of fielding fewer but more capable and versatile nuclear systems. The new 1,550 limit for deployed nuclear warheads on no more than 700 deployed strategic nuclear delivery vehicles is lower than any previous treaty, but each side possesses thousands of additional warheads in storage, undergoing maintenance, or in the form of shorter-range nuclear systems. The 7-year implementation timeline gives Russia and the United States ample time to gradually continue reducing their totals while modernizing their remaining arsenals. Furthermore, the provisions give Russia and the United States considerable flexibility to determine how to structure their nuclear arsenals within these aggregate limits. Both sides can continue to keep a strategic triad of ICBMs, SLBMs, and strategic bombers, distributing the warheads among these three legs as they prefer. The United States and Russia are even allowed to keep an additional 100 non-deployed ICBM and SLBM launchers and heavy bombers equipped for nuclear armaments, a provision designed to deal with the problem of the U.S. "phantom" systems — those missile launchers and strategic bombers that are no longer usable but still counted under the original START, because they had not been eliminated according to its procedures.

The treaty's proposed verification regime would be less intrusive and costly than the elaborate requirements of the 1991 START Treaty, yet it still includes on-site inspections of nuclear weapons facilities, mandated exhibitions of delivery vehicles, obligatory exchanges of data, and advanced notifications of some activities related to Russian and American nuclear weapons policies. Other provisions would facilitate treaty monitoring by prohibiting acts that could disrupt national technical means of verification and by mandating the continued exchange of some missile testing telemetry.

NATO foreign ministers discussed the future of the alliance's TNWs at an April 22-23, 2010, informal meeting in Tallinn, Estonia. The issue had become divisive within the alliance as some governments were pressing for unilaterally ending NATO nuclear sharing, while others were insisting on retaining it. Although not empowered to make conclusive decisions, the foreign ministers nevertheless agreed on "some clear themes" to guide their approach to the TNW issue:

- NATO member states will not make "unilateral moves" on nuclear weapons issues;
- Members would share the burdens of maintaining a safe and credible nuclear deterrent;
- The alliance would balance maintaining a credible nuclear deterrent with the need to contribute to general arms control and disarmament.[67]

According to NATO Spokesman James Appathurai, the foreign ministers did indicate one way in which NATO could reduce its TNWs — if Russia agreed to eliminate some of its much larger stockpile of these weapons, as well as relocate any TNWs its does keep away from neighboring NATO countries, and make these holdings more transparent. Secretary of State Hilary Clinton told the foreign ministers that:

> In [seeking] any future reductions, our aim should be to seek Russian agreement to increase transparency on non-strategic nuclear weapons in Europe, relocate those weapons away from the territory of NATO members, and include non-strategic nuclear weapons

in the next round of U.S.-Russian arms control discussions.[68]

Apparthurai observed that, while NATO might take actions affecting its nuclear weapons policies without a direct Russian input, "Russia had to be taken into account when looking at the broader issue of reducing the total holdings of nuclear weapons in Europe."[69] Nonetheless, Apparthurai acknowledged that the Russians have not shown interest in negotiating formal limits on their TNWs, and that the allies have yet to propose initiating formal negotiations with the Russians.

Indeed, Russian officials have expressed little interest in entering into TNW reduction negotiations with NATO. Instead, they have regularly denounced the alliance's nonstrategic weapons as being threatening to Russia and have persistently urged NATO to relocate all foreign (i.e., American) TNWs to their home territories. In this regard, Russian Government representatives often refer to how Moscow has already eliminated the majority of the nonstrategic systems that it inherited from the Soviet Union and relocated the remainder in secure storage exclusively within Russian territory.[70] In late 2003, General Baluyevsky observed that the hundreds of U.S. air-deliverable TNWs in Europe "are for Russia acquiring a strategic nature since theoretically they could be used on our command centers and strategic nuclear centers."[71] In June 2005, Defense Minister Ivanov said that Russia was "prepared to start talks about tactical nuclear weapons only when all countries possessing them keep these weapons on their own territory."[72] In March 2010, Foreign Minister Sergey Lavrov said that ending the forward-positioning of U.S. TNWs "should be the starting point in any conversation on this topic."[73]

The main Russian military newspaper, *Krasnaya Zvezda*, has published several articles this year underscoring that Russia wanted the United States to remove all its TNW from Europe even before Moscow would consent to enter into nonstrategic arms control talks. One author explained:

> Before the beginning of official discussions on this theme, Washington and Moscow must take the same starting position in the negotiations. [The United States must agree] to withdraw all of its TNW from the European continent and bring them back to its own territory. That is, it must do what Russia did 15 years ago.[74]

American officials have traditionally responded to this Russian argument by noting that U.S. nonstrategic nuclear weapons play an essential role in sustaining NATO's nuclear deterrence and discouraging efforts by additional NATO members to acquire their own nuclear weapons.

On those rare occasions when prominent Russian policymakers have gone beyond this party-line position, they have laid out stringent conditions for even initiating nonstrategic arms control talks — these conditions are unlikely to be soon realized unless NATO proves willing to make vary generous unilateral concessions. On September 3, 2007, Russian Colonel General Vladimir Verkhovtsev, head of the Defense Ministry's 12th Main Directorate (*Glavnoye Upravleniye Ministerstvo Oborony* — GUMO), which is responsible for Russia's nuclear weapons, told reporters that Russia would consider negotiating additional restrictions on nonstrategic nuclear weapons, "but it must take place with the participation in the process of other countries, above all Britain and France."[75] Since France and Britain characterize their nuclear-armed ballistic missiles as strategic rather than nonstrategic weapons, they and other NATO governments, including Washington, have resisted their inclusion in any nonstrategic negotiations. The following year, General Nikolai Makarov, General Baluyevsky's replacement as head of the Russian General Staff, told ITAR-TASS that the Russian Armed Forces had no intention of eliminating its TNWs "as long as Europe is unstable and packed with armaments" — a condition that could be used indefinitely to characterize the military situation on the Continent pending universal disarmament (though Makarov probably meant the continued existence of NATO and its robust conventional forces).[76]

Russians outside the executive branch have been somewhat more creative and flexible in considering how to achieve some TNW arms control — suggesting linking talks on reducing Russian TNWs, an area of Russian advantage, in return for U.S. and NATO concessions regarding strategic offensive nuclear weapons (especially by reducing the larger number of U.S. non-deployed nuclear warheads), strategic defenses, or the conventional force imbalance in Europe, which presently favors NATO.[77] Western analysts have offered similar proposals, linking Russian concessions regarding TNWs to NATO's accepting limits on its conventional superiority through an enhanced Conventional Forces in Europe (CFE) Treaty.[78] Other Western analysts have proposed extending the provisions of the bilateral INF Treaty to encompass both shorter-range missiles and additional countries.[79] Before assuming office, a senior advisor to Secretary of State Clinton suggested removing some or all U.S. TNWs from NATO Europe in return for encouraging Russia simply to concentrate its large number of TNWs in more secure locations.[80] Russian officials have also expressed alarm about U.S. prompt global strike plans — the arming of traditionally nuclear-armed strategic delivery systems with conventional warheads — so they might want to restrict those further in return for constraining TNWs.[81]

Russian government officials might be seeking to avoid nonstrategic arms control talks in anticipation that European governments might at some point decide to request the removal of U.S. TNWs in any case given a lack of widespread popular support for NATO's nuclear mission. Some Russian analysts also seem concerned that any formal negotiations on the issue would raise the prominence of the issue within Europe and lead NATO members concerned about Russian military power to demand that the alliance either keep the NATO TNWs or take other steps to bolster their defenses against Moscow.[82] Finally, several Russian writers have expressed concern that discussing limitations on nonstrategic nuclear weapons could undermine the prospects for reforming Russia's conventional forces. Not only could opponents of reform cite the resulting anti-Russian rhetoric of East European NATO members fearful of Moscow, but they could object to exposing Russian vulnerabilities during the unstable transition period that would arise between when the existing structure was dismantled and the new one was fully operational.[83]

Even if Russia were to agree to enter into formal nonstrategic negotiations with NATO, it is unclear how these talks could best be structured. TNW issues could be discussed in bilateral Russia-U.S. talks devoted solely to that issue, though Russia has always resisted that approach and Washington's NATO allies would not welcome their exclusion. They could also be dealt with as part of the NATO-Russia dialogue regarding a new European security architecture. Moscow would like to draw up a new European Security Treaty along the lines of the draft text proposed by Russian President Medvedev. These could occur within the framework of the NATO-Russia Council, but Appathurai said during his April 22 Tallinn news conference that: "I don't think that that is on the immediate agenda. That's not the forum in which that kind of discussion, I think, would be held, and certainly not now."[84]

Furthermore, the TNW issues could be negotiated as part of follow-on negotiations to the New START, which would cover other issues set aside in the rush to negotiate the recently signed treaty (non-deployed nuclear warheads, strategic defense systems, and the use of conventional warheads on traditionally strategic delivery vehicles such as long-range ballistic missiles). Finally, they might be considered as part of the discussions to strengthen the NPT against further nuclear proliferation (many NPT parties consider NATO's nuclear-sharing arrangement a violation of the first two articles of the treaty).

What results one might reasonably hope to achieve from such negotiations is unclear. Even an American offer to redeploy all U.S. nuclear weapons in Europe to the United States might prove insufficient to convince the Russian Government to agree to additional TNW arms control measures. The United States could return its short-range nuclear weapons to Europe in a few hours unless their storage sites and related infrastructure had also been destroyed. In addition, it would prove difficult to verify any agreement since attack aircraft, the main NATO delivery system for U.S. nonstrategic nuclear weapons, are typically dual-use systems that can also launch conventional strikes.

Any proposals for increased transparency or TNW consolidation would need to overcome Russian fears about NATO preemption, since placing the weapons in a few designated places would make them easier to attack, creating opportunities (and incentives) for a preemptive first strike that would destroy the weapons before they could be dispersed to their launch sites. Any proposals for less than total reductions would need to address U.S. congressional concerns about the imbalance in the Russian-U.S. TNWs, which would become especially salient were both countries to negotiate further reductions in the size of their strategic nuclear arsenals. The warhead and launcher limits in the New START may already be lower than the size of Russia's residual TNWs, though the latter are by definition less threatening to the U.S. homeland and compensated for by NATO's superior conventional forces.

Even if the parties are unable to secure the elimination of all NATO and Russian TNW, or if some weapons were exempt from the transparency arrangements to enhance deterrence through the increased uncertainty, mutual TNW reductions could provide several advantages, including reducing the number of possible terrorist targets, saving money that would have to be spent on having to modernize a larger number of weapons, allowing NATO to remove the TNWs from countries no longer eager to host them (which might leave U.S. TNWs in only Turkey and perhaps Italy), and demonstrating NATO and Russian commitment to making progress toward nuclear nonproliferation. Yet, securing Russian Government approval for even partial reductions looks unlikely for the indefinite future.

CONCLUSION: NUCLEAR POSSIBILITIES AND ILLUSIONS

In recent years, a number of American and international security experts, including several who held prominent U.S. Government positions during the Cold War, have supported various proposals leading toward general nuclear disarmament.[85] In his April 2009 speech in Prague, President Obama declared his ultimate objective to be the complete elimination of all nuclear weapons. Russian officials have publicly offered general support for eliminating nuclear weapons at some point. At his September 2008 meeting in Sochi with foreign experts of Russia who were members of the Valdai Discussion Club, Prime Minister Putin gave conditional support for abolishing nuclear weapons. Although Putin acknowledged that, until a few years ago, he would have considered achieving the practical elimination of nuclear weapons "absolutely impossible," he now professed that: "Today I consider it almost realistic" given that the conventional weapons capabilities of nuclear weapons states, like Russia, had improved sufficiently to deter any aggressor.[86] Medvedev and Obama reaffirmed in their April 1 joint statement their ultimate goal of abolishing all nuclear weapons. Additionally, Putin responded affirmatively to a question at a joint news conference with visiting German Foreign Minister Frank-Walter Steinmeier when asked whether he could imagine a Russia without nuclear weapons, though Putin indicated he would expect for the United States to also eliminate its own nuclear forces.[87]

Nonetheless, many foreign observers of the Russian defense community doubt that the Russian government would want to relinquish one of the last

401

remaining props of Russia's great power status, and create a situation in which American and NATO conventional military superiority would be unchecked by Russian nuclear weapons.[88] Influential Russians have also expressed unease at transitioning to a nuclear-free world. In April 2009, Sergey Rogov, the director of the USA and Canada Institute of the Russian Academy of Sciences, published a commentary in the Russian newspaper *Kommersant* explicitly warning that, the lower the level of Russia and American nuclear forces, the more significant the conventional imbalance of forces will become.[89] Like Putin, President Medvedev has described Russia's possession of nuclear weapons as the main bulwark guaranteeing the country's ability to pursue an independent foreign policy in an international system heavily dominated by the United States.[90]

On April 20, 2009, Medvedev directly addressed Obama's April 5 Prague speech in which Obama called for the eventual elimination of nuclear weapons. Medvedev said that a number of "conditions" must be achieved for universal nuclear disarmament. These prerequisites include: banning the deployment of nuclear weapons in outer space; ensuring that nuclear weapons removed from operational deployment were destroyed rather than simply stockpiled; and, preventing a compensating buildup in conventional arms following a reduction in nuclear forces. Medvedev further warned that the unilateral deployment of missile defense systems also "complicates nuclear disarmament."[91] The Russian people also favor their country's retention of a robust nuclear force. For example, a recent poll by the Russia Public Opinion Research Center (VTsIOM) found that, unlike in the years immediately following the end of the Cold War, a majority of Russian respondents (60 percent) now oppose further nuclear disarmament. Most cited a concern with assuring Russia's security in case of war, while a quarter of the respondents favored preserving Russia's nuclear weapons to showcase Russia's political power. Only 4 percent said that nuclear weapons were essential for countering U.S. military strength, though such a perspective may be encompassed in the above responses and appears common among Russia's current generation of foreign and defense policy leaders.[92]

Most Americans would probably not presently favor eliminating the U.S. nuclear arsenal. In its April 2010 *Nuclear Posture Review Report*, the Obama administration itself sets very high standards for realizing a nuclear-free world:

> The conditions that would ultimately permit the United States and others to give up their nuclear weapons without risking greater international instability and insecurity are very demanding. Among those are the resolution of regional disputes that can motivate rival states to acquire and maintain nuclear weapons, success in halting the proliferation of nuclear weapons, much greater transparency into the programs and capabilities of key countries of concern, verification methods and technologies capable of detecting violations of disarmament obligations, and enforcement measures strong and credible enough to deter such violations. Clearly, such conditions do not exist today. But we can — and must — work actively to create those conditions.[93]

Realizing these conditions in Russia's case would require a transformation in the threat perceptions, security culture, and defense ambitions of Russian leaders comparable to that which occurred in Germany and Japan in the generations after World War II. Although these cases show that these types of security revolutions are possible—and Russia might have come close to experiencing one during the few years immediately following the demise of the Soviet Union and its inherently antagonistic Communist ideology—they are also very rare. Russia will likely remain a nuclear weapons power for decades to come, with nonstrategic weapons serving as a prominent tool in its portfolio.

ENDNOTES - CHAPTER 8

1. Nikolai Sokov, "Issue Brief: Tactical Nuclear Weapons (TNW)," *Nuclear Threat Initiative*, May 2002, available from *www.nti.org/e_research/e3_10a.html*.

2. *Ibid*.

3. Wade Boese, "Deeper Nuclear Cuts Unlikely for Now," *Arms Control Today*, Vol. 35, No. 6, July/August 2005, p. 36; and "Press Conference with Stephen Rademaker, Acting Assistant Secretary of State for Security and Nonproliferation Issues," Official Kremlin International News Broadcast, April 12, 2006, available from *www.sgpproject.org/Personal%20Use%20Only/G8Rademaker4.12.06.htm*.

4. Robert S. Norris and Hans M. Kristensen, "U.S. Nuclear Forces, 2010," *Bulletin of the Atomic Scientists*, March/April 2010, p. 65.

5. *Nuclear Posture Review Report*, Washington, DC: U.S. Department of Defense, April 2010, p. 29.

6. "Yadernoe Oryzhie Rossii - Protivoves Vooryzheniyam v Evrope," *Oryzhie Rossii*, 2010, available from *www.arms-expo.ru/site.xp/049051124053055052049.html*; and Igor Korotchenko, "Voennyi Disparitet s NATO RF Neitralizyet Yadernym Oryzhiem," December 12, 2008, available from *news.km.ru/voennyj_disparitet_s_nato_rf_nej*.

7. Sergei Zhuravlev, "On Combat Readiness: The 1,000,000-Strong Army Cannot Fight," *Nezavisimoe voennoe obozrenie*, April 2, 2010.

8. Nikolai Poroskov, "O Probleme Sokrasheniya Takticheskogo Yadernogo Oryzhiya," *Evropeiskaya Bezopasnost': Sobytiya, Ozenki, Prognozy*, No. 11, March 2004, available from *www.inion.ru/product/eurosec/st1vp11.htm#1*.

9. "Alexei Arbatov: v Yadernom Arsenale RF ne Menee 10 Tysyach Boezaryadov," *RiaNovosti*, July 6, 2010, available from *www.rian.ru/defense_safety/20100706/252532909.html*.

10. Alexei Arbatov, "Takticheskoe Yadernoe Oryzhie - Problemy i Resheniya," May 5, 2010, *Voenno-Promyshlennyi Kyr'er*, available from *vpk.name/news/39071_takticheskoe_yadernoe_oruzhie__problemyi_i_resheniya.html*; and "Kolichestvo Nositelei i Boezaryadov Strategicheskix Yadernyx Sil U.S. i Rossii," *Novosti VPK*, March 30, 2010, available from *vpk.name/news/37967_kolichestvo_nositelei_i_boezaryadov_strategicheskih_yadernyih_sil_ssha_i_rossii.html*.

11. Norris and Kristensen, p. 74.

12. *Ibid.*, p.79.

13. "Rol Takticheskogo Yadernogo Oruzhiya na Mnogotselevykh APL Vozrastet – VMF" ("The Role of Tactical Nuclear Weapons on Multipurpose Submarines Set to Grow — the Navy,") *RIA-Novosti*, August 23, 2009, available from *www.rian.ru/defense_safety/20090323/165742858.html*.

14. Norris and Kristensen, p. 79.

15. Miles A. Pomper, William Potter, and Nikolai Sokov, *Reducing and Regulating Tactical (Nonstrategic) Nuclear Weapons in Europe*, Monterey: CA: Monterey Institute of International Studies, James Martin Center for Nonproliferation Studies, December 2009, p. 14.

16. *Voennaya Doktina Rossiyskoy Federatsii (Military Doctrine of the Russian Federation)*, Russian President's website, February 5,

2010, available from *news.kremlin.ru/ref_notes/461*. See also "NATO Predstavlyaet Dostatochno Ser'eznyu Ygrozy dlya Rossii," *Rambler Novosti*, February 9, 2010, available from *news.rambler.ru/Ukraine/r/5285633/*; and Sergei Tyrchenko and Petr Vladimirov, "Nikolai Patryshev: Rossiya Imeet Pravo na Preventivnyi Yadernyi Ydar. Sekretar' Sovbeza RF Napomnil, Chto y Atomnoi Dybinki, Kotoroi Tak Lubyat Razmaxivat' US, Est' i Vtoroi Konez," *Svobodnaya Pressa*, October 14, 2009, available from *svpressa.ru/society/article/15470/*.

17. *Voennaya Doktrine Rossiyskoy Federatsii, (Military Doctrine of the Russian Federation)*, April 21, 2000, available from *www.nationalsecurity.ru/library/00003/index.htm*.

18. "The Basic Provisions of the Military Doctrine of the Russian Federation," adopted by Edict No. 1833 of the President of the Russian Federation, November 2, 1993, available from *www.fas.org/nuke/guide/russia/doctrine/russia-mil-doc.html*.

19. Matthew Day, "Russia 'Simulates' Nuclear Attack on Poland," *The Telegraph*, November 2, 2009, available from *www.telegraph.co.uk/news/worldnews/europe/poland/6480227/Russia-simulates-nuclear-attack-on-Poland.html*; and Pomper, Potter, and Sokov, p. 14.

20. See, for example, "Head of the General Staff: the RF Develops a New Military Doctrine and Plans Military Measures Against the U.S. BMD," *Newsru.com*, May 7, 2007, available from *www.newsru.com/russia/07may2007/baluevskij.html*.

21. Timofey Borisov, "Nikolay Patrushev: The Draft of the New Document, which Defines the Country's Defense Capability, Has Been Prepared," *Rossiyskaya Gazeta*, November 20, 2009. See also Vladimir Mamontov, "Security Council's Nikolai Patrushev Interviewed on Military Doctrine," *Izvestiya*, October 14, 2009.

22. See, for example, Dmitry Gorenburg, "Russia's New Military Doctrine: An Exercise in Public Relations," February 8, 2010, available from *russiamil.wordpress.com/2010/02/08/russias-new-military-doc*; and Marcel de Haas, "Doctrinal Stipulations and Political Realities. What Should Be the Western Response to the New Doctrine?" *Nezavisimaya Gazeta*, February 2, 2010, available from *www.ng.ru/realty/2010-02-26/1_doktrina.html*.

23. See for example: "The National Security Concept of the Russian Federation," adopted by the Decree of the President of the Russian Federation No. 1300 of December 17, 1997, in the "Edited Version of the Presidential Decree No. 24 of January 10, 2000," available from *www.iss.niiit.ru/doktrins/doktr01.htm*; and "The Law of the Russian Federation on Defense," adopted by the State Duma on April 24, 1996, and Approved by the Federation Council on May 15, 1996, available from *www.hro.org/docs/rlex/defence/index.htm*.

24. Sergey Ivanov, "Military Doctrine: Russia Must Be Strong," *Vedomosti*, January 12, 2006.

25. Sergey Ivanov, "Russia Reserves the Right to Preemptive Strikes," *Moscow Agentstvo Voennykh Novoste*i, February 7, 2007.

26. "Sergey Ivanov raskryl britantsam tseli I zadachi rossiyskikh yadernykh sil," July 14, 2004, available from *www.rol.ru/news/misc/news/04/07/14_010.htm*.

27. Viktor Litovkin, "General Gareyev: Russia Changing its Military Doctrine," *RIA Novosti*, Part 2, January 18, 2007, available from *en.rian.ru/analysis/20070118/59307373.html*. See also Makhmut Gareyev, "New Conditions—New Military Doctrine," *Nezavisimoe Voennoe Obozrenie*, February 2, 2007.

28. "Strategiya natsional'noy bezopasnosti RF do 2020 goda," May 12, 2009, available from *www.nsnbr.ru/strategiya_nb_rf.html*.

29. Vera Sitnina, "Voina Mozhet Vspykhnut Vnezapno," *Vremya Novostei*, September 29, 2008.

30. Viktor Myasnikov, "Starie osnovi novoy doktriny," *Nezavisimaya gazeta*, December 19, 2006.

31. Alexei Arbatov, "Advancing U.S.-Russian Security Cooperation," transcript of presentation at the Carnegie Endowment for International Peace, April 1, 2010, available from *www.carnegieendowment.org/files/0402carnegie-russia1.pdf*.

32. Cited in Peter Finn, "Antimissile Plan By U.S. Strains Ties With Russia," *Washington Post,* February 21, 2007, available from *www.washingtonpost.com/wp-dyn/content/article/2007/02/20/AR2007022001431.html?nav=rss_world/Europe.*

33. Vladimir Socor, "Ukraine's Top Three Leaders Request NATO Membership Action Plan," January 18, 2008, available from *www.jamestown.org/single/?no_cache=1&tx_ttnews%5Btt_news%5D=33304.*

34. Luke Harding, "Putin Issues Nuclear Threat to Ukraine over Plan to Host US Shield," *The Guardian*, February 13, 2008, available from *www.guardian.co.uk/world/2008/feb/13/russia.putin.*

35. Cited in "Russia Might Target U.S. Missile Defenses in Europe," Global Security Newswire, September 21, 2006, available from *204.71.60.35/d_newswire/issues/2006/9/21/129e3869-dfe9-4e90-bd29-da75bf307a26.html.*

36. Nikolai Sokov, "Russia's Newest Submarine-Launched Missile Fails in Tests, but Tests of Other Systems Succeed: Defense Minister Ivanov Raises Questions on Status of Russian Sea-Based Tactical Nuclear Weapons," *WMD Insights*, No. 10, November 2006, pp. 30-31; and Vladimir Mukhin, "Bulava kak zerkalo oboronki" ("Bulava is Like a Defense Circle"), *Nezavisimaya Gazeta*, September 12, 2006.

37. "Russia Could Use Tactical Nuclear Weapons to Defeat U.S. Missile Defenses in Europe, Experts Say," Global Security Newswire, September 22, 2006, available from *www.nti.org/d_newswire/issues/2006_9_22.html.*

38. "Deployment of U.S. Missile Defense in Europe Is Threat to Russia — Military Chief," October 18, 2006, available from *www.mosnews.com/news/2006/10/18/usthreat.shtml.*

39. "Russia Could Target Missiles at Sites in Central Europe," *RIA Novosti*, September 10, 2008, available from *en.rian.ru/russia/20080910/116678626.html.*

40. Thom Shanker and Nicholas Kulish, "Poland-U.S. Missile Deal Draws Anger from Russia," *New York Times*, August 15, 2008,

available from *www.nytimes.com/2008/08/15/world/europe/15iht-missile.3.15333406.html.*

41. "Rice to Visit Poland to Sign Missile Shield Deal," Agence-France Press, August 17, 2008, available from *afp.google.com/article/ALeqM5gLzVO9YmRVo2zJXJwfNJ0XQRZQWg.*

42. "Russian Missiles Near Poland to 'Offset' U.S. Shield - NATO Envoy," *RIA Novosti*, November 5, 2008, available from *en.rian.ru/russia/20081105/118146144.html.*

43. "Russia's Iskander Best Answer to U.S. Missiles in Europe - Analyst," *RIA Novosti*, November 5, 2008, available from *en.rian.ru/russia/20081105/118140039.html.*

44. "Russian Missile Move Worries NATO Member Estonia," Radio Free Europe/Radio Liberty, July 20, 2010, available from *www.rferl.org/content/Russian_Missile_Move_Worries_NATO_Member_Estonia/2105076.html.*

45. Cited in "Russia to Buy 17 ICBMs in 2007 - Minister," *RIA Novosti*, November 16, 2006, available from *en.rian.ru/russia/20061116/55705839.html.*

46. For a probably exaggerated assessment of the U.S. capacity to launch an effective first strike against Russia and China, see Kier A. Leiber and Daryl G. Press, "The Rise of U.S. Nuclear Primacy," *Foreign Affairs*, Vol. 85, No. 2, March-April 2006, pp. 42-54; and Keir A. Lieber and Daryl G. Press, "The End of MAD? The Nuclear Dimension of U.S. Primacy," *International Security*, Vol. 30, No. 4, Spring 2006, pp. 7-44. Russian responses to their assessment are surveyed in Arthur Blinov and Igor Plugatarev, "Guaranteed Unilateral Destruction," *Nezavisimaya Gazeta*, March 23, 2006; and Pavel K. Baev, "Moscow Puts PR Spin on its Shrinking Nuclear Arsenal," *Eurasia Daily Monitor*, April 17, 2006, available from *www.jamestown.org/single/?no_cache=1&tx_ttnews%5Btt_news%5D=31591.* Other critiques appeared in the September-October 2006 issue of *Foreign Affairs*.

47. "Rossii Nyzhno Dat' Pravo na Primenenie Ydernogo Oryzhiya – Expert," *RIA Novosti*, March 12, 2008, available from *nuclearno.ru/text.asp?12665.*

48. Viktor Myasnikov, Vladimir Ivanov, and Anton Khodas-evich, "Novaya strategicheskaya initsiativa," *Nezavisimaya Gazeta,* June 26, 2006.

49. According to one authoritative source, "De-escalation of aggression" is defined as "forcing the enemy to halt military ac-tion by threat to deliver or by actual delivery of strikes of varying intensity with reliance on conventional and (or) nuclear weap-ons." Sergey Ivanov, *Priority Tasks of the Development of the Armed Forces of the Russian Federation,* Moscow, Russia: Ministry of De-fense, October 2, 2003, p. 70, available from *www.pircenter.org/in-dex.php?id=184.*

50. "The Basic Provisions of the Military Doctrine of the Rus-sian Federation," adopted by Edict No. 1833 of the President of the Russian Federation, November 2, 1993, available from *www. fas.org/nuke/guide/russia/doctrine/russia-mil-doc.html.*

51. Aleksei Arbatov, "Tactical Nuclear Weapons - Problems and Prospects," *Voenno-promyshlennyi kuryer,* May 5, 2010, avail-able from *www.carnegie.ru/publications/?fa=40747.*

52. This debate is reviewed in Nikolai Sokov, "Moderniza-tion of Strategic Nuclear Weapons in Russia: The Emerging New Posture," May 1998, available from *www.nti.org/db/nisprofs/over/ modern.htm;* and Frank Umbach, *Future Military Reform: Russia's Nuclear & Conventional Forces,* Camberley, UK: Conflict Studies Research Centre, Defence Academy of the United Kingdom, Au-gust 2002, pp. 11-14.

53. "Transcript of the Press Conference for the Russian and Foreign Media," January 31, 2006, available from *www.kremlin.ru/ eng/speeches/2006/01/31/0953_type82915type82917_100901.shtml.* In an interview with NBC News, Putin likewise observed: "How can we talk about ensuring global security and address the issues of nonproliferation and disarmament if we do not include Russia, which is one of the biggest nuclear powers?" available from *krem-lin.ru/eng/speeches/2006/07/12/1443_type82916_108525.shtml.*

54. "Opening Remarks at Meeting with Heads of the Rus-sian Nuclear Weapons and Nuclear Energy Complexes," *Novo-*

Ogaryovo, June 9, 2006, President of Russia Official Web Portal, available from *www.kremlin.ru/eng/text/speeches/2006/06/09/1952_type82912type82913_106757.shtml.*

55. Nabi Abdullaev, "Russia Won't Seek Nuclear Parity with West," *Defense News*, April 10, 2006, p. 12.

56. Vladimir Putin, "Annual Address to the Federal Assembly of the Russian Federation," May 10, 2006, available from *www.kremlin.ru/eng/speeches/2006/05/10/1823_type70029type82912_105566.shtml.*

57. "The Bulava Should Be Put in the Kremlin: It Does Not Fly," *Moskovskiy Komsomolets*, August 2, 2009.

58. Aleksei Pyshkov, "Perezagryzka-Smena Politiki ili Smena Ritoriki?" *Izvestia*, July 5, 2009, available from *www.izvestia.ru/comment/article3130323/.*

59. Vladimir Putin, "Annual Address to the Federal Assembly of the Russian Federation," May 10, 2006, available from *www.kremlin.ru/eng/speeches/2006/05/10/1823_type70029type82912_105566.shtml.*

60. See, for example, Robin Cook and Robert McNamara, "Is it Time to Dismantle the Cold War's Nuclear Legacy?" *Financial Times*, June 23, 2005; and Daryl G. Kimball, "Small, Portable, Deadly, and Absurd: Tactical Nuclear Weapons," *International Herald Tribune*, May 3, 2005.

61. Nikolai Poroskov, "O Probleme Sokrasheniya Takticheskogo Yadernogo Oryzhiya," *Evropeiskaya Bezopasnost': Sobytiya, Ozenki, Prognozy*, available from *www.inion.ru/product/eurosec/st1vp11.htm#1.*

62. Olga Oliker and Tanya Charlick-Paley, *Assessing Russia's Decline: Trends and Implications for the United States and the U.S. Air Force*, Santa Monica, CA: RAND, 2002, pp. 81-83.

63. Pierre Claude Nolin, *The Security of WMD Related Material in Russia*, Brussels, Belgium: NATO Parliamentary Assembly, November 2005, p. 7, available from *www.nato-pa.int/Default.*

asp?SHORTCUT=695; John Edwards and Jack Kemp, eds., *Russia's Wrong Direction: What the United States Can and Should Do*, New York: Council on Foreign Relations, 2006, pp. 48-49.

64. Office of the Assistant Secretary of Defense, Public Affairs, U.S. Department of Defense, "Testimony for the Senate Foreign Relations Committee regarding the Moscow Treaty as Delivered by Secretary of Defense Donald H. Rumsfeld," July 17, 2002, available from *www.defenselink.mil/speeches/2002/s20020717-secdef1.html*.

65. Cited in Wade Boese, "Deeper Nuclear Cuts Unlikely for Now," *Arms Control Today*, Vol. 35, No. 6, July/August 2005, p. 36.

66. "Whither U.S.-Russia Relations?" Carnegie International Nonproliferation Conference, April 6, 2009, available from *www.carnegieendowment.org/events/?fa=eventDetail&id=1305&prog=zgp&proj=zted*.

67. "Press briefing by NATO Spokesman James Appathurai at the Informal meeting of NATO Foreign Ministers - Tallinn, Estonia," April 22, 2010, available from *www.nato.int/cps/en/SID-E0A8F737-39D940A7/natolive/opinions_62906.htm*.

68. Arshad Mohammed and David Brunnstrom, "U.S. signals its nuclear arms stay in Europe for now," *Reuters*, April 22, 2010; available from *www.washingtonpost.com/wp-dyn/content/article/2010/04/22/AR2010042202712.html*.

69. "Press briefing by NATO Spokesman James Appathurai at the Informal meeting of NATO Foreign Ministers - Tallinn, Estonia."

70. See, for example, Sergei B. Ivanov, "Speech at the 46th Munich Security Conference," Munich Security Conference, February 6, 2010, available from *www.securityconference.de/Ivanov-Sergey-B.457.0.html?&L=1*.

71. Cited in Robert S. Norris and Hans M. Kristensen, "U.S. Nuclear Forces, 2004," *Bulletin of the Atomic Scientists*, Vol. 60, No. 3, May/June 2004, p. 69.

72. "Russia Warns U.S. about Weapons in Space," Associated Press, June 3, 2005, available from *www.msnbc.msn.com/id/8073961/*.

73. "Tactical Nuclear Weapons Next Target for Arms Control - Lavrov," *RIA Novosti*, March 26, 2010, available from *en.rian.ru/russia/20100326/158322926.html*.

74. Vladimir Kozin, "TNW: Ill-Conceived Messages from the Foreign Ministers of Poland and Sweden," *Krasnaya Zvezda*, February 21, 2010. See also Viktor Ruchkin, "Old Bombs and New Problems," *Krasnaya Zvezda*, March 16, 2010.

75. "Britain, France Must be Included in Weapons Talks: Russian General," Agence-France Presse, September 3, 2007, available from *www.france24.com/france24Public/en/archives/news/world/20070903-Russia-France-Britain-nuclear-power-reduce-weapons.php*.

76. "Russian Military Chief Defends Nonstrategic Nukes," Global Security Newswire, December 17, 2008, available from *gsn.nti.org/gsn/nw_20081217_4724.php*.

77. These proposals are reviewed in Johan Bergenäs, Miles A. Pomper, William Potter, and Nikolai Sokov, *Reducing and Regulating Tactical (Non-strategic) Nuclear Weapons in Europe: Moving Forward?*, Washington, DC: The James Martin Center for Nonproliferation Studies, April 2010, p. 13.

78. *Ibid.*, p. 42.

79. Catherine M. Kelleher and Scott L. Warren, "Getting to Zero Starts Here: Tactical Nuclear Weapons," *Arms Control Today*, October 2009, available from *www.armscontrol.org/act/2009_10/Kelleher*.

80. Martin Matishak, "U.S. Could Pull Back Europe-Based Nukes, State Department Official Says," Global Security Newswire, August 5, 2009, available from *www.globalsecuritynewswire.org/gsn/nw_20090805_4929.php*.

81. Ministry of Foreign Affairs of the Russian Federation, "Transcript of Remarks and Response to Media Questions by Russian Minister of Foreign Affairs Sergey Lavrov at Joint Press Conference with Minister of Foreign Affairs Radoslaw Sikorski, Warsaw, Poland, September 11, 2008," available from *www.mid.ru/brp_4.nsf/e78a48070f128a7b43256999005bcbb3/cd9a026910cb657b c32574c3003c69a2?OpenDocument.*

82. Fedor Lukyanov, "Last Treaty: Russia and United States Have Exhausted Potential for Two-Way Nuclear Disarmament," *Vremya Novostey,* March 30, 2010.

83. Sergei Karaganov, "Nuclear Free World is a Dangerous Concept That Ought to be Abandoned," *Rossiyskaya Gazeta,* April 23, 2010.

84. "Press Briefing by NATO Spokesman James Appathurai at the Informal Meeting of NATO Foreign Ministers - Tallinn, Estonia."

85. George P. Shultz, Sidney D. Drell, and James E. Goodby, eds., *Reykjavik Revisited: Steps Toward a World Free of Nuclear Weapons,* Stanford, CA: Hoover Institution Press, 2008. See also George P. Shultz, William J. Perry, Henry A. Kissinger, and Sam Nunn, "A World Free of Nuclear Weapons," *The Wall Street Journal,* January 4, 2007, available from *www.fcnl.org/issues/item.php?item_id=2252&issue_id=54;* George P. Shultz, William J. Perry, Henry A. Kissinger, and Sam Nunn, "Toward a Nuclear-Free World," *The Wall Street Journal,* January 15, 2008, available from *online.wsj.com/public/article_print/SB120036422673589947.html.*

86. Andrei Zolotov Jr., "Three Hours with Vladimir Putin," *Russia Profile,* September 12, 2008, available from *www.russiaprofile.org/page.php?pageid=Politics&articleid=a1221223275.*

87. "Putin Could Imagine a Russia with no Nuclear Weapons," *Deutche Welle,* June 10, 2009, available from *www.dw-world.de/dw/article/0,,4315776,00.html.*

88. Pavel Felgenhauer, "Russia Will Retain as Many Nuclear Weapons as Possible," *Eurasia Daily Monitor,* April 9, 2009, available from *www.jamestown.org/programs/edm/single/?tx_ttnews%5Btt_*

news%5D=34834&tx_ttnews%5BbackPid%5D=407&no_cache=1;
Brian Whitmore, "Arms Control Redux: Let The Games Begin," RFE/RL, April 24, 2009, available from *www.rferl.org/content/Arms_Control_Redux_Let_The_Games_Begin/1615455.html*; and Michael Bohm, "Finished From the START," *Moscow Times*, June 11, 2009, available from *www.themoscowtimes.com/article/1016/42/378486.htm*.

89. Sergey Rogov, *Kommersant*, April 15, 2009.

90. "Rossia ne Bydet Yvelichivat' Potenzial Yadernogo Sderzhivaniya," *Rossiiskaya Gazeta*, March 5, 2010, available from *www.rg.ru/2010/03/05/rossiya-anons.html*.

91. Brett Young and Denis Dyomkin, "Russia Gives Cautious Response to Obama Nuclear Plan," *Reuters*, April 20, 2009, available from *www.reuters.com/article/worldNews/idUSLK21213720090420*.

92. "Most of Russians against nuclear disarmament – poll," *RIA Novosti*, July 15, 2010, available from *en.rian.ru/mlitary_news/20100715/159825463.html*.

93. *Nuclear Posture Review Report*, pp. 48-49.

CHAPTER 9

NEW START AND NONPROLIFERATION:
SUITORS OR SEPARATE TABLES?

Stephen J. Cimbala

INTRODUCTION

In the spring of 2010, the diplomatic atmosphere was an apparent success story for those seeking to reduce nuclear danger. The signing of the New Strategic Arms Reduction Treaty (START) agreement in April 2010 took place almost exactly 1 year after President Barack Obama's landmark speech calling for nuclear abolition. New START was followed by the successful outcome of the Nuclear Non-Proliferation Treaty (NPT) review conference in May 2010, in marked contrast to the acrimonious denouement of the 2005 meeting.[1] In addition, a U.S. Nuclear Posture Review and a revised Russian Military Doctrine made public in the spring of 2010 also seemed to reduce the role of nuclear weapons in the respective military strategies and national security policies of the two states. Russia, the United States, and the North Atlantic Treaty Organization (NATO) talked of cooperation on missile defense and other issues, and Obama pushed forward an ambitious agenda of multilateral control measures, including ratification of the Comprehensive Test Ban Treaty (CTB) and global support for a Fissile Materials Cutoff Treaty (FMCT). Only Maurice Chevalier, strolling and singing on a boulevard in Paris, was lacking for suitable background music.

Diplomatic atmospheres come and go, but the bankers of policy and strategy demand payment in hard currency. Russian-American strategic nuclear arms reductions neither preclude, nor guarantee, favorable prospects for multilateral disarmament or nonproliferation. This discussion first reviews the New START agreement and its implications for deterrence stability and arms control. Second, we develop and test the viability of a hypothetical, post-New START agreement with significantly lower numbers of operationally deployed strategic nuclear weapons. Third, we model a constrained nuclear nonproliferation regime, based on the post-New START agreement described earlier. A fourth section summarizes pertinent conclusions.

POLICY

New START Gets Done.

U.S. President Obama and Russian President Dmitry Medvedev signed the New START agreement April 8, 2010, in Prague, Czech Republic. Replacing the START I that had already expired in December 2009, the New START agreement called for reductions in the number of deployed long range nuclear weapons and their delivery systems: intercontinental missiles and heavy bombers. Part of the "reset" in U.S.-Russian relations following the acrimony of the Vladimir Putin and George W. Bush presidencies, the New START agreement was seen as a prelude to further Russian and American nuclear force reductions and to broader cooperation between Moscow and Washington on other nuclear related matters, including nonproliferation.

Under the new START agreement, each state would be required to reduce its number of deployed strategic warheads to a maximum of 1,550 and its number of launchers to a maximum of 800 – 700 deployed – within 7 years of treaty ratification and entry into force.[2] In theory, these limits were below the ceiling of 2,200 set by the preceding Strategic Offensive Reductions Treaty (SORT) in 2002 for deployed strategic warheads, and also below the START I maximum limit of 1,600 for long range delivery systems. Due to idiosyncrasies in the counting rules for weapons and the prior reductions by both states in their number of deployed weapons and launchers, neither the United States nor Russia would be required to make drastic changes in either existing or planned nuclear forces.[3]

Getting to New START from where they began in 2009 required the United States and Russia to make some compromises inside and outside of the actual START negotiation process.[4] Russia made concessions on the issues of missile defenses and "upload potentials" for stored, but not deployed, warheads. With respect to missile defenses, Russian treaty negotiators attempted to obtain an American commitment to limit future missile defense deployments in Europe, and/ or to involve Russia in the planning and implementing of future defenses. The treaty includes statements attesting to the importance of the relationship between offensive and defensive weapons, but it places no limits on future U.S. ballistic missile defense (BMD) modernization or deployment.[5] This compromise was made possible by the prior U.S. decision, apart from START negotiations, in the fall of 2009 to reboot the George W. Bush administration's plan to deploy missile defenses in Poland and in the Czech Republic, creating tension with Russia throughout 2007 and 2008. Writing in the *Wall Street Journal* in May, 2010, U.S. Secretary of Defense Robert M. Gates emphasized that the New START will not constrain American defenses:

The U.S. will continue to deploy and improve the interceptors that defend our homeland—those based in California and Alaska. We are also moving forward with plans to field missile defense systems to protect our troops and partners in Europe, the Middle East, and Northeast Asia against the dangerous threats posed by rogue nations like North Korea and Iran.[6]

The question of "upload potentials" raised some serious strategic issues. Russian START negotiators, doubtlessly reflecting the suspicions of their military, were concerned that the United States could first remove downloaded weapons consistently with START requirements and then, having decided to abrogate the treaty at a later date, rapidly upload the same weapons to achieve a surge or even a position of overwhelming nuclear superiority against Russia.[7] Theoretically, Russia would have a similar option to withdraw from the treaty and reload previously disarmed weapons. Compared to the American nuclear force modernization program, the Russian program was expected to provide fewer opportunities for timely reload on account of the disparity in suitable launchers, especially in submarine launched ballistic missiles (SLBMs). Russia's nuclear ballistic missile submarine (SSBN) and SLBM modernization programs fell well behind schedule in the preceding decade, and the test results for the planned Bulava SLBM, to be deployed with the newest *Borey* class of SSBNs, have been disappointing.[8]

Russia's concerns about U.S. relative nuclear advantage were not entirely based on arguments about upload potentials for current or future launchers. Three other issues played into Russian pessimism on this point. The first, already acknowledged, was the

U.S. plan for missile defenses deployed in Europe, adjusted by the Obama administration to a new approach that was presumably more acceptable to Russia than was the original Bush plan. The revised European BMD plan was a phased, adaptive approach built around sea and land-based missile interceptors for theater or shorter range ballistic missiles launched from Iran or other Middle Eastern locations.[9] Although the Obama European BMD plan was apparently less contentious than the Bush plan, Russian pessimists were not entirely mollified. They feared that the revised BMD plan left open the possibility of future enhancements to the antimissile systems that would degrade or even nullify Russia's nuclear deterrent.[10] The current probability of nuclear war between the United States and Russia is acknowledged by leaders of both states as being low to nonexistent, but Russia might still fear future political coercion on the part of the United States as supported by improved strategic defenses.[11] Russian doubts about U.S. intentions could be increased if improved American and/or NATO antimissile defenses were complemented by newly deployed systems for non-nuclear prompt global strike.

Conventional and Nuclear Deterrence.

A second source of Russian concern about the appearance of U.S.-Russian nuclear parity, and about the future viability of Russia's nuclear deterrent, resided in American plans for improving non-nuclear global strike capabilities. The George W. Bush administration had already introduced the notion of a "new triad" of conventional and nuclear offensive weapons, missile defenses, and improved nuclear infrastructure. The *Obama Nuclear Posture Review Report (NPR) of 2010* noted that U.S. policy was generally to reduce reliance on nuclear weapons over time, and specifically to forego nuclear weapons as an option for retaliation against non-nuclear weapons states that were fully in compliance with the NPT.[12] Presumably this nuclear abstinence would even hold in the face of attacks by a non-nuclear state with chemical or biological weapons, although the 2010 NPR included an escape clause for any future biological attacks with catastrophic consequences. Although the Obama NPR fell short of a commitment to "no first use" of nuclear weapons under any conditions, it did chart a preferred course toward the use of nuclear weapons only for deterrence of a nuclear attack or in retaliation for one.[13] Daryl G. Kimball, executive director of the Arms Control Association, offered a favorable appraisal of the Obama NPR for narrowing the conditions under which the United States might use nuclear weapons, and for reducing the overall salience of nuclear weapons in U.S. security policy. But he also cautioned against NPR euphoria with respect to arms control:

> Assigning U.S. nuclear weapons any role beyond 'core nuclear deterrence' is both unnecessary and counterproductive. The United States, as well as Russia, should adopt a 'sole purpose' policy now rather than later. Reserving the option to use nuclear force in non-nuclear situations provides little or no deterrent value at high cost. It undermines the credibility of conventional deterrence, complicates our nonproliferation diplomacy and can be used by other countries to justify the pursuit or improvement of nuclear weapons.[14]

The Obama administration's intent to de-emphasize the role of nuclear weapons in U.S. political and military strategy invites the development and eventual deployment of weapons for conventional prompt global strike.[15] According to the 2010 NPR, the Department of Defense will retain a margin above the minimum force required for nuclear deterrence "for the possible addition of non-nuclear prompt-global strike capabilities" that would be accountable under the New START treaty.[16] START-accountable non-nuclear prompt global strike systems could include conventionally-armed intercontinental ballistic missiles (ICBMs), SLBMs, or purpose-built aerospace planes.

In theory, conventional precision guidance systems (PGS) would permit timely attacks on terrorist bases, launch-ready missile parks, weapons of mass destruction (WMD) storage sites, or other time urgent or important targets without the collateral damage and moral opprobrium of nuclear weapons. Russian negotiators at New START, and in other Russian and U.S. discussions with the George W. Bush and Obama administrations, had expressed reservations about conventional PGS weapons mounted on ballistic missiles or other launchers that also carried some part of the U.S. nuclear arsenal. One objection was that conventionally armed long-range ballistic missiles might pose a threat to nuclear crisis stability. Nuclear warning and response systems might not be able to distinguish between a conventional PGS launch and a nuclear first strike. In response to Russian concerns, New START negotiators agreed to a treaty provision that requires the decommissioning of one U.S. nuclear missile for every conventional PGS weapon deployed.[17]

In addition to the problem of nuclear crisis stability that is possibly implicit in conventional PGS systems, another Russian concern is that U.S. advanced conventional PGS systems could be combined with a nuclear offense and with improved missile defenses to create a conventional-nuclear first strike capability against Russia. Although this possibility might seem paranoid in a time when the United States and Russia have an official non-hostile political relationship, the scenario of an American nuclear first strike capability has received close attention from U.S. analysts and from Russian military experts.[18] However, politics drives strategy—including domestic politics in the United States and Russia. In the case of Russia, domestic politics includes a General Staff and officer corps determined to preserve their status and power in the face of threatened military modernization to improve Russia's conventional forces. This domestic political debate within Russia about conventional force modernization is a third force, in addition to U.S. missile defenses and conventional PGS systems, that makes some Russians less relaxed about the appearance of nuclear-strategic parity.

Russian Perspectives.

The Russian ruling tandem of President Medvedev and Prime Minister Vladimir Putin, along with Russian Defense Minister Anatoly Serdyukov, have recognized the need for military reform in order to improve the quality of Russia's Armed Forces. Improvements are needed in both conventional and nuclear forces, to be sure.[19] But, compared to the former Soviet Union, the decline in the quality of Russia's conventional forces relative to those of the United States and NATO has been more obvious and noticeable. Problems include both the quantity and quality of enlisted personnel, a top-heavy officer corps, and insufficient numbers of modern weapons and hours of training for personnel in the Ground Forces, Navy, and Air Force.[20] Russia's need for military modernization is not prompted exclusively by perceived threats from its western and southern directions. Russia's strategic east faces a growing military and economic power in China, whose own military modernization "has moved the PLA [People's Liberation Army] from a mass industrial army built to fight people's war to a force seeking to rearm as an advanced conventional force and conduct their own version of net-centric warfare."[21]

The Russian Defense Ministry's plan for modernization and reform is ambitious on paper. It anticipates a broad transformation, departing from the historical experience of the Soviet Union in the 20th century with mass mobilization, conscript based forces, and trained for protracted interstate wars of attrition.[22] Instead, future emphasis will be placed on the creation of light, rapidly deployable, and elite units of permanent readiness, staffed by specially trained contract soldiers instead of draftees. Additionally: the brigade, instead of the division, will be the focal operational-tactical unit of action; the officer corps will be downsized; and, emphasis will be placed on improving the command-control and network centric warfare capabilities of ready forces.[23] The post-reform brigades will be the drivers of a new Russian military that is trained for the kinds of wars that Russia is more likely to have to fight in the 21st century: small wars, including counterinsurgency and counterterrorism operations, near or within Russia's borders.

Skeptics question whether Russia has the necessary financial resources to fund this program for military transformation, and others have pointed to demographic problems in making available the numbers of eligible contract troops as well as draftees to achieve transformative goals in the next decade.[24] But this skepticism is, among some quarters within Russia, fueled by the self-interest of a bloated military bureaucracy that seeks to preserve positions for general officers by resisting reform. One strategy for resistance is to adhere strictly to expired threat assessments and retro geopolitics, defining NATO and the United States as major enemies of Russia. Even the revised Russian Military Doctrine of 2010, which may suggest a lesser emphasis on its nuclear weapons for covering a wide variety of contingencies, compared to earlier versions (and thus, may be more compatible with the thrust of Obama's NPR than those earlier editions of Russian military doctrine), nevertheless includes NATO enlargement among the dangers that Russia must take seriously and for which it must plan.[25]

Russian geostrategic thinking welcomes the emergence of a multipolar international order in which the leading military and economic state actors reach decisions by consensus.[26] Ranking highest among Russia's state priorities are the growth of its economy and an increase in the respect and deference accorded to Russian foreign and security policy, especially in its "near abroad" of former Soviet states, and particularly in Europe.[27] From this perspective, Russia's military clash with Georgia in August 2008 demonstrated Russia's sensitivity, not only to Georgia's perceived provocations, but also to the Russian leaders' view of Georgia as a Trojan horse for U.S. and NATO political influence and military penetration. Although Russia's conventional forces rapidly overpowered Georgian resistance and declared a postwar separatism from Georgia on behalf of Abkhazia and South Ossetia as an accomplished fact, obvious problems marked Russia's military performance during this brief and one-sided war. The conflict also served as a warning to Georgia about poorly timed and ill-considered military brinkmanship. The war advertised how far away Russia's conventional military forces are from those suited to the aspirations of a major regional or global military power.

Among some Russian government officials and other elites, it is now recognized that broad changes in foreign policy must accompany, if not precede, the accomplishment of significant military reform. On this point, in May 2010 the Russian edition of *Newsweek* magazine published a draft document from the Russian foreign ministry that was prepared earlier in February for President Medvedev.[28] According to press reports, the foreign ministry document calls for a new Russian foreign policy, emphasizing improved relations with the United States and the European Union (EU) in order to expedite technology development and a more favorable climate for investment in Russia.[29] Dmitri Trenin of the Moscow Carnegie Center, writing in the *Moscow Times*, assessed the draft doctrine and its implications thus:

> Russia is losing ground in the global pecking order by falling behind in terms of its industrial, technological, and scientific capabilities. All the proceeds from Gazprom's sales notwithstanding, Russia is sorely lacking what it takes to be a major global economic and political force in the 21st century. Relative energy abundance and nuclear arsenals are simply not enough.[30]

An alternative perspective on the draft document was provided by Andrei Tsygankov, who regarded its interpretation as a pro-Western shift in Russian foreign policy as "not incorrect" but "insufficient." Tsygankov argues that Russia's rapprochement with the

427

West is taking place within a larger context of a more decentralized, and less West-centric, world order. As he puts it, the post-Western world "has in store not only expertise and capital from advanced countries, but (also) new opportunities for improving Russia's welfare and security in Asia, the Middle East and Latin America."[31] Edward Lozansky also supports the idea that Russia's drive for economic and technology modernization is an all-azimuths one. The document, in his judgment, is "oriented toward West, East, South, North, and any other direction that has a potential for promoting Russian interests."[32] Putting the document in historical perspective, Stephen J. Blank cautions against euphoria with regard to Western expectations for Russian foreign policy transformation:

> Indeed, it is a time-honored tradition of Russian and Soviet foreign policy to signal a détente based on common economic interests, the main goal of which is that Russia obtains foreign technology (which, because of its economic-political structure, it cannot optimally utilize) in return for sham or cosmetic concessions.[33]

Thus Russia's nuclear and conventional force modernization depend both upon closing the gap between Russian performance and that of the other leading state economies.

The conclusion of New START also provides symbolic benefits for Russia, by treating Russia as an equal negotiating partner with the United States for purposes of establishing a hierarchy of nuclear weapons states. So established, Russia has an additional hand to play at the head of the table among G-8 (the United States, Japan, Germany, France, the United Kingdom [UK], Canada, Italy, and Russia) and G-20 (South Africa, Canada, Mexico, the United States, Argentina,

Brazil, China, Japan, South Korea, India, Indonesia, Saudi Arabia, Russia, Turkey, France, Germany, Italy, the UK, Australia, and the European Union) major powers, despite its insufficiencies in non-nuclear forces. For the United States and its NATO allies, the impression of nuclear-strategic parity, as between the United States and Russia, should make Russia a more reliable partner for resolving conflicts short of war. In case of an outbreak of conventional war in or near Europe, Russia's self-confidence, as a strategic nuclear partner of the United States, might delay Russia's reach for its nuclear means of threat or actual nuclear use. Absent this reassurance, the gap between Russian and U.S.-NATO conventional forces creates a perilous temptation for prompt nuclear threat or use, once conventional war has begun. Into this double helix of escalation ladders fall U.S.-NATO and Russian sub-strategic nuclear weapons.

Sub-strategic Weapons and Alliance Politics.

The conclusion and eventual ratification of New START will leave unsettled the status of sub-strategic nuclear weapons deployed by the United States and Russia in Europe. Sub-strategic weapons are those deployed on other than strategic launchers, i.e., missiles or bombers of less than intercontinental range. In practice, this includes delivery systems at or below the outer limit of intermediate range missiles (5,500 kilometers), sometimes referred to as "battlefield," "tactical," "operational," or "theater" missiles depending on actual ranges. U.S. sub-strategic nuclear weapons are presently located in five other NATO member countries: Belgium, Germany, Italy, the Netherlands, and Turkey. The rationale for these forward deployed

U.S nuclear weapons during the Cold War was to support the "coupling" of American and NATO European strategic commitments against Soviet intimidation or nuclear blackmail. Now decades beyond the Cold War, leading military experts and politicians within NATO Europe have recommended that these weapons should be removed and dismantled.[34]

Both the political and military rationales for U.S. sub-strategic weapons deployed in allied NATO states have been called into question. The political rationale of deterrence "coupling" seems beside the point if NATO and Russia are no longer declared or de facto enemies. The military rationale, or the need for a tactical nuclear option as part of an escalation "ladder" that would allow NATO to skirmish with Russia in increments, but short of total war, demands nuanced performance from command, control, and communications (C3) systems, and commanders on both sides. Otherwise escalation control turns into mutual confusion. Although current Russian military doctrine stipulates that NATO is a "danger" instead of a "threat," Russian military concerns about a NATO conventional first strike option near Russia or within its state territory argue against a long pause between rungs of its escalation ladder.[35]

Some Russian strategists support the use of a small number of tactical nuclear weapons for the de-escalation of a conventional war based on the shock value of a nuclear "first use" option to obtain a favorable war termination. But such a use, as opposed to the threat of nuclear force employment, could backfire, causing a retaliatory and larger escalation by the opponent.[36] As Pavel Baev noted, "deficiencies in Russia's conventional military forces might increase the appeal of nuclear weapons under the exigent circumstances of perceived battlefield desperation."[37] Additionally, as Nikolai Sokov has explained:

> The continuing weakness of Russian conventional forces vis-à-vis U.S. and combined NATO power as well as the close proximity of NATO forces to Russian territory (making limited use of force both more feasible and more effective) have led Russian military planners to rely on nuclear weapons for the purpose of de-escalation — the threat of a limited nuclear strike in response to a conventional attack that cannot be repelled by conventional forces is supposed to deter the attack in the first place.[38]

The group of experts tasked in 2010 to prepare guidelines for the revision of NATO's strategic concept nevertheless endorsed the alliance's deployment of U.S. sub-strategic nuclear weapons by noting that, as long as nuclear weapons "remain a reality in international relations," NATO should retain a nuclear component to its deterrent strategy at the minimum level required by the international security environment.[39] The rationales for this position are that the retention of some U.S. forward deployed nuclear weapons on European territory will support "extended nuclear deterrence and collective defense."[40] Having it both ways, as it were, the NATO group of experts also calls for "an ongoing nuclear dialogue with Russia" to expedite the further reduction, and possible elimination, of "the entire class of sub-strategic weapons."[41]

Proposals from European politicians calling for the removal of U.S. sub-strategic nuclear weapons from NATO Europe, especially in the absence of some *quid pro quo* from Russia, are certain to meet with resistance across the Atlantic.[42] Russia will be cautious about reciprocating. The "going in" position for Russia will be that the first step should be taken by the United

States to repatriate or destroy all its nuclear weapons deployed outside of U.S. national territory, as did Russia with its nuclear weapons deployed in former Soviet states after the Cold War (with U.S. assistance). The U.S. argument will be that Russia must dismantle or relocate some of its own tactical nuclear weapons that are forward deployed in Russia's western military districts and, in particular, near to the borders of NATO member states.

Russia considers the assumption of symmetrical reductions in tactical nuclear weapons with NATO to be unfair because NATO already has superior conventional forces relative to Russia. Therefore, Russian tactical nuclear weapons provide reassurance against NATO escalation dominance, in case of any situation of threat or outbreak of local war. In addition, elimination of sub-strategic nuclear weapons calls for levels of transparency even beyond the inspection and verification regimes required for strategic nuclear weapons, as under New START, and steps on the national sensitivities of American NATO allies. Outside the realm of Russia's public diplomacy, but surely on the minds of Russian military planners, as Jacob Kipp has noted, is the undoubted role of Russia's sub-strategic nuclear weapons in deterring any conventional war against China or, in the event of deterrence failure, in contributing to a war termination on favorable terms.[43]

The Obama Nuclear Agenda.

President Obama's extended agenda for nuclear marginalization (and, in theory, eventual abolition) goes beyond further START reductions and limitations on NATO and Russian tactical nuclear weapons.[44] In addition, Obama wants the United States and other outliers to ratify the Comprehensive Test Ban Treaty

(CBT); to mobilize international support in favor of a Fissile Materials Cutoff Treaty (FMCT); to extend and strengthen the Nuclear Non-Proliferation Treaty (NPT); and, most importantly, to draw bright lines for preventing Iran from becoming a nuclear weapons state and for reversing North Korea's nuclear weapons status.[45] This is an ambitious, although not impossible, agenda for nonproliferation, and it requires considerable cooperation from existing legally recognized and de facto nuclear weapons states. However, the United States and Russia have a special responsibility for leadership in this regard: they hold more than 90 percent of the world's nuclear weapons and, as well, the historical responsibility for godfathering the nuclear revolution in military affairs. Their management of nuclear forces during and after the Cold War, despite some scary moments and embarrassing political posturing here and there, provide "lessons learned" for other, and especially newer, members of the nuclear weapons club.

One of these lessons is that further progress in horizontal nuclear risk reduction (the spread of nuclear weapons among additional states) requires the simultaneous commitment by leading nuclear weapons states to vertical risk reduction (limiting the growth of existing arsenals, or preferably, reducing them in size). The preceding point does not depend upon the allegedly naive argument that a good example set by the United States and by Russia automatically translates into vertical or horizontal nuclear risk reduction. Critics of nuclear risk reduction attack a straw man here. The United States and Russia are not reducing their numbers of long-range nuclear weapons and launchers because of altruism. They are taking this step because excessive numbers of nuclear weapons are politically pointless and militarily useless.

In doing so, the leaders of Russia and the United States commit themselves to a process of reciprocal nuclear risk management and support for stable deterrence and reassurance, a necessary step for further cooperation on vertical and horizontal disarmament. However, the United States and Russia cannot proceed to lower-than-New START reductions without tacit and explicit cooperation on the part of other current nuclear weapons states, and even some nuclear weapons-ready or virtual nuclear weapons states. As Henry Sokolski has explained:

> In addition to making roughly equal reductions with Russia, then, the United States will have to keep other nuclear-armed states, such as China and India, from trying to catch up with U.S. nuclear weapons deployment levels and—as in the case of India and China, Pakistan and India, and Japan and China—from trying to catch up with each other. This means that additional nuclear restraints, either in the form of nuclear weapons reductions or further limits on the production or stockpiling of weapons-usable fuel, will need to be reached with Russia, of course, but also with China, India, and Pakistan. As a practical matter, this also means that other nuclear weapons-ready or virtual weapons states (e.g., Japan) will have to be persuaded to curtail or end their production of weapons-usable materials or to dispose of some portion of what they currently have.[46]

Obama's vision of a nuclear free world, as he admits, may not be realized in his lifetime—if ever. But the avoidance of nuclear war, and the preservation of a nuclear taboo that has existed since Nagasaki, is a sufficiently challenging crusade for the rest of the present century.[47] Managing toward that end will require international cooperation in nuclear arms control, nonproliferation, and disarmament that connect linear to nonlinear strategies for risk reduction. Serial progress in U.S. and Russian nuclear arms limitation is a realistic expectation, but not a guaranty of nonlinear success stories in nonproliferation or in disarmament. To achieve broader objectives in nuclear renunciation, states will have to leapfrog beyond purely statist models of defense and deterrence into more communitarian and regional, or even global, paradigms of reference. The shared space of nuclear danger includes threats, not only from existing and aspiring nuclear weapons states, but also from nonstate actors such as terrorists with apocalyptic or other anti-systemic agendas.[48] The two dangers are linked in theory and in practice: the more states with nuclear weapons and with anti-systemic grievances, the more vulnerable are the commons to lapses in nuclear security and, perhaps, nuclear terrorism. States that fail, individually and collectively, to embrace nuclear risk reduction or elimination could find themselves in the target coordinates of future extremists who are beyond deterrence.

METHODOLOGY

Approach.

The preceding discussion sets the stage for the following analysis. The methodology will proceed in two principal steps. First, a statistical model is used to test the adequacy of projected U.S. and Russian strategic nuclear forces that are New START-compliant. As part of this framework, an examination is provided to determine if smaller forces for either state could meet the criteria for deterrence sufficiency and stability. The comparison with possible post-New START forces is not an idle academic exercise. Both the United States and Russia have indicated that the door is open to reducing the numbers of deployed strategic nuclear weapons below the levels agreed in the treaty signed on April 8, 2010.

In a second step of the analysis, the connection between nuclear arms reductions and nonproliferation will be examined through the use of a pertinent "what if" illustration of one hypothetical, but realistic, world environment. If, for example, the United States and Russia can agree to lower-than-New START levels of strategic retaliatory forces, their remaining maximum levels for deployed nuclear weapons could be the basis for a constrained nuclear proliferation system among the existing recognized and de facto nuclear weapons states. This connection between American and Russian vertical disarmament and responsibility for leadership on nonproliferation is not hypothetical or academic, but legal and operational.[49]

As acknowledged nuclear weapons states under the protocols of the nuclear NPT, the United States and Russia (among others) are required to engage in nuclear arms reductions and arms limitation. Operationally, the United States and Russia have the largest nuclear arsenals, the most experience with nuclear force operations, and the most experience in negotiating nuclear arms control agreements. In short, the connection between U.S.-Russian nuclear arms reductions and downstream success in controlling the spread of nuclear weapons is explicit, despite the denials of cynics, nay sayers, and prophets of inevitable nuclear proliferation and doomsday. On the other hand, accepting responsibility for action is not the same thing as accomplishing it. The United States and Russia cannot necessarily get the rest of the nuclear club to march in step with their ambitions, even when Washington and Moscow are agreed.

Data Analysis.

Current and New START accountable U.S. and Russian strategic nuclear forces are summarized in Table 9-1.

Russia

	July 2009 Old START launchers	2010 Actual Operationally Deployed Launchers (total launchers)	Ca. 2020 New START operationally deployed launchers (total launchers)- estimate	Ca. 2020 New START warheads (estimate)
ICBMs				
SS-25	176	171	0	0
SS-27 Silo	50	50	60	60
SS-27 Road	15	18	27	27
RS-24			85	255
SS-19	120	70	0	0
SS-18	104	59	20	200
Total ICBMs	465	367	192	542
SLBMs				
Delta III/ SS-N-18	6/96	4/64	0	0
Delta IV/ SS-N-23	6/96	4/64 (6/96)	4/64	256
Typhoon/ SS-N-20	2/40	0	0	0
Borey/ Bulava	2/36	0	4/64	384
Total SLBMs	268	128 (164)	128	640
Bombers				
Tu-160	13	13	13	13
Tu-95MS	63	63	63	63
Total Bombers	76	76	76	76
TOTAL	809	571(603)	396(396)	1258

United States

	July 2009 Old START launchers	2010 Actual Operationally Deployed Launchers (total launchers)	Ca. 2020 New START operationally deployed launchers (total launchers)-estimate	Ca. 2020 New START warheads (estimate)
ICBMs				
Minute-man III	500	450	350	350
MX	50	0	0	0
Total ICBMs	550	450	350	350
SLBMs				
Trident I/C-4	4/96	0	0	0
Trident II/D-5	14/336	12/288 (14/336)	12/288 (14/336)	1152
Total SLBMs	268	288 (336)	288 (336)	1152
Borey/ Bulava	2/36	0	4/64	384
Total SLBMs	268	128 (164)	128	640
Bombers				
B-1	47	0	0	0
B-2	18	16 (18)	16 (18)	16
B-52	141	44 (93)	32 (93)	32
Total Bombers	206	60 (111)	48 (111)	48
TOTAL	1188	798 (897)	686 (797)	1550

Source: Pavel Podvig, "New START Treaty in Numbers," from his blog, *Russian strategic nuclear forces*, April 9, 2010, available from *russianforces.org/blog/2010/03/new_start_treaty_in_numbers.shtml*.

Notes:

1. New START counting rules count each bomber as a single weapon (warhead) although bombers actually carry more than one weapon.

2. Under New START each state is permitted to deploy a maximum number of 700 operational launchers and to maintain up to 100 additional nondeployed launchers.

Table 9-1. Russian and U.S. Strategic Nuclear Forces. Past and Projected.

Using the numbers in Table 3-1 as points of departure, we construct hypothetical, but not unrealistic,
U.S. and Russian strategic nuclear forces for the period 2017-2020 that are consistent with New START
guidelines and related policy statements made by officials of both states.[50] These guidelines include:

(1) the expectation that both the United States
and Russia will maintain a triad of strategic nuclear
launchers, including land-based ICBMs, SLBMs, and
heavy bombers;

(2) no limitations on future defenses deployed by
either side, although a notification and withdrawal
clause exists that could allow either party to depart
the treaty for this or other reasons;

(3) counting rules that underrepresent the numbers of weapons deployed on long-range bombers;

(4) postponement of the issues of stored nuclear
weapons and their related upload potential; and,

(5) a two step limitation on the numbers of deployed intercontinental or transoceanic launchers—700 deployed and 100 additional nondeployed.[51]

Figure 9-1 provides a drawdown curve of second
strike surviving and retaliating strategic nuclear warheads for U.S. forces under New START deployment
limits of 1,550 weapons for each state.[52] Surviving and
retaliating warheads are calculated under each of four
operational conditions of alertness and launch readiness:

(1) forces are on generated alert and launched on
warning (GEN, LOW);

(2) forces are on generated alert and ride out the
attack before retaliating (GEN, ROA);

(3) forces are on day-to-day alert and launch on
warning (DAY, LOW); and,

(4) forces are on day to day alert and ride out the attack (DAY, ROA).

The drawdown curve graphs the numbers of total, available, alert, surviving, and arriving weapons for each operational condition.

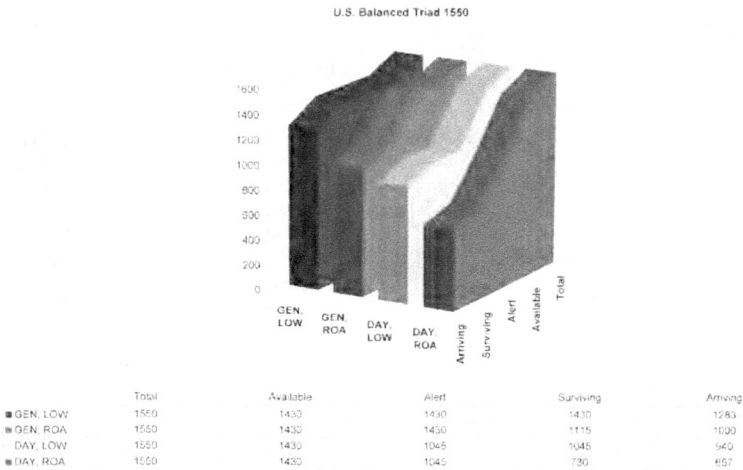

U.S. Balanced Triad 1550

	Total	Available	Alert	Surviving	Arriving
■ GEN, LOW	1550	1430	1430	1430	1283
■ GEN, ROA	1550	1430	1430	1115	1000
DAY, LOW	1550	1430	1045	1045	940
■ DAY, ROA	1550	1430	1045	730	657

Figure 9-1. U.S. Surviving and Retaliating Warheads, 1,550 Deployment Limit.

In Figure 9-2, the numbers of surviving and retaliating Russian second strike warheads are tabulated and depicted for each of the four operational conditions under New START deployment limits of 1,550 weapons. The graph shows the numbers of total, available, alert, surviving, and arriving weapons for each operational condition, following the same schematic as shown in Figure 9-1 for U.S. forces.

440

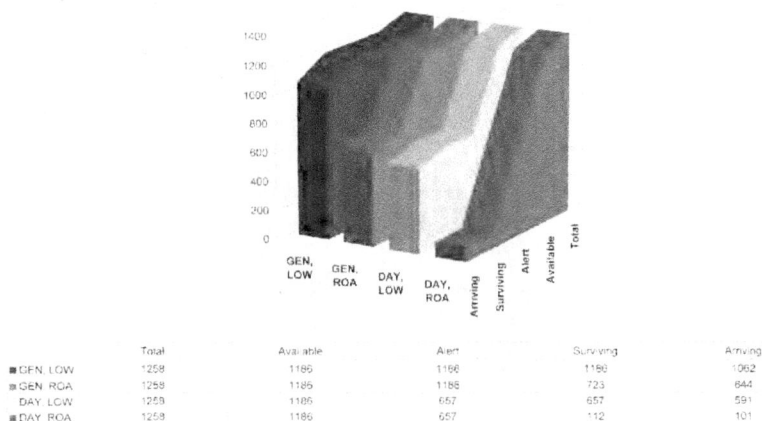

RF Balanced Triad 1550

	Total	Available	Alert	Surviving	Arriving
■ GEN. LOW	1258	1186	1186	1186	1062
■ GEN. ROA	1258	1186	1186	723	644
DAY. LOW	1258	1186	657	657	591
■ DAY. ROA	1258	1186	657	112	101

Figure 9-2. Russian Surviving and Retaliating Warheads, 1,550 Deployment Limit.

A close inspection of Figures 9-1 and 9-2 reveals that U.S. and Russian New START-compliant forces can easily satisfy requirements for mutual deterrence based on assured retaliation. Each, under a variety of operational conditions, has sufficient numbers of surviving and retaliating warheads to guarantee unacceptable societal damage to the first striker. In addition to this "assured destruction" or "assured retaliation" metric, each side can also provide for additional warheads with which to attack nuclear, other forces, and command-control systems. The addition of defensive weapons to the equation for both sides does not change this picture fundamentally, although it does reduce the flexibility of targeting for each side in retaliation.

What happens if the maximum number of strategic nuclear weapons permitted for each side is reduced to

441

1,000 instead of 1,550? In Figures 9-3 and 9-4, the numbers of U.S. and Russian second strike surviving and retaliating warheads for the four operational conditions outlined in Figures 9-1 and 9-2 are summarized.

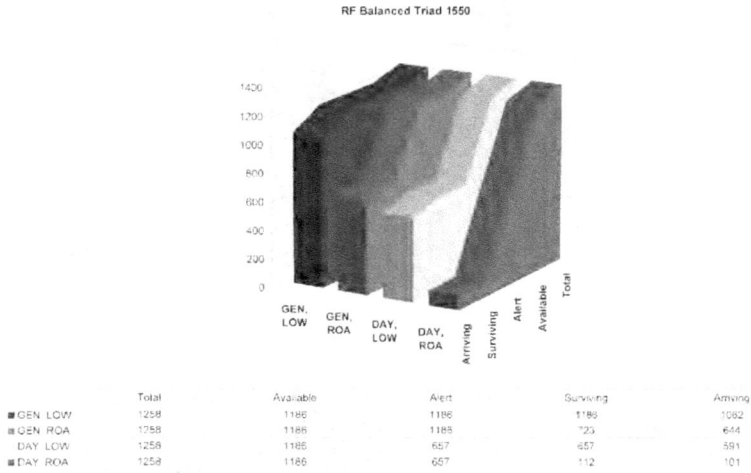

RF Balanced Triad 1550

	Total	Available	Alert	Surviving	Arriving
■ GEN LOW	1258	1186	1186	1186	1082
■ GEN ROA	1258	1186	1188	723	644
DAY LOW	1258	1186	657	657	591
■ DAY ROA	1258	1186	657	112	101

**Figure 9-3. U.S. Surviving and Retaliating
Warheads, 1,000 Deployment Limit.**

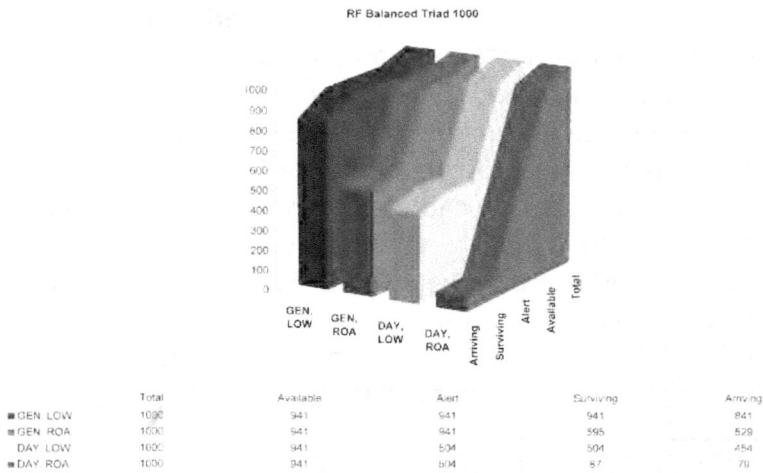

RF Balanced Triad 1000

	Total	Available	Alert	Surviving	Arriving
■ GEN LOW	1000	941	941	941	841
■ GEN ROA	1000	941	941	595	529
DAY LOW	1000	941	504	504	454
■ DAY ROA	1000	941	504	87	79

**Figure 9-4. Russian Surviving and Retaliating
Warheads, 1,000 Deployment Limit.**

The results summarized in Figures 9-3 and 9-4 show that the United States and Russia can, within a maximum deployment limit of 1,000 weapons and under almost all conditions of operational alertness and launch readiness, provide for the assured destruction-assured retaliation mission, and then some. Each has more than 400 surviving and retaliating weapons under all operational conditions, except for Russia under the "worst case" for a retaliator: with the retaliator's forces postured on day-to-day alert, and riding out the attack. Neither Russian nor American forces would probably be in this condition during the kind of political crisis in which the use of nuclear weapons was seriously considered by each side. In addition, the reason for the greater degree of symmetry between the two sides in outcomes for the 1,000 warhead deployment limit, compared to the New START 1,550 maximum, lies in the fact that our 1,000 (hypothetical) illustration uses a Russian force that is closer in size and quality to the U.S. force than is the case in New START. In terms of strategic impact, however, this is a distinction without a difference.

Why bother demonstrating what some scholars and defense analysts regard as self evident: that the United States and Russia have more than enough deployed long-range nuclear weapons, currently and prospectively, to maintain stable deterrence and to avoid the possibility of a nuclear first strike by the other side? The problem is more subtle than the question implies. The abstract possibility of a nuclear first strike capability by the United States against Russia has been used as a bargaining chip in Russian domestic politics by disgruntled conservatives in its military, by researchers in Russian think tanks, and by Kremlin-supportive media sources.[53] This constellation of hawkish views outside of official Russian ministries, but acting in possible concert with sympathetic Kremlin sources, allows the Medvedev-Putin tandem to have it both ways. Official channels trumpet the "reset" in U.S.-Russian relations, while supposedly independent hawkish commentators fan the flames of public opinion in defining the United States and NATO as major enemies of Russia.[54] Nor were doubts about New START and further progress in nuclear arms control confined to skeptical Russians. During hearings before the U.S. Senate Foreign Relations Committee in May 2010, various Senators expressed doubts about New START, including the possibility that it would limit future American missile defense options.[55]

The first section of this chapter argued that there was a direct connection in policy and strategy between the bilateral U.S.-Russian nuclear arms reductions and the problem of multilateral nonproliferation management. If so, could the lower of the two illustrations for the U.S.-Russian force limitations, a maximum of 1,000 deployed warheads for each side, serve as a basis for organizing a constrained nonproliferation system among the existing nuclear weapons states? Let us assume that, in this constrained nuclear proliferation system, Iran is prevented from deploying nuclear weapons and North Korean nuclear proliferation is rolled back by diplomatic agreement. The remaining nuclear weapons states (the United States, Russia, UK, France, China, India, Pakistan, and Israel) agree to a tiered structure that provides for a maximum of 1,000 deployed weapons for the United States and for Russia; a maximum of 500 each for Britain, France, and China; and a maximum of 300 for India, Israel, and Pakistan. Notional forces are assigned to each of these powers in Figure 9-5, and the numbers of second strike retaliating warheads provided by each force are estimated in Figure 9-6. These numbers are obviously not intended as predictions of actual forces to be deployed by these states in the 2017-20 time frame. Instead, they are heuristics to allow for broad comparisons and illustrations of possible second strike survivability under canonical conditions.

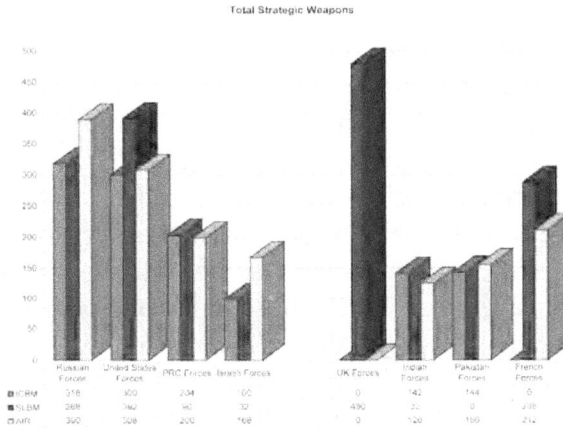

Total Strategic Weapons

	Russian Forces	United States Forces	PRC Forces	Israeli Forces	UK Forces	Indian Forces	Pakistan Forces	French Forces
ICBM	316	300	204	00	0	141	144	0
SLBM	268	360	40	32	430	32	0	248
AIR	390	508	200	168	0	120	160	212

Figure 9-5. Constrained Proliferation Model. Total Strategic Weapons.

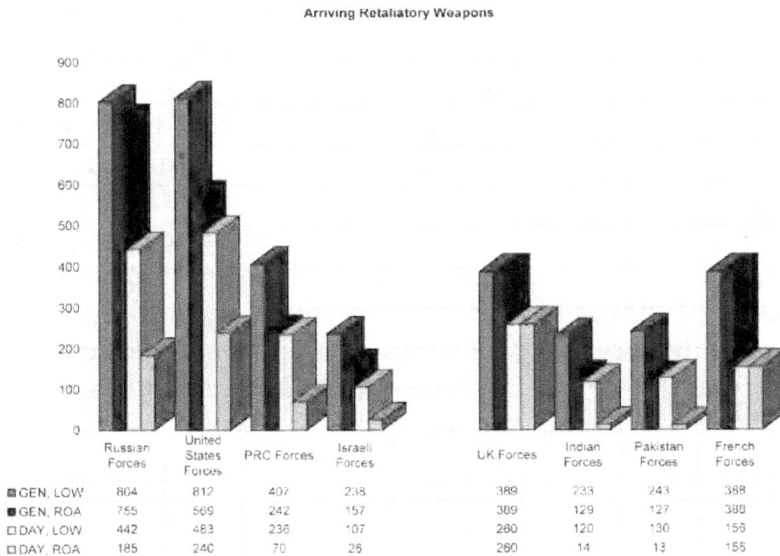

Arriving Retaliatory Weapons

	Russian Forces	United States Forces	PRC Forces	Israeli Forces	UK Forces	Indian Forces	Pakistan Forces	French Forces
GEN, LOW	804	812	407	236	389	233	243	388
GEN, ROA	755	569	242	157	389	129	127	388
DAY, LOW	442	483	236	107	260	120	130	156
DAY, ROA	185	240	70	26	260	14	13	156

Figure 9-6. Constrained Proliferation Model, Surviving and Retaliating Weapons.

445

The findings in Figure 9-6 show that within a three-tiered constrained nuclear proliferation system, under an umbrella of U.S. and Russian forces each capped at 1,000 deployed long-range weapons, it is possible (although not guaranteed) to construct a deterrence and crisis-stable pyramid if — always the big "if" — negotiations can produce acceptable bargains, monitoring, and verification can be accomplished with necessary transparency, and those outliers seeking to bash their way into the club can be excluded. Is this fair? Neither nonproliferation nor any other serious goal in international politics is likely to be obtained by means that are entirely fair, but a less than entirely fair system might still meet the criteria of decision rationality. Those criteria include the premise that consensus on major points of agreement has been reached across the boundaries of diverse state interests and priorities.

In addition, trade-offs and side payments to reach that consensus should not leave any nuclear armed state in a constrained proliferation system with incentives for cheating on the agreed numbers or, even worse, for overturning the entire structure in favor of nuclear adventurism. No arrangement of numbers can restrict the elbow room of states and their leaders to do harm, or good, based on domestic political motives and the structure of the international system. Arms control cannot substitute for politics; it can only take advantage of favorable political climates to reduce the probability of war or the disutility of war, if it occurs.[56] In the case of nuclear war or nuclear weapons spread, the avoidance is to be preferred to the alternatives.

CONCLUSION

New START and other manifestations of U.S.-Russian nuclear arms control are embedded in (at least) three overlapping levels of conceptual analysis. The first level is the need for reconceptualization of geostrategic space, especially Euro-strategic space, in order to extend the concept of a "European" security community from the Atlantic to the Urals, and from Svalbard to Sinope. This truly transcontinental security space must be approached by the United States, Russia, and NATO as a positive-sum policy and strategy game, instead of zero-sum competition. *Cooperative* security is an empty vessel without active *collaborative* security procedures and institutions to support it — as recent arms control experience has shown. Movement from cooperative into collaborative security will require persistent policymakers who are determined to overcome bureaucratic inertia in Washington, Moscow, and Brussels.

The second level of analysis involves the necessary transformation in foreign policy orientations on the part of the United States, NATO, and Russia. The United States needs to discard its recent excursions into unilateralism, preemptive military doctrines, and omnivorous statements of foreign policy objectives, based on an oxymoronic cocktail of liberal internationalism and neoconservatism. Instead, the United States should pursue its traditional policy of being an "offshore balancer," supplemented by preemptive leadership for (multilateral) conflict prevention and management, supported by America's unique capabilities for systems integration and global military reach. Russia needs to adjust its military DNA to a world in which NATO is part of the solution, not the problem, from a Russian perspective: cooperation on missile defenses would be a step in this direction. NATO needs to adjust its near term goals, away from the acquisition of additional territories and dependencies (read: Ukraine and Georgia) and toward a "Great Northern Alliance" concept that includes Russia as a security partner, if not a member.

The third level of analysis, derivative of the first two, is further Russian-American movement on nuclear arms reductions, with the potential for spillover into nonproliferation. Will the New START agreement, once ratified and brought into force lead necessarily, or inevitably, to progress on nuclear nonproliferation under the leadership of Moscow and Washington? A great deal depends on the priorities placed by each side on nonproliferation, compared to other foreign policy issues.[57] The United States and Russia can do little without cooperation from other nuclear weapons states, especially the other permanent members of the UN Security Council (P-5): the UK, France, and China. Iran and North Korea are imminent test cases for the viability of the current nuclear nonproliferation regime, but even the most favorable outcomes in these cases do not preclude other challenges.[58] Regardless the trials and tribulations of interstate proliferation, nonstate actors, especially terrorists, present additional challenges guaranteeing sleepless nights.

ENDNOTES - CHAPTER 9

1. Eben Harrell, "A Surprising Consensus on Nuclear Nonproliferation," Time.com, June 2, 2010, available from *www.time.com/time/printout/0,8816,1993339,00.html*.

2. Rose Gottemoeller, Assistant Secretary, Bureau of Verification, Compliance and Implementation, "The New START Trea-

ty," Opening Statement before the Senate Foreign Relations Committee, Washington, DC, June 15, 2010, available from *www.state.gov/t/vci/rls/143159.htm*.

3. Peter Baker, "Russia and U.S. Sign Nuclear Arms Reduction Pact," *New York Times*, April 8, 2010, available from *www.nytimes.com/2010/04/09/world/europe/09prexy.html*; and "Obama, Medvedev sign historic arms deal," Associated Press, April 8, 2010, available from *www.msnbc.msn.com/id/36254613/ns/politics-white_house/print*. For expert analysis and projections, see Pavel Podvig, "New START Treaty in Numbers," from his blog, *Russian strategic nuclear forces*, April 9, 2010, available from *russianforces.org/blog/2010/03/new_start_treaty_in_numbers.shtml*.

4. The text of the New START treaty appears in *Treaty between the United States of America and the Russian Federation on Measures for the Further Reduction and Limitation of Strategic Offensive Arms*, Washington, DC: U.S. Department of State, April 8, 2010, available from *www.state.gov/documents/organization/140035.pdf*. Contrasting appraisals of New START appear in Steven Pifer, "New START: Good News for U.S. Security," *Arms Control Today*, May 2010, available from *www.armscontrol.org/print/4209*; Keith B. Payne, "Evaluating the U.S.-Russian Nuclear Deal," *Wall Street Journal*, April 8, 2010, in Johnson's Russia List 2010, #69, April 8, 2010, available from *davidjohnson@starpower.net*; Jonathan Schell, "Nuclear balance of terror must end," CNN, April 8, 2010, in Johnson's Russia List 2010, #69, April 8, 2010, *davidjohnson@starpower.net*; and Alexander Golts, "An Illusory New START," *Moscow Times*, March 30, 2010, in Johnson's Russia List 2010, #62, March 30, 2010, available from *davidjohnson@starpower.net*.

5. On current and prospective U.S. missile defense programs, see Unclassified Statement of Lieutenant General Patrick J. O'Reilly, Director, Missile Defense Agency, before the House Armed Services Committee, Subcommittee on Strategic Forces, Regarding the Fiscal Year 2011 Missile Defense Programs, Washington, DC: House Armed Services Committee, U.S. House of Representatives, April 15, 2010, esp. p. 18 on absence of New START constraints. See also Walter Pincus, "Arms treaty shouldn't constrain U.S. missile defenses," *Washington Post*, April 20, 2010, p. A13, available from *www.washingtonpost.com/wp-dyn/content/article/2010/04/19/AR2010041904602_*.

6. Robert M. Gates, "The Case for the New START Treaty," *Wall Street Journal*, May 13, 2010, in Johnson's Russia List 2010, #94, May 13, 2010, available from *davidjohnson@starpower.net*.

7. An informative discussion of this appears in Alexei Arbatov, "The New START—A View from Moscow," question and answer format, Washington, DC: Carnegie Endowment for International Peace, April 6, 2010, available from *www.carnegieendowment.org/publications/index.cfm?fa=view&id=40506*.

8. Pavel Felgenhauer, "The Bulava Blunder," *Novaya Gazeta*, July 25, 2009, in Johnson's Russia List 2009, #140, July 27, 2009, available from *davidjohnson@starpower.net*. According to Alexander Golts, the "Bulava fiasco" is more a matter of managerial incompetence than it is a technological failure. Golts, "The High Price of Feeding Russia's Ambitions," *Moscow Times*, July 28, 2009, in Johnson's Russia List 2009, #141, July 28, 2009, available from *davidjohnson@starpower.net*.

9. Robert M. Gates, "A Better Missile Defense for a Safer Europe," *New York Times*, September 19, 2009, available from *www.nytimes.com/2009/09/20/opinion/20gates.html*. The Obama Phased Adaptive Approach to missile defense will retain and improve some technologies deployed by the George W. Bush administration, but shift emphasis to other interceptors supported by improved battle management, command-control-communications (BMC3) systems, and launch detection and tracking. See Unclassified Statement of Lieutenant General Patrick J. O'Reilly, USA, Director, Missile Defense Agency, Before the House Armed Services Committee, Washington, DC: U.S. House of Representatives, House Armed Services Committee, October 1, 2009. Prompt reactions to the Obama missile defense plan include George Friedman, "The BMD Decision and the Global System," STRATFOR, September 21, 2009, in Johnson's Russia List 2009, #175, September 22, 2009, available from *davidjohnson@starpower.net*; Alexander Golts, "Calling Moscow's Bluff on Missile Defense," *Moscow Times*, September 22, 2009, in Johnson's Russia List 2009, #175, September 22, 2009, available from *davidjohnson@starpower.net*; Alexander L. Pikayev, "For the Benefit of All," *Moscow Times*, September 21, 2009, in Johnson's Russia List 2009, #174, September 21, 2009, available from *davidjohnson@starpower.net*; and Strobe

Talbott, "A better base for cutting nuclear weapons," *Financial Times*, September 21, 2009, in Johnson's Russia List 2009, #174, September 21, 2009, available from *davidjohnson@starpower.net*.

10. A critical expert appraisal of the Obama missile defense plan appears in George N. Lewis and Theodore A. Postol, "A Flawed and Dangerous U.S. Missile Defense Plan," *Arms Control Today*, May 2010, available from *www.armscontrol.org/print/4244*. See also William J. Broad and David E. Sanger, "Review Cites Flaws in U.S. Antimissile Program," *New York Times*, May 17, 2010, available from *www.nytimes.com/2010/05/18/world/18missile. html*. For a favorable expert assessment of the Obama missile defense plan, see Hans Binnendijk, "A Sensible Decision: A Wider Protective Umbrella," *Washington Times*, September 30, 2009, in Johnson's Russia List 2009, #181, September 30, 2009, available from *davidjohnson@starpower.net*. Expert Russian commentary on prospects for U.S.-Russian missile defense cooperation and on related strategic issues also appears in Sergei Rogov, "Concepts: The Window of Opportunity is Open," *Nezavisimoye Voyennoye Obozreniye*, May 28, 2010, in Johnson's Russia List 2010, #114, June 11, 2010, available from *davidjohnson@starpower.net*. Continuing Russian doubts about BMD are noted in "Russia Still Suspicious of U.S. Missile Defense Plans," Reuters, September 29, 2009, in Johnson's Russia List 2009, #181, September 30, 2009, available from *davidjohnson@starpower.net*.

11. Nikolai Sokov, "Nuclear Weapons in Russian National Security Strategy," paper presented at conference on "Strategy and Doctrine in Russian Security Policy," Ft. McNair, National Defense University, Washington, DC, June 28, 2010, p. 30.

12. *Nuclear Posture Review Report*, Washington, DC: U.S. Department of Defense, April 2010, p. 15.

13. Pertinent and spirited commentary on NPR and related nuclear security issues appears on the blog *ArmsControlWonk* edited by Dr. Jeffrey Lewis. See, for example, Jeffrey Lewis, "Grading the NPR: Transparency," April 13, 2010; Lewis, "The Pivot," April 7, 2010; and Joshua Pollack, "Where the NPR Meets in the Middle," April 6, 2010, all available from *www.armscontrolwonk. com/category/nuclear-weapons/*.

14. Daryl G. Kimball, "Obama's Nuclear Doctrine Could Boost Reset," *Moscow Times*, April 13, 2010, in Johnson's Russia List 2010, #72, April 13, 2010, available from *davidjohnson@starpower. net*. See also Daryl G. Kimball and Greg Thielmann, "Obama's NPR: Transitional, Not Transformational," *Arms Control Today*, May 2010, available from *www.armscontrol.org/print/4223*.

15. Craig Whitlock, "U.S. developing new non-nuclear missiles," *Washington Post*, April 8, 2010, available from *www.msnbc. msn.com/id/36253190/ns/us_news-washington_post/print/1/*.

16. *Nuclear Posture Review Report*, p. 20.

17. David E. Sanger and Thom Shanker, "U.S. Faces Choice on New Weapons for Fast Strikes," *New York Times*, April 23, 2010, p. A1. According to the same source, the Obama precision global strike concept envisions that Russia would regularly inspect PGS silos to reassure itself that the weapons were non-nuclear, and that American PGS launchers would be located far from those tasked for strategic nuclear forces.

18. Keir A. Lieber and Daryl G. Press, "The Rise of U.S. Nuclear Primacy," *Foreign Affairs*, March/April 2006, available from *www.foreignaffairs.org/20060301faessay85204/keir-a-lieber-daryl-g-press/html*. For rejoinders to Lieber and Press, see Peter C. W. Flory, Keith Payne, Pavel Podvig, and Alexei Arbatov, "Nuclear Exchange: Does Washington Really Have (or Want) Nuclear Primacy?" *Foreign Affairs*, September/October 2006, available from *www.foreignaffairs.com/print/61931*.

19. Nuclear weapons, according to Nikolai Sokov, have three partially overlapping roles in Russian national security policy: (1) as a status symbol; (2) for existential deterrence; and, (3) as part of contingent plans for use or threat of use to deter large scale conventional attacks on Russia. Sokov, "Nuclear Weapons in Russian Security Strategy," paper presented at conference on "Strategy and Doctrine in Russian Security Policy," Ft. McNair, National Defense University, Washington, DC, June 28, 2010, p. 5.

20. Dale R. Herspring, "Putin, Medvedev, and the Russian Military," Chap. 12, in Stephen K. Wegren and Dale R. Herspring, eds., *After Putin's Russia: Past Imperfect, Future Uncertain*, Fourth Ed., Lanham, MD: Rowman and Littlefield, 2010, pp. 265-290.

21. Jacob W. Kipp, "Russia's Nuclear Posture and the Threat That Dare not Speak Its Name," paper presented at conference on "Strategy and Doctrine in Russian Security Policy," Ft. McNair, National Defense University, Washington, DC, June 28, 2010, p. 5.

22. I gratefully acknowledge Dale Herspring for insights into this issue. He is not responsible for arguments here. See also, on the seriousness of Russian military reform, Keir Giles, "The Military Doctrine of the Russian Federation 2010," *NATO Research Review*, Rome, Italy: NATO Defense College, February, 2010, esp. p. 3.

23. Roger N. McDermott, "Russia's Conventional Armed Forces, Reform and Nuclear Posture to 2020," paper presented at conference on "Strategy and Doctrine in Russian Security Policy," Ft. McNair, National Defense University, Washington, DC, June 28, 2010.

24. Projections suggest that between now and 2025, Russia's pool of draft age manpower will decline at an even faster rate than the rate for the general population. The implications of this for the size and composition of Russia's future forces are traced in Olga Oliker, Keith Crane, Lowell H. Schwartz, and Catherine Yusupov, *Russian Foreign Policy: Sources and Implications*, Santa Monica, CA; RAND, 2009, pp. 145-151.

25. For an assessment of the 2010 doctrine on this point, see Nikolai Sokov, "The New, 2010 Russian Military Doctrine: The Nuclear Angle," Monterey, CA: Center for Nonproliferation Studies, Monterey Institute of International Studies, February 5, 2010, available from *cns.miis.edu/stories/100205_russian_nuclear_doctrine.htm*. See also, *The Military Doctrine of the Russian Federation*, available from *www.Kremlin.ru*, February 5, 2010, in Johnson's Russia List 2010, #35, February 19, 2010, available from *davidjohnson@starpower.net*.

26. Sokov, "Nuclear Weapons in Russian Security Strategy," p. 5.

27. According to some experts, Russians do not have a unified view of their foreign policy objectives, but a broad consensus emerged during Putin's second term about Russia's foreign policy goals. See Oliker *et. al.*, *Russian Foreign Policy*, pp. 83-138, esp. p. 87. See also Anders Aslund and Andrew Kutchins, *The Russia Balance Sheet*, Washington, DC: Peterson Institute for International Economics and Center for Strategic and International Studies, April, 2009; and Stephen J. Blank, *Russia and Arms Control: Are There Opportunities for the Obama Administration?* Carlisle, PA: Strategic Studies Institute, U.S. Army War College, March 2009, for additional perspective on Russian objectives pertinent to national security and nuclear arms control.

28. See "Russia Profile Weekly Experts Panel: Russia's New Foreign Policy Doctrine," introduction by Vladimir Frolov, in *Russia Profile*, May 21, 2010, available from *www.russiaprofile.org*, in Johnson's Russia List 2010, #101, May 24, 2010, available from *davidjohnson@starpower.net*.

29. *Ibid.*

30. Trenin, quoted in Frolov *et al.*, *Russia Profile*, May 24, 2010.

31. Tsygankov commentary in "Russia Profile Weekly Experts Panel: Russia's New Foreign Policy Doctrine," introduction by Vladimir Frolov, in *Russia Profile*, May 21, 2010, available from *www.russiaprofile.org*, in Johnson's Russia List 2010, #101, May 24, 2010, available from *davidjohnson@starpower.net*.

32. Lozansky commentary in *Ibid*.

33. Blank commentary in *Ibid*.

34. For an expert assessment, see Malcolm Chalmers and Simon Lunn, *NATO's Tactical Nuclear Dilemma*, London, UK: Royal United Services Institute, Occasional Paper, March 2010, available from *www.rusi.org*. Pertinent historical and technical background is given in Hans M. Kristensen, *U.S Nuclear Weapons in Europe: A Review of Post-Cold War Policy, Force Levels, and War Planning*, Washington, DC: Natural Resources Defense Council, February 2005.

35. "Military dangers" create conditions where threats are possible, whereas "military threats" exist where there is "a realistic possibility of armed conflict arising." See Giles, pp. 4-5; and, *The Military Doctrine of the Russian Federation Approved by Russian Federation Presidential Edict*, February 5, 2010, Part I, No. 6, English translation available from *www.sras.org/military_doctrine_russian_federation_2010*.

36. Richard Weitz, "Strategy and Doctrine in Russian Security Policy," paper presented at conference on "Strategy and Doctrine in Russian Security Policy," Ft. McNair, National Defense University, Washington, DC, June 28, 2010, pp. 25-27, provides an insightful discussion.

37. Pavel K. Baev, "Russia's Security Relations with the U.S.: Futures Planned and Unplanned," paper presented at conference on "Strategy and Doctrine in Russian Security Policy," Ft. McNair, National Defense University, Washington, DC, June 28, 2010, p. 8.

38. Sokov, "Nuclear Weapons in Russian Security Strategy," pp. 7-8. See also Weitz, "Strategy and Doctrine in Russian Security Policy," pp. 25-27; and Baev, "Russia's Security Relations with the U.S.: Planned and Unplanned," pp. 7-8.

39. *NATO 2020: Assured Security; Dynamic Engagement, Analysis and Recommendations of the Group of Experts on a New Strategic Concept for NATO*, Brussels, Belgium: North Atlantic Treaty Organization, May 17, 2010, p. 43.

40. *Ibid.*

41. *Ibid.*

42. Mark Landler, "U.S. Resists Push by Allies for Tactical Nuclear Cuts," *New York Times*, April 22, 2010, available from *www.nytimes.com/2010/04/23/world/europe/23diplo.html*.

43. Kipp, "Russia's Nuclear Posture and the Threat That Dare not Speak Its Name. See also *Ibid.*, p. 3, for Russian nuclear deployments on non-European strategic axes, including (among others) the Siberian and Far Eastern federal districts.

44. See George Perkovich, "After Prague: What's Next for Arms Control?" *International Herald Tribune*, April 7, 2010, available from *www.carnegieendowment.org/publications/index.cfm?fa=view&id=40532*.

45. On Iran's progress toward the capability for nuclear weaponization and related issues, see *Iran's Nuclear and Missile Potential: A Joint Threat Assessment by U.S. and Russian Technical Experts*, New York: East-West Institute, May 2009, available from *www.ewi.info*; and "Iran's Nuclear Timetable," *Iran Watch*, updated February 23, 2010, and regularly, available from *www.iranwatch.org/ourpubs/articles/iranucleartimetable.html*. For possible scenarios if diplomacy fails, see Anthony Cordesman, *Iran, Israel and the Effects of a Nuclear Conflict in the Middle East*, Washington, DC: Center for Strategic and International Studies, June 1, 2009, esp. pp. 5-8 and 32-46. On North Korea, see Leon V. Sigal, "Let's Make a Deal," *The American Interest Magazine*, January-February 2010, available from *the-american-interest.com/article-bd.cfm?piece=767*; and Andrew Scobell and John M. Sanford, *North Korea's Military Threat: Pyongyang's Conventional Forces, Weapons of Mass Destruction, and Ballistic Missiles*, Carlisle, PA: U.S. Army War College, Strategic Studies Institute, April 2007.

46. Henry Sokolski, "Moving Toward Zero and Armageddon?" Chap. 5, in Sokolski, ed., *Reviewing the Nuclear Nonproliferation Treaty*, Carlisle, PA: Strategic Studies Institute, U.S. Army War College, May 2010, pp. 77-101, citation from p. 87.

47. For possible dangers and pathways to nuclear first use, see George H. Quester, *Nuclear First Strike: Consequences of a Broken Taboo*, Baltimore, MD: Johns Hopkins University Press, 2006. On the concept of a nuclear taboo, see Nina Tannenwald, *The Nuclear Taboo: The United States and the Non-Use of Nuclear Weapons Since 1945*, Cambridge UK: Cambridge University Press, 2007, esp. pp. 327-360.

48. See Graham Allison, *Nuclear Terrorism: The Ultimate Preventable Catastrophe*, New York: Henry Holt, Times Books, 2004, pp. 61-63.

49. For informative discussion on this point, see Blank, *Russia and Arms Control*; and Joseph Cirincione, *Bomb Scare: The History*

and Future of Nuclear Weapons, New York: Columbia University Press, 2007.

50. For U.S. force modernization plans pertinent to the New START agreement of April, 2010, see *Nuclear Posture Review Report*, pp. 19-27. For Russian possibilities, see Podvig, "New START Treaty in Numbers," from his blog, *Russian strategic nuclear forces*, April 9, 2010, available from *russianforces.org/blog/2010/03/new_start_treaty_in_numbers.shtml*; and Podvig, "Russia's new arms development," *Bulletin of the Atomic Scientists*, January 16, 2009, available from *thebulletin.org/web-edition/columnists/pavel-podvig/russias-new-arms-development*.

51. *Treaty between the United States of America and the Russian Federation on Measures for the Further Reduction and Limitation of Strategic Offensive Arms*, Washington, DC: U.S. Department of State, April 8, 2010, available from *www.state.gov/documents/organization/140035.pdf*.

52. Grateful acknowledgment is made to Dr. James Scouras for use of his AWSM® model for making calculations and drawing graphs pertinent to this study. He is not responsible for any arguments or opinions here. Additional information about this model with pertinent illustration appears in Stephen J. Cimbala and James Scouras, *A New Nuclear Century*, Westport, CT: Praeger Publishers, 2002, pp. 25-73.

53. For pertinent references and commentary on this point, see Michael Bohm, "The Kremlin's Shock Troops," *Moscow Times*, May 6, 2010, in Johnson's Russia List 2010, #89, May 6, 2010, available from *davidjohnson@starpower.net*.

54. Bohm, "The Kremlin's Shock Troops."

55. Rachel Oswald, "GOP Senators Remain Wary of U.S.-Russian Arms Control Deal," available from *www.globalsecuritynewswire.org*, in Johnson's Russia List 2010, #87, May 4, 2010, available from *davidjohnson@starpower.net*.

56. An argument in favor of a multi-causal explanation for Cold War and post-Cold War outcomes in nuclear policy and strategy is effectively presented in Michael Krepon, *Better Safe than Sorry: The Ironies of Living with the Bomb*, Stanford, CA: Stanford University Press, 2009.

57. In addition to sources previously cited, excellent discussions on this topic appear in Alexei Arbatov, "Terms of Engagement: Weapons of Mass Destruction Proliferation and U.S.-Russian Relations," Chap. 5, pp. 139-168; and Stephen J. Blank, "Prospects for Russo-American Cooperation in Halting Nuclear Proliferation," Chap. 6, pp. 169-284, both in Stephen J. Blank, ed., *Prospects for U.S.-Russian Security Cooperation*, Carlisle, PA: Strategic Studies Institute, U.S. Army War College, March 2009.

58. Although official U.S. policy holds that Iran should not be permitted to obtain nuclear weapons, the United States also hedges against the possibility of a nuclear Iran, including plans for missile detection and defense systems and other military ties to Persian Gulf states and Obama's revised missile defense plan for Europe. See "U.S. Considers Options Against Nuclear Iran," Associated Press, April 23, 2010, available from *www.cbsnews.com/ stories/2010/04/20/politics/main6414377.shtml*.

CHAPTER 10

RUSSIA'S NUCLEAR POSTURE AND THE THREAT THAT DARE NOT SPEAK ITS NAME[1]

Jacob W. Kipp

The overwhelming focus of the limited Western writings on the contemporary Russian military and its nuclear forces is predominantly European. This exists in spite of the fact that Russia under Vladimir Putin and Dmitri Medvedev has proclaimed itself a Eurasian power. Western commentary on the Russo-Georgian Conflict of August 2008 highlights this tendency. The conflict in this context becomes about Georgia's desire to join the West via membership in the North Atlantic Treaty Organization (NATO) and Russia's military response—although aimed at the Georgian government under President Mikhail Saakashvilli and the Georgian Armed Forces—intended to undermine U.S. and NATO interests in Europe.[2] The same can be said about the Obama administration's "reset" of U.S.-Russian relations and the emphasis placed upon reaching an agreement on offensive nuclear forces, which are a legacy of the militarized Cold War confrontation in Europe. Obama's address in Prague in 2009 spoke of the promise of a "global zero" for nuclear weapons, but the approach to Russia focused upon strategic offensive nuclear forces to the exclusion of tactical and theater nuclear arms. The language of the treaty stresses measures to ensure strategic stability between the two signatories, even as the global security environment has moved from bipolar, through unipolar to an emerging multipolar system. The recently published *National Security Strategy* does seem to recognize this multipolar context and speaks of Russia as a regional partner along with China, India, and other "increasingly influential nations" such as Brazil, South Africa, and Indonesia.[3] The document speaks of Russia as a partner for the United States in Europe and Asia in the context of fighting terrorism and providing stability for Afghanistan but not in terms of larger Asian security themes, leaving the impression that the White House does not envision an Asian dimension to the partnership.[4]

Indeed, while the post-Cold War world has moved from a bipolar system, through a unipolar one, to multipolarity, the U.S.-Russian security dialogue has been remarkably Euro-centric, whether it was about strategic partnership, NATO-Russian cooperation, Russian hostility to NATO expansion and out-of-area operations, or the U.S. deployment of anti-ballistic missile (ABM) assets into Central Europe.[5] In fact, this silence in the West can be put at Moscow's own door. Only this spring, a group of NATO "elders" visited Moscow to discuss NATO's new "Strategic Concept" shortly after the publication of Russia's new *Military Doctrine*, which had once again treated NATO as a "danger and threat" because of the actions it had taken on the periphery of Russia, including NATO expansion.[6] During the conversations led by former U.S. Secretary of State Madeleine Albright and the Vice Chair of the Expert Group, Jeroen van der Veer, the former Chief Executive Officer (CEO) of Royal Dutch Shell, the "elders" had asked the Russian officials and scholars with whom they met about Russian perceptions of the growing power and influence of the People's Republic of China (PRC). The official and unofficial Russian response was a studied silence. The conversation did not transcend the issues dividing Russian and NATO perspectives on European security.[7]

Russian foreign policy commentary on Chinese-Russian relations continues to stress the elements of partnership comprise the interests of the two states in multipolarity to counter American hegemony, even as U.S. policy under Obama has stressed international engagement and a "reset" with Russia, and even though neither Moscow nor Beijing desired that the Shanghai Cooperation Organization (SCO) would become an anti-Western military alliance. The only negative point made by Aleksandr Lukin in an assessment of those bilateral relations was that China would, from time to time, encourage Russia to take anti-Western actions that China itself would not do.[8] Two Canadian scholars in a recent review of Sino-Russian relations concluded that the "strategic partnership" between Moscow and Beijing was based on realpolitik focused on countering U.S. influence and the scholars did not see any prospect for a deepening relationship in the short- or mid-term future because of the continuing distrust between China and Russia.[9] Western observers have seen more tension between Russia and China in Central Asia. Jeffrey Mankoff and Leland R. Miller have written of the bilateral competition between China and Russia, thereby affording the United States more room to maneuver politically and economically in that region.[10]

Some Russian authors have raised an alarm over an emerging security challenge to Russia's Far East from a Chinese military that already has the marks of a military superpower in comparison with Russia's own conventional forces. Aleksandr' Khramchikhin spoke of a Chinese military that combined mass and modern technology deployed along Russia's eastern frontiers at a time when it was evident that China no longer had to contemplate using military force to regain Taiwan.[11]

461

For well over 2 decades, Soviet and Russian military planners have looked upon tactical nuclear forces as the ultimate guarantor of Russian security in the East. For the last 15 years, the national political and military elite have been agreed that there was no conventional military threat from China, because of improved relations. But that situation has been changing rapidly over the last several years. Indeed, even as Russia's Ministry of Defense and General Staff prepare to conduct a strategic-operational exercise this summer, Vostok-2010, there has been remarkable silence on the exercise's scenario.[12]

The issue of advanced Chinese conventional capabilities has forced a reconsideration of Moscow's military response. These tensions, in conjunction with other emerging military transformations among non-European nuclear powers, should highlight the difficulties associated with stability outside of the main European framework, which become even more complex in Russia's Asian frontiers. Nuclear disarmament, which does address the military-technical revolution associated with advanced conventional weapons, informatization, and network-centric warfare will not address the much more complicated role that nuclear weapons will be expected to play as an instrument of theater deterrence.

In this context, Russia's nuclear arsenal remains, however, a key variable in Eurasian security. At present, that arsenal is estimated to be significantly smaller than the 40,000 that existed at the end of the Cold War, but is certainly in excess of 14,000 weapons, including 3,113 strategic warheads and 2,079 nonstrategic warheads deployed and another 8,000 in storage or waiting to be dismantled as of 2008.[13] A significant portion of these are stored east of the Urals and form a major component of Russia's geostrategic posture in the non-European strategic axes which include the Caucasus, Central Asia, Siberia, the Russian Far East, and the Arctic.[14] With regard to Asian security, the nuclear weapons deployed and stored in the Siberian Federal and the Far Eastern Federal Okrugs form the basis of Russia's theater nuclear forces. These forces include the nuclear weapons of the Russian Pacific Fleet, Air Force, Strategic Rocket Forces, and the Army.[15] The theater role that these forces will play in case of armed conflict with the PRC has been candidly described by Aleksandr Khramchikhin.[16]

At present, the Russian Ministry of Defense and the General Staff are in the process of redefining those strategic axes, and they are reducing the number of military districts from six to four, and they are creating operational-strategic commands in each. They include: the Western, covering Europe with its headquarters in St. Petersburg; the Southern, covering the Black Sea, Caucasus, and Caspian with its headquarters in Rostov-on-Don; the Central, covering Central Asia with its headquarters in Yekaterinburg; and the Eastern, covering the Far East and Pacific Ocean with its headquarters in Khabarovsk. This concept was tested in conjunction with Vostok-2010, a major exercise in Siberia that the Russian Far East Command conducted in late June and early July.[17] Since 1999, Russia has conducted operational-strategic exercises dealing with its western strategic direction on a regular basis. Those exercises have included the first use of nuclear weapons to de-escalate and bring about conflict termination in a scenario involving a conventional attack upon Russia from the West by coalition forces that enjoy tactical-technical qualitative superiority over Russian conventional forces. The limited nuclear strikes seemed to have been designed to disrupt command, control, communications, computers, and intelligence, surveillance, and reconnaissance (C4ISR) and precision strike capabilities of the aggressor forces in order to halt the attack.[18] Vostok-2010 was the first to address the Eastern strategic direction and has been associated with the implementation of the military "new look" championed by Minister of Defense Anatoly Serdyukov and Chief of the General Staff General Nikolai Makarov as part of the transformation of the Russian military into a brigade-centric force, capable of conducting advanced conventional operations and network-centric warfare.[19] As one of the Russian reformers described the "new look," it was a gamble on the nature of the future war, which the Russian Army would face.[20]

The motivation behind this shift in direction is not military-technological development in the West but a deep reappraisal of the security situation in Russian Siberia and the Far East. In an article devoted to Russia's "Eastern Vector," General Makhmut Gareev pointed to the emergence of NATO as a global security organization with a footprint in Central Asia as a result of the Afghan War, and he predicted that there will be rising tensions between a U.S.-led NATO and the PRC. While he focused on NATO's nonmilitary means of exerting influence, particularly on the model of the "color revolutions" in Ukraine and Georgia that had brought regimes hostile to Russia to power, his primary focus was on the unleashing of armed conflict in regions where Russia was lacking in combat potential, especially combat readiness.[21] Gareev returned to the theme of combat readiness in a follow-on article about lessons learned from the Great Patriotic War. In addition to citing the surprise attack of Nazi Germany in 1941, Gareev pointed to the outbreak of local fighting between the Soviet Union and the PRC along the Amur River in 1969 that forced the mobilization of an entire military district. He also noted the risks involved when national political leadership did not appreciate the military-political situation they were addressing when they ordered the use of force. Gareev drew attention to the decision to intervene militarily in Afghanistan in 1979 and the decision to intervene in Chechnya in 1994. In both Afghanistan and Chechnya, the governments blundered into wars that they did not want, because they failed to understand the implied tasks that followed from the initial order and failed in their political guidance to take into account the real situation on the ground. The relevance of these lessons from all four conflicts is the nature of the true connection between politics and strategy:

> The final and decisive word belongs to the political leadership but in the working out of the most important military-political decisions, military professionals and other specialists must take part, otherwise policy will not apply to the real life. And the main point is that politicians and diplomats are obliged to create favorable conditions for the actions of the Armed Forces.[22]

On the issue of "new look," Gareev endorsed its content, i.e., the creation of precision-strike weapons and the necessary technological base to support the conduct of network-centric warfare. At the same time, he called for the working out and implementation of a more active and decisive strategy, and operational art, and tactics so as to impose upon the enemy those actions, including contact warfare, which he most seeks to avoid. [23] In this regard, combat readiness becomes one of the primary concerns of military professionals, since combat potential, when not linked to actual combat readiness, can create a false appreciation of the military power available. Here the nation's capacity to mobilize additional military power defines its ability to manage the escalation of a local conflict toward a decision in keeping with national interests.[24]

This is supposed to be the exact focus of Vostok-2010.[25] The "new look" military, which the Ministry of Defense has set out to create via a brigade-based ground force capable of launching precision strikes and conducting network-centric warfare faces a particular challenge in Siberia and the Far East, where Chinese military modernization has moved the People's Liberation Army (PLA) from a mass industrial army built to fight people's war to that of an army seeking to rearm itself as an advanced conventional force and to conduct their own version of network-centric warfare. A year ago, informed Russian defense journalists still spoke of the PLA as a mass industrial army seeking niche advanced conventional capabilities. Looking at the threat environment that was assumed to exist under Zapad 2009, defense journalist Dmitri Litovkin spoke of Russian forces confronting three distinct types of military threats:

> ...an opponent armed to NATO standards in the Georgian-Russian confrontation over South Ossetia last year. In the eastern strategic direction Russian forces would likely face a multi-million-man army with a traditional approach to the conduct of combat: linear deployments with large concentrations of manpower and firepower on different axes. In the southern strategic direction, Russian forces expect to confront irregular forces and sabotage groups fighting a partisan war against 'the organs of Federal authority,' i.e., internal troops, the border patrol, and the Russian Federal Security Service (FSB).[26]

By the spring of 2009, a number of those involved in bringing about the "new look" were speaking of a PLA that was moving rapidly towards a high-tech conventional force with its own understanding of network-centric warfare.[27] Moreover, the PLA conducted a major exercise, "Stride-2009," which looked to some Russian observers like a rehearsal for military intervention against Central Asia and/or Russia.[28]

Speaking about the deployment of two newly-organized brigades along the Russian-Chinese border on the Irkutsk-Chita Axis, Lieutenant-General Vladimir Valentinovich Chirkin, the recently appointed commander of the Siberian Military District, stated that the brigades were deployed there to counter the presence of five PLA combined arms armies across the border. From 2003 to 2007, Chirkin commanded an army in the Siberian military district. On the rationale for the deployment, Chirkin stated: "We are obligated to keep troops there because on the other side of the order are five Chinese armies, and we cannot ignore that operational direction." He added that the Ministry of Defense intended to develop an army headquarters for command and control of the brigades.[29] In a related report, Chirkin described the PLA forces across the border as composed of three divisions and 10 tank, mechanized, and infantry brigades, which he described as not little, but also "not a strike force." As to the role of the new brigades, Chirkin put them as part of a deterrent force aimed as friendly reminder to the PRC that: ". . . despite the friendly relations with China, our army command understands that friendship is possible only with strong countries, that is whose (sic) who can quiet a friend down with a conventional or nuclear club."[30]

The gamble on the nature of future war described by Aleksandr' Kondrat'ev in supporting the development of network-centric warfare capabilities, comes down to the issue of Russia's capacity to arm, create, train, deploy, and keep combat ready forces capable of conducting advanced conventional warfare. In the absence of such forces, the deterrence equation is reduced to the credibility of the nuclear option for deterring conventional attacks. Given the economic and demographic realities of Siberia and the Russian Far East, Russia seeks by non-military means to preclude the emergence of a Chinese military threat. However, Russian observes also are aware of the fact that an imminent military threat from Beijing can emerge out of regional instability, which is beyond Russia's unilateral means to control.

As the most recent Russian *Military Doctrine* of 2010 states, nuclear weapons remain the primary instrument for deterrence against both nuclear and conventional attacks upon Russia and in defense of Russian interests, territorial integrity, and sovereignty.[31] The doctrine does not explicitly state that Russia will use nuclear weapons in a preemptive attack against such threats, as had been discussed by senior members of the Security Council in the fall of 2009, but leaves the decision to use such weapons in the hands of the President of the Russian Federation. The context of use, however, is defined by the nature of the challenges and threats that Russia faces across Eurasia. A second classified document, "The Foundations of State Policy in the Area of Nuclear Deterrence to 2020," which was issued at the same time as the *Military Doctrine*, has had portions leaked to the mass media. These describe two types of threats that could lead to the use of nuclear weapons: 1) attacks upon vital economic and political structures, early warning systems, national command and control, and nuclear weapons systems, which fits a U.S.-led NATO threat involving conventional forces cable of conducting global strikes against such targets; and 2) during an invasion by an enemy's ground units onto Russian territory if Russia's Armed Forces are incapable of stopping the enemy progress and it penetrates deep into the country through conventional means of waging war, which fits more closely with an assault by the PLA against the Russian Far East.[32]

The first concept resembles one popularized by General-Major Vladimir Slipchenko in his discussions of sixth-generation warfare and no-contact warfare on the model of NATO's campaign against Kosovo, but applied on a global scale.[33] Slipchenko speculated on the use of long-range precision-strike systems for attacks upon enemy economic, administrative, and military infrastructure. The second concept, which was not contained in the 2000 version of Russian *Military Doctrine* is quite new and reflects what the Russian military recognizes is an emerging threat from the PRC. In a polemic with Slipchenko in 2005, General Gareev discussed such a conflict which would require the development of a mass mobilization base to conduct a protracted war, which employed precision-strike systems, but did not achieve annihilation of the opponent's forces.[34] Both Slipchenko and Gareev agreed that nuclear deterrence had become self-deterrence in the post-Cold War era.

FACING WEST AND EAST

For Russia, which inherited the Soviet nuclear arsenal, but has faced a serious change in its international position, the nuclear equation is, in fact, shaped by Russia's status as a regional power in a complex Eurasian security environment, where nuclear issues are not defined exclusively by the U.S.-Russian strategic nuclear equation but by security dynamics involving interactions with Russia's immediate periphery. On the one hand, Russia's security responses have been shaped by a post-Soviet decade of sharp internal political crises, economic transformation, social instability, demographic decline, and the collapse of conventional military power. The impact of these developments has been uneven across Russia, leading to very distinct security environments, which have demanded regional responses. The initial focus of security concerns for both the Soviet Union and the Russian Federation was primarily upon European security. This was the primary focus of the U.S.-Soviet strategic competition and the place where its militarization was most evident.

The end of the Cold War began with the attempt to reform the Soviet system under Mikhail Gorbachev by means of *perestroika* and *glasnost* and embraced the idea of getting time and space for reform by removing the ideological roots of East-West confrontation from Europe. As presented by Aleksandr Yakovlev, one of Gorbachev's key advisors, the policy involved the removal of the primary driver of East-West conflict, the military confrontation between NATO and the Warsaw Treaty Organization (WTO).[35] Demilitarization of the Cold War in Europe and Soviet military disengagement from international conflicts, especially Afghanistan, were part of an effort to save a system that had lost the capacity to innovate and only survived on the basis of bureaucratic inertia and coercion. Reform risked both domestic and international complications.[36] In Europe, the first real indicator of successful demilitarization was the Intermediate Range Nuclear Forces (INF) Treaty of 1987 which abolished entire classes of intermediate-range nuclear forces with operational-strategic impact on the European theater, followed by moves under the Organization for Security and Cooperation in Europe (OSCE) toward greater military transparency, and was then consummated by the Conventional Forces in Europe Treaty of 1990 which set limits on forward deployed conventional forces in Central Europe and on its flanks from the Atlantic to the Urals.[37]

Political developments, however, made this security regime obsolete when the Velvet Revolutions of 1989 replaced governments allied with the Soviet Union and led to the abolition of the WTO in December 1991. In the meantime, political discontent and rising nationalism within the Union of Soviet Socialist Republics (USSR) undermined Gorbachev's program of gradual reform and led to a confrontation between hardliners opposed to further reform and nationalists calling for both the abolition of Soviet power and the end of the Soviet Union. Boris Yeltsin, elected President of the Russian Socialist Federal Soviet Republic (RSFSR) in June 1991, became the spokesman for national democratic opposition to the existing Soviet order. The attempted coup by hardliners in August 1991 failed, and Boris Yeltsin emerged as leader of a Russian Federation that was willing to see the Soviet Union abolished, which occurred on December 31, 1991. In a matter of months, the Cold War bilateral international system had shifted to a unipolar order dominated by a U.S.-led Atlantic-European community. The Russian Federation found itself dealing with the dismemberment of the Soviet Union and the regathering of the Soviet nuclear arsenal under its control and preventing the proliferation of nuclear weapons, fissionable materials, and nuclear weapons expertise, a policy supported by the George H.W. Bush and Bill Clinton administrations. Hope of a strategic partnership, which flourished in Washington and Moscow in the early 1990s, was cooling by the second half of the decade.

On the other hand, the emergence of the United States as the sole superpower put a distinct complication in Russia's responses to these regional issues and led to efforts to cultivate the creation of a multipolar counterbalance to U.S. influence. As framed by Foreign Minister Evgenii Primakov, the new order was supposed to rest on cooperation among Moscow, Beijing, and New Delhi to balance Washington's global influence. Neither New Delhi nor Beijing endorsed a policy of trilateral balancing, but Moscow and Beijing did move towards a de facto security system with the signing of the five-power Treaty on Deepening Military Trust in Border Regions in 1996. The agreement, a part of the relaxation of tensions associated with the end of the Cold War, was seen in Moscow as the foundation for balancing in a relatively benign environment in Central Asia and the Far East. Russia embraced arms sales to the PRC as a desperation measure to keep its own military industrial complex from complete collapse. In the absence of domestic orders, foreign sales kept design bureaus and production facilities operational. A case in point was the sale of Su-27M fighters to the PRC in 1992, which kept the design bureau in Moscow and the production plant at Komsomosk-na-Amur open.[38] Russia did not see the PRC as an immediate military threat. Consequently, it was interested in reducing its own forces deployed in the Far East, and was most concerned with averting the total collapse of its defense industry. Primakov's vision of a trilateral balancing mechanism among Moscow, Beijing, and New Delhi did not depend upon arms sales, but it provided geopolitical justification for such sales to China and India. Primakov's vision assumed relatively stable and benign relations among all three actors would exist.[39]

The Putin decade of recovery, which began in 1999 and still continues under the Medvedev-Putin Tandem, was marked by a significant economic recovery, internal stability, state recentralization, and until very recently only marginal improvements in conventional military power. For much of the decade, favorable oil and gas prices allowed Russia to practice Putin's own brand of energy diplomacy across Eurasia by cultivating supplier-consumer relations with major powers, while exercising energy discipline with the states on its own periphery.[40] The decade began with a fundamental shift in the content of the Russian security relationship in Asia. The point of departure was the disillusionment with Euro-Atlantic engagement after NATO expansion and the NATO-conducted air campaign against Yugoslavia and in the face of Russia's vigorous objections to military actions undertaken without a mandate from the United Nations Security Council (UNSC). At the same time, deteriorating security in the Caucasus and Central Asia invoked the need to create a new security regime to cover Asiatic Russia.[41] On the one hand, renewed war in Chechnya raised the prospect of increased involvement by radical Islamic elements there and across the Caucasus. In Central Asia, the spread of Islamic radicalism by the Taliban out of Afghanistan had called into question the existing security structures provided by the Commonwealth of Independent States (CIS). Russia, which had intervened in the Tajik civil war of 1992-97 and helped with the United States to broker a peace settlement there, now found itself faced by a more general regional Islamic threat, which had actually helped to drive the opposing Tajik factions into cooperation. That threat was the spread of jihad from Afghanistan into Central Asia. The PRC, which faced its own Islamic separatist threat among the Uyghur population, which made up a large percentage of the population in Xinjiang, China's frontier region with Central Asia, had its own reasons to support collective security arrangements in the late 1990s.

In this context, in 2001, Russia joined with four other Central Asian states (Kazakhstan, Kyrgyzstan, Tajikistan, and Uzbekistan), and China to form the Shanghai Cooperation Organization (SCO) with an expressed mandate to cooperate against "terrorism, separatism, and extremism."[42] In addition to this regional security function, the SCO also became a vehicle for Moscow and Beijing to express their concerns over U.S. hegemony in the international system and to create a counterweight to NATO as the alliance moved more actively into out-of-area operations affecting Central Asia, especially after its intervention in Afghanistan and the U.S. development of bases in the region, especially Uzbekistan and Kyrgyzstan. The tensions became particularly acute after the U.S. intervention in Iraq when it appeared that the United States was planning for a long-term presence in both Iraq and Afghanistan. The acquisitions of nuclear

474

weapons by India and Pakistan in 1998 had intensified the India-Pakistan conflict and brought with it the possibility of a new "great game" in Central and South Asia, played by nuclear armed states and increasing tensions among Moscow, Beijing, and New Delhi with the United States and NATO—were directly engaged in Afghanistan.[43]

For most of the decade, Russian official literature discussing foreign policy, national security strategy, and military doctrine focused upon the United States and NATO as the chief sources of challenges and threats to Russian national security, with secondary attention given to internal sources of instability (extremism and separatism) and to international terrorism. This official position masked what were developing concerns regarding the security of its own Eastern Siberian and Far Eastern domains. Those security concerns are rooted in Russia's historical experience with this distant and relatively isolated territory.

Russian Cossacks pushed into the Far East in the mid-17th century, and a network of settlements spread. These remotes lands were more connected with Moscow by sea than by land, with the Russian Navy maintaining a nominal presence to enforce Russian claims. The integration of these regions into Imperial Russia took a quantum leap in the last decade of the 19th century with the construction of the Trans-Siberian railroad under the leadership of the Minister of Finances Sergei Witte. Witte saw the railroad as the key to the Russian development of Siberia and as access to the Chinese market. However, before those benefits could be reaped, Russia found itself drawn into imperial rivalries over Manchuria and Korea, leading to war with Japan and defeat. During the war, the railroad became the chief means of Russian strategic mobility and underscored the need for the development of more infrastructure in Eastern Siberia and in the Far East. But the tsarist regime collapsed in the course of another war, and foreign powers (the United States and Japan) found it easy to intervene there during the Russian civil war, which followed the Bolshevik seizure of power and the decision to make peace with the Central Powers. Bolshevik power was slow to consolidate its control in the Far East, which did not come until 1922, when the Japanese military withdrew and the Far Eastern Republic, which had served as a buffer between Soviet territory and the Japanese zone of occupation, was abolished.

Under Joseph Stalin, there was a major effort at developing the Soviet Far East, which included the mobilization of the Komsomol (young communist) cadre to set up new settlements; the creation of vast mining and forestry projects under the Russian People's Commissariat of Internal Affairs (NKVD); and, composing the islands in the Gulag Archipelago. After the Japanese occupation of Manchuria in 1931, intensive efforts were made to strengthen the defenses of the Soviet Far East and the Mongolian People's Republic, an ally of the Soviet Union from its establishment in 1924. Soviet forces fought limited border engagements with the Japanese Kwantung Army in 1938 at Lake Khasan, near Vladivostok, and at Khalkhin-Gol in the Manchuko-Mongolian border in 1939. During World War II, the Soviet Far East was the arrival point for lend-lease materials from the United States—shipped on Soviet-flagged ships—and served as the staging area for the Soviet offensive of August 1945 which announced Soviet entry into the war against Japan and led to the Soviet occupation of Manchuria and North Korea and the seizure of the southern Sakhalin and the

Kuril islands. In both Manchuria and North Korea, the Soviet military presence facilitated the establishment of local Communist regimes. In the postwar period, the Soviet Far East continued to be a major part of the Gulag until Stalin's death and the dismantling of the camp system.

During the Cold War, the Soviet Far East was the staging area for support to North Korean and Chinese Communist forces engaged in the Korean War. With the emergence of the Sino-Soviet conflict and especially after the border incidents with China in 1969, the Far East became a military bastion and remained so until the collapse of the USSR. In the decade that followed the collapse of the USSR, the Russian Far East experienced demographic decline and economic crisis, from which it began a slow recovery. The region has endured an energy crisis, criminality, and corruption. Tensions between Moscow and the Far East grew sharp with the global economic downturn and the decline in world energy prices, particularly when Moscow sought to impose a tariff on imported automobiles, which had been a thriving business in Vladivostok. In December 2008, local protestors took to the streets under the slogan: "Authorities: Raise the Standard of Living, not the Tariff." They were met by Ministry of Internal Affairs (MVD) riot police sent from Moscow to restore order by applying their batons to the demonstrators' bodies.[44]

In part, these crises were a legacy of the collapse of the Soviet system, which had treated those regions as the forward bastions of its security in the context of deteriorating relations with the PRC. Moscow had invested heavily in maintaining a military presence and infrastructure in the region, including the Baikal-Amur Main Line (*Magistral*), which was to provide the transportation infrastructure to give the region strategic depth for defense but was never completed. With the collapse of the Soviet Union, that military infrastructure was allowed to decay, since Moscow had no resources to fund it. In the absence of continuing investment credits, Moscow granted the regions local self-government and looked to economic transformation on the basis of international trade to revive the area. There was much hope expressed in Moscow that Japanese capital, Chinese workers, and Russian raw materials would make the Russian Far East into a part of the dynamic Asia-Pacific economy. Instead, the Far East saw a radical decline in population (7.9 million in 1989) and economic activity, leading to a total population in the Far East of 6.7 million by the 2002 census and making the region one of the most under-populated regions in the world in terms of persons per square mile. In fact, however, most of the population in the Russian Far East is concentrated in a 90-mile belt of settlement from Chita in the West to Vladivostok on the Pacific with the Trans-Siberian Railroad providing the single corridor for transregional transportation through it. Russia did move to resolve border disputes with the PRC under President Boris Yeltsin, which led to a general agreement in 1995 but left the settlement of conflicting claims over certain strategic islands in the areas of Chita and Khabarovsk unresolved. In 2005, these issues were resolved with the transfer of about half the disputed territory to China. In spite of the fact that islands near Khabarovsk were directly across from this major Russian city and defense center, military authorities downplayed any military threat to the city, although the Border Guards did express concern about possible illegal immigration.[45] In the general climate of improved Sino-Russian relations, no military threat seemed to exist.

There were, of course, all sorts of concerns about illegal Chinese settlers coming into the Far East. Viktor Ishaev, the Governor of Khabarovsk Krai from 1991 to 2009, repeatedly raised the issue of Chinese migration into the region as part of plan for the "peaceful capture" of the Russian Far East.[46] But unlike under Yeltsin, a stronger central government was able to keep local problems and perceptions from impacting the conduct of bilateral relations. Likewise, pertaining to nuclear issues, if the great concern had been regionalism and the actions of local officials in regard to supporting and protecting existing nuclear infrastructure from decay, criminal penetration, and incompetent management in the 1990s, when the center was weak under Putin, the center reestablished control and co-opted local political leaders to the center's interests, reducing the risks of crisis between the center and the Far Eastern periphery.[47] Putin's strategy, which has continued under President Medvedev, was to seek to bring about the economic integration of Russia into the global economic processes that have turned Asia into an engine of globalization. Russia has formally engaged with regional organizations such as the Asia-Pacific Economic Council (APEC), which it joined in 1998, and fostered a partnership with the Association of Southeastern Asian Nations (ASEAN). However, Russia has not achieved its goals as of 2010.

In the Far East, Russia's primary gamble was on the prospect of good relations with China. Until to 2009, China was consistently described as Russia's strategic partner, the primary engine of Asia's economic transformation and growing global influence. Russia was to serve as a source of advanced military technology and raw materials and to provide China with a stable rear supporting its international position.[48] No mention of China as a strategic threat came from official sources, although commentators might worry about a yellow peril of Chinese settlers in the Far East or complain of Chinese goods driving out domestic products in local markets. Konstantin Pulikovsky, a former general and President Putin's envoy to the Far Eastern Federal Okrug from 2000 to 2009, spoke of Chinese investment as vital to the future of the region.[49] Russia's residual influence in North Korea had declined rapidly after the collapse of the Soviet Union as the issue of North Korean nuclear weapons development emerged. In 2000, President Putin invited Kim Jong Il to visit Russia, which he did in the summer of 2000. Pulikovsky, who accompanied Kim in his rail trip to Moscow, became the Russian official with the closest ties to Kim Jong Il and appreciated the importance of North Korea to Russia's own security interests and appreciated China's strongest influence in Pyongyang.[50] After Kim Jong Il's visit to Russia in 2000, some spoke of the personal ties between Kim and President Putin as redefining Russian-North Korean relations, but developments over the rest of the decade confirmed China's greater access and influence during the Six Party Talks over North Korea's nuclear program. Russia's approach to that ongoing crisis has been to support its legitimate security interests in Northeast Asia via preserving peace and stability on the Korean Peninsula.[51] In this capacity, Russia has engaged in the Six Party Talks. Russia could and did develop economic ties with South Korea over the last 2 decades, while it kept its limited influence in North Korea. This balancing has been evident in Moscow's approach to the crisis set off by the sinking of the South Korean patrol corvette, the *Cheonan*, by an acoustic torpedo, which an international investigation carried out by U.S. and

Australian experts concluded was fired by North Korean forces.[52] What Moscow wants most to avoid is a regional crisis becoming an armed conflict and inviting the intervention of other powers, especially the United States and the PRC in support of South and North Korea.

Over the last 2 decades, Russia has looked to Japanese investment even in the face of the lack of progress in resolving the territorial dispute over the Kurile Islands, which had kept Japanese-Soviet and now Japanese-Russian relations frozen—the Soviet Union and then Russia offered a two of four split of the island chain, with Russia retaining the northern and Japan getting the southern islands. Japan demanded the return of all four islands, which Russia refused. Russian energy diplomacy under Putin favored Chinese interests over Japanese. Realists in Moscow saw no major movement in Tokyo's security regime with Washington and simply gave a lower priority to the improvement of bilateral political relations even though Moscow continued to court Japanese investment in the Russian Far East. Border incidents and disputes over fishing rights led to periodic flare-ups but no major crisis, so Moscow was willing to keep its policy towards Japan in line with that of Beijing. Moscow supported the Six Party Talks but with the clear understanding that Beijing had the best leverage with Pyongyang. Moscow supported counterproliferation initiatives, but has worried that U.S. impatience and/or North Korea provocations could lead to war and greater instability in northeast Asia and even risk a Sino-American confrontation. The Russian concern about Sino-American conflict grows in conjunction with the two major points of contentions between the two powers: Taiwan and the Korean peninsula. The concerns have become greater as the conduct of the North Korean regime has become more erratic.

Strategic nuclear weapons loomed very large in the Yeltsin era when the strategic arsenal was expected to play a major political role in assuring that Russia would establish and retaining a strategic partnership with the United States and obtain a major say in the emerging post-Cold War order in Europe. Since 1999, Russia has emphasized the deterrent function of its strategic nuclear forces, but has focused its posture on conflict management to discourage military intervention in Russia's periphery. For two decades, the Russian military has placed the likelihood of nuclear war at a very low level and has even seen the possibility of a general coalition war at a low probability. That being said, the Russian government has also recognized that its immediate periphery is quite unstable, fraught with local conflicts that can turn into local wars, and lead to foreign military interventions against the national interests, territorial integrity, and sovereignty of Russia. The question of the "near abroad," a euphemism for the independent states that emerged on Russia's periphery with the breakup of the USSR, has been closely tied to Russian national interests, a Russian sphere of influence, and the protection of Russian minorities living in the successor states. Russian intervention in ethnic conflicts in this region has been seen by the West as one of the primary areas of conflict with Russia, especially in the aftermath of the Russo-Georgian War of August 2008.[53] For Russian leaders, the Russo-Georgian conflict revealed a number of problems associated with the command and control of modern conventional forces, especially the integration of air-land combat, which became a driver for the Ministry of Defense's "new look."[54] At the same time, however, Chinese military modernization made the gamble on strategic partnership less inviting if China was intent upon developing large-scale theater warfare capabilities that embrace advanced conventional weapons and network-centric operations. The default military gamble on nonstrategic nuclear forces to deter a remote Chinese threat became less appealing. Thus, in June and July, the Russian Military Defense and General Staff conducted Vostok-2010 with the intent of assessing Russia's capacity to mobilize and deploy its "new look" conventional forces to defeat a military intervention against the Russian Far East, and tested both the combat capabilities and combat readiness of these forces to deal with that threat.[55] The outcome of that exercise was a major test for the "new look" and began the process of redefining the role of theater nuclear forces in the Far East from the perspective of the necessity toward a true second order response, giving Moscow the capacity to manage such a conflict toward a political solution that does not put into risk the territorial integrity of Russia or its survival as a sovereign state. Continued progress in this direction depends upon Russia's capacity to rearm its forces with advanced conventional capabilities, which will depend on the adaptability of its military industrial complex, and on its capacity to escape its relative geostrategic isolation in the Far East if relations with China should deteriorate.

Vostok-2010 underscored the existing geostrategic isolation of Russia in that region, even as the Ministry of Defense and the General Staff evaluated Russia's "new look" military. One conspicuous feature of the exercise was the description of opposing forces as those of "a hypothetical enemy." Roger McDermott, a prominent Western commentator on the "new look" reforms of the Russian military, offered an excellent overview of Vostok-2010 as an operational-strategic exercise. McDermott correctly pointed to the role of the exercise in testing concepts associated with the "new look" reforms of the Russian Armed Forces and called attention to the testing of the speed of deployment of brigades, their combat readiness, and their capacity to engage in combined arms combat in an air-land battle, and their logistical support to sustain combat actions. He also noted that while the scenario dealt with a wide range of combat actions, including anti-piracy, to counterterrorism, the senior military leadership, including Chief of the General Staff General Nikolai Makarov, stated that the opponent was hypothetical and was not intended to simulate "any one country or bloc." McDermott, however, concluded that the actual objective of the exercise was a test of the defenses of Siberia and the Far East from attack by the PLA of China. McDermott raised the very threat about which the Russian political and military elite could not speak openly.[56] To understand this silence, one needs to understand the political-military context of this exercise.

Anyone who has been involved in the construction of a scenario for a wargame or exercise knows that the creation of the documents for the conduct of such an operational-strategic exercise involves the creation of a road to war, which brings about conflict between the contending sides, usually labeled "red" and "blue" in the case of Russian war games — with "blue" being the color associated with the aggressor forces against which Russian "red" forces defend. In the case of the "Vostok-2010," the Russian forces involved in the exercise were facing a "hypothetical opponent" (*uslovnyi protivnik*). At a press conference at the start of the exercise, General Makarov stated that: "First I would note that this particular exercise, like last years, is not directed against any concrete nation or military-political bloc. It has a strictly defense orientation to maintain security and defense of the state's national interests along its Far Eastern borders from a hypothetical enemy."[57]

Even a hypothetical opponent has to have some military capabilities in order to execute acts of aggression, which bring about the responses of the "red" defenders in the Russian case.[58] An operational-strategic exercise is composed of many distinct tactical vignettes, which are used to test the training of the forces involved in the exercise. Vostok- 2010 not only involved air, ground, and naval forces of the Russian Ministry of Defense but also included forces of the Internal Troops of the MVD, FSB, Border Guards, Ministry of Extraordinary Situations, Federal Security Service (FSO), and Federal Service for Execution of Punishments (FSIN).[59] Its scale was quite large in terms of troops, equipment, and the number of training areas in Siberia and the Far East that were involved. When asked about the opponent that drove these vignettes, General Makarov replied:

> We did not look at any particular country and did not look at any particular enemy. We are talking about what direction we will create our own operational-strategic situation in the course of which somewhere a group of terrorists or large group of separatists are active, which is quite characteristic for low-intensity conflicts. For instance we selected such scenarios. But by quantity—here a brigade, there a battalion, here a small groups of warships. I will say once again, we did not attempt to assemble huge forces and means in any district. We want to look at the capacity of execut-

485

ing tasks with small subunits. We have to understand how our troops must act, and most important what armaments they will need.[60]

According to Minister of Defense Dmitri Serdyukov, Vostok-2010 was designed particularly to test the deployment of forces and the operational command and control of the new brigade-based force structure. Vostok-2010 did not pit two opposing armies in linear combat. Instead, it involved isolated combat and noncombat episodes testing various forces. Fighter aviation conducted long-range deployments from European Russia to the Far East, employing in-air refueling from tanker aircraft. Air defense forces launched surface to air (SAM) missile strikes against "enemy bombers seeking to attack Khabarovsk." Special forces cooperated with the camp guards to prevent the release of a special prisoner from a labor camp near Chita. Combined naval forces, including ships from the Pacific, Northern, and Black Sea Fleets, engaged enemy surface and subsurface forces at sea and conducted air assault and amphibious landings. Other troops beat back an enemy landing on one of the Kuril Islands. Motorized rifle and tank brigades in the Siberian Military District engaged separatists seeking to cut off the Russian Far East and they defeated the enemy by combined arms maneuver through the depths of the enemy, culminating in forcing the Onon River and imposing upon the enemy retreat and the assumption of a tactical defense. In Primorye (the Maritime Province), Russian forces simulated the flight of refugees from North Korea. At the same time, President Medvedev used his visit to the Far East in conjunction with the exercise to praise the evident progress made in the "new look" and to underscore the government's commitment to make Russia into an integrated part of the Asia-Pacific world. Observing the naval exercise, Medvedev took time to decorate sailors from the *Marshal Shaposhnikov*, who had taken part in the recapture of the tanker *Moscow University* and the liberation of its crew.

Russian commentators have concluded that, in spite of all the extensive press coverage of the exercise, the government failed to articulate one message and stay on point. The military, including the Minister of Defense and the Chief of the General Staff were set upon emphasizing the progress made in creating the "new look" Armed Forces and to disarm critics who have charged that the Serdyukov reforms had broken the military.[61] On the other hand, the political leadership in the person of President Medvedev had as its primary message Russia's economic drive for regional integration as a vital national objective. Medvedev emphasized the Asia-Pacific region's continued economic growth even during the current global economic crisis, and spoke of Russia's integration with the entire Asia-Pacific region and not just the PRC, and he even listed integration of the Brazil-Russia-India-China (BRIC) bloc as a national objective.[62]

Aleksandr' Sadchikov described Medvedev's policy as "the fourth campaign to the East," recalling three earlier campaigns: Russia's rivalry with England and France for position in the Far East in the middle of the 19th century; the Russo-Japanese War of 1904-05; and, the "socialist expansion under the Soviet Union," which culminated in the territorial gains achieved as a result of the August 1945 war against Japan. Sadchikov made reference to the political forecast made by Vyacheslav Nikonov about the advantages to Russia in leaning to the east to escape the pressure of the

American superpower. In 2002, Nikonov had written of a China already transforming itself economically and strategically focusing on the unification of Taiwan with the PRC as its primary strategic objective. Nikonov projected a relatively slow transformation of the Chinese military over the next 25 years, making the East in the form of the PRC relatively low risk in terms of security. Sadchikov characterizes the fourth campaign to the East as an adaptation of Beijing's strategy to Russian circumstances: "In its time, China formulated its own strategy: lean on the north, stabilize the west, and expand to the south and east. According to Nikonov, Moscow's present strategy must be lean on the west, stabilize the south, and go east."[63] With the military addressing a separatist threat that obtains armed assistance from abroad and the political leadership committed to going East, one must still ask what were the underlying threats driving the General Staff's accumulation of vignettes.

Looking at the various episodes that made up the scenario for Vostok-2010, one could conclude that going east has its own peculiar risks for Russia. The refugee scenario for North Korea highlights the instability of that regime and the likelihood of conflict developing out of its disintegration or from its desperate acts to sustain its position. Fear that a U.S.-Chinese conflict in the wake of the collapse of North Korea would impose difficult strategic choices upon Moscow has been a regular theme for press commentary concerning Korea. The sharp exchange between Moscow and Tokyo over the exercise in the disputed Kuril Islands highlights the troubled state of Russo-Japanese relations and brings into the strategic calculation the U.S.-Japanese Treaty of Mutual Cooperation and Security.[64] Just as President Medvedev was visiting the nuclear cruiser *Petr Velikii* to observe a mock naval battle and amphibious landing, naval officers there informed the media that the tactical problem of the exercise was the destruction of "an American squadron" and that the probable enemy was unchanged. Commenting on the meteorological conditions at the time of this naval exercise, which involved heavy mist and low visibility, the author described Vostok-2010 as "covered in fog," a categorization which would fit the confused military and political signals being sent.[65] Finally, the air and ground exercises near Chita and Khabarovsk make no sense except as responses to some force threatening the territorial integrity of Eastern Siberia and the Far East. The only forces with the military potential to carryout air and ground attacks that deep into Russian territory are the PLA in support of the so-called separatists identified in the scenario. Reflecting on the vignettes that made up Vostok-2010, Aleskandr' Khramchikhin concluded that the hypothetical opponent in these ground and air operations was, indeed, Russia's probable opponent, the PLA. And he stated in his assessment of the exercise that: "The probable opponent will defeat us in a serious conflict."[66]

The one branch of the Russian military not involved in direct combat operations during Vostok-2010 was the Strategic Rocket Forces, which carried out no operational launches. Their only role was the defense of their bases from attacks by terrorists. However, according to press reports, the exercise did end with a tactical nuclear strike. As Khramchikhin noted, such a strike was hardly in keeping with a fight against separatists and bandits.[67] This seems to suggest that conventional forces could not handle such a challenge to the territorial integrity of the Russian state in so vulnerable a region as the Far East. However, the scenario had left open the intervention of a powerful hypothetical opponent in support of the separatists after their defeat on the Onon.

CONCLUSION

Short of a diplomatic revolution to end Russia's international isolation in the Far East, we can expect the continuation of a Janus-like policy of looking to economic integration with the rest of the Asia-Pacific world, while exercising against these unnamed hypothetical opponents. Russia's Vostok-2010 exercise did not define the role of theater nuclear forces in the Far East—whether they will be the response of necessity or become a true second order response—giving Moscow the capacity to manage such a conflict toward a political solution that does not put into risk the territorial integrity of Russia or its survival as sovereign state. Much will depend upon Russia's capacity to rearm its forces with advanced conventional capabilities, which will depend on the adaptability of its military industrial complex and on its capacity to escape its relative geostrategic isolation in the Far East if relations with China should deteriorate.

In recent articles, Aleksandr' Khramchikhin raised two issues that make this problem particularly difficult. First, he did a strategic assessment of the threats faced by Russia on all strategic axes and then examined the military capabilities available to deal with them. He noted conventional military deficiencies in the west, the south, and north, but said that Russia's defenses in the east were clearly the weakest of all. In this, he included the defenses covering Sakhalin and the Kuril Islands, but focused on the Sino-Russian border in Siberian and the Far East. There he described Russia as effectively defenseless against Chinese aggression. Against a massive array of PLA conventional, ground, and air forces, the Siberian and Far Eastern military districts contain only one tank, eight motorized rifle, two air assault, three missile, four artillery, two rocket-artillery, one covering, and four air defense brigades, and about 300 combat aircraft with their bases located close to the border. China has much greater capacity to reinforce its units in the theater by rail movement, while Russia must face the fact that the trans-Siberian railroad is vulnerable to air interdiction in Siberia and direct attack in the Far East.[68] The second point concerned the conduct of Russian policy in the context of military weakness, where Russia invites confrontations with the United States even as it faces threats on other axes, on which its very weakness provokes the emergence of new threats.[69]

The new tenor of relations between Moscow and Beijing was evident at the recent SCO summit in Tashkent, where Moscow and Beijing discretely jockeyed for position. Moscow has put greater emphasis on security in Central Asia and has revived military cooperation with Kazakhstan, Kyrgyzstan, Tajikistan, and Uzbekistan there under the Collective Security Treaty Organization (CSTO), just as joint military exercises under the SCO have declined since 2007. China has emphasized economic penetration via investment and follows a coherent long-range policy of regional integration with China's economy. James Nixey of Chatham House commented on the recent summit that Russia now recognizes China as a major security concern but is unwilling to say so openly.[70] Moreover, the threat is not just to Central Asia. Tensions between Russia and China have mounted over the Russian Far East. Press reports, citing sources in the Russian Border Guards, speak of Chinese efforts to dredge the Ussuri near Khabarovsk and change the navigational flow to China's advantage in order to get additional territory ceded to China.[71]

Such incidents are not the real challenge to Russian sovereignty over its Far Eastern territories. The real challenge is to be found in the very contradictory claims about the Far East coming out of Moscow, where some see the region as the economic engine and source of raw materials to pull Russia into the 21st century, while others see the region as already being lost and as a de facto part of the Chinese economy. Dr. Viktor Larin, Director of the Institute of History, Archeology, and Ethnography of the Peoples of the Far East, took these conflicting opinions as the point of departure for a major analytical report on "The Asia-Pacific Region in the Early 21st Century: Challenges, Threats, and Chances of Pacific-Ocean Russia." Colleagues saw this piece as an intellectual provocation and an invitation for reflection on the current situation. Larin is skeptical about the government's declarations about investment in the region and questions its willingness to sustain such investments in the region's oil, gas, and transportation infrastructure. He notes that there is nothing inevitable about a Russian presence in the Far East. Other European colonial powers have failed to keep their Asian empires. Why should Russia be any different? Over the last 2 decades, government programs and foreign investments have not led to improvements in the lives of the local population—Larin cites oil and gas development in Sakhalin as an example. Russia is still really on the margins of the emerging Asia-Pacific economy. The center talks about investment in the Far East because it fears that it will lose the region. Moscow is motivated by external threats, but the real problem is that the remaining population in the region has no stake in its future with Russia. Looking back 15 years, Russians spoke of a "yellow peril" from Chinese immigration, but that is not the case today. The real Chinese presence today is in pervasive economic penetration into Russia's Far Eastern and Siberian markets for consumer goods and food stuffs. Russia missed the train for European economic integration and is likely to miss the Asian train as well. If Moscow does not stop thinking of the Far East as a colony to be milked and start thinking about it as a fully-integrated part of the Russian and Asian-Pacific economies, it will, at some time in the not-too-distant future, face the real threat of separatism. The Soviet answer of treating the Far East as a military bastion has no prospect of success.[72]

These developments may fundamentally shift the geostrategic context of President Obama's global zero initiative on nuclear weapons. For the last 2 decades, Russia's nuclear arsenal in Asia was first seen internationally as a problem of management and control as it declined in size and operational readiness. Operationally, even in its reduced capacity, it was for Russia the only military option open in case of attack in a region effectively denuded of conventional military power. China's relative military inferiority made that prospect remote. Both Moscow and Beijing could look to strategic partnership without the prospect of an emerging military threat. Chinese military modernization has in the last year changed that perception in Moscow. Now, with the emergence of a potential conventional threat from its former strategic partner, Russia is in the process of evaluating whether its reformed conventional forces might achieve s viable deterrence in case of attack from a modernized Chinese military. In the absence of such a capability, Russia will be forced to gamble even more on theater nuclear forces and be even less willing to consider reductions in its nonstrategic nuclear forces. In the context of an increasing military confrontation on the Korean peninsula and periodic tensions between Washington and Beijing over Taiwan, Russia's increased fear of China's growing power and its military response adds one further complication to Eurasian security for all parties and makes Asian nuclear force reductions an even more complex problem for Washington to manage. Recent Russian statements on global zero have made it clear that Moscow expects the process to be long, out to 2045 and to involve multilateral discussions about nonstrategic nuclear weapons among all nuclear powers as part of a matrix of global security.[73]

There is now more evidence of a debate within the Russian national security elite on China's role in Russian national security. Recently, Sergei Kazennov, geopolitics expert with the Russian Academy of Sciences, and Vladimir Kumachev, with the Russian Government's Institute of National Security and Strategic Research, took issue with Khramchikhin's pessimistic reading of Russia's military capacity to resist China. They did not disagree with his analysis of Chinese military progress or his assessment of the balance of conventional forces, but said that Russia had sufficient nuclear-armed missile forces to engage in both counterforce and countervalue targeting against China.[74] In fact, they accused Khramchikhin of hyping a hypothetical conflict between Russia and the PRC, when such a conflict was not even a remote possibility. The authors did drag out the well-worn threat of a Sino-U.S. conspiracy to divide Russia in something like the Molotov-Ribbentrop Pact of 1939. They accused Khramchikhin of "playing with soldiers" when the real pieces were in clear view in "secret little boxes," a thinly veiled reference to nuclear weapons as the weapon of immediate resort in the absence of conventional defense capabilities. Rehashing "massive retaliation" for the 21st century, the authors found their way out by pointing to Russia as a key supplier of critical raw materials to the world and therefore an economic guarantee that no one would want to disrupt a good thing. Khramchikhin did not depict China as an aggressor. What he pointed to was Russia's relative geopolitical isolation in a region, where he sees rising tensions. Kazennov and Kumachev's final words were that a "master pattern maker" could cover any threadbare parts of the geopolitical fabric with material (in this case nuclear weapons and energy exports) from another area to secure Russia's national security well into the future.

These developments may fundamentally shift the geostrategic context of President Obama's global zero initiative on nuclear weapons. For the last 2 decades, Russia's nuclear arsenal in Asia was first seen internationally as a problem of management and control as it declined in size and operational readiness. Operationally, even in its reduced capacity, it was for Russia the only military option open in case of attack in a region effectively denuded of conventional military power. China's relative military inferiority made that prospect remote. Both Moscow and Beijing could look to strategic partnership without the prospect of an emerging military threat. Chinese military modernization has in the last year changed that perception in Moscow. Now, with the emergence of a potential conventional threat from its former strategic partner, Russia is in the process of evaluating whether its reformed conventional forces might achieve s viable deterrence in case of attack from a modernized Chinese military. In the absence of such a capability, Russia will be forced to gamble even more on theater nuclear forces and be even less willing to consider reductions in its nonstrategic nuclear forces. In the context of an increasing military confrontation on the Korean peninsula and periodic tensions between Washington and Beijing over Taiwan, Russia's new posture adds one further complication to Eurasian security for all parties and makes Asian nuclear force reductions an even more complex problem for Washington to manage.

ENDNOTES - CHAPTER 10

1. This chapter draws heavily upon research done for the paper, "Asian Drivers of Russia's Nuclear Force Posture," which will be published shortly by the Nonproliferation Education Center of Washington, DC. The author wishes to express his appreciation to Henry Sokolski, who provided invaluable comments and suggestions on that paper.

2. Ronald D. Asmus, *A Little War that Shook the World: Georgia, Russia, and the Future of the West*, New York: Palgrave Macmillan, 2010.

3. *The National Security Strategy of the United States*, Washington, DC: White House, May 27, 2010, p. 3, available from *www.whitehouse.gov/sites/default/files/rss_viewer/national_security_strategy.pdf*.

4. *Ibid.*, p. 44.

5. The obvious exception to this view is Zbigniew Brzezinski. His book, *The Grand Chessboard: American Primacy And Its Geostrategic Imperatives*, reflected the assumptions of its time, which assumed America's status as a superpower in a unipolar landscape, where the United States could forge arrangements with other regional powers. Brzezinski forecast China's sphere of influence

that included not only the Russian Far East but also eastern Siberia and left the impression among Russian readers that what he was purposing was a new geopolitical recasting of the board to Russia's disadvantage. The book was particularly popular in Russia in 1999 during NATO's campaign against Serbia when it was taken as an accurate portrayal of American policy goals. See Zbigniew Brzezinski, *The Grand Chessboard: American Primacy And Its Geostrategic Imperatives*, New York: Basic Books, 1998.

6. Prezident Rossii, *Voennaia doktrina Rossiiskoi Federatsii (Military Doctrine of the Russian Federation)*, February 5, 2010.

7. Andrei Terekhov, "Mudretsy NATO napomnili Moskve o Kitaiskom vyzove," *Nezavisimaia gazeta*, February 12, 2010.

8. A. Lukin, "Russian-Chinese Relations: Keeping up the Pace," *International Affairs*, No. 1, 2010, p.27.

9. Christina Yeung and Nebojda Bjelakovic, "The Sino-Russian Strategic Partnership: Views from Beijing and Moscow," *The Journal of Slavic Military Studies*, Vol. XXIIII, No 2, April-June 2010, pp. 243-281.

10. Jeffrey Mankoff and Leland R. Miller, "China-Russia Competition Opens a Door for America," *Forbes*, April 22, 2010, available from *www.forbes.com/2010/04/22/china-russia-politics-tension-markets-economy-oil-gas.html?boxes=marketschannelnews*.

11. Aleksandr' Khramchikhin, "Milliony soldat plius sovremennoe vooruzhenie," *Nezavisimoe voennoe obozrenie*, October 9, 2009.

12. Roger McDermott, "Russian Military Prepares for Vostok-2010," *Eurasia Daily Monitor*, June 2, 2010.

13. Robert S. Norris and Hans S. Kristensen, "Russian Nuclear Forces, 2008," *Bulletin of the Atomic Scientists*, Vol. 64, No. 2, May-June 2008, pp. 54-57, 62.

14. Iurii Mikhailov, "Sistema ugroz bezopasnosti Rossiiskoi Feederatsii in ee obespechenie," *Orientir*, No. 5, May 2010, pp. 49-52.

15. On the facilities in these two okrugs, see the two chapters by Christina Chuen and Dmitry Kovchegin in James Clay Moltz, Vladimir A. Orlov, and Adam M. Stulberg, eds., *Preventing Nuclear Meltdown: Managing Decentralization of Russia's Nuclear Complex*, Aldershot, UK, and Burlington, VT: Ashgate, 2004, pp. 105-134, 184-210.

16. Aleksandr' Khramchikhin, "Neadekvatnyi vostok," *Nezavisimoe voennoe obozrenie*, July 27, 2010.

17. "The Quantity of Military Districts in Russia Will Be Reduced from Six to Four by December 1 and Operational Strategic Commands Will Be Formed," *Defense & Security*, May 31, 2010.

18. Jacob W. Kipp, "Russian Non-Strategic Nuclear Weapons," *Military Review*, Vol. 81, No. 3, May-June 2001, pp. 27-38.

19. Aleksei Nikolsky, "To Be Assessed by East," *Vedomosti,* March 9, 2010, p. 2. On the "new look" as a gamble on advanced technology and network-centric warfare, see Aleksandr Kondrat'ev, "Stavka na 'voiny budushchego'," *Nezvasimoe voennoe obozrenie*, June 27, 2008.

20. Kondrat'ev, "Stavka na 'voiny budushchego'."

21. Gennadii Miranovich, "Vostochnyi vektor," *Krasnaia zvezda*, March 3, 2010.

22. Makhmut Gareev, "Opyt pobeditelei v Velikoi voine ne mozhet ustaret'," *Nezavisimoe voennoe obozrenie*, March 9, 2010.

23. *Ibid*.

24. *Ibid*.

25. Alesksei Nikol'skii, "Otsenku dast 'Vostok'," *Vedomosti*, March 9, 2010.

26. Dmitri Litovkin, "Ucheniia popali v seti," *Izvestiia*, September 28, 2009.

27. Aleksandr' Kondrat'ev, "Nekotorye osobennosti realizatsii kontseptsii 'setetsentricheskaia voina' v vooruzhennykh silakh KNR," *Zarubezhnoe voennoe obozrenie*. No. 3, March 2010, pp. 11-17.

28. "Ucheniia," *Zarubezhnoe voennoe obozrenie* , No. 8, July 31, 2009; and Aleksandr' Khramchikhin, "Starye osnovy novoi doktriny," *Voenno-Promyshlennyi Kuryer,* Bo. 6, February 17, 2010, p. 5.

29. "Novosti," *VPK-Voennopromyshlennyi kur'er*, March 3, 2010.

30. "Russia Strengthens the Border with China," *Argumenty nedeli*, March 4-10, 2010.

31. Prezident Rossii, *Voennaia Doktrina Rossiiskoi Federatsii (Military Doctrine of the Russian Federation),* February 5, 2010.

32. Vladimir Mokhov, "Osnovy natsional'noi bezopasnosti," *Krasnaia zvezda*, February 6, 2010.

33. Vladimir Slipchenko, *Beskontaktnye voiny*, Moscow, Russia: "Gran-Press," 2001, pp. 29-39.

34. Vladimir Slipchenko and Makhmut Gareev, *Future War*, Ft. Leavenworth, KS: Foreign Military Studies Office, 2007, pp. 67-68.

35. Christopher Shulgan, *The Soviet Ambassador: The Making of the Radical Behind Perestroika*, London, UK: McClelland and Stewart, 2008.

36. Jacob W. Kipp, "Perestroyka and Order [Poryadok]: Alternative Futures and Their Impact on the Soviet Military," *Military Review*, No. 12, December 1989, pp. 2-16.

37. George L. Rueckert, *Global Double Zero: The INF Treaty From Its Origins to Implementation*, Westport, CT: Greenwood Press, 1993; John Borawski, *From the Atlantic to the Urals: Negotiating Arms Control at the Stockholm Conference*, Washington, DC: Pergamon-Brassey International Defense Publishers, 1988; Ivo H.

Daalder, *The CFE Treaty: An Overview and an Assessment*, Washington, DC: The Johns Hopkins Foreign Policy Institute, 1991; and Michael R. Beschloss and Strobe Talbott, *At the Highest Levels: The Inside Story of the End of the Cold War*, Boston, MA: Little, Brown, and Company, 1993.

38. V. Usol'tsev. "'Golubye molnii' i Rosssiiskie letchiki edut v Kitai," *Krasnaia zvezda*, April 11, 1992.

39. Richard Weitz, "The Shanghai Cooperation Organization: The Primakov Vision and Central Asian Realities," *Fletcher Forum of World Affairs*, Vol. 31, No. 1, 2007, pp. 103-118.

40. Marshall I. Goldman, *Petrostate: Putin, Power and the New Russia*, New York: Oxford University Press, 2008.

41. Roy Allison and Lena Jonson, eds. *Central Asian Security*, London, UK: Royal Institute of International Affairs, 1991.

42. "Shanghai Cooperation Organization Charter," *China Daily*, June 12, 2006, available from *www.chinadaily.com.cn/china/2006-06/12/content_614628.htm*.

43. Feroz Hassan Khan, "The New Great Game in Central Asia/South Asia: Continuity and Change," in Charles Hawkins and Robert L. Love, eds., *The New Great Game: Chinese Views on Central Asia*, Ft. Leavenworth, KS: Foreign Military Studies Office, 2006, pp. 1-16.

44. G. A. Ziuganov, "Rasprava vo Vladivostoke ne dolzhena ostat'sia beznakazannoi," *Pravda*, December 15, 2008.

45. Sergei Blagov, "Russia Hails Border Deal with China Despite Criticism, *Eurasian Daily Monitor*, Vol. 2, No. 102, May 25, 2005, available from *www.jamestown.org/single/?no_cache=1&tx_ttnews%5Btt_news%5D=30445*.

46. Jeanne L. Wilson, *Strategic Partners: Russian-Chinese Relations in the Post-Soviet Era*, Armonk, NY: M. E. Sharpe, 2004, pp. 126-127.

47. This process has been addressed in the work of Christina Chuan, "Nuclear Issues in the Far Eastern Federal Okrug," in James Clay Molts, Vladimir A. Olav, and Adam M. Stolberg, eds., *Preventing Nuclear Meltdown: Managing Decentralization of Russia's Nuclear Complex*, Aldershot, UK, and Burlington, VT: Ashgate, 2004, pp. 105-134.

48. Vladimir Pyle, "Spasitel'myi Kitai?" *Orientir*, No. 3, March 2009, pp. 8-11.

49. "Far East looks to China for investment," *The Russian Journal*, October 10, 2003, available from *www.russiajournal.com/node/16455*.

50. Konstantin Preobrazhensky, "Through Russia With Kim Jong Il," *North Korean Review*, Vol. 1, No. 1, February 29, 2004, available from *www.jamestown.org/single/?no_cache=1&tx_ttnews%5Btt_news%5D=26321*.

51. Alexander Vorontsov, "Current Russia-North Korea Relations: Challenges and Achievements," Washington, DC: The Brookings Institution, February 2007, available from *www.brookings.edu/papers/2007/02northkorea_vorontsov.aspx*.

52. "Russian Specialists Arrive in S. Korea to Probe Warship Sinking," *RIA Novosti*, May 31, 2010; "Russia, N. Korea to Continue Consultations to Settle Inter-Korean Conflict, *RIA Novosti*, May 28, 2010; and "Russia, South Korea to Discuss Cheonan Issue Thursday," *RIA Novosti*, June 2, 2010.

53. Asmus, *A Little War that Shook the World*.

54. Mikhail Barabanov, Anton Lavrov, and Viacheslav Tseluiko, *Tanki augusta: Sbornik statei*, Moscow, Russia: Tsentr Analiza Strategii i tekhnologii, 2009.

55. Valerii Shcheblanin, "Voennaia bezopasnost' na vostok Rossii budet obespechena," *Buriatiia*, February 20, 2010.

56. Roger McDermott, "'Virtual' Defense of the Russian Far East, Vostok 2010," *Eurasian Daily Monitor*, Vol. VII, No. 129, July 6, 2010.

57. "Vostok-2010 bez konkretnykh protivnikov," *Interfax*, June 28, 2010 .

58. Hypothetical opponents are not new and are not the product of post-modern political correctness. Those familiar with the exercises of the U.S. Army after World War II will remember "FM 30-102, *Handbook on Aggressor Military Forces*," published in 1947, which stated: "The country, peoples and forces described herein are entirely fictitious. Any resemblance to existing countries or forces is inadvertent and coincidental." That notional opponent, "Circle Trigon" with its Esperanto-speaking opposing forces continued to be used in US Army exercises into the 1970s. Such an official orientation did not prevent U.S. forces from exercising against a notional opponent that looked something like the Red Army, and by the 1980s the OPFOR (opposing force) at the National Training Center had evolved into a very good replication of a Soviet motorized rifle regiment. Thus, hypothetical opponents can over time evolve into probable opponents.

59. "V Rossii nachinaiutsia masshtabnye ucheniia 'Vostok-2010'," *RBC.ru*, June 29, 2010.

60. "Opiat' bez protivnika?" *Nezavisimoe voennoe obozrenie*, July 2, 2002.

61. "Serdiukov ne vevel ustraivat' voinu dvukh armii," *Nezavisimoe voennoe obozrenie*, July 9, 2010.

62. "Dmitrii Medvedev postavil pered dal'nom vostokom glavnye zadachi," *Respublika Armeniia*, July 7, 2010.

63. Aleksandr' Sadchikov, "Chetvertyi pokhod na Vostok," *Izvestiia*, July 9, 2010.

64. "V khode uchenii 'Vostok-2010' Rossiiskie voennye obideli Iaponiiu s osobym pazmakhom," *NEWSru*, July 7, 2010.

65. Aleksandr' Kolesnichenko, "Ucheniia, ukrytye tumanom," *Novye izvestiia*, July 5, 2010.

66. Aleksandr' Khramhikhin. "Neadekvatnyi vostok," *Nezavisimoe voennoe obozrenie*, July 27, 2010.

67. *Ibid.*

68. Aleksandr' Khramchikhin. "Chetyre vektora Rossiiskoi oborony," *Nezavisimoe voennoe obozrenie*, May 21, 2010.

69. Aleksandr' Khramchikhin, "Slabost' provotziruet sil'nee, chem moshch'," *Nezavisimoe voennoe obozrenie*, March 19, 2010.

70. Bruce Pannier. "Unspoken Russian-Chinese Rivalry Is Subtext of SCO Summit," *RFE/RL*, June 10, 2010.

71. Kitaitsy odvigaiut granitsu s Rossiei," *Vremia i den'gi*, June 8, 2010.

72. Natal'ia Ostrovskaia, "Zachem Rossii Dal'nyi Vostok?" *Komsomol'skaia pravda*, May 28, 2010.

73. Sergei Lavrov, "Novyi dogovor o SNV v matritse global'noi bezopasnosti," *Mezhdunarodnaia zhizn'*, No. 7, July 2010. On the notion of a process lasting to 2045, see Vladimir Kozin, "6 Obstacles to Nuclear Zero," *Moscow Times*, August 3, 2010.

74. Sergei Kazennov and Vladimir Kumachev, "Ne nado absoliutizirovat' 'ukgrazu s vostoka'," *Nezavisimoe voennoe obozrenie*, August 13, 2010, p. 12.

ABOUT THE CONTRIBUTORS

STEPHEN J. BLANK has served as the Strategic Studies Institute's expert on the Soviet bloc and the post-Soviet world since 1989. Prior to that he was Associate Professor of Soviet Studies at the Center for Aerospace Doctrine, Research, and Education, Maxwell Air Force Base, AL; and taught at the University of Texas, San Antonio; and at the University of California, Riverside. Dr. Blank is the editor of *Imperial Decline: Russia's Changing Position in Asia*, coeditor of *Soviet Military and the Future*, and author of *The Sorcerer as Apprentice: Stalin's Commissariat of Nationalities, 1917-1924*. He has also written many articles and conference papers on Russia, the Commonwealth of Independent States, and Eastern European security issues. Dr. Blank's current research deals with proliferation and the revolution in military affairs, and energy and security in Eurasia. His two most recent books are *Russo-Chinese Energy Relations: Politics in Command*, London, UK: Global Markets Briefing, 2006; and *Natural Allies? Regional Security in Asia and Prospects for Indo-American Strategic Cooperation*, Carlisle, PA: Strategic Studies Institute, U.S. Army War College, 2005. Dr. Blank holds a B.A. in history from the University of Pennsylvania, and an M.A. and Ph.D. in history from the University of Chicago.

PAVEL K. BAEV is a Research Professor at the Peace Research Institute, Oslo (PRIO); he is also affiliated with the Centre for the Study of Civil War at PRIO. He worked in a research institute in the USSR Defence Ministry, and then worked in the Institute of Europe, Moscow, before joining PRIO in October 1992. In 1995-2001, he was the editor of PRIO's quarterly journal, *Security Dialogue*, and in 1998-2004, he was a member of the PRIO Board. Dr. Baev's research on the transformation of the Russian military is supported by the Norwegian Defence Ministry; other research interests include the energy and security dimensions of the Russian-European relations and post-Soviet conflict management in the Caucasus and the greater Caspian area. His weekly column appears in *Eurasia Daily Monitor* and his latest book, *Russian Energy Policy and Military Power*, was published by London, UK: Routledge, 2008. Dr. Baev holds an MA in political geography from the Moscow State University and a Ph.D. in international relations from the USA & Canada Institute, USSR Academy of Sciences.

STEPHEN J. CIMBALA is Distinguished Professor of Political Science at Penn State University-Brandywine and has contributed to the literature in U.S. national security policy, nuclear arms control, and other topics for many years. Dr. Cimbala is a past winner of the university's Eisenhower Award for distinguished teaching and has served as a consultant to various U.S. Government agencies and defense contractors. He most recently edited and contributed a chapter for The George W. Bush Defense Program (Falls Church, VA: Potomac, 2010).

DANIEL GOURE is a Vice President with the Lexington Institute, a nonprofit public-policy research organization headquartered in Arlington, Virginia. Dr. Goure has held senior positions in both the private sector and the U.S. Government. Prior to joining the Lexington Institute, he was the Deputy Director, International Security Program at the Center for Strategic and International Studies. Dr. Goure spent 2 years in the U.S. Government as the director of the Office of Strategic Competitiveness in the Office of the Secretary of Defense. He also served as a senior analyst on national security and defense issues with the Center for Naval Analyses, Science Applications International Corporation, SRS Technologies, R&D Associates, and System Planning Corporation. Dr. Goure holds a B.A. in Government and History from Pomona College, and Masters and Ph.D. degrees in international relations and Russian studies from Johns Hopkins University.

DALE R. HERSPRING is a University Distinguished Professor at Kansas State University, a member of the Council on Foreign Relations, and a retired U.S. diplomat and Navy captain. He is the author of 13 books and close to 100 articles. His forthcoming publications include a book to be entitled *Shared Responsibility and Civil-Military Relations: The American, Canadian, German and Russian Cases* and "Creating Shared Responsibility Through Respect for Military Culture: the Russian and American Cases," *Public Administration Review*, July 2011.

JACOB KIPP taught at Kansas State University from 1971 to 1985. In 1986, he joined the Soviet Army Studies Office (SASO) at Ft. Leavenworth, KS. In 1991, SASO became the Foreign Military Studies Office (FMSO). From 2003 to 2006, Dr. Kipp served as Director of FMSO. In 2006 he took the position of Deputy Director of the School of Advanced Military Studies (SAMS). He retired from federal service in 2009. Dr. Kipp has written extensively on Russian and Soviet military and naval history, aviation, strategy, operational art, and military doctrine. He served as deputy editor of *Military Affairs*, as assistant editor of the *Journal of Slavic Military Studies*, as founding co-editor of *European Security*, and as a member of the editorial board of the *Modern War Studies Series* of the University Press of Kansas. He is a member of the Russian Academy of Natural Sciences. At present, he is an adjunct professor of History, and Russian and Eurasian Studies at the University of Kansas and a contributor to the Jamestown Foundation's *Eurasian Daily Monitor*. Dr. Kipp worked closely with Mary Fitzgerald on several projects relating to Soviet and Russian military affairs. Dr. Kipp holds a Ph.D. from the Pennsylvania State University.

ROGER N. MCDERMOTT is a graduate of the University of Oxford specializing in defense and security issues in the Commonwealth of Independent States (CIS). He is a Senior Fellow in Eurasian Military Studies, Jamestown Foundation, Washington, DC; Senior International Fellow, Foreign Military Studies Office, Fort Leavenworth; and, Affiliated Senior Analyst, Danish Institute for International Studies, Copenhagen. Mr. McDermott is on the editorial board of *Central Asia and the Caucasus* and the scientific board of the *Journal of Power Institutions in Post-Soviet Societies*. His articles appear in scholarly journals including the *Journal of Slavic Military Studies*, and his weekly assessments of security developments in Central Asia, *Eurasia Daily Monitor* (Jamestown Foundation), are read by policy planners. He is also the co-editor of the book, *Russian Military Reform 1992-2002* (London, UK/Portland, MD: Frank Cass, 2003). Mr. McDermott is also conducting extensive policy oriented research into Russian defense reform and will publish a book on the "new look" Russian armed forces, as well as a seminal chapter in a forthcoming book, published by Routledge, based on an FOI (Freedom of Information) conference in Sweden (October 4-5, 2010), in which he examines Russian perspectives on network-centric warfare.

ANDREI SHOUMIKHIN is Senior Analyst at the National Institute for Public Policy. His previous assignments were as Director of the Washington Office of the Moscow Public Science Foundation and coordinator of the Foundation's projects in the United States; he was associated with the Institute of USA and Canada Studies of the Russian Academy of Sciences and headed the USA Institute's Center for the Middle East and Conflict Resolution. Dr. Shoumikhin was responsible for analyses of U.S. foreign policy and the preparation of analyses and recommendations for use by the Russian president, parliamentary committees, and various ministries, with special emphasis on conflict resolution and the relationship between the United States, Russia, and the developing world. He was President of the Center for Conflict Resolution and also served as an interpreter for the United Nations Secretariat and the Central Committee of the Communist Party in Moscow. Dr. Shoumikhin is a graduate of the Moscow Institute for Foreign Languages and the United Nations Translation and Interpreter Course. He holds a Ph.D. in political science from the Institute of USA and Canada Studies.

NIKOLAI N. SOKOV is a Senior Research Associate at James Martin Center for Nonproliferation Studies at Monterey Institute of International Studies, a Graduate School of Middlebury College. He worked at the Institute of U.S. and Canadian Studies and the Institute of World Economy and International Relations in Moscow. From 1987-92 he worked at the Ministry for Foreign Affairs of the Soviet Union and later Russia, and participated in START I and START II negotiations as well as in a number of summit and ministerial meetings. Dr. Sokov has published extensively on international security and arms control. He is the author of *Russian Strategic Modernization: Past and Future* (Lanham, MD: Rowman and Littlefield, 2000), co-author and co-editor of the first Russian-language college-level textbook on nuclear nonproliferation (*Yadernoe Nerasprostranenie*, Vol.I-II, PIR Center, 1st Ed., 2000, 2nd Ed., 2002), and several monographs. Dr. Sokov graduated from Moscow State University in 1981 and holds a Ph.D. from the University of Michigan and the Soviet equivalent of a Ph.D. Candidate of Historical Sciences degree from the Institute of World Economy and International Relations.

RICHARD WEITZ is Senior Fellow and Director of the Center for Political-Military Analysis at Hudson Institute. His current research includes regional security developments relating to Europe, Eurasia, and East Asia as well as U.S. foreign, defense, and homeland security policies. Dr. Weitz is also a non-resident Senior Advisor at the Project on National Security Reform (PNSR), where he oversees case study research. He is a non-resident Senior Fellow at the Center for a New American Security (CNAS), where he contributes to various defense projects. Dr. Weitz has published or edited several books and monographs, including *The Russian Military Today and Tomorrow* (2010); *Global Security Watch-Russia* (2009); a volume of *National Security Case Studies* (2008); *China-Russia Security Relations* (2008); *Kazakhstan and the New International Politics of*

Eurasia (2008); *Mismanaging Mayhem: How Washington Responds to Crisis* (2008); *The Reserve Policies of Nations: A Comparative Analysis* (2007); and *Revitalising US–Russian Security Cooperation: Practical Measures* (2005).

www.ingramcontent.com/pod-product-compliance
Lightning Source LLC
Chambersburg PA
CBHW080041280326

41935CB00014B/1756